C12

Thro
E

The value to scholars of a text which can be used with confidence is obvious, while the nonspecialist reader will find Jim's adventures as enthralling as any in the literature of the American West. It is of special interest and significance that Beckwourth was of Negro heritage and that his book was one of the few by a mulatto to be published before the Civil War. Indeed, Beckwourth stands as a representative folk hero for the other men of his race whose share in the development of the West has not yet been recognized.

A native of Idaho, DELMONT R. OSWALD holds his B.A. from Idaho State University and his advanced degrees from Brigham Young University, where he now teaches history. His previous publications include an article on Beckwourth in volume six of *The Mountain Men and the Fur Trade* (1968).

THE LIFE AND ADVENTURES OF

JAMES P. BECKWOURTH

The Life and Adventures of James P. Beckwourth

as told to

Thomas D. Bonner

Introduced and with notes and an epilogue by

Delmont R. Oswald

UNIVERSITY OF NEBRASKA PRESS · LINCOLN

CONTENTS

INTRODUCTION

James Pierson Beckwourth played a role—and often a strenuous one—in some of the most significant and exciting events in nineteenth-century American history. A friend and associate of men like William H. Ashley, Jim Bridger, and Kit Carson, he participated in the development of the fur trade of the Far West, the Seminole and Mexican wars, and the California gold rush, and lived for several years as a member of the Crow Indian tribe. What is perhaps even more important to historians, Beckwourth left his own record of his packed and colorful life. First published as *The Life and Adventures of James P. Beckwourth, Mountaineer, Scout, and Pioneer, and Chief of the Crow Nation of Indians*, it has served to make him both a significant source in the early history of the Rocky Mountain West and one of its most controversial figures.

Estimates of Beckwourth's character and of the truthfulness of his recital of his exploits have varied considerably, not only among his own acquaintances but among those who have known him only through his autobiography and other published sources. When the autobiography first appeared, men in the mining camps were more than a little skeptical of "old Jim's" veracity;[1] but even before then, ten years before the book was published, the revered historian Francis Parkman, basing his opinon on hearsay, called Beckwourth "a ruffian of the worst stamp; bloody

1. See Epilogue.

and treacherous, without honor or honesty."[2] Another derogatory judgment came from Hiram Chittenden, who noted in his monumental work on the fur trade that "it is idle to treat as reliable history the ingenious collection of heroic achievements which [Beckwourth] has dignified under the style of 'autobiography.' The whole book is replete with fable, and there is probably not a single statement in it that is correct as given."[3] On the other hand, Col. Henry Inman, who was personally acquainted with many frontiersmen, stated that "Colonel Boone, the Bents, Carson, Maxwell, and others ascribed to him no such traits as those given by Parkman, and as to his honesty, it is an unquestionable fact that Beckwourth was the most honest trader in the business."[4]

Opinions are as widely varied among more recent scholars and writers. Wright Howes regards the autobiography as "highly colored, but basically authentic," yet J. Frank Dobie says flatly that Beckwourth was "the champion of all western liars."[5] While Bernard De Voto states that he

2. Francis Parkman, *The Oregon Trail* (Garden City: Doubleday & Co., 1946), p. 106. Originally published as *The California and Oregon Trail*, this work first appeared in March, 1849. It should be noted that Parkman did admit the possibility of personal bias and acknowledged that some of the stories about Beckwourth might be true. Referring to a story told him by the son of Pierre Dorion at Fort Laramie, Parkman said that he did not believe it "until I had heard it confirmed from so many independent sources that my skepticism was almost overcome." Ibid.

3. Hiram Martin Chittenden, *The American Fur Trade of the Far West*, 2 vols. (New York: Barnes & Noble, 1935), 2: 680. First published in 1902.

4. Col. Henry Inman, *The Old Santa Fe Trail* (Topeka: Crane & Co., 1916), p. 337.

5. Wright Howes, comp., *U. S.iana (1690-1950): A Selective Bibliography* (New York: R. R. Bowker for the Newberry Library,

"gave our literature its goriest lies," the anthropologist Robert Lowie finds that Beckwourth "reproduces with admirable correctness the martial atmosphere of the Crow life in the 'twenties and 'thirties of the last century"; and J. Cecil Alter points out that "it is remarkable how closely historians follow him when other sources give out. . . . thank goodness for Beckwourth."[6] Alter's point can be proven by simply examining the works of recognized historians such as LeRoy Hafen, Dale Morgan, Ray Allen Billington, David Lavender, and others.

Beckwourth dictated his memoirs to Thomas D. Bonner, an itinerant justice of the peace in the California gold camps. After Bonner polished up Beckwourth's rough narrative, the book was published by Harper and Brothers in 1856 to meet the growing public demand for literature about the West. The work seems to have been well received, for an English edition appeared the same year, published by S. Low, Son and Company, and a second printing was issued by Harpers in 1858. Two years later a French translation, entitled *Le chasseur; scénes de la vie sauvage en Amérique*, was published in Paris by E. Dentu. Since then there have been three editions—in 1892, 1931, and 1965—of which only the first two re-

---

1962), p. 65; J. Frank Dobie, *Guide to Life and Literature of the Southwest* (Dallas: Southern Methodist University Press, 1952), p. 71.

6. Bernard De Voto, *The Year of Decision, 1846* (Boston: Houghton Mifflin Co. 1943), p. 63; Robert H. Lowie, *The Crow Indians* (New York: Farrar & Rinehart, 1935), pp. 335-36; J. Cecil Alter, *Jim Bridger* (Norman: University of Oklahoma Press, 1962), pp. 69-70.

quire comment here.[7]

The 1892 edition was edited by an Englishman, Charles G. Leland, for the Unwin Adventure Series.[8] Leland, who had become fascinated with the rugged frontier types he met on a visit to St. Louis, added a flowery introduction and provided a few footnotes on matters he had verified. He concluded that everything in the book was the gospel truth.

A better attempt at a constructive evaluation of the Beckwourth-Bonner account was made by Bernard De Voto in 1931. Although, as he said, it was not his purpose to produce a scholarly work on the subject, he was the first to show any interest in doing so. Still it is clear that De Voto had mixed feelings about Beckwourth's material, for after stating that the book is neither history nor fiction, but mythology, he remarks a few pages farther on that "it reveals more of Indian human nature than can be found in any other book of the time."[9] De Voto also rashly criticizes Chittenden for relying upon Beckwourth as a source despite his unfavorable judgment upon the

7. The 1965 edition, published by Ross & Haines, is a photo-offset reproduction of the 1856 edition with a brief introduction by Stan Nelson and an index. In addition portions of the Beckwourth-Bonner book have been extracted and reprinted for the popular market: for example, five chapters of the original edition appear under the title *The Smiling Pioneer* with a preface by Henry Carr (Los Angeles: United States Library Assoc., 1932), and brief selections were published in Joseph Arnold Foster, comp., *The Life and Adventures of James P. Beckwourth, Selections,* (Claremont, Calif.: Scripps College, 1950).

8. T. D. Bonner, *The Life and Adventures of James P. Beckwourth,* ed. Charles G. Leland (London: T. Fisher Unwin, 1892).

9. T. D. Bonner, *The Life and Adventures of James P. Beckwourth,* ed. Bernard De Voto (New York: Alfred A. Knopf, 1931), pp. xxvi-xxvii, xxv.

memoirs, and then asserts that "one of the most flagrantly erroneous passages in Chittenden's history is his account of General Ashley's emergence from the canyons of the Green River. It is based on Beckwourth."[10] But, as later scholarship has demonstrated, Chittenden and Beckwourth were right and De Voto was wrong.[11]

The present edition reproduces the text of the 1856 edition, with new notes intended to show as comprehensively as possible what parts of Beckwourth's story are authentic, what parts are questionable or at least not susceptible to proof, and what parts are unreliable or deliberate lies. The main faults of Beckwourth's work are the result of a poor memory for dates and recklessness with statistics, his desire for self-glorification which led to his stretching the truth and making himself the hero of adventures which happened to others, and just plain lying for the sake of a good story. In Jim's behalf, however, it should be said that he was typical of his breed when he indulged in self-glorification, for it seems to have been a characteristic of most mountain men to exaggerate their prowess. Moreover, the art of tale telling was held in high esteem;[12] and for men like Beckwourth, as Dale L. Morgan has written, "to be a liar was as much a part of mountain honor as hard drinking or straight shooting. Embroider your adventures, convert to use any handy odyssey, and spin it all out in the firelight, the only sin is the sin of being dull."[13] Nonetheless, after the obvious tall tales,

10. Ibid., p. xx.

11. Dale L. Morgan, "A New Ashley Document," *Westerners New York Posse Brand Book* 12 (1966) : 73-88.

12. Beckwourth openly admits a desire to gain "renown." See page 405 below.

13. Dale L. Morgan, *Jedediah Smith and the Opening of the West* (New York: Bobbs-Merrill Co., 1953), p. 156.

the exaggerations, and the inadvertent errors have been discounted, what remains is a work of substantial value to the historian, the anthropologist, and the student of Western Americana.

In annotating this edition I have made use of the most recent data discovered by others as well as my own research findings. Whenever possible I have corrected the chronology and statistics (as, for example, the population of tribes referred to). Throughout I have tried to show both where Beckwourth is telling the truth and where he is romanticizing or is guilty of deliberate falsification. Admittedly there are statements which remain questionable and which cannot be independently verified, and I have tried to indicate their possibilities or limitations. After the notes, which follow the text, I have added an epilogue which carries on Jim's story from the period covered by his memoirs to his death.

The value of Beckwourth's memoirs already has been demonstrated through its wide use in the literature of the fur trade and other aspects of nineteenth-century American history. It is hoped that this edition will provide the scholar with a text which can be used with confidence and that it will help to end many of the controversies which have developed since the book was first published almost a hundred and twenty years ago. It is also my hope that it will give the nonspecialist reader a better picture of Beckwourth himself, without marring the original account which has given enjoyment to so many devotees of Western Americana. I have certainly not intended to express any judgment on Beckwourth's character or deeds, only to put them in the context of his own times and to distinguish fact from fiction. I believe that by doing so

I have made it easier to see that James P. Beckwourth—trapper, hunter, guide, tale teller, friend and foe of the Indian—deserves a place in history alongside men like Jedediah Smith, Kit Carson, and Jim Bridger.

                                        Delmont R. Oswald

Brigham Young University

THE

LIFE AND ADVENTURES

OF

JAMES P. BECKWOURTH,

MOUNTAINEER, SCOUT, AND PIONEER,

AND

CHIEF OF THE CROW NATION OF INDIANS.

With Illustrations.

WRITTEN FROM HIS OWN DICTATION,

BY T. D. BONNER.

NEW YORK:

HARPER & BROTHERS, PUBLISHERS,

FRANKLIN SQUARE.

1856.

PREFACE.

Buried amid the sublime passes of the Sierra Nevada are old men, who, when children, strayed away from our crowded settlements, and, gradually moving farther and farther from civilization, have in time become domiciliated among the wild beasts and wilder savages—have lived scores of years whetting their intellects in the constant struggle for self-preservation; whose only pleasurable excitement was found in facing danger; whose only repose was to recuperate, preparatory to participating in new and thrilling adventures. Such men, whose simple tale would pale the imaginative creations of our most popular fictionists, sink into their obscure graves unnoticed and unknown. Indian warriors, whose bravery and self-devotion find no parallels in the preserved traditions of all history, end their career on the "war-path," sing in triumph their death-song, and become silent, leaving no impression on the intellectual world.

Among the many men who have distinguished themselves as mountaineers, traders, chiefs of great Indian nations, and as early pioneers in the settlement of our Pacific coast, is James P. Beckwourth, whose varied and startling personal adventures would have found no record but for the accident of meeting with a wanderer in the mountains of California, who became interested in the man, and, patiently listening to his story, proceeded, as it fell from his lips, to put it upon paper.

This autobiography was thus produced, and was the result of some months' labor in the winter of 1854–55. In prosecuting the task, the author has in no instance departed from the story of the narrator, but it was taken down literally as it was from day to day related. Beckwourth kept no journal, and, of course, relied upon his memory alone; consequently dates are often wanting, which it was impossible to give with accuracy when recurring to events transpiring in the course of very many years. Beckwourth is personally known to thousands of people " living on both sides of the mountains," and also, from his service under the United States government, has enjoyed the acquaintance of many officers of the United States Army, who have been stationed in Florida, Mexico, and California. In his long residence with the Indians he adopted their habits, and was in every respect conformed to their ways: the consequence was, from his great courage and superior mental endowments, he rose rapidly in their estimation, and finally became their chief. As an Indian, therefore, he speaks of their customs, and describes their characteristics; and probably, from his autobiography, we have more interesting particulars than were ever before given of the aborigines.

Beckwourth, after ten thousand adventures, finally became involved in the stream that set toward the Pacific, and, almost unconsciously, he established a home in one of the pleasant valleys that border on Feather River. Discovering a pass in the mountains that greatly facilitated emigrants in reaching California, his

house became a stopping-place for the weary and dis-
pirited among them, and no doubt the associations
thus presented have done much to efface his natural
disposition to wander and seek excitement among the
Indian tribes.

In person he is of medium height, of strong muscular power, quick of apprehension, and, for a man of his
years, very active. From his neck is suspended 'a
perforated bullet, with a large oblong bead each side
of it, secured by a thread of sinew : this amulet is just
as he wore it while chief among the Crows. With
the exception of this, he has now assumed the usual
costume of civilized life, and, in his occasional visits to
San Francisco, vies with many prominent residents in
the dress and manners of the refined gentleman.

It is unnecessary to speak of the natural superiority
of his mind : his autobiography every where displays
it. His sagacity in determining what would please the
Indians has never been surpassed; for on the most trying occasions, where hundreds of others would have
fallen victims to circumstances, he escaped. His courage is of the highest order, and probably no man ever
lived who has met with more personal adventure involving danger to life, though in this respect he is not
an exception to all mountaineers and hunters who early engaged in the fur trade and faced the perils of an
unknown wilderness.

CONTENTS.

8

CHAPTER VII.

CHAPTER VIII.

CHAPTER IX.

CHAPTER X.

CHAPTER XI.

CHAPTER XII.

CHAPTER XIII.

CHAPTER XIV.

CHAPTER XV.

CHAPTER XVI.

CHAPTER XVII.

CHAPTER XVIII.

CHAPTER XIX.

CHAPTER XX.

10 CONTENTS.

CHAPTER XXI.

CHAPTER XXII.

CHAPTER XXIII.

CHAPTER XXIV.

CHAPTER XXV.

CHAPTER XXVI.

CHAPTER XXVII.

CHAPTER XXVIII.

CHAPTER XXIX.

CHAPTER XXX.

CHAPTER XXXI.

CHAPTER XXXII.

CHAPTER XXXIII.

CHAPTER XXXIV.

AUTOBIOGRAPHY

OF

JAMES P. BECKWOURTH.

CHAPTER I.

Birth-place and Childhood.—Removal to St. Louis.

I was born in Fredericksburg, Virginia, on the 26th of April, 1798. My father's family consisted of thirteen children, seven sons and six daughters. I was the third child, having one sister and one brother older than myself.

My father had been an officer in the Revolutionary War, and had held a major's commission. He served throughout that glorious struggle which

> " Raised the dignity of man,
> And taught him to be free."

I well recollect, when a small boy, the frequent meetings of the old patriots at my father's house, who would sit down and relate the different battles in which they had taken part during "those days that tried men's souls." According to the custom of those days, their meetings were occasionally enlivened with some good old peach brandy; the same kind, I presume, as that with which the old Tory treated M'Donald when he delivered his splendid charger "Selim" to him for presentation to Colonel Tarleton, which circumstance was very frequently spoken of by the old soldiers.

Often during these reminiscences every eye would

dim, and tears course down the cheeks of the old veterans, as they thus fought their battles o'er again, and recalled their sufferings during the struggles they had passed through.

My youthful mind was vividly impressed with the stirring scenes depicted by those old soldiers; but time and subsequent hardship have obliterated most of their narratives from my memory. One incident I recollect, however, related by my father, when he formed one of a storming party in the attack on Stony Point made under General Wayne.

When I was but about seven or eight years of age, my father removed to St. Louis, Missouri, taking with him all his family and twenty-two negroes. He selected a section of land between the forks of the Mississippi and Missouri Rivers, twelve miles below St. Charles, which is to this day known as "Beckwourth's Settlement."

At this early period of our history (1805–6) the whole region of country around was a "howling wilderness," inhabited only by wild beasts and merciless savages. St. Louis, at that time, was but a small town, its inhabitants consisting almost wholly of French and Spanish settlers, who were engaged in trafficking with the Indians the commodities of civilization, such as *fire-water*, beads, blankets, arms, ammunition, &c., for peltry.

For protection against the Indians, who were at that time very troublesome and treacherous, it became necessary for the whites to construct block-houses at convenient distances. These block-houses were built by the united exertions of the settlers, who began to gather from all quarters since the "Jefferson Purchase" had been effected from the French government. The settlers or inhabitants of four adjoining sections would unite and build a block-house in the centre of their possessions, so that in case of alarm they could all repair to it as a place of refuge from the savages.

It was necessary to keep a constant guard on the plantations, and while one portion of the men were at work, the others, with their arms, were on the alert watching the wily Indian. Those days are still fresh in my memory, and it was then that I received, young as I was, the rudiments of my knowledge of the Indian character, which has been of such inestimable value to me in my subsequent adventures among them.

There were constant alarms in the neighborhood of some of the block-houses, and hardly a day passed without the inhabitants being compelled to seek them for protection. As an illustration of our mode of life, I will relate an incident that befell me when about nine years old.

One day my father called me to him, and inquired of me whether I thought myself man enough to carry a sack of corn to the mill. The idea of riding a horse, and visiting town, possessed attractions which I could not resist, and I replied with a hearty affirmative. A sack of corn was accordingly deposited on the back of a gentle horse selected for the purpose, and " Young Jim" (as I was called) was placed upon the sack, and started for the mill two miles distant. About midway to the mill lived a neighbor having a large family of children, with whom I frequently joined in boyish sports. On my way I rode joyously up to the little fence which separated the house from the road, thinking to pass a word with my little playmates. What was my horror at discovering all the children, eight in number, from one to fourteen years of age, lying in various positions in the door-yard with their throats cut, their scalps torn off, and the warm life-blood still oozing from their gaping wounds! In the door-way lay their father, and near him their mother, in the same condition; they had all shared the same fate. I found myself soon back at my father's house, but without the sack of corn—how I managed to get it off I never discovered—and related the circumstance to my father. He immediately gave the alarm throughout the settlement, and a body of men started in pursuit of the savages who had perpetrated this fearful tragedy; my father, with ten of his own men, accompanying them. In two days the band returned, bringing with them eighteen Indian scalps; for the backwoodsman fought the savage in Indian style, and it was scalp for scalp between them.

The day when I beheld the harrowing spectacle of my little murdered playmates is still as fresh in my memory as at the time of its occurrence, and it never will fade from my mind. It was the first scene of Indian cruelty my young eyes had ever witnessed, and I wondered how even savages could possess such relentless minds as to wish to bathe their hands in the blood of little innocents against whom they could have no cause of quarrel. But my subsequent experience has better acquainted me with the Indian character, as the reader will learn in the course of the following pages.

I also recollect a large body of Indians assembling in their war costume on the opposite side of the Mississippi River, in what is now the State of Illinois. This was at Portage de Soix, twenty-five miles above St. Louis, and about two miles from my father's house; and their intention was to cut off all the white inhabitants of the surrounding country. The alarm was given; a large party of the settlers collected, crossed the river, and after a severe engagement defeated the Indians with great loss, and frustrated their bloody purposes.

Three days after this battle, a woman came into the settlement who had been three years captive among the Indians. She had made her escape during the confusion attending their defeat, and reached her friends in safety, after they had long supposed her dead. The name of this woman I do not remember, but I have no doubt there are old settlers in that region who yet recollect the circumstance, and the general rejoicing with which her escape was celebrated.

The news that she brought was of the most alarming nature. She related how several of the Indian tribes had held a grand council, and resolved upon a general attack upon St. Louis and all the surrounding country, with the view to butcher indiscriminately all the white inhabitants, French and Spanish excepted. This intelligence produced the greatest alarm among the inhabitants, and every preparation was made to repel the attack. New block-houses were erected, old ones repaired, and every thing placed in the best posture for defense. The Indians soon after appeared in great force opposite St. Louis. Blondo, an interpreter, was dispatched across the river to them, to inform them of the preparations made for their reception. He informed them of the intelligence communicated by the woman fugitive from their camp; and represented to them that the people of St. Louis were provided with numerous " big guns mounted on wagons," which, in case of attack, could not fail to annihilate all their warriors. They credited Blondo's tale, and withdrew their forces.

At the period of which I speak, the major part of the inhabitants of St. Louis were French and Spanish. These were on friendly terms with all the Indian tribes, and wished to confine their long-established traffic with the Red men to themselves. For this reason they discountenanced the settlement of Americans among them, as they considered it an invasion of their monopoly of the traffic with the Indians; and St. Louis being the grand trading depôt for the regions of the West and Northwest, the profits derived from the intercourse were immense. The Indians, too, thinking themselves better dealt with by the French and Spanish, united with the latter in their hostility to the influx of the Americans.

When about ten years of age I was sent to St. Louis to attend school, where I continued until the year 1812. I was then apprenticed to a man in St. Louis named George Casner, to learn the trade of blacksmith. (This man had a partner named John L. Sutton, who is yet a resident in St. Louis.)

I took to the trade with some unwillingness at first, but becoming reconciled to it, I was soon much pleased with my occupation. When I had attained my nineteenth year, my sense of importance had considerably expanded, and, like many others of my age, I felt myself already quite a man. Among other indiscretions, I became enamored of a young damsel, which, leading me into habits that my *boss* disapproved of, resulted finally in a difficulty between us.

Being frequently tempted to transgress my *boss's* rules by staying from home somewhat late of an evening, and finding the company I spent my time with so irresistibly attractive that I could not bring myself to obedience to orders, I gave way to my passion, and felt indifferent whether my proceedings gave satisfaction or otherwise. One morning I was assailed by my principal in language which I considered unduly harsh and insulting, and on his threatening to dismiss me his house, I was tempted to reply with some warmth, and acknowledge that his doing so would exactly square with my wishes.

Provoked at this, he seized a hammer and flung at me. I dodged the missile, and threw it back at him in return. A scuffle then ensued, in which I, being young and athletic, came off master of the ground, and, accepting his polite dismissal, walked straight to my boarding-house. But a few moments elapsed before my assailant walked in and forbade my landlady to entertain me farther on his account.

I replied that I had plenty of money, and was competent to pay my own board.

This provoked him to a second attack, in which he again came off worsted.

Hereupon resolving to leave the house, I began to prepare for my departure; but, before I had completed my preparations, a one-armed constable presented himself at the stairs, and demanded to see me. Well knowing his errand, I took a well-loaded pistol in my hand, and went to meet him, assuring him that if he ascended the steps to capture me I would shoot him dead. In my exasperated state of mind, I really believe I should have executed my threat; the constable, perceiving my resolute bearing, after parleying a while, went away. Feeling confident that he had gone for another officer, who I feared might capture me, I expedited my departure, and, taking refuge in the house of a friend, concealed myself for three days, and then shipped on board a keel-boat, proceeding to the mines on Fever River. But I was discovered by my *boss* and detained, he holding himself responsible for my appearance until my father's decision was learned.

Accordingly, I went home to my father, and related the difficulty I had recently had with my master. He counseled me to return to my apprenticeship, but I declared my determination never to be reconciled again. My father then wished me to set up in business in his settlement, but I expressed disinclination, and declared a growing wish to travel. Seeing my determination, my father finally consented to my departure. He admonished me with some wholesome precepts, gave me five hundred dollars in cash, together with a good horse, saddle, and bridle, and bade me God speed upon my journey.

Bidding adieu to all my friends, I proceeded to the boat and went on board. The object for which the boat was dispatched up the Fever River was to make a treaty with the Sac Indians, to gain their consent to our working the mines, at that time in their possession. The expedition was strictly of a pacific character, and was led by Colonel R. M. Johnson. A brother of the colonel's accompanied us, and several other gentlemen went in the boat as passengers.

CHAPTER II.

Expedition to the Mines.—Am Hunter to the Party.—First Trip to New Orleans. — Sick with Yellow Fever. — Return Home. — First Trip to the Great West.

THE expedition consisted of from six to eight boats, carrying probably about one hundred men. The party in our boat numbered some eight or ten men, among whom were Colonel Johnson, his son Darwin Johnson, Messrs. January, Simmes, Kennerley, and others, whose names have escaped me. I engaged in the capacity of hunter to the party.

We pushed off, and after a slow and tedious trip of about twenty days, arrived at our place of destination (Galena of the present day). We found Indians in great numbers awaiting our disembarkation, who were already acquainted with the object of our expedition. The two tribes, Sacs and Foxes, received us peaceably, but, being all armed, they presented a very formidable appearance. There was a considerable force of United States troops quartered in that region, under the command of Colonel Morgan, stationed in detachments at Prairie du Chien, Rock Island, St. Peter's, and Des Moines.

After nine days' parleying, a treaty was effected with them, and ratified by the signatures of the contracting parties. On the part of the Indians, it was signed by Black Thunder, Yellow, Bank, and Keokuk (father to the Keokuk who figured in the Black Hawk war). On the part of the United States, Colonels Morgan and Johnson attached their signatures. This negotiation concluded, the mines were then first opened for civilized enterprise.

During the settlement of the preliminaries of the treaty, there was great difficulty with the Indians, and it was necessary for each man of our party to be on his guard against any hostile attempts of the former, who were all armed to the teeth. On the distribution of presents, which followed the conclusion of the treaty, consisting of casks of whisky, guns, gunpowder, knives, blankets, &c., there was a general time of rejoicing. Pow-wows, drinking, and dancing diversified the time, and a few fights were indulged in as a sequel to the entertainment.

The Indians soon became very friendly to me, and I was indebted to them for showing me their choicest hunting-grounds. There was abundance of game, including deer, bears, wild turkey, raccoons, and numerous other wild animals. Frequently they would accompany me on my excursions (which always proved eminently successful), thus affording me an opportunity of increasing my personal knowledge of the Indian character. I have lived among Indians in the Eastern and Western States, on the Rocky Mountains, and in California; I find their habits of living, and their religious belief, substantially uniform through all the unmingled races. All believe in the same Great Spirit; all have their prophets, their medicine men, and their soothsayers, and are alike influenced by the appearance of omens; thus leading to the belief that the original tribes throughout the entire continent, from Florida to the most northern coast, have sprung from one stock, and still retain in some degree of purity the social constitution of their primitive founders.

I remained in that region for a space of eighteen

months, occupying my leisure time by working in the mines. During this time I accumulated seven hundred dollars in cash, and, feeling myself to be quite a wealthy personage, I determined upon a return home.

My visit paid, I felt a disposition to roam farther, and took passage in the steam-boat Calhoun, Captain Glover, about to descend the river to New Orleans. My stay in New Orleans lasted ten days, during which time I was sick with the yellow fever, which I contracted on the way from Natchez to New Orleans. It was midsummer, and I sought to return home, heartily regretting I had ever visited this unwholesome place. As my sickness abated, I lost no time in making my way back, and remained under my father's roof until I had in some measure recruited my forces.

Being possessed with a strong desire to see the celebrated Rocky Mountains, and the great Western wilderness so much talked about, I engaged in General Ashley's Rocky Mountain Fur Company. The company consisted of twenty-nine men, who were employed by the Fur Company as hunters and trappers.

We started on the 11th of October with horses and pack-mules. Nothing of interest occurred until we approached the Kansas village, situate on the Kansas River, when we came to a halt and encamped.

Here it was found that the company was in need of horses, and General Ashley wished for two men to volunteer to proceed to the Republican Pawnees, distant three hundred miles, where he declared we could obtain a supply. There was in our party an old and experienced mountaineer, named Moses Harris, in whom the general reposed the strictest confidence for his knowledge of the country and his familiarity with Indian life. This Harris was reputed to be a man of "great leg,"* and capable, from his long sojourning in the mountains, of enduring extreme privation and fatigue.

There seemed to be a great reluctance on the part of the men to undertake in such company so hazardous a journey (for it was now winter). It was also whispered in the camp that whoever gave out in an expedition with Harris received no succor from him, but was abandoned to his fate in the wilderness.

Our leader, seeing this general unwillingness, desired me to perform the journey with Harris. Being young, and feeling ambitious to distinguish myself in some important trust, I asked leave to have a word with Harris before I decided.

Harris being called, the following colloquy took place:

"Harris, I think of accompanying you on this trip."

"Very well, Jim," he replied, scrutinizing me closely, "do you think you can stand it?"

"I don't know," I answered, "but I am going to try. But I wish you to bear one thing in mind: if I should give out on the road, and you offer to leave me to perish, as you have the name of doing, if I have strength to raise and cock my rifle, I shall certainly bring you to a halt."

Harris looked me full in the eye while he replied, "Jim, you may precede me the entire way, and take your own jog. If I direct the path, and give you the lead, it will be your own fault if you tire out."

"That satisfies me," I replied: "we will be off in the morning."

The following morning we prepared for departure. Each man loading himself with twenty-five pounds of

---

* i. e., a great traveler ; able to go a great distance in a day.

provisions, besides a blanket, rifle, and ammunition each, we started on our journey. After a march of about thirty miles, I in advance, my companion bringing up the rear, Harris complained of fatigue. We halted, and Harris sat down, while I built a large, cheering fire, for the atmosphere was quite cold. We made coffee, and partook of a hearty supper, lightening our packs, as we supposed, for the following day. But while I was bringing in wood to build up the fire, I saw Harris seize his rifle in great haste, and the next moment bring down a fat turkey from a tree a few rods from the camp. Immediately reloading (for old mountaineers never suffer their guns to remain empty for one moment), while I was yet rebuilding the fire, crack went his rifle again, and down came a second turkey, so large and fat that he burst in striking the ground. We were thus secure for our next morning's meal. After we had refreshed ourselves with a hearty supper, my companion proposed that we should kill each a turkey to take with us for our next day's provision. This we both succeeded in doing, and then, having dressed the four turkeys, we folded ourselves in our blankets, and enjoyed a sound night's rest.

The following morning we breakfasted off the choicest portions of two of the turkeys, and abandoned the remainder to the wolves, who had been all night prowling round the camp for prey. We started forward as early as possible, and advanced that day about forty miles. My companion again complained of fatigue, and rested while I made a fire, procured water, and performed all the culinary work. The selected portions of last evening's turkeys, with the addition of bread and coffee, supplied us with supper and breakfast.

After a travel of ten days we arrived at the Republican Pawnee villages, when what was our consternation and dismay to find the place entirely deserted! They had removed to their winter quarters. We were entirely out of provisions, having expected to find abundance at the lodges. We searched diligently for their *caches* (places where provisions are secured), but failed in discovering any. Our only alternative was to look for game, which, so near to an Indian settlement, we were satisfied must be scarce.

I would break my narrative for a while to afford some explanation in regard to the different bands of the Pawnee tribe; a subject which at the present day is but imperfectly understood by the general reader— the knowledge being confined to those alone who, by living among them, have learned their language, and hence become acquainted with the nature of their divisional lands.

The reader, perhaps, has remarked, that I related we were on a visit to Republican Pawnee villages. This is a band of the Pawnee tribe of Indians, which is thus divided:

The Grand Pawnee Band.
" Republican Pawnee Band.
" Pawnee Loups or Wolf Pawnees.
" Pawnee Pics or Tattooed Pawnees, and
" Black Pawnees.

The five bands constitute the entire tribe. Each band is independent and under its own chief, but for mutual defense, or in other cases of urgent necessity, they unite into one body. They occupy an immense extent of country, stretching from beyond the Platte River to south of the Arkansas, and, at the time I speak of, could raise from thirty thousand to forty thousand warriors. Like all other Indian tribes, they have dwindled away from various causes, the small-pox and war having carried them off by thousands. Some of the bands have been reduced to one half by this fatal disease (in many instances introduced designedly among them by their civilized brethren); a disease more particularly fatal to the Indians from their entire ignorance of any suitable remedy. Their invariable treatment for all ailments being a cold-water immersion, it is not surprising that they are eminently unsuccessful in their treatment of the small-pox. Horse-stealing, practiced by one band upon the other, leads to exterminating feuds and frequent engagements, wherein great numbers are mutually slain.

The following interesting episode I had from the lips of the interpreter:

Some thirty-two years ago, during Monroe's administration, a powerful Indian named *Two Axe*, chief counselor of the Pawnee Loup band, went to pay his "Great Father," the President, a visit. He was over six feet high and well proportioned, athletic build, and as straight as an arrow. He was delegated to Washington by his tribe to make a treaty with his Great Father.

Being introduced, his "father" made known to him, through the interpreter, the substance of his proposal. The keen-witted Indian, perceiving that the proposed treaty "talked all turkey" to the white man and "all crow" to his tribe, sat patiently during the reading of the paper. The reading finished, he arose with all his native dignity, and in that vein of true Indian eloquence in which he was unsurpassed, declared that the treaty had been conceived in injustice and brought forth in duplicity; that many treaties had been signed by Indians of their "Great Father's" concoction, wherein they bartered away the graves of their fathers for a few worthless trinkets, and afterward their hearts cried at their folly; that such Indians were fools and women. He expressed his free opinion of the "Great Father," and all his white children, and concluded by declaring that he would sign no paper which would make his own breast or those of his people to sorrow.

Accordingly, Two Axe broke up the council abruptly, and returned to his home without making any treaty with his "Great Father."

CHAPTER III.

Return from the deserted Pawnee Villages.—Sufferings on the Way. —Prospect of Starvation.—Fall in with the Indians most opportunely.—Safe Arrival at Ely's Trading-post at the mouth of the Kansas.

My companion and myself took counsel together how to proceed. Our determination was to make the best of our way to the Grand Ne-mah-haw River, one of the tributaries of the Missouri. We arrived at that river after nine days' travel, being, with the exception of a little coffee and sugar, entirely without provisions. My companion was worn out, and seemed almost disheartened. I was young, and did not feel much the worse for the journey, although I experienced a vehement craving for food. Arrived at the river, I left Harris by a good fire, and, taking my rifle, went in quest of game, not caring what kind I met.

As Fortune would have it, I came across an elk, and my rifle soon sent a leaden messenger after him. We encamped near him, promising ourselves a feast. He was exceedingly poor, however, and, hungry as we were, we made a very unsavory supper off his flesh.

The next morning we continued our journey down the Ne-mah-haw, traveling on for five days after I had kill-ed the elk without tasting food. The elk had been so rank that we carried no part of him with us, trusting to find some little game, in which we were disappoint-ed. We had thrown away our blankets to relieve ourselves of every burden that would impede our prog-ress, which, withal, was extremely slow.

On the fifth day we struck a large Indian trail, which bore evident marks of being fresh. My com-panion now gave entirely up, and threw himself to the ground, declaring he could go no farther. He pro-nounced our position to be thirty miles from the trad-ing-post. I endeavored to arouse him to get up and proceed onward, but he could only advance a few rods at a time. I felt myself becoming weak; still, I had faith that I could reach Ely's, if I had no hinderance; if I lingered for Harris, I saw we should both inevi-tably perish. He positively declared he could advance not a step farther; he could scarcely put one foot be-fore the other, and I saw he was becoming bewildered.

In the dilemma I said to him, "Harris, we must both perish if we stay here. If I make the best of my way along this trail, I believe I can reach Ely's some time in the night" (for I was aware that the In-dians, whose trail we were following, were proceeding thither with their peltry).

But Harris would not listen to it.

"Oh, Jim," he exclaimed, "don't leave me; don't leave me here to die! For God's sake, stay with me!"

I did my best to encourage him to proceed; I as-sisted him to rise, and we again proceeded upon our journey.

I saw, by the progress we were making, we should

never get on; so I told him, if I had to advance and leave him, to throw himself in the trail, and await my return on the following day with a good horse to carry him to the trading-post. We walked on, I a hundred yards in advance, but I became convinced that if I did not use my remaining strength in getting to Ely's, we should both be lost.

Accordingly, summoning all my forces, I doubled my speed, determined to reach the post before I stopped. I had not proceeded half a mile ere I heard the report of two rifles, and, looking in the direction of the sound, I saw two Indians approaching with demonstrations of friendship.

On reaching me, one of them exclaimed, "You are dead—you no live!"

I explained to him that I had left my companion behind, and that we were both nearly starved to death. On this they spoke a few words to each other in their own language, and one started off like a race-horse, along the trail, while the other returned with me to my companion.

As we approached him I could hear him moaning, "Ho, Jim! come back! come back! don't leave me!"

We went up to him, and I informed him that we were safe; that I had met the Indians, and we should soon be relieved.

After waiting about three hours, the rattling of hoofs was heard, and, looking up, we discovered a troop of Indians approaching at full speed. In another moment they were by our side. They brought with them a portion of light food, consisting of corn-meal made into a kind of gruel, of which they would give us but a small spoonful at short intervals. When Harris was sufficiently restored to mount a horse with the assistance of the Indians, we all started forward for the post.

It appeared that the two Indians whom I had so fortunately encountered had lingered behind the main party to amuse themselves with target-shooting with their rifles. The one that started along the trail overtook the main body at a short distance, and, making our case known to them, induced them to return to our succor.

We encamped with them that night, and they continued the same regimen of small periodic doses of gruel. Several times a large Indian seized hold of an arm of each of us, and forced us into a run until our strength was utterly exhausted. Others of the party would then support us on each side, and urge us on till their own strength failed them. After this discipline, a spoonful or two of gruel would be administered to us. This exercise being repeated several times, they at length placed before us a large dish containing venison, bear-meat, and turkey, with the invitation to eat all we wanted. It is unnecessary to say that I partook of such a meal as I never remember to have eaten before or since.

Early the next day we arrived at the trading-post of Ely and Curtis, situate on the Missouri River, near the mouth of the Kansas. As I entered the house, I heard some one exclaim, "Here comes Jim Beckwourth and Black Harris," the name he went by where he was known.

Ely sprang up to welcome us. "Sure enough," said he, "it is they; but they look like corpses."

Another voice exclaimed, "Halloo, Jim! what is the matter with you? Is it yourselves, or only your ghosts? Come along and take some brandy, any way; living or dead, you must be dry."

We accepted the invitation, and took each a glass, which, in our greatly reduced state, quite overpowered us. Left to my reflections, I resolved that, if I survived my present dangers, I would return to civilized life. The extremities I had been reduced to had so moderated my resentments that, had I encountered my former *boss*, I should certainly have extended my hand to him with ready forgiveness.

The Indians we had so opportunely fallen in with belonged to the Kansas band of the Osage tribe, and were on the way, as we had surmised, to dispose of their goods at the trading-post. Their wares consisted principally of peltry, obtained by their sagacity in trapping, and their skill in hunting the wild animals of the plains. In purchasing their skins of them, Messrs. Ely and Curtis rewarded the Indians very liberally with *government stores* for their humanity in succoring us when exhausted, and as an encouragement to relieve others whom they might chance to find similarly distressed.

After thoroughly recruiting at the trading-post, where I received every attention from Messrs. Ely and Curtis, I started for St. Louis. On my arrival at G. Chouteau's trading-post, I calculated the intervening distance to St. Louis, and abandoned my intention of proceeding thither, delaying my return till the spring, when the ice would break up in the Missouri. Mr. Chouteau engaged me to assist in packing peltries during the winter, at twenty-five dollars per month.

When the river was free from ice, I took passage in a St. Louis boat, and, after a quick run, arrived safe in the city early in the evening of the fifth day.

Shortly after my arrival I fell in with General Ashley, who had returned to the city for more men. The general was greatly surprised to see me, he having concluded that my fate had been the same with hundreds of others, engaged to fur companies, who had perished with cold and starvation. The general informed me that he had engaged one hundred and twenty men, who were already on their road to the mountains. He declared I was just the man he was in search of to ride after and overtake the men, and accompany them to the mountains, and added that I must start the next morning.

My feelings were somewhat similar to those of a young sailor on his return from his first voyage to sea. I had achieved one trip to the wild West, and had returned safe, and now I was desirous of spending a long interval with my father. I suffered the arguments of the old general to prevail over me, however, and I re-engaged to him, with the promise to start on the following morning. This afforded me short time to visit my friends, to whom I just paid a flying visit, and returned to the city in the morning.

After attending to the general's instructions, and receiving eight hundred dollars in gold to carry to Mr. Fitzpatrick (an agent of General Ashley then stationed in the mountains), I mounted a good horse, and put on in pursuit of the party, who were five or six days' journey in advance.

I may here remark that the general had been recently married, and, feeling some reluctance to tear himself away from the delights of Hymen, he sent me on for the performance of his duties. The general followed after in about a week, and overtook the party at Franklin, on the Missouri.

It was early May when I commenced my journey. Unfolding Nature presented so many charms that my previous sufferings were obliterated from my mind. The trees were clothing themselves with freshest verdure, flowers were unveiling their beauties on every side, and birds were caroling their sweetest songs from every bough. These sights and sounds struck more pleasantly upon my senses than the howl of the wolf and the scream of the panther, which assailed our ears in the forests and prairies of the wild West.

After being joined by our general, we proceeded up the Missouri to Council Bluffs, and thence struck out for the Platte country. Soon after our arrival on the Platte we had the great misfortune to lose nearly all our horses, amounting to about two hundred head, stolen from us by the Indians. We followed their trail for some time, but, deeming it useless to follow mounted Indians while we were on foot, our general gave up the pursuit. We could not ascertain what tribe the robbers belonged to, but I have since been convinced they were either the I-a-tans or the Arrap-a-hos.

Our general then gave orders to return to the Missouri and purchase all the horses we needed, while he returned to St. Louis to transact some affairs of business, and possibly pay his devotions to his very estimable lady.

We succeeded in obtaining a supply of horses after retracing about two hundred miles of our journey, paying for them with drafts upon General Ashley in St. Louis. We then again returned to our camp on the Platte. This adventure occupied nearly the whole summer; and we guarded against a repetition of the misfortune by strictly watching the horses day and night. While a portion of the company were engaged in making purchase of our second supply of horses, the other portion remained on the ground to hunt and trap, and gather together a supply of provision for our consumption. They met with excellent success, and caught a great number of beavers and otters, together with a quantity of game.

General Ashley rejoined us in September, and by his orders Fitzpatrick and a Robert Campbell proceeded to the Loup fork, taking with them all the men. except eight, who remained behind with the general, to ascend the Platte in quest of the company he left there the preceding winter, from which Harris and myself had been detached on our expedition to the Pawnee camp.

After several days' travel we found the company we were seeking. They were all well, had been successful in trapping, and had made some good trades with straggling parties of Indians in the exchange of goods for peltry. They had fared rather hard a part of the time, as game, which was their sole dependence, was often difficult to obtain.

I should here mention that we found Harris in the course of our second trip, who rejoined our company, well and hearty.

Fur companies in those days had to depend upon their rifles for a supply of food. No company could possibly carry provisions sufficient to last beyond the most remote white settlements. Our food, therefore, consisted of deer, wild turkeys (which were found in great abundance), bear-meat, and, even in times of scarcity, dead horses. Occasionally a little flour, sugar, and coffee might last over to the mountains; but those who held these articles asked exorbitant prices for them, and it was but few who tasted such luxuries.

We were now in the buffalo country, but the In-

dians had driven them all away.   Before we left the
settlements, our party made free use of the bee-hives,
pigs, and poultry belonging to the settlers ; a marauding practice commonly indulged in by the mountaineers, who well knew that the strength of their party
secured them against any retaliation on the part of the
sufferers.

There were two Spaniards in our company, whom
we one morning left behind us to catch some horses
which had strayed away from the camp.   The two men
stopped at a house inhabited by a respectable white
woman, and they, seeing her without protection, committed a disgraceful assault upon her person.   They
were pursued to the camp by a number of the settlers,
who made known to us the outrage committed upon
the woman.   We all regarded the crime with the utmost abhorrence, and felt mortified that any of our
party should be guilty of conduct so revolting.   The
culprits were arrested, and they at once admitted their
guilt.   A council was called in the presence of the settlers, and the culprits offered their choice of two punishments : either to be hung to the nearest tree, or to
receive one hundred lashes each on the bare back.
They chose the latter punishment, which was immediately inflicted upon them by four of our party.   Having no cat-o'-nine-tails in our possession, the lashes
were inflicted with hickory withes.   Their backs were
dreadfully lacerated, and the blood flowed in streams
to the ground.   The following morning the two Spaniards, and two of our best horses, were missing from
the camp ; we did not pursue them, but, by the tracks
we discovered of them, it was evident they had started
for New Mexico.

CHAPTER IV.

Severe Sufferings in the Camp.—Grand Island.—Platte River.—Up the South Fork of the Platte.—The Dog, the Wolf, and the first Buffalo.

ON our arrival at the upper camp, related in the preceding chapter, we found the men, twenty-six in number, reduced to short rations, in weakly condition, and in a discouraged state of mind. They had been expecting the arrival of a large company with abundant supplies, and when we rejoined them without any provisions, they were greatly disappointed. General Ashley exerted himself to infuse fresh courage into their disconsolate breasts, well knowing himself, however, that, unless we could find game, the chances were hard against us.

We remained in camp three or four days, until we were well refreshed, and then deliberated upon our next proceeding. Knowing there must be game farther up the river, we moved forward. Our allowance was half a pint of flour a day per man, which we made into a kind of gruel; if we happened to kill a duck or a goose, it was shared as fairly as possible. I recalled to mind the incidents of our Pawnee expedition.

The third evening we made a halt for a few days. We had seen no game worth a charge of powder during our whole march, and our rations were confined to the half pint of flour per day.

We numbered thirty-four men, all told, and a duller encampment, I suppose, never was witnessed. No jokes, no fire-side stories, no fun; each man rose in the morning with the gloom of the preceding night filling his mind; we built our fires and partook of our scanty repast without saying a word.

At last our general gave orders for the best hunters to sally out and try their fortune. I seized my rifle and issued from the camp alone, feeling so reduced in strength that my mind involuntarily reverted to the extremity I had been reduced to with Harris. About three hundred yards from camp I saw two teal ducks; I leveled my rifle, and handsomely decapitated one. This was a temptation to my constancy; and appetite and conscientiousness had a long strife as to the disposal of the booty. I reflected that it would be but an inconsiderable trifle in my mess of four hungry men, while to roast and eat him myself would give me strength to hunt for more. A strong inward feeling remonstrated against such an invasion of the rights of my starving messmates; but if, by fortifying myself, I gained ability to procure something more substantial than a teal duck, my dereliction would be sufficiently atoned, and my overruling appetite, at the same time, gratified.

Had I admitted my messmates to the argument, they might possibly have carried it adversely. But I received the conclusion as valid; so, roasting him without ceremony in the bushes, I devoured the duck alone, and felt greatly invigorated with the meal.

Passing up the stream, I pushed forward to fulfill my obligation. At the distance of about a mile from the camp I came across a narrow deer-trail through some rushes, and directly across the trail, with only the centre of his body visible (his two extremities being hidden by the rushes), not more than fifty yards distant, I saw a fine large buck standing. I did not

wait for a nearer shot. I fired, and broke his back.
I dispatched him by drawing my knife across his
throat, and, having partially dressed him, hung him on
a tree close by. Proceeding onward, I met a large
white wolf, attracted, probably, by the scent of the
deer. I shot him, and, depriving him of his meal, devoted him for a repast to the camp. Before I returned, I succeeded in killing three good-sized elk, which,
added to the former, afforded a pretty good display of
meat.

I then returned near enough to the camp to signal
to them to come to my assistance. They had heard
the reports of my rifle, and, knowing that I would not
waste ammunition, had been expecting to see me return with game. All who were able turned out to
my summons; and when they saw the booty awaiting
them, their faces were irradiated with joy.

Each man shouldered his load; but there was not
one capable of carrying the weight of forty pounds.
The game being all brought into camp, the fame of
"Jim Beckwourth" was celebrated by all tongues.
Amid all this gratulation, I could not separate my
thoughts from the duck which had supplied my clan-
destine meal in the bushes. I suffered them to appease their hunger with the proceeds of my toil before
I ventured to tell my comrades of the offense I had
been guilty of. All justified my conduct, declaring my
conclusions obvious. As it turned out, my proceeding was right enough; but if I had failed to meet with
any game, I had been guilty of an offense which would,
ever after, have haunted me.

At this present time I never kill a duck on my
ranche, and there are thousands of teal duck there, but
I think of my feast in the bushes while my compan-

ions were famishing in the camp. Since that time I have never refused to share my last shilling, my last biscuit, or my only blanket with a friend, and I think the recollection of that "temptation in the wilderness" will ever serve as a lesson to more constancy in the future.

The day following we started forward up the river, and, after progressing some four or five miles, came in sight of plenty of deer-sign. The general ordered a halt, and directed all hunters out as before. We sallied out in different directions, our general, who was a good hunter, forming one of the number. At a short distance from the camp I discovered a large buck passing slowly between myself and the camp, at about pistol-shot distance. As I happened to be standing against a tree, he had not seen me. I fired ; the ball passed through his body, and whizzed past the camp. Leaving him, I encountered a second deer within three quarters of a mile. I shot him, and hung him on a limb. Encouraged with my success, I climbed a tree to get a fairer view of the ground. Looking around from my elevated position, I perceived some large, dark-colored animal grazing on the side of a hill, some mile and a half distant. I was determined to have a shot at him, whatever he might be. I knew meat was in demand, and that fellow, well stored, was worth more than a thousand teal ducks.

I therefore approached, with the greatest precaution, to within fair rifle-shot distance, scrutinizing him very closely, and still unable to make out what he was. I could see no horns ; and if he was a bear, I thought him an enormous one. I took sight at him over my faithful rifle, which had never failed me, and then set it down, to contemplate the huge animal still farther.

Finally, I resolved to let fly; taking good aim, I pulled trigger, the rifle cracked, and I then made rapid retreat toward the camp. After running about two hundred yards, and hearing nothing in movement behind me, I ventured to look round, and, to my great joy, I saw the animal had fallen.

Continuing my course on to the camp, I encountered the general, who, perceiving blood on my hands, addressed me, "Have you shot any thing, Jim?"

I replied, "Yes, sir."

"What have you shot?"

"Two deer and something else," I answered.

"And what is the something else?" he inquired.

"I do not know, sir."

"What did he look like?" the general interrogated. "Had he horns?"

"I saw no horns, sir."

"What color was the animal?"

"You can see him, general," I replied, "by climbing yonder tree."

The general ascended the tree accordingly, and looking through his spy-glass, which he always carried, he exclaimed, "A buffalo, by heavens!" and, coming nimbly down the tree, he gave orders for us to take a couple of horses, and go and dress the buffalo, and bring him into camp.

I suggested that two horses could not carry the load; six were therefore dispatched, and they all came back well packed with his remains.

There was great rejoicing throughout the camp at such bountiful provision, and all fears of starvation were removed, at least for the present. The two deer were also brought in, besides a fine one killed by the general, and ducks, geese, and such like were freely added by the other hunters, who had taken a wider circuit.

It appears strange that, although I had traveled hundreds of miles in the buffalo country, this one was the first I had ever seen. The conviction weighing upon my mind that it was a huge bear I was approaching had so excited me that, although within fair gunshot, I actually could not see his horns. The general and my companions had many a hearty laugh at my expense, he often expressing wonder that my keen eye could not, when close to the animal, perceive the horns, while he could see them plainly near two miles distant.

A severe storm setting in about this time, had it not been for our excellent store of provisions we should most probably have perished of starvation. There was no game to be procured, and our horses were beginning to die for want of nourishment. We remained in this camp until our provisions were all expended, and our only resource was the flesh of the horses which died of starvation and exposure to the storm. It was not such nutritious food as our fat buffalo and venison, but in our present circumstances it relished tolerably well.

Were General Ashley now living, he would recollect the hardships and delights we experienced in this expedition.

When the storm was expended we moved up the river, hoping to fall in with game. We, unfortunately, found but little on our course. When we had advanced some twenty miles we halted. Our position looked threatening. It was mid-winter, and every thing around us bore a gloomy aspect. We were without provisions, and we saw no means of obtaining any. At this crisis, six or seven Indians of the Pawnee Loup

band came into our camp. Knowing them to be friendly, we were overjoyed to see them. They informed
our interpreter that their village was only four miles
distant, which at once accounted for the absence of
game. They invited us to their lodges, where they
could supply us with every thing that we needed;
but on our representing to them our scarcity of horses,
and the quantity of peltry we had no means of packing, they immediately started off to their village (our
interpreter accompanying them) in quest of horses, and
speedily returned with a sufficient number. Packing
our effects, we accompanied them to their village, Two
Axe, of whom I have previously made mention, and a
Spaniard named Antoine Behele, chief of the band,
forming part of our escort.

Arrived at their village, which we found well provided with every thing we needed, the Indians gave
us a hospitable reception, and spread a feast which, as
they had promised, " made all our hearts glad." Our
horses, too, were well cared for, and soon assumed a
more rotund appearance. We purchased for our future use beans, pumpkins, corn, cured meat, besides
some beaver-skins, giving them in exchange a variety
of manufactured goods used in the Indian trade, of
which we had a great plenty. We replaced our lost
horses by purchasing others in their stead; and now,
every thing being ready for departure, our general in-
timated to Two Axe his wish to get on.

Two Axe objected. "My men are about to surround the buffalo," he said; "if you go now, you will
frighten them. You must stay four days more, then
you may go."

His word was law, so we staid accordingly.

Within the four days appointed they made "the

surround," and killed fourteen hundred buffaloes. The tongues were counted by General Ashley himself, and thus I can guarantee the truth of the assertion.

To the reader unacquainted with the Indian mode of taking these animals, a concise description may not be uninteresting.

There were probably engaged in this hunt from one to two thousand Indians, some mounted and some on foot. They encompass a large space where the buffaloes are contained, and, closing in around them on all points, form a complete circle. Their circle at first inclosed may measure perhaps six miles in diameter, with an irregular circumference determined by the movements of the herd. When "the surround" is formed, the hunters radiate from the main body to the right and left until the ring is entire. The chief then gives the order to charge, which is communicated along the ring with the speed of lightning; every man then rushes to the centre, and the work of destruction is begun. The unhappy victims, finding themselves hemmed in on every side, run this way and that in their mad efforts to escape. Finding all chance of escape impossible, and seeing their slaughtered fellows drop dead at their feet, they bellow with affright, and in the confusion that whelms them, lose all power of resistance. The slaughter generally lasts two or three hours, and seldom many get clear of the weapons of their assailants.

The field over, the "surround" presents the appearance of one vast slaughter-house. He who has been most successful in the work of devastation is celebrated as a hero, and receives the highest honors from the "fair sex," while he who has been so unfortunate as not to kill a buffalo is jeered and ridiculed by the whole band. Flaying, dressing, and preserving the meat next engages their attention, and affords them full employment for several weeks.

The "surround" accomplished, we received permission from Two Axe to take up our line of march. Accordingly, we started along the river, and had only proceeded five miles from the village when we found that the Platte forked. Taking the south fork, we journeyed on some six miles, when we encamped. So we continued every day, making slow progress, some days not advancing more than four or five miles, until we had left the Pawnee villages three hundred miles in our rear. We found plenty of buffalo along our route until we approached the Rocky Mountains, when the buffalo, as well as all other game, became scarce, and we had to resort to the beans and corn supplied us by the Pawnees.

CHAPTER V.

Sufferings on the Platte.—Arrive at the Rocky Mountains.—Fall out with General Ashley.—Horses again stolen by the Crow Indians. —Sickness of our General.—Rescue of the General from a wounded Buffalo. — Remarkable Rescue of the General from the Green River "Suck."

NOT finding any game for a number of days, we again felt alarmed for our safety. The snow was deep on the ground, and our poor horses could obtain no food but the boughs and bark of the cotton-wood trees. Still we pushed forward, seeking to advance as far as possible, in order to open a trade with the Indians, and occupy ourselves in trapping during the finish of the season. We were again put upon reduced rations, one pint of beans per day being the allowance to a mess of four men, with other articles in proportion.

Here I had a serious difficulty with our general, which arose in the following manner. The general desired me to shoe his horse, which I cheerfully proceeded to do. I had finished setting three shoes, and had yet one nail to drive in the fourth, when, about to drive the last nail, the horse, which had been very restless during the whole time, withdrew his foot from me. My patience becoming exhausted, I applied the hammer several times to his belly, which is the usual punishment inflicted by blacksmiths upon unruly horses. The general, who was standing near, flew into a violent rage, and poured his curses thick and fast upon me. Feeling hurt at such language from the lips of a man whom I had treated like my own brother, I retorted, reminding him of the many obligations he owed me. I told him that his language to me was harsh and unmerited; that I had thus far served him faithfully; that I had done for him what no other man would do, periling my life for him on several occasions; that I had been successful in killing game when his men were in a state of starvation; and, warming at the recapitulation, I added, "There is one more nail to drive, general, to finish shoeing that horse, which you may drive for yourself, or let go undriven, for I will see you dead before I will lift another finger to serve you."

But little more was said on either side at that time.

The next morning the general gave orders to pack up and move on. He showed me a worn-out horse, which he ordered me to pack and drive along. I very well knew that the horse could not travel far, even without a pack.

Still, influenced by the harsh language the general had addressed to me on the previous day, I said, "General, I will pack the horse, but I wish you to understand that, whenever he gives out, there I leave him, horse and pack."

"Obey my orders, and let me have none of your insolence, sir," said the general.

I was satisfied this was imposed upon me for punishment. I, however, packed the horse with two pigs of lead and sundry small articles, and drove him along in the rear, the others having started a considerable time previous. The poor animal struggled on for about a mile, and then fell groaning under his burden. I unpacked him, assisted him to rise, and, repacking him, drove him on again in the trail that the others had left in the snow. Proceeding half a mile farther, he again fell. I went through the same ceremony as before. He advanced a few yards, and fell a third time. Feeling mad at the general for imposing such a task upon me, my hands tingling with cold through handling the snowy pack-ropes, I seized my hammer from the pack, and, striking with all my power, it penetrated the poor animal's skull.

"There," said I, "take that! I only wish you were General Ashley."

"You do, do you?" said a voice from the bushes on the side of the trail.

I well knew the voice: it was the general himself; and another volley of curses descended uninterruptedly upon my head.

I was not the man to flinch. "What I said I meant," I exclaimed, "and it makes no odds whether you heard it or not."

"You are an infernal scoundrel, and I'll shoot you;"

and, suiting the action to the word, he cocked his piece and leveled it.

I cocked my rifle and presented it also, and then we stood at bay, looking each other direct in the eye.

"General," I at length said, "you have addressed language to me which I allow no man to use, and, unless you retract that last epithet, you or I must surely die."

He finally said, "I will acknowledge that it was language which never should be used to a man, but when I am angry I am apt to speak hastily. But," he added, "I will make you suffer for this."

"Not in your service, general," I replied. "You can take your horse now, and do what you please with him. I am going to return to St. Louis."

The general almost smiled at the idea.

"You will play —— going back to St. Louis," he said, "when, in truth, you were afraid of being killed by the Indians, through being left too far behind with that old horse."

I left general, horse, and pack, and started on to overtake the advanced party, in order to get my saddle-bags before leaving them. Approaching the party, I advanced to Fitzpatrick (in whose possession they were) and addressed him: "Hold up, Fitzpatrick; give me my saddle-bags. I am going to leave you, and return to St. Louis."

"What!" exclaimed he, "have you had more words with the general?"

"Yes," I replied, "words that will never be forgiven—by *me*, at least, in this life. I am bound to return."

"Well," said he, "wait till we encamp, a few hundred yards ahead. Your things are in the pack; when we stop you can get them."

I accompanied them till they encamped; then, taking my goods from the pack, I was getting ready to return, when the general came up.

Seeing me about to carry my threat into execution, he addressed me: "Jim, you have ammunition belonging to me; you can not take *that* with you."

Luckily, I had plenty of my own, so I delivered up all in my possession belonging to him.

"Sir," I said, "as Fortune has favored me with plenty, I deliver up yours; but, if I had had none of my own, I would have retained a portion of yours, or died in the attempt. And it seems to me that you must have a very small soul to see a man turned adrift without any thing to protect him against hostile savages, or procure him necessary food in traversing this wide wilderness."

He then said no more to me, but called Fitzpatrick, and requested him to dissuade me from leaving. Fitzpatrick came, and exerted all his eloquence to deter me from going, telling me of the great distance before me, the danger I ran, when alone, of being killed by Indians—representing the almost certain fact that I must perish from starvation. He reminded me that it was now March, and the snows were already melting; that Spring, with all its beauties, would soon be ushered in, and I should lose the sublime scenery of the Rocky Mountains.

But my mind was bent upon going; all my former love for the man was forfeited, and I felt I could never endure his presence again.

Fitzpatrick's mission having failed, the general sent a French boy to intercede, toward whom I felt great

attachment.   He was named Baptiste La Jeunesse,
and was about seventeen years of age.   I had many
times protected this lad from the abuse of his countrymen, and had fought several battles on his account,
for which reason he naturally fled to me for protection,
and had grown to regard me in the light of a father.

When this boy saw that I was in earnest about
leaving, fearing that all attempts at persuasion would
be useless, he hung his nether lip, and appeared perfectly disconsolate.

The general, calling this lad to him, desired him to
come to me and persuade me from the notion of leaving.   He pledged his word to Baptiste that he would
say no more to displease me ; that he would spare no
efforts to accommodate me, and offered me free use of
his horses, assigning as a reason for this concession
that he was unwilling for word to reach the States that
he had suffered a man to perish in the wilderness
through a little private difficulty in the camp.

At this moment Le Pointe presented himself, manifesting by his appearance that he had something of importance to communicate.

" General," said he, " more than half the men are
determined to leave with Beckwourth ; they are now
taking ammunition from the sacks and hiding it about.
What. is to be done ?"

" I will do the best I can."   Then turning to the
lad, he said, " I took Jim's ammunition, thinking to deter him from going; had he insisted upon going, I should
have furnished him with plenty.   Go now," he added,
" and tell him I want him to stay, but if he insists
upon going, to take whatever he wants."

Baptiste left the group which surrounded the general, and made his way to me, with his head inclined.

"Mon frère," said the lad, addressing me as I sat, "the général talk much good. He vant you stay. I tell him you no stay; dat you en colère. I tell him if mon frère go, by gar, I go too. He say, you go talk to Jim, and get him stay. I tell you vat I tink. You stay leetle longer, and if de général talk you bad one time more, den ve go, by gar. You take von good horse, me take von good horse too; ve carry our planket, ve take some viande, and some poudre—den ve live. Ve go now—ve take noting—den ve die."

I knew that the boy gave good advice, and, foregoing my former resolve, I concluded to remain.

My decision was quickly communicated to the whole camp, and the hidden parcels of ammunition were restored to their proper places. The storm in the camp ceased, and all were ready to proceed.

I have heard scores of emigrants (when stopping with me in my "hermitage," in Beckwourth Valley, California) relate their hair-breadth escapes from Indians, and various hardships endured in their passage across the Plains. They would dwell upon their perilous nights when standing guard; their encounters with Indians, or some daring exploit with a buffalo. These recitals were listened to with incredulous ears; for there is in human nature such a love of the marvelous, that traditionary deeds, by dint of repetition, become appropriated to the narrator, and the tales that were related as actual experience now mislead the speaker and the audience.

When I recurred to my own adventures, I would smile at the comparison of their sufferings with what myself and other men of the mountains had really endured in former times. The forts that now afford protection to the traveler were built by ourselves at the constant peril of our lives, amid Indian tribes nearly double their present numbers. Without wives and children to comfort us on our lonely way; without well-furnished wagons to resort to when hungry; no roads before us but trails temporarily made; our clothing consisting of the skins of the animals that had fallen before our unerring rifles, and often whole days on insufficient rations, or entirely without food; occasionally our whole party on guard the entire night, and our strength deserting us through unceasing watching and fatigue; these are sufferings that made theirs appear trivial, and ours surpass in magnitude my power of relation.

Without doubt, many emigrants were subjected to considerable hardship, during the early part of the emigration, by the loss of cattle, and the Indians came in for their full share of blame. But it was through extreme carelessness that so many were lost; and those who have charged their losses upon the Indians have frequently found their stock, or a portion of it, harnessed to wagons either far in advance of them, or lagging carelessly in their rear. The morality of the whites I have not found to exceed very much that of the red man; for there are plenty of the former, belonging to trains on the routes, who would not hesitate to take an ox or two, if any chance offered for getting hold of them.

But to return. At the time when I had concluded to proceed with the party, we were encamped in the prairie, away from any stream (having passed the fork of the Platte), and were again in a starving condition. Except an occasional hare or rabbit, there was no sign of supplying ourselves with any kind of game.

We traveled on till we arrived at Pilot Butte, where

two misfortunes befell us. A great portion of our horses were stolen by the Crow Indians, and General Ashley was taken sick, caused, beyond doubt, by exposure and insufficient fare. Our condition was growing worse and worse; and, as a measure best calculated to procure relief, we all resolved to go on a general hunt, and bring home something to supply our pressing necessities. All who were able, therefore, started in different directions, our customary mode of hunting. I traveled, as near as I could judge, about ten miles from the camp, and saw no signs of game. I reached a high point of land, and, on taking a general survey, I discovered a river which I had never seen in this region before. It was of considerable size, flowing four or five miles distant, and on its banks I observed acres of land covered with moving masses of buffalo. I hailed this as a perfect Godsend, and was overjoyed with the feeling of security infused by my opportune discovery. However, fatigued and weak, I accelerated my return to the camp, and communicated my success to my companions. Their faces brightened up at the intelligence, and all were impatient to be at them.

The general, on learning my intelligence, desired us to move forward to the river with what horses we had left, and each man to carry a pack on his back of the goods that remained after loading the cattle. He farther desired us to roll up snow to provide him with a shelter, and to return the next day to see if he survived.

The men, in their eagerness to get to the river (which is now called Green River), loaded themselves so heavily that three or four were left with nothing but their rifles to carry. Though my feelings toward the general were still unfriendly (knowing that he had expressed sentiments concerning me that were totally unmerited), I could not reconcile myself to deserting him in his present helpless condition. Accordingly, I informed him that if he thought he could endure the journey, I would make arrangements to enable him to proceed along with the company.

He appeared charmed with the magnanimty of the proposal, and declared his willingness to endure any thing in reason. His consent obtained, I prepared a light litter, and, with the assistance of two of the unladen men, placed him upon it, in the easiest position possible; then, attaching two straps to the ends of the litter-bars, we threw them over our shoulders, and, taking the bars in our hands, hoisted our burden, and proceeded with all the ease imaginable. Our rifles were carried by the third man.

The anxiety of the general to remain with us prevented his giving utterance to the least complaint, and we all arrived in good season on the banks of Green River. We were rejoiced to find that our companions who preceded us had killed a fine buffalo, and we abandoned ourselves that evening to a general spirit of rejoicing. Our leader, in a few days, entirely recovered, and we were thus, by my forethought in bringing him with us, spared the labor of a return journey.

We all feasted ourselves to our hearts' content upon the delicious, coarse-grained flesh of the buffalo, of which there was an unlimited supply. There were, besides, plenty of wild geese and teal ducks on the river—the latter, however, I very seldom ventured to kill.

One day several of us were out hunting buffalo, the general, who, by the way, was a very good shot, being among the number. The snow had blown from the level prairie, and the wind had drifted it in deep mass-

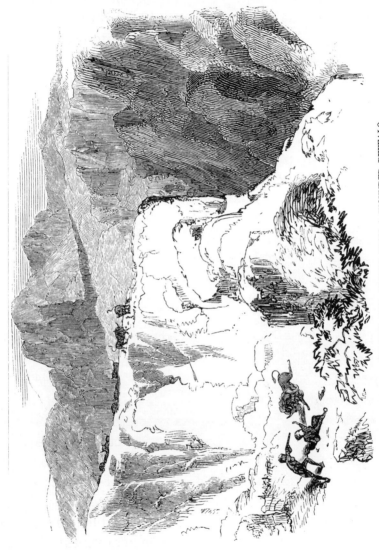

BECKWOURTH RESCUES GEN. ASHLEY FROM A WOUNDED BUFFALO.

es over the margins of the small hills, through which
the buffalo had made trails just wide enough to admit
one at a time. These snow-trails had become quite
deep—like all snow-trails in the spring of the year—
thus affording us a fine opportunity for lurking in one
trail, and shooting a buffalo in another. The general
had wounded a bull, which, smarting with pain, made
a furious plunge at his assailant, burying him in the
snow with a thrust from his savage-looking head and
horns. I, seeing the danger in which he was placed,
sent a ball into the beast just behind the shoulder, instantly dropping him dead. The general was rescued
from almost certain death, having received only a few
scratches in the adventure.

After remaining in camp four or five days, the general resolved upon dividing our party into detachments
of four or five men each, and sending them upon different routes, in order the better to accomplish the object of our perilous journey, which was the collecting
all the beaver-skins possible while the fur was yet
valuable. Accordingly, we constructed several boats
of buffalo hides for the purpose of descending the river and proceeding along any of its tributaries that
might lie in our way.

One of our boats being finished and launched, the
general sprang into it to test its capacity. The boat
was made fast by a slender string, which snapping
with the sudden jerk, the boat was drawn into the
current and drifted away, general and all, in the direction of the opposite shore.

It will be necessary, before I proceed farther, to
give the reader a description, in as concise a manner
as possible, of this "Green River Suck."

We were encamped, as we had discovered during

our frequent excursions, at the head of a great fall of
the Green River, where it passes through the Utah
Mountains. The current, at a small distance from
our camp, became exceedingly rapid, and drew toward
the centre from each shore. This place we named the
Suck. This fall continued for six or eight miles, making a sheer descent, in the entire distance, of upward
of two hundred and fifty feet. The river was filled
with rocks and ledges, and frequent sharp curves, having high mountains and perpendicular cliffs on either
side. Below our camp, the river passed through a
canyon, or *cañon*, as it is usually written, a deep river-
pass through a bluff or mountain, which continued below the fall to a distance of twenty-five or thirty miles.
Wherever there was an eddy or a growth of willows,
there was sure to be found a beaver lodge; the cunning creatures having selected that secluded, and, as
they doubtless considered, inaccessible spot, to conceal
themselves from the watchful eye of the trapper.

To return to the general. His frail bark, having
reached the opposite shore, encountered a ledge of
rocks, and had hardly touched, when, by the action
of the rolling current, it was capsized, and he thrown
struggling into the water. As Providence would have
it, he reached the bluff on the opposite side, and, holding on to the crevices in the high and perpendicular cliff,
sung out lustily for assistance. Not a moment was to be
lost. Some one must attempt to save him, for he could
not hold his present position, in such cold water, long. I
saw that no one cared to risk his life amid such imminent peril, so, calling to a Frenchman of the name of Dor-
way, whom I knew to be one of the best swimmers, to
come to the rescue, I threw off my leggins and plunged

in, supposing he would follow. I swam under water as far as 1 could, to avail myself of the under current (this mode is always practiced by the Indians in crossing a rapid stream). I struck the bluff a few feet above the general. After taking breath for a moment or two, I said to him (by the way, he was no swimmer), "There is only one way I can possibly save you, and I may fail in that; but you must follow my directions in the most minute degree, or we are certainly both lost."

"Any thing you say, James, I will follow," said he.

"Then," I continued, "when I float down to you, place your hands on my shoulder, and do not take hold of my neck. Then, when I give you the word, kick out with all your might, and we may possibly get across."

I then let myself down to the general, who was clinging to the rocks like a swallow. He did as I had directed, and I started, he kicking in my rear like the stern-wheel of a propeller, until I was obliged to bid him desist; for, with such a double propelling power as we produced, I could not keep my mouth out of water. We swam to within a few yards of the opposite shore, where the main suck caught us, and, my strength becoming exhausted, we began slowly to recede from the shore toward inevitable death. At this moment Fitzpatrick thrust a long pole toward us, to the end of which he attached a rope which the party on shore retained possession of. I seized the pole with a death-grip, and we were hauled out of our perilous situation; a few moment's delay, and the world had seen the last of us.

After this rescue, the general remarked to Fitzpatrick, "That Beckwourth is surely one of the most sin-

gular men I ever met. I do not know what to think
of him ; he never speaks to me except when absolutely unavoidable ; still, he is the first and only man to
encounter peril on my behalf. Three times he has
now saved my life when not another man attempted
to succor me. He is a problem I can not possibly
solve."

Agreeably to previous arrangement, on the following
morning our company proposed to disperse in different
directions. While preparing to leave our comfortable
camp to take our chance in the mountains, I happening to be out among the stock, the general inquired for
me, and I was pointed out to him where I stood.

" He is a singular being," he exclaimed ; " he
knows we are about to separate, yet he does not trouble himself to come and bid me good-by. I must go
to him."

Approaching me, he said, "James, we are now about
to part ; these toilsome enterprises in the mountains
are extremely hazardous ; although I hope to see you
again, perhaps we may never meet more. I am under great obligations to you. You have several times
rescued me from certain death, and, by your skill in
hunting, you have done great service to my camp.
When my mind was irritated and harassed, I was betrayed into the use of language toward you which I
regretted immediately after, and still regret. I wish
you to forgive me, and desire to part in friendship. So
long as you continue to use the same precaution you
have hitherto used, I can securely hope you will escape
all accident, and look forward to meeting you again
under more auspicious circumstances ;" and he concluded by bidding me good-by.

I bade him good-by, and we separated.

Previous to this, and after his rescue from the
" Suck," he mentioned to Fitzpatrick that I ought to
have the lead of a party, and that he believed I was as
capable as any one in the company for it.   Fitzpatrick
told him he did not believe I would accept the responsibility.   The general bade him ask me.   He came and
communicated to me our general's wish, and asked me
if I would take the leadership of one of our detached
parties.

I declined the offer, assigning as my reason that I
was too young to undertake the responsibilities of the
charge; that this was my first trip to the mountains,
and I had but little experience in trapping, and that
there were older men better qualified for the duty.

The leadership of a party of a fur company is a very
responsible post.   Placed similarly to a captain of a
whaling vessel, where all depends upon his success,
if a captain is fortunate, and returns from a profitable
voyage, of course, in the eyes of the owners, he is a
first-rate officer, and stands well for the future.   But
if he has experienced unusual hardships, and returns
more or less unsuccessful, he is disgraced in his command, and is thrust aside for a more fortunate man.
It is just similar with trappers in the mountains;
whatever is their fortune, good or bad, the leader is the
person on whom the praise or blame falls.

CHAPTER Vl.

We separate into six Detachments, and start out.—Trapping on Green
River.—Narrow Escape from a Massacre by the Arrap-a-hos.—One
Man murdered in Camp.—Retreat.—Fall in with a Detachment of
our Company.—Great Joy at the Meeting.—Return of the Detachments to the Place of Rendezvous at the " Suck."

AFTER "caching" our peltry and goods by burying
them in safe places, we received instructions from our
general to rendezvous at the " Suck" by the first of
July following. Bidding each other adieu, for we could
hardly expect we should meet again, we took up our
different lines of march.

Our party consisted, led by one Clements, of six,
among whom was the boy Baptiste, he always insist-
ing on remaining with his brother (as he called me).
Our route was up the river—a country that none of us
had ever seen before—where the foot of the white man
had seldom, if ever, left its print. We were very successful in finding beaver as we progressed, and we obtained plenty of game for the wants of our small party.
Wherever we hauled up a trap, we usually found a
beaver, besides a considerable number we killed with
the rifle.

In moving up the river we came to a small stream
—one of the tributaries of Green River—which we
named " Horse Creek," in honor of a wild horse we
found on its banks. The Creek abounded with the
objects of our search, and in a very few days we succeeded in taking over one hundred beavers, the skins
of which were worth ten dollars per pound in St. Lou-

is. Sixty skins, when dried, formed a pack of one hundred pounds. After having finished our work on Horse Creek, we returned to the main river, and proceeded on, meeting with very good success, until we encountered another branch, which we subsequently named Le Brache Creek, from our comrade who was murdered by the Indians. Our success was much greater here than at any point since leaving the Suck, and we followed it up until we came to a deep *cañon*, in which we encamped.

The next day, while the men were variously engaged about the camp, happening to be in a more elevated position than the others, I saw a party of Indians approaching within a few yards, evidently unaware of our being in their neighborhood. I immediately shouted, " Indians! Indians! to your guns, men!" and leveled my rifle at the foremost of them. They held up their hands, saying, " Bueno! bueno!" meaning that they were good or friendly; at which my companions cried out to me, " Don't fire! don't fire! they are friendly—they speak Spanish." But we were sorry afterward we did not all shoot. Our horses had taken fright at the confusion and ran up the cañon. Baptiste and myself went in pursuit of them. When we came back with them we found sixteen Indians sitting around our camp smoking, and jabbering their own tongue, which none of us understood. They passed the night and next day with us in apparent friendship. Thinking this conduct assumed, from the fact that they rather " overdid the thing," we deemed it prudent to retrace our steps to the open prairie, where, if they did intend to commence an attack upon us, we should have a fairer chance of defending ourselves. Accordingly, we packed up and left, all the Indians following us.

The next day they continued to linger about the camp. We had but slight suspicion of their motives, although, for security, we kept constant guard upon them. From this they proceeded to certain liberties (which I here strictly caution all emigrants and mountaineers against ever permitting), such as handling our guns, except the arms of the guard, piling them, and then carrying them together. At length one of the Indians shouldered all the guns, and, starting off with them, ran fifty yards from camp. Mentioning to my mates I did not like the manœuvres of these fellows, I started after the Indian and took my gun from him, Baptiste doing the same, and we brought them back to camp. Our companions chided us for doing so, saying we should anger the Indians by doubting their friendship. I said I considered my gun as safe in my own hands as in the hands of a strange savage; if they chose to give up theirs, they were at liberty to do so.

When night came on, we all lay down except poor Le Brache, who kept guard, having an Indian with him to replenish the fire. Some of the men had fallen asleep, lying near by, when we were all suddenly startled by a loud cry from Le Brache and the instant report of a gun, the contents of which passed between Baptiste and myself, who both occupied one bed, the powder burning a hole in our upper blankets. We were all up in an instant. An Indian had seized my rifle, but I instantly wrenched it from him, though, I acknowledge, I was too terrified to shoot. When we had in some measure recovered from our sudden fright, I hastened to Le Brache, and discovered that a tomahawk had been sunk in his head, and there remained. I pulled it out, and in examining the ghastly wound.

buried all four fingers of my right hand in his brain. We bound up his head, but he was a corpse in a few moments.

Not an Indian was then to be seen, but we well knew they were in the bushes close by, and that, in all probability, we should every one share the fate of our murdered comrade. What to do now was the universal inquiry. With the butt of my rifle I scattered the fire, to prevent the Indians making a sure mark of us. We then proceeded to pack up with the utmost dispatch, intending to move into the open prairie, where, if they attacked us again, we could at least defend ourselves, notwithstanding our disparity of numbers, we being but five to sixteen.

On searching for Le Brache's gun, it was nowhere to be found, the Indian who had killed him having doubtless carried it off. While hastily packing our articles, I very luckily found five quivers well stocked with arrows, the bows attached, together with two Indian guns. These well supplied our missing rifle, for I had practiced so much with bow and arrow that I was considered a good shot.

When in readiness to leave, our leader inquired in which direction the river lay; his agitation had been so great that his memory had failed him. I directed the way, and desired every man to put the animals upon their utmost speed until we were safely out of the willows, which order was complied with. While thus running the gauntlet, the balls and arrows whizzed around us as fast as our hidden enemies could send them. Not a man was scratched, however, though two of our horses were wounded, my horse having received an arrow in the neck, and another being wounded near the hip, both slightly. Pursuing our course, we arrived soon in the open ground, where we considered ourselves comparatively safe.

Arriving at a small rise in the prairie, I suggested to our leader that this would be a good place to make a stand, for if the Indians followed us we had the advantage in position.

"No," said he, "we will proceed on to New Mexico."

I was astonished at his answer, well knowing— though but slightly skilled in geography—that New Mexico must be many hundred miles farther south. However, I was not captain, and we proceeded. Keeping the return track, we found ourselves, in the afternoon of the following day, about sixty miles from the scene of murder.

The assault had been made, as we afterward learned, by three young Indians, who were ambitious to distinguish themselves in the minds of their tribe by the massacre of an American party.

We were still descending the banks of the Green River, which is the main branch of the Colorado, when, about the time mentioned above, I discovered horses in the skirt of the woods on the opposite side. My companions pronounced them buffalo, but I was confident they were horses, because I could distinguish white ones among them. Proceeding still farther, I discovered men with the horses, my comrades still confident I was in error; speedily, however, they all became satisfied of my correctness, and we formed the conclusion that we had come across a party of Indians. We saw by their manœuvres that they had discovered us, for they were then collecting all their property together.

We held a short council, which resulted in a determination to retreat toward the mountains. I, for one, was tired of retreating, and refused to go farther. Baptiste joining me in my resolve. We took up a strong position for defense, being a place of difficult approach; and having our guns, and ammunition, and abundance of arrows for defense, considering our numbers, we felt ourselves rather a strong garrison. The other three left us to our determination to fall together, and took to the prairie; but, changing mind, they returned, and rejoined us in our position, deeming our means of defense better in one body than when divided. We all, therefore, determined to sell our lives as dearly as possible should the enemy attack us, feeling sure that we could kill five times our number before we were overpowered, and that we should, in all probability, beat them off.

By this time the supposed enemy had advanced toward us, and one of them hailed us in English as follows:

" Who are you ?"

" We are trappers."

" What company do you belong to ?"

" General Ashley's."

" Hurrah! hurrah! hurrah!" they all shouted, and we, in turn, exhausted our breath in replying.

" Is that you, Jim Beckwourth ?" said a voice from the party.

" Yes. Is that you, Castenga ?" I replied.

He answered in the affirmative, and there arose another hurrah.

We inquired where their camp was. They informed us it was two miles below, at the ford. Baptiste and myself mounted our horses, descended the bank, plunged into the river, and were soon exchanging salu-

tations with another of the general's old detachments.
They also had taken us for Indians, and had gathered
in their horses while we took up our position for defense.

The night was spent in general rejoicing, in relating
our adventures, and recounting our various successes
and reverses.   There is as much heartfelt joy experienced in falling in with a party of fellow-trappers in
the mountains as is felt at sea when, after a long voyage, a friendly vessel just from port is spoken and
boarded.   In both cases a thousand questions are asked; all have wives, sweethearts, or friends to inquire
after, and then the general news from the States is
taken up and discussed.

The party we had fallen in with consisted of sixteen
men.   They had been two years out; had left Fort
Yellow Stone only a short time previously, and were
provided with every necessary for a long excursion.
They had not seen the general, and did not know he
was in the mountains.   They had lost some of their
men, who had fallen victims to the Indians, but in
trapping had been generally successful.   Our little
party also had done extremely well, and we felt great
satisfaction in displaying to them seven or eight pack-
ets of sixty skins each.   We related to them the murder of Le Brache, and every trapper boiled with indig-
nation at the recital.   All wanted instantly to start in
pursuit, and revenge upon the Indians the perpetration
of their treachery; but there was no probability of
overtaking them, and they suffered their anger to cool
down.

The second day after our meeting, I proposed that
the most experienced mountaineers of their party should
return with Baptiste and myself to perform the burial

rites of our friend. I proposed three men, with our-selves, as sufficient for the sixteen Indians, in case we should fall in with them, and they would certainly be enough for the errand if we met no one. My former comrades were too tired to return.

We started, and arrived at our unfortunate camp, but the body of our late friend was not to be found, though we discovered some of his long black hair clot-ted with blood.

On raising the traps which we had set before our precipitate departure, we found a beaver in every one except four, which contained each a leg, the beavers having amputated them with their teeth. We then returned to our companions, and moved on to Willow Creek, where we were handy to the *caches* of our ren-dezvous at the "Suck." It was now about June 1st, 1822.

Here we spent our time very pleasantly, occupying ourselves with hunting, fishing, target-shooting, foot-racing, gymnastic, and sundry other exercises. The other detachments now came in, bringing with them quantities of peltry, all having met with very great success.

CHAPTER VII.

Arrival of General Ashley and Party.—His Relation of their Sufferings
after leaving the Rendezvous.—Their Excursion to Salt Lake.—Fall
in with a Fur Company before unknown to the Mountaineers.—His
final Fortune, and return to St. Louis.

SITTING in camp one beautiful summer morning—
for the month of June is always lovely in northern
latitudes—an Indian lass stepped up to me, and wished me to kill a deer or an antelope, and bring her the
brains, wherewith to dress a deer-skin, offering me, in
compensation, a handsome pair of moccasins. Thinking to save two dollars by a few minutes' exertion, I
took my rifle and alone left camp. After traveling
two miles, I obtained sight of a fine antelope, which
had also seen me, and kept himself at a respectful distance. In following him up to get a fair shot, I at
length found myself about ten miles from camp, with
small prospect of getting either brains or moccasins.

While among the wild sage, still trying to approach
the antelope, I observed a horse and rider coming in
my direction. Feeling satisfied that the rider was an
Indian, I at once made up my mind to run no farther
after the antelope, but to shoot him, and take his
brains to the squaw, as she would know no difference. I therefore concealed myself in the sage until
he should come within range of my rifle. Becoming
impatient, at length, at his tardy approach, I raised
my head to take a look, when, to my utter astonishment, I saw General Ashley in the act of mounting
his horse at a few paces' distance. He had stopped

to adjust something belonging to his saddle, and to this trifling circumstance he was indebted for his life. On seeing who it was, I became so excited at the narrow escape he had made, that my rifle fell from my hand. If I had shot him, it being well known in camp that I was not entirely reconciled to him, I should, most undoubtedly, have been charged with his murder. I told the general of the narrow escape he had just made. He was surprised at my mistaking him for an Indian, and inquired if I did not know that they never traveled singly.

I then inquired after his health, and the success he had met with, and then related to him our own losses and success generally. He inquired where the camp was. I told him it was close at hand. In conducting the general thither, he pronounced my " close at hand" rather distant.

Arrived at camp, the general related their adventures in descending the Green River over the rapids, through the Suck and *cañon*, in the following narrative:

" We had a very dangerous passage down the river, and suffered more than I ever wish to see men suffer again. You are aware that we took but little provision with us, not expecting that the *cañon* extended so far. In passing over the rapids, where we lost two boats and three guns, we made use of ropes in letting down our boats over the most dangerous places. Our provisions soon gave out. We found plenty of beaver in the *cañon* for some miles, and, expecting to find them in as great plenty all the way, we saved none of their carcasses, which constituted our food. As we proceeded, however, they became more and more scarce, until there were none to be seen, and we were entirely out of provisions. To retrace the river was impossible, and to ascend the perpendicular cliffs, which hemmed us in on either side, was equally impossible. Our only alternative was to go ahead.

"After passing six days without tasting food, the men were weak and disheartened. I listened to all their murmurings and heart-rending complaints. They often spoke of home and friends, declaring they would never see them more. Some spoke of wives and children whom they dearly loved, and who must shortly become widows and orphans. They had toiled, they said, through every difficulty; had risked their lives among wild beasts and hostile Indians in the wilderness, all which they were willing to undergo; but who could bear up against actual starvation?

"I encouraged them all in my power, telling them that I bore an equal part in their sufferings; that I, too, was toiling for those I loved, and whom I yet hoped to see again; that we should all endeavor to keep up our courage, and not add to our misfortunes by giving way to despondency.

"Another night was passed amid the barren rocks. The next morning, the fearful proposition was made by some of the party for the company to cast lots, to see which should be sacrificed to afford food for the others, without which they must inevitably perish. My feelings at such a proposition can not be described. I begged of them to wait one day more, and make all the way they could meanwhile. By doing so, I said, we must come to a break in the cañon, where we could escape. They consented, and, moving down the river as fast as the current would carry us, to our inexpressible joy, we found a break, and a camp of trappers therein.

"All now rejoiced that they had not carried their

fearful proposition into effect. We had fallen into good hands, and slowly recruited ourselves with the party, which was under the charge of one Provo, a man with whom I was well acquainted. By his advice, we left the river and proceeded in a northwesterly direction. Provo was well provided with provisions and horses, and he supplied us with both. We remained with his party until we arrived at the Great Salt Lake. Here I fell in with a large company of trappers, composed of Canadians and Iroquois Indians, under the command of Peter Ogden, in the service of the Northwest Fur Company. With this party I made a very good bargain, as you will see when they arrive at our camp, having purchased all their peltry on very reasonable terms."

The general concluded his narrative, and was congratulated by all present on his safe arrival. We were all rejoiced to hear that, during an absence of six or seven weeks, he had not lost a man.

We then proceeded to *uncache* our goods, which we had buried at the " Suck," and prepared to move up the river to a point where the Canadians and Indians had engaged to meet him with their peltry. The general appointed me captain of a party to meet the Canadians, and escort them to the rendezvous which he had proposed to them, while he and some few others remained to bring up the goods, consisting of flour, sugar, coffee, blankets, tobacco, whisky, and all other articles necessary for that region.

There were at this time assembled at our camp about two hundred men, besides many women and children—for many of the Frenchmen were accompanied with a squaw. I took with me eighty men, with their women, children, and effects, leaving for the general a strong guard of one hundred and twenty men, to escort the goods up the river.

Two days after we had started, being about a mile from the river, we stopped to dress a buffalo. While resting, a party of four hundred Indians passed at full speed between us and the river, driving a large number of horses. We mounted with all haste and started after them, but not in time to recapture the whole of the horses, which they had just stolen, or, rather, forced from the general in the presence of his men.

We fired on the Indians, and, after a smart skirmish, in which I received an arrow in the left arm, we recaptured twenty-seven of the animals, the Indians running off the remainder, amounting to seventy or eighty head; a severe loss, for we needed them to carry our peltry. We found three dead Indians on the field, whom we scalped, leaving them for the wolves to feed on. I ordered a camp to be formed wherein to leave the women and children, with a guard, and then, mustering all the horses, we took the return track to the camp, fearing that the party had been surprised and perhaps all massacred. On the road we met a party which the general had dispatched to us, he having similar apprehensions in regard to us. They informed us that the Indians had broken in upon them in broad daylight, unawares, and stampeded one hundred head of horses; that two of their men were wounded, of whom Sublet (since well known to the Western people) was one. It seems he was with the horses at the time the Indians rushed in upon them; he fired at one, but missed him; then clubbing his piece, he struck the Indian, nearly knocking him off his horse. The Indian rallied again and fired at Sublet, wounding him slightly. Both the wounded men were doing well.

Arrived at the camp, we related our exploit to the general. He was overjoyed to hear that we had re-captured so many horses without the loss of a single man. This was my first engagement with Indians in the capacity of officer; and never did Generals Scott or Taylor feel more exultation at their most signal tri-umph than did I in this trifling affair, where a score or so of horses were captured at the expense of myself and two of my men receiving slight wounds.

We all moved on together, feeling ourselves a match for a thousand Indians, should they dare to assail us. On arriving at the rendezvous, we found the main body of the Salt Lake party already there with the whole of their effects. The general would open none of his goods, except tobacco, until all had arrived, as he wish-ed to make an equal distribution; for goods were then very scarce in the mountains, and hard to obtain.

When all had come in, he opened his goods, and there was a general jubilee among all at the rendez-vous. We constituted quite a little town, number-ing at least eight hundred souls, of whom one half were women and children. There were some among us who had not seen any groceries, such as coffee, sugar, &c., for several months. The whisky went off as freely as water, even at the exorbitant price he sold it for. All kinds of sports were indulged in with a heartiness that would astonish more civilized societies.

The general transacted a very profitable trade with our Salt Lake friends. He purchased all their beaver, of which they had collected a large quantity, so that, with his purchases and those of our own collection, he had now one hundred and ninety-one packs, all in excellent order, and worth $1000 per pack in St. Louis.

There lay the general's fortune in one immense pile, collected at the expense of severe toil, privation, suffering, peril, and, in some cases, loss of life. It was supposed the general was indebted in the mountains and elsewhere to the amount of $75,000. The skins he had purchased of the Northwest Company and free trappers had cost him comparatively little; if he should meet with no misfortune on his way to St. Louis, he would receive enough to pay all his debts, and have an ample fortune besides.

In about a week the general was ready to start for home. The packs were all arranged; our Salt Lake friends offered him the loan of all the horses he wanted, and engaged to escort him to the head of Wind River, one of the branches of the Yellow Stone. The number selected to return with the general was twenty men, including my humble self; thirty men were to accompany us as a guard, and to return the horses we had borrowed.

The night previous to our departure, I and my boy Baptiste were sleeping among the packs, as were also some of the other men, when the sentinel came to me to tell me that he had seen something which he believed to be Indians. I arose, and satisfied myself that he was correct. I sent a man to acquaint the general, at the same time waking the boy and two men near me. We noiselessly raised ourselves, took as good aim as possible, and, at a signal from me, all four fired. We saw two men run. By this time the whole camp was aroused; the general asked me what I had fired at. I told him I believed an Indian.

"Very good," said he; "whenever you see an Indian about the camp at night, you do right to shoot him."

Our whole force was on guard from that time till the morning, when we discovered two dead Indians lying where we had directed our aim in the night. We knew they had been killed by our guns, for the other two men fired with shot-guns loaded with buck-shot. One had been killed with a ball through the arm and body; the other was shot through the head. We at first supposed that the two Indians belonged to the Black Feet, but we subsequently found they were Crows. One of them wore a fine pair of buckskin leggins, which I took from him and put on myself.

We started with an escort of fifty men, following the Wind River down to the Yellow Stone, where we built our boats to descend the river. On the sixth day after leaving camp, while we were packing our effects for an early start, the alarm of "Indians!" was given, and, on looking out, we saw an immense body of them, well mounted, charging directly down upon our camp. Every man seized his rifle, and prepared for the living tornado. The general gave orders for no man to fire until he did. By this time the Indians were within half pistol shot. Greenwood (one of our party) pronounced them Crows, and called out several times not to shoot. We kept our eyes upon our general; he pulled trigger, but his gun missed fire, and our camp was immediately filled with their warriors. Most fortunate was it for us that the general's gun did miss fire, for they numbered over a thousand warriors, and not a man of us would have escaped to see the Yellow Stone.

Greenwood, who knew the Crows, acted as interpreter between our general and the Indian chief, whose name was Ap-sar-o-ka Bet-set-sa, *Sparrow-Hawk Chief.*

After making numerous inquiries about our success in hunting, the chief inquired through the interpreter where we were from.

"From Green River," was the reply.

"You killed two Black Feet there?"

"Yes."

"Where are their scalps? My people wish to dance."

"Don't show them!" cried Greenwood to us.

Turning to the Indian: "We did not take their scalps."

"Ugh! that is strange."

During this colloquy I had buried my scalp in the sand, and concealed my leggins, knowing they had belonged to a Crow. The chief gave orders to his warriors to move on, many of them keeping with us on our road to their camp, which was but a short distance off.

Soon after reaching there, an Indian woman issued from a lodge and approached the chief. She was covered with blood, and, crying in the most piteous tones, addressed the chief: "These are the men that killed my son on Green River, and will you not avenge his death?"

She was almost naked, and, according to their custom when a near relative is slain, had inflicted wounds all over her body in token of her deep mourning.

The chief, turning to the general, then said,

"The two men that were killed in your camp were not Black Feet, but my own warriors; they were good horse-thieves, and brave men. One of them was a son of this woman, and she is crying for his loss. Give her something to make her cease her cries, for it angers me to see her grief."

The general cheerfully made her a present of what things he had at hand, to the value of about fifty dollars.

"Now," said the chief to the woman, "go to your lodge and cease your crying." She went away seemingly satisfied.

During the day two other Indians came to the encampment, and, displaying each a wound, said, "See here what you white people have done to us; you shot us; white people shoot good in the dark."

These were the two whom we had seen run away after our night-discharge on the Green River. They had been wounded by the other two men's shot-guns, but their wounds were not serious. They said that their intention had been to steal our horses, but our eyes were too sharp for them. The general distributed some farther presents among these two men.

Happening to look among their numerous horses, we recognized some that had been stolen from us at the time the general was sick, previous to our discovery of the Green River.

The general said to the chief, "I believe I see some of my horses among yours."

"Yes, we stole them from you."

"What did you steal my horses for?"

"I was tired with walking. I had been to fight the Black Feet, and, coming back, would have called at your camp; you would have given me tobacco, but that would not carry me. When we stole them they were very poor; they are now fat. We have plenty of horses; you can take all that belong to you."

The chief then gave orders for them to deliver up all the horses taken from our camp. They brought in eighty-eight—all in excellent condition—and delivered them up to the general, who was overjoyed at their recovery, for he had never expected to see his horses again.

On our issuing from their camp, many of the Indians bore us company for two days, until we came to a pass in the mountains called Bad Pass, where we encamped. Several of the party being out with their guns searching for game, a man by the name of Baptiste—not the boy—having a portion of a buffalo on his horse, came across a small stream flowing near the trail, when he halted to get a drink. While stooping to drink, a grizzly bear sprang upon him, and lacerated him in a shocking manner. Passing that way, I came across his dismounted horse, and, following his tracks down to the river, discovered the poor fellow with his head completely flayed, and several dangerous wounds in various parts of his body. I quickly gave the alarm, and procured assistance to carry him to the camp. Soon after reaching the camp we heard a great rush of horses, and, looking in the direction of the noise, perceived a party of our half-breeds charging directly toward our camp, and driving before them another bear of enormous size. All the camp scattered and took to trees. I was standing by the wounded man at the time, and became so terrified that I hardly knew whether I was standing on the ground or was in a tree. I kept my eye on the bear, not supposing that he would enter our camp; but he held his course directly for me. I withdrew to look for a tree, but for some reason did not climb. Every man was calling to me, "To a tree, Jim! to a tree!" but by this time the bear was in camp, and the horsemen at his heels. On his seeing the wounded man lying there all covered with blood, he made a partial halt. I profited by the incident, and put a ball directly into his heart, killing his bearship instantly. The general fired at the same moment, his ball also taking good effect.

The next day we went through Bad Pass, carrying our wounded companion on a litter, who, notwithstanding his dreadful wounds, recovered. On arriving at the "Big Horn," as it is called there, we set about preparing boats, which, after five days, were ready for launching. There were fur-trappers with us, who, having made a boat for themselves, went on in advance, intending to trap along down until we should overtake them. They accordingly started. When we went down we found their boat and traps, which had been broken, but no remains of the trappers. By the appearance of the ground, it was evident that the Indians had surprised and murdered them, and afterward removed their bodies. Nothing else of consequence occurred during our run down the Big Horn and Yellow Stone to the junction of the latter with the Missouri, thus running a distance of eight hundred miles in our boats.

In effecting a landing at the junction of these two rivers we unfortunately sunk one of our boats, on board of which were thirty packs of beaver-skins, and away they went, floating down the current as rapidly as though they had been live beavers. All was noise and confusion in a minute, the general, in a perfect ferment, shouting to us to save packs. All the swimmers plunged in after them, and every pack was saved. The noise we made attracted a strong body of U. S. troops down to the river, who were encamped near the place, and officers, privates, and musicians lined the shore. They were under the command of General Atkinson, then negotiating a treaty with the Indians of that re-

gion on behalf of the government. General Atkinson
and our general happened to be old acquaintances, and
when we had made every thing snug and secure, we
all went into camp, and freely indulged in festivities.
"Hurrah for the Mountains!" rung through the camp
again and again.

The next morning we carried all our effects from the
boats to the encampment, and our hunters went out in
search of game. Not a day passed but we brought in
great quanties of buffalo, venison, mountain-sheep, etc.
Of the latter, we caught some very young ones alive,
one of which I presented to Lieutenant (now General)
Harney, which circumstance, I have no doubt, he still
bears in mind.

After a stay of about a week, General Atkinson
furnished us a boat of sufficient size to carry all our
effects, and, breaking up the encampment, afforded us
the pleasure of the company of all the troops under
his command—we, gentlemen mountaineers, traveling
as passengers. At our camping-places we very willingly supplied the party with game.

At one of our encampments an amusing accident
occurred. We were out hunting buffalo, and had succeeded in wounding a bull, who, furious with his wound,
made, with the speed of lightning, directly for the camp,
leaving a cloud of dust in his track. The troops, perceiving his approach, scattered in all directions as
though an avalanche was bursting upon them. On
went the buffalo, overturning tents, baggage, and guns
—leaping every impediment that arrested his course;
then, turning, he plunged into the river and gained
the opposite prairie, leaving more than a hundred soldiers scared half to death at his visitation. They certainly discharged their pieces at him, but, for all the

injury they inflicted, he will probably live to a good old age.

Previous to our arrival at Fort Clarke we met with another serious misadventure. The boat containing all our general's effects, running on a snag, immediately sunk. Again all our packs were afloat, and General Atkinson, witnessing the accident, ordered every man overboard to save the peltry, himself setting the example. In an instant, mountaineers, United States officers and soldiers plunged in to the rescue. Fortunately it was shoal water, not more than waist high, and all was speedily saved.

General Atkinson related a difficulty he had had with the Crow nation in the course of a treaty with them at Fort Clarke, on his way up the river. The Crows, in a battle with the Black Feet, had taken a half-breed woman and child, whom they had captured on the Columbia River some time previously. General Atkinson ordered them to liberate the captives, which they refused to do, saying that they had taken them from their enemies, the Black Feet, and that they clearly belonged to them. The general persisted in his demand, and the Indians refused to comply, even offering to fight about the matter. The general declined fighting that day, but desired them to come on the morrow and he would be prepared.

The next day the Indian force presented themselves for the onset, they bringing a host of warriors. One of the chiefs visited the military camp for a "talk." He had an interview with Major O'Fallen, who ordered him to give up the captives or prepare to fight. The chief boastingly replied, through Rose, the interpreter, that the major's party was not a match for the Crows; that he would whip his whole army. On this, the major, who was a passionate man, drew his pistol and snapped it at the chief's breast. It missed fire, and he then struck the Indian a violent blow on the head with the weapon, inflicting a severe gash. The chief made no resistance, but remained sullen. When this occurrence reached the ears of the Indian warriors, they became perfectly infuriated, and prepared for an instant attack. General Atkinson pacified them through Rose, who was one of the best interpreters ever known in the whole Indian country. During the hubbub, the Indians spiked the general's guns with wooden spikes, and stuffed them with grass.

Their principal chief, "Long Hair," then visited the camp, and addressed the general:

" White Chief, the Crows have never yet shed the blood of the white people; they have always treated them like brothers. You have now shed the first blood; my people are angry, and we must fight."

The general replied, " Chief, I was told by my friend, the great Red-haired Chief, that the Crows were a good people; that they were our friends. We did not come to fight the Crows; we came as their friends."

" The Red-haired Chief!" exclaimed Long Hair, in astonishment; " are you his people?"

" Yes," replied the general.

" The Red-haired Chief is a great chief, and when he hears that you have shed the blood of a Crow, he will be angry, and punish you for it. Go home," he added," and tell the Red-haired Chief that you have shed the blood of a Crow, and, though our people were angry, we did not kill *his* people. Tell him that you saw Long Hair, the Crow chief, to whom he gave the red plume many winters ago."

Long Hair and Rose then went out and harangued

the warriors, who immediately withdrew, and soon the woman and child were brought into camp. The general made them a present of a great number of guns, and ammunition in abundance, at which they were highly delighted.

The reader who has perused "Lewis and Clarke's Travels" will please to understand that the "Red-haired Chief" spoken of above was none other than Mr. Clarke, whom the Crows almost worshiped while he was among them, and who yet hold his name in the highest veneration. He was considered by them to be a great "medicine man," and they supposed him lord over the whole white race.

The loss of the boat being supplied, and all to rights again, we continued our course down the Missouri, still in company with the troops, until we reached Fort Look-out, where we encamped for the night. There was a trading-post at this fort, belonging to the American Fur Company, in charge of Major Pitcher. The major made General Ashley present of a large grizzly bear for a plaything, and a pretty plaything we found him before we were done with him. He was made fast with a chain to the cargo-box on deck, and seemed to think himself captain ; at any rate, he was more imperious in his orders than a commodore on a foreign station. He would suffer no one on deck, and seemed literally to apply the poet's words to himself,

"I am monarch of all I survey,
My right there is none to dispute."

We continued our course down the river, encamping on shore every night. We had a jovial time of it, telling stories, cracking jokes, and frequently making free with Uncle Sam's "O be joyful," of which there was great plenty for the supply of rations to the troops. The soldiers listened with astonishment to the wild adventures of the mountaineers, and would, in turn, engage our attention with recitals of their own experience.

At length we arrived at Council Bluffs, where we remained three days, feeling ourselves almost at home. We of course had a good time at the Bluffs, and the three days passed in continual festivities.

Providing ourselves with a good boat, we bade adieu to the troops, who stayed behind at the Bluffs, and continued our descent of the river. The current of the Missouri is swift, but to our impatient minds a locomotive would have seemed too tardy in removing us from the scenes of hardship and privation we had just gone through to the homes of our friends, our sweethearts, our wives and little ones.

Those who reside in maritime places, and have witnessed the hardy tars step ashore in their native land, can form an adequate idea of the happy return of the mountaineers from their wanderings on the Plains to St. Louis, which is their great sea-port; or, if a pun is admissible, I may perhaps say *see*-port; for there we *see* our old friends, there we *see* our fun and merriment, and there we sometimes " *see* sights."

Arrived at St. Charles, twenty miles above St. Louis, the general dispatched a courier to his friends, Messrs. Warndorf and Tracy, to inform them of his great success, and that he would be in with his cargo the next day about noon.

When we came in sight of the city we were saluted by a piece of artillery, which continued its discharges until we landed at the market-place. There were not less than a thousand persons present, who hailed our landing with shouts which deafened our ears. Those who had parents, brothers and sisters, wives or sweet-hearts, met them at the landing; and such a rushing, crowding, pulling, hauling, weeping, and laughing I had never before witnessed. Every one had learned our approach by the courier.

My father, who had moved to St. Louis, was in the crowd, and was overjoyed to see me. He had lost a part of his property by being surety for other men, and I could see that age had left its traces upon him during the little time that I had been absent.

Our cargo was soon landed and stored, the men receiving information that they would be paid off that afternoon at the store of Messrs. Warndorf and Tracy. We accordingly repaired thither in a body to receive our pay. The full amount was counted out in silver to each man, except three, namely, La Roche, Pellow, and myself. To us the general gave twenty-five dollars each, telling us he would see us there again. I immediately thought of my difficulty with him in the mountains, and concluded that the remainder of my pay was to be withheld on that account. We took our twenty-five dollars each, and went away, asking no farther questions, though we took no trouble to conceal our thoughts. Before we left the counting-room, the general told us to repair to any hotel we chose, and have whatever we liked to call for until the next morning, and he would pay the bill.

Accordingly, we all repaired to Le Barras's hotel, and had a glorious time of it. The house was thronged with our friends besides, who all felt themselves included in the general's hospitality. General Ashley called on us the next morning, and, perceiving that we had "run all night," told us to keep on another day at his expense, adding that, if we wished to indulge in a ride, he would pay for carriages. We profited by his hint, and did not fail to take into our party a good share of lasses and mountaineers.

The next morning the general again visited us, and, seeing we were pretty sober, paid the bill (not a trifling matter), and desired us to call on him at the store at ten o'clock. We went as appointed, not knowing yet how he would treat us. When we were assembled, he paid us our wages in full, made us a present of three hundred dollars each, and desired us to purchase a first-rate suit of clothes each at his expense.

" I give you this extra," he said, " for your faithful services to me in the mountains ; for your watchfulness over my property and interest while there ; for your kindness in caring for me while sick and helpless, carrying me when unable to walk, and not leaving me to perish in the camp alone."

I forgot to mention the disembarkation of Grizzly at the proper time, but will do so here. After the peltry was all landed and stored, the bear still occupied his station. Hundreds were yet gazing at him, many of whom had never seen one of the kind before. The general said to me, " James, how, under the sun, are we to get that animal off the boat ?" I, having a few glasses of " artificial courage" to back me, felt exceedingly valorous, and thought myself able to throw a mill-stone across the Mississippi. Accordingly, I volunteered to bring him ashore. I procured a light stick, walked straight up to the bear, and, speaking very sharp to him (as he had to us all the way down the river), deliberately unfastened his chain. He looked me in the eyes for a moment, and, giving a low whine, drooped his head. I led him off the boat along a staging prepared for the purpose, the crowd instantly falling back to a respectful distance. Landing him without accident, the general wished me to lead him to the residence of Major Biddle, distant a quarter of a mile from the landing. Courageous as ever, I led him on, though some of the time he would lead his leader, Bruin often looking round at the crowd that was following up at a prudent distance behind. I arrived safe at the residence, and made Grizzly fast to an apple-tree that stood there. I had scarcely got to the length of his chain, when he made a furious spring at me ; the chain, very fortunately, was a strong one, and held him fast.

I then called at the major's house, and, delivering our general's compliments to him, informed him he had sent a *pet* for his acceptance. He inquired what kind of a *pet*, and, taking him to the tree where I had made fast the bear, I showed the huge beast to him. The major almost quaked with fear. While we stood looking at him, a small pig happened to pass near the bear, when Grizzly dealt him such a blow with his paw that he left him not a whole bone in his body, and piggy fell dead out of the bear's reach.

The major then invited me in, and, setting out some of his *best*, I drank his health according to the custom of those days, and left to rejoin my companions.

CHAPTER VIII.

Unexpected Return to the Rocky Mountains.—Camp removed.—Final
Success in finding our party in the Mountains.—Joyful Meeting.—
Horses stolen by the Pun-nak Indians.—A Battle, and six Indians
killed.—We recapture our Horses.

I HAD been in St. Louis only one week, when Gen.
Ashley came to me, and desired me to return to the
mountains immediately, to carry dispatches to Mr. W.
L. Sublet, captain of the trappers, and offering me the
magnificent sum of one thousand dollars for the trip.
I consented to go; La Roche and Pellow were to accompany me. A journey to the mountains was then
called two thousand miles, through a country considered dangerous even for an army. I left St. Louis
this time with extreme reluctance. It is a severe trial
to leave one's friends; but the grief of separating from
father and all other relatives sank into insignificance
when contrasted with the misery of separating from
one in particular—one in whom all my affections were
reposed, and upon whom all my hopes of the future
were concentrated. The contemplation of the anguish
I was about to inflict by the announcement filled my
heart with sorrow. One week more, and the happy
event that would make one of two loving hearts would
have been consummated.

The general's business was urgent, and admitted of
no delay; after I had engaged, not a day, scarcely an
hour was to be lost. The thousand dollars I was to
receive looked large in my eyes; and that, added to
what I already possessed, would the better prepare me

for a matrimonial voyage. I comforted myself with the reflection that my services were confined to the mere delivering of the dispatches; that service performed, I was free to return immediately.

I bid my aged father farewell—it was the last time I saw him. To my other friends I said cheerfully *au revoir*, expecting to return to them shortly.

But my greatest conflict was to come. I had encountered perils, privation, and faced death itself; I had fought savages and the wild beasts of the mountains; but to approach this tender heart, that had been affianced to my own for years, unmanned me. That heart that was then so light, so buoyant with hope, so full of confidence in the future, that I must plunge in utter darkness by the intelligence that in a few short hours I must leave her! Could I have communicated it to her by fighting a score of Indians, how much my pain would have been mitigated! But time was urgent, and the sacred obligation to the lady must be performed.

I called on my sweetheart; she looked more lovely than ever. She remarked my troubled looks. "James," she said, "you look saddened; what is the matter? Are you unwell?"

"No, Eliza, I am well; but—"

"But what, James? What has happened? Speak!"

Knowing that I had no time for delay, I felt it my duty to break the news to her at once.

"My dear girl," I said, "I have loved you long and ardently. I have waited to see if the affection which you shared with me in childhood would stand the proof of maturer years. We are now both matured in years, and are capable of judging our own hearts. Through all my sufferings and dangers, my devotion to you has grown with my growth and strengthened with my strength. We have decided on the day for our indissoluble union. But, Eliza, I am yet young; my means of supporting you as I could wish are inadequate. I have just received a very tempting offer from General Ashley."

"What to do, James?"

"He offers me one thousand dollars to carry dispatches to the mountains, which admits of my immediate return."

"And are you going?"

"That is what I have come to inform you, Eliza. Understand my motive—it is solely to obtain the means to enable us to start the fairer in life."

"I care not for money, James," she said, bursting into a flood of tears.

My heart sought relief from its overcharged feeling in the same way. I left her amid her sobs, promising to make a speedy return, and that we would part no more till death should separate us.

The general had furnished us with two good saddle-horses each, and one stout mule to carry our bedding. We mounted, and, leaving St. Louis, were soon some miles on our journey. We proceeded up the Missouri River, left the last white settlement, and issued out into the wilderness. We proceeded with the utmost caution; always halting before dark, we built a fire and ate our supper; then moving on farther to a secure camping-place, we lit no fire, to avoid attracting the Indians to us. On arriving at the forks of the Platte, we held a council, and resolved to follow up the north branch to its source, thence cross over to Green River, thus striking it much higher up than we had ever been on that stream before. We proceeded accordingly—

crossed Green River, and held our course to the head of Salt River. Here we found a party belonging to the general's company. Winter was now beginning to set in, and it was time for the whole company to go into winter quarters. As nearly as I can recollect, this was the end of October, 1823.

A place of rendezvous had been previously agreed upon, and as it was certain that the various parties would soon assemble, I concluded to proceed to the rendezvous, and wait the arrival of Sublet, for the delivery of my dispatches, rather than undertake a search for him in the mountain wilderness. I and my companions, therefore, continued with the party until we reached the rendezvous. The parties, one after the other, came slowly in, and Sublet's was the last to arrive. It was now too late for me to return, and I had no alternative but to wait until spring.

Our present rendezvous was in Cache Valley, but Sublet gave orders for all to remove to Salt Lake, which was but a few miles distant, and then go into winter quarters. We accordingly moved to the mouth of "Weaver's Fork," and established ourselves there. When all were collected together for the winter, our community numbered from six to seven hundred souls (from two to three hundred consisting of women and children), all strong and healthy as bears, and all having experienced very good success.

Shortly after we had become well settled down, we had the misfortune to lose about eighty horses, stolen one dark, stormy night by the *Pun-naks*, a tribe inhabiting the head-waters of the Columbia River. On missing them the next day, we formed a party of about forty men, and followed their trail on foot—the ground was covered with snow at the time. I volunteered with the rest, although fortunately my horses were not among the missing. After a pursuit of five days we arrived at one of their villages, where we saw our own horses among a number of others. We then divided our forces, Fitzpatrick taking command of one party, and a James Bridger of the other.

The plan resolved upon was as follows : Fitzpatrick was to charge the Indians, and cover Bridger's party, while they stampeded all the horses they could get away with. I formed one of Captain Bridger's party, this being the first affair of the kind I had ever witnessed. Every thing being in readiness, we rushed in upon the horses, and stampeded from two to three hundred, Fitzpatrick at the same time engaging the Indians, who numbered from three to four hundred. The Indians recovered a great number of the horses from us, but we succeeded in getting off with the number of our own missing, and forty head besides. In the engagement, six of the enemy were killed and scalped, while not one of our party received a scratch. The horses we had captured were very fine ones, and our return to the camp was greeted with the liveliest demonstrations.

We found, on our return from the above marauding expedition, an encampment of Snake Indians, to the number of six hundred lodges, comprising about two thousand five hundred warriors. They had entirely surrounded us with their encampments, adding very materially to our present population. They were perfectly friendly, and we apprehended no danger from their proximity. It appears this was their usual resort for spending the winter ; and, after pitching their lodges, which are composed of skins, they proceeded to build a large " medicine lodge."

The word *medicine* (or, as they call it, *Barchk-Parchk*) signifies a prophet or dreamer, and is synonymous with the word prophet as employed in the Old Testament. The Indian form of government is a theocracy, and the *medicine man* is the high-priest. His dreams or prophecies are sacred; if his predictions are not verified in the result, the fault is with themselves; they had disregarded some of his instructions. When by accident his dreams are exactly verified, their confidence in their prophet exceeds all belief. The " medicine lodge" is the tabernacle of the wilderness, the habitation of the Great Spirit, the sacred ark of their faith.

Our long residence with the Snake tribe afforded us an excellent opportunity of acquainting ourselves with the domestic character of the Indians. They often invited us into their medicine lodge to witness their religious ceremonies and listen to their prophesyings. The name of the old prophet was *O-mo-gua*, which in English means woman's dress. One evening he delivered a prophecy for us.

" I can see," said he, " white people on Big Shell (Platte River); I see them boring a hole in a red bucket; I see them drawing out medicine water (whisky); I see them fighting each other; but Fate (Sublet) has gone down on the other side of the river: he does not see them. He has gone to the white lodges. Where are you going?"

" We are going," answered Fitzpatrick, " to trap on Bear Head and the other small streams in the country of the Black Feet."

" No," said the prophet, " you will go to Sheep Mountain; there you will find the snow so deep that you can not pass. You will then go down Port Neif to Snake River. If you are fortunate you will discover the Black Feet before they see you, and you will beat them. If they discover you first, they will rub you all out—kill you all. Bad Hand (Fitzpatrick), I tell you there is blood in your path this grass. If you beat the Black Feet, you will retrace your steps and go to Bear River, whose water you will follow until you come to Sage River. There you will meet two white men who will give you news."

To return to my narrative: Mr. Sublet, having left the camp in company with my old companion, Mr. Harris, before we returned, had left a letter of instructions for Fitzpatrick, desiring him to remove our camp as early in the spring as possible back to Cache Valley, and to repair to Weaver's Lake, where he would rejoin him. Sublet and Harris had parted for St. Louis, which they reached in safety after a journey in mid-winter.

We spent the winter very comfortably, and at the opening of spring we all moved—whites and Indians —back to Cache Valley. Soon after we arrived we commenced digging *caches* to secure seventy-five packs of beaver-skins in the possession of our party. While digging a *cache* in the bank, the earth caved in, killing two of our party, who were Canadians. The Indians claimed the privilege of burying them, which ceremony they performed by hoisting them up in trees. This has ever been the method of disposing of the dead with most, if not all, of the Rocky Mountain tribes. The body is securely wrapped in blankets and robes fastened with thongs, in which are inclosed the war implements, pipes, and tobacco of the deceased. If he had been a warrior, his war-horse is killed and buried, together with his saddle and other implements, at the foot of the same tree.

One more accident occurred, which at first occasioned us considerable alarm, before we quitted Cache Valley on our excursion. One of our men was out hunting, and coming across an antelope, as he supposed, fired at the animal's head, and killed it. On going to cut the animal's throat, to his surprise he found he had killed one of the Snake Indians, who had put on this disguise to decoy the antelopes near him. This was an accident that we deeply lamented, as the Snakes were very friendly toward us. Before the Indians discovered the accident, we held a council, and resolved to make a precipitate retreat, as we felt very distrustful of the consequences. While we were preparing to start, the chief came among us, and was greatly surprised at our sudden departure, especially as we had given him no previous notice. We excused ourselves by saying we were going to engage in hunting and trapping. He then asked what ailed us, saying we all looked terrified, and wished to know what had happened. Fitzpatrick at length told him what had taken place, and how it came to pass.

" Oh," said the chief, " if that is what you are alarmed at, take off your packs and stay. The Indian was a fool to use a decoy when he knew the antelope came into the sage every day, and that the white men shoot all they see."

He then made a speech to his warriors, telling them what had happened, and ordered some of his men to bring in the dead Indian. Then turning to us, he said, " You and the Snakes are brothers; we are all friends; we can not at all times guard against accident. You lost two of your warriors in the bank, the Snakes have just lost one. Give me some red cloth to wrap up the body. We will bury the fallen brave."

We gave the chief a scarlet blanket, as he had desired, and all was well again.

CHAPTER IX.

The Company removes from Cache Valley on a Hunting and Trapping Excursion.—Discovery of a Band of Black Feet.—A Battle ensues with them.—Description of the Battle.—Return to Rendezvous.—Fulfillment of the Medicine Chief's Prophecy.

THE peltry and other things not required in our expedition being all safely *cached*, our whole party—numbering two hundred and fifty, besides women and children—left Cache Valley for the country of the Black Feet, expecting to make a profitable hunt. I had engaged to the Fur Company for the spring hunt for the sum of five hundred dollars, with the privilege of taking for servant the widow of one of the men who had been killed in the bank. She was of light complexion, smart, trim and active, and never tired in her efforts to please me, she seeming to think that she belonged to me for the remainder of her life. I had never had a servant before, and I found her of great service to me in keeping my clothes in repair, making my bed, and taking care of my weapons.

We kept on till we came to Sheep-horn Mountain, but, finding it impassable for the snow, we changed our course, and proceeded down the Port Neif until we arrived at its junction with the Snake River, one of the main branches of the Columbia. No trappers having preceded us on the Port Neif, we met with excellent success all the way to the junction, a course which occupied us three weeks. An advanced party arriving at the junction before the main body came up, immediately upon landing discovered Indians coming down the Snake River. They were not perceived by the Indians, who were as yet at a considerable distance. Our whole force was soon prepared to meet them. Leaving one hundred men in camp, the remaining one hundred and fifty marched up the river, keeping in the timber; our policy being to retain our foes in the open prairie, while we kept the protection of the woods. At last they perceived us; but, seeing that we had the advantage of them, they made signs of great friendship.

Not wishing to be the aggressors, we contented ourselves with observing the enemy, and retired toward our camp, without any hostile demonstration on either side. Seeing signal-smokes arising on every side, we knew an attack on our little band was meditated by their thousands of mounted warriors. We therefore determined on a retreat as the safest course. There being many Indians about our camp, it required a strict watch to be maintained, every man having his gun constantly in hand, and the priming well looked to. We were able to converse with them, as many of our men could speak their language; but they still pretended to entertain toward us feelings of the "most distinguished consideration." We encamped that night, keeping a strong guard, and saw all around us, as far as the eye could extend, numerous signal-fires.

At daylight one of our men shouted, "Stop the Indians! stop the Indians! My rope is cut!" On looking, we found that three of our best horses had been stolen, notwithstanding our unceasing vigilance. The cry then passed around, "The ropes are cut! Shoot them down! shoot them down!" Rifles began to crack, and six of the Indians fell, five of whom were instantly scalped (for the scalps are taken off with greater ease

while the bodies are warm); and the remaining Indian, having crawled into the river after receiving his wound, his scalp was lost. One of their chiefs was among the slain. He was shot in our camp before he had time to make his retreat with the others, who all ran as soon as our camp was alarmed.

Not a moment was then to be lost. We knew that their signal-fires would cover the whole prairie with savages, for we were in the very heart of their country. Packing up, in a few minutes we were on the retreat, which we pressed all day. We encamped the same night, as the Indians did not see fit to follow us.

Soon after this occurrence a party of fur-trappers, consisting of twelve men, under the charge of one Logan, left our company to try their fortune, but were never heard of afterward. Every exertion was subsequently made to obtain some clew to the cause of their disappearance, but nothing was ever learned of them. Beyond doubt, they fell victims to the treachery of the Black Feet.

Our party continued trapping up the Port Neif until we came to Sheep Mountain, which we passed without difficulty, the snow having by this time disappeared. We proceeded on to Bear River, and continued trapping upon that stream and its tributaries until we reached Sage River, where, very unexpectedly, and to our utter surprise, we met "two white men," Black Harris and my old friend Portuleuse.

This verification of the prediction of the old chief was, to say the least, a remarkable coincidence, and one not easily accounted for.

Our two friends informed us that they were from St. Louis, and had left General Ashley and Sublet but a short distance in the rear. We took up our traps and moved immediately to Weaver Lake, and formed a rendezvous to wait the arrival of the general and Sublet.

While resting there, a party of sixteen Flat Heads came to our camp, and informed us that there were thirty white men, with women and children, encamped on a creek twelve or fifteen miles distant. They stated that the party had twenty-six guns, but that their ammunition was expended. Having some splendid horses, in the very best condition, I proposed to go and take them some ammunition, in the event of their having need for it on their way to our camp. Provo, Jarvey, and myself mounted three of our fleetest steeds, and found the party in camp. As we had expected, we found they were Campbell's party, among whom were many of our personal friends. They had met with very good fortune in their *cruise*, and had lost none of their men. We encamped with them that night, and escorted them to the rendezvous the next day.

On our way to the rendezvous we heard singing in our rear, and, looking in the direction of the noise, we discovered a party of five hundred mounted Indians coming directly toward us. "Flat Heads! Flat Heads!" was shouted; and, believing them to be such, I and my two friends wheeled to go and meet them. Approaching within a short distance, to our horror and surprise we discovered they were Black Feet—a tribe who prize white scalps very highly. Wishing to take us all together, probably, they ordered us back—an order we obeyed with alacrity, and we speedily gave the alarm. Placing the women and children in advance, and directing them to make all speed to a patch of willows six miles in front, and there to secure themselves, we formed to hold the Indians in check. The women made good time, considering the jaded state of their animals, for they were all accustomed to horse-back-riding.

By this time the Indians had commenced charging upon us, not so furiously as was their wont, but they doubtless considered their prey sure, and, farther, did not care to come into too close proximity to our rifles. Situated as we were, it was impossible for them to surround us, for we had a lake on one side and a mountain on the other. They knew, however, that we must emerge into the open country, where their chance of attack would be improved. When they approached too near, we used our rifles, and always with effect; our women the mean while urging on their animals with all the solicitude of mothers, who knew that capture was certain death to their offspring.

The firing continued between both parties during the whole time of our retreat to the willows; in fact, it was a running fight through the whole six miles. On the way we lost one man, who was quite old. He might have saved himself by riding to the front, and I repeatedly urged him to do so, telling him that he could not assist us; but he refused even to spur on his horse when the Indians made their charges. I tarried with him, urging him on, until I found it would be certain death to delay longer. My horse had scarcely made three leaps in advance when I heard him cry, "Oh God, I am wounded!" Wheeling my horse, I called on my companions to save him. I returned to him, and found an arrow trembling in his back. I jerked it out, and gave his horse several blows to quicken his pace; but the poor old man reeled and fell from his steed, and the Indians were upon him in a moment to tear off his scalp. This delay nearly cost two more lives, for myself and Jarvey were surrounded with the Black Feet, and their triumphant yells told us they felt certain of their prey. Our only chance of escape was to leap a slough fifteen feet from bank to bank, which we vaulted over at full speed. One Indian followed us, but he was shot in the back directly upon reaching the bank, and back he rolled into the ditch. We passed on around the slough in order to join our companions, but in doing so were compelled to charge directly through a solid rank of Indians. We passed with the rapidity of pigeons, escaping without any damage to ourselves or horses, although a shower of arrows and bullets whistled all around us. As we progressed, their charges became more frequent and daring; our ammunition now grew very short, and we never used a charge without we were sure of its paying for itself.

At length we gained the willows. If our ammunition had been plenty, we would have fought them here as long as they might have wished. When all was gone, what were we to do with an enemy more than ten times our number, who never grants or receives quarter?

Eroquey proposed one bold charge for the sake of the women and children. "Let us put our trust in God," he exclaimed, "and if we are to die, let us fall in protecting the defenseless. They will honor our memory for the bravery they witnessed."

Sixteen of us accordingly mounted our horses, leaving the remainder to hold out to the last. Eroquey led the charge. In our fierce onset we broke through two ranks of mounted Indians, killing and overturning every thing in our way. Unfortunately, my beautiful horse was killed in his tracks, leaving me alone amid a throng of Indians. I was wounded with an arrow in the head, the scar of which, with many other wounds received since, I shall carry to my grave. My boy Baptiste, seeing my danger, called upon his comrades to assist him to save his brother. They charged a second time, and the Indians who surrounded me were driven back. At that moment Baptiste rode up to me; I sprang on the saddle behind him, and retreated in safety to the willows. The foe still pressed us sorely, but their shots produced little effect except to cut off the twigs of the bushes which formed our hiding-place; as for charging in upon us, they showed some disinclination.

To hold out much longer was impossible. Immediate assistance must be had, and it could come from no other place than our camp. To risk a message there seemed to subject the messenger to inevitable death; yet the risk must be encountered by some one. "Who'll go? who'll go?" was asked on all sides. I was wounded, but not severely; and, at a time so pressing, I hardly knew that I was wounded at all. I said, "Give me a swift horse, and I will try to force my way. Do not think I am anxious to leave you in your perilous position."

"You will run the greatest risk," said they. "But if you go, take the best horse."

Campbell then said that two had better go, for there might be a chance of one living to reach the camp. Calhoun volunteered to accompany me, if he had his choice of horses, to which no one raised any objection. Disrobing ourselves, then, to the Indian costume, and tying a handkerchief round our heads, we mounted horses as fleet as the wind, and bade the little band adieu. "God bless you!" shouted the men; the women cried, "The Great Spirit preserve you, my friends."

Again we dashed through the ranks of the foe before they had time to comprehend our movement. The balls and arrows flew around us like hail, but we escaped uninjured. Some of the Indians darted in pursuit of us, but, seeing they could not overtake us, returned to their ranks. Our noble steeds seemed to fully understand the importance of the mission they were going on. When about five miles from the camp we saw a party of our men approaching us at a slow gallop. We halted instantly, and, taking our saddle-blankets, signaled to them first for haste, and then that there was a fight. Perceiving this, one man wheeled and returned to the camp, while the others quickened their pace, and were with us in a moment, although they were a mile distant when we made the signal. There were only sixteen, but on they rushed, eager for the fray, and still more eager to save our friends from a horrible massacre. They all turned out from the camp, and soon the road was lined with men, all hurrying along at the utmost speed of the animals they bestrode. My companion and I returned with the first party, and, breaking once more through the enemy's line, rode back into the willows, amid the cheers of our companions and the loud acclamations of the women and children, who now breathed more freely again. The Indians were surprised at seeing a re-enforcement, and their astonishment was increased when they saw a whole line of men coming to our assistance. They instantly gave up the battle and commenced a retreat. We followed them about two miles, until we came to the body of Bollière—the old man that had been slain; we then returned, bringing his mangled remains with us.

On our side we lost four men killed and seven

wounded. Not a woman or child was injured. From the enemy we took seventeen scalps, most of them near the willows; those that we killed on the road we could not stop for. We were satisfied they had more than a hundred slain; but as they always carry off their dead, we could not ascertain the exact number. We also lost two packs of beavers, a few packs of meat, together with some valuable horses.

After attending to our wounded, we all proceeded to camp, where the scalp-dance was performed by all the half-breeds and women, many of the mountaineers taking part in the dance. The battle lasted five hours, and never in my whole life had I run such danger of losing my life and scalp. I now began to deem myself Indian-proof, and to think I never should be killed by them.

The reader will wonder how a contest could last that length of time when there were but thirty to oppose five hundred men, and we not meet with a greater loss. It is accounted for by the Indian mode of warfare. The Indian is a poor marksman with a gun, more especially on horseback, and, to kill with their arrows, they must be near their mark. They often shoot their arrows when their horse is in full speed, and, unless they are very near their object, they seldom take effect. When they hunt the buffalo, their horses are trained to keep by the side of their destined victim until the arrow is discharged; then springing directly away, he escapes the charge of the infuriated animal, which becomes dangerous as soon as wounded. Unlike the Indians, we seldom discharged our guns unless sure of our man, for we had no ammunition to waste.

Our victory was considered, under the circumstances, a glorious one, and all who participated in the battle our companions lauded to the skies. The women, too, hailed us as the " bravest of the brave," knowing that we had preserved them from a captivity to which death were preferable.

Two days after the battle we were again rejoined by our friends, the Snakes, to the number of four thousand. They all took part in our scalp-dance, and such a scene of rejoicing as we held has seldom been witnessed in the mountains. They deeply lamented that they had not come in season to take part in the battle, so that not one of the Black Feet could have escaped. Their wishes for battle, however, were soon after gratified.

The absent parties began to arrive, one after the other, at the rendezvous. Shortly after, General Ashley and Mr. Sublet came in, accompanied with three hundred pack mules, well laden with goods and all things necessary for the mountaineers and the Indian trade. It may well be supposed that the arrival of such a vast amount of luxuries from the East did not pass off without a general celebration. Mirth, songs, dancing, shouting, trading, running, jumping, singing, racing, target-shooting, yarns, frolic, with all sorts of extravagances that white men or Indians could invent, were freely indulged in. The unpacking of the *medicine water* contributed not a little to the heightening of our festivities.

We had been informed by Harris, previous to the arrival of the general, that General Ashley had sold out his interest in the mountains to Mr. Sublet, embracing all his properties and possessions there. He now intended to return to St. Louis, to enjoy the fortune he had amassed by so much toil and suffering, and in which he had so largely shared in person.

CHAPTER X.

Great Battle with the Black Feet.—Departure of General Ashley.—
His Farewell Speech to the Mountaineers.—Removal of our Ren-
dezvous.—Peace between the Flat Heads and Black Feet.—Trad-
ing-post at their Village.—I become Son-in-law to the Black Foot
Chief.—Trouble in the Family.—Wife punished for Disobedience.
—Troubled Waters finally stilled.

Two days after the arrival of the general, the *tocsin*
again sounded through our whole camp, " The Black
Feet! the Black Feet!" On they came, making the
very earth tremble with the tramp of their fiery war-
horses. In their advance they surprised three men
and two women belonging to the Snakes, who were
out some distance from camp, gathering roots. The
whole five were instantly overtaken, killed, and scalped.

As soon as the alarm was given, the old prophet
came to our camp, and, addressing Mr. Sublet, said,

"Cut Face, three of my warriors and two women
have just been killed by the Black Feet. You say
that your warriors can fight — that they are great
braves. Now let me see them fight, that I may know
your words are true."

Sublet replied, "You shall see them fight, and then
you will know that they are all braves—that I have no
cowards among my men, and that we are all ready to
die for our Snake friends."

"Now, men," added he, turning to us, "I want every brave man to go and fight these Black Feet, and
whip them, so that the Snakes may see that we can
fight, and let us do our best before them as a warning

to them. Remember, I want none to join in this battle who are not brave. Let all cowards remain in camp."

Every man was impatient to take part; but, seeing that his camp would be deserted and his goods exposed, he detained quite a number, as well to guard the goods as to keep the general company, he not wishing to take part in the battle.

There were over three hundred trappers mounted in a few moments, who, with Captain Sublet at their head, charged instantly on the enemy. The Snake warriors were also on hand, thirsting to take vengeance on the Black Feet for the five scalps of their friends. After retreating before us about five miles, they formed in a place of great security, in a deep hollow on the border of the lake. At our arrival, the battle recommenced in good earnest. We and our allies fought them for about six hours, they certainly displaying great intrepidity, for they would repeatedly issue from their stronghold and make a bold sortie against us. When intrenched in their position, they had a great advantage over us, as it was difficult for a man to approach them without being shot, and to charge on them as they were situated would have occasioned us great loss of life. One Indian issuing from their position was shot through the back bone, thus depriving his legs of all power of motion. Seeing him fall, Sublet said to me, "Jim, let us go and haul him away, and get his scalp before the Indians draw him in."

We went, and, seizing each a leg, started toward our lines with him: the wounded Indian grasping the grass with both hands, we had to haul with all our strength. An Indian, suddenly springing over their breast-work, struck me a heavy blow in the back with his gun, causing me to loose hold of my leg and run. Both I and my companion were unarmed; and I, not knowing how many blows were to follow, deemed discretion on this particular occasion the better part of valor. Sublet made a strong demonstration against my assailant with his fists, at the same time calling me back and cursing me for running. I returned, and, together, we dragged the Indian to one of our men, also wounded, for him to dispatch. But the poor fellow had not strength sufficient to perforate the Indian's skin with his knife, and we were obliged to perform the job ourselves.

After six hours' fighting, during which time a number of the enemy were slain, we began to want nourishment. Sublet requested our allies "to rub out" all their foes while we went and procured refreshment; but on our leaving, they followed us, and we all arrived in camp together. On our return to the field of battle we found the Black Feet were gone, having departed precipitately, as they had left a number of their dead, a thing unusual with the Indians. The fruits of our victory were one hundred and seventy-three scalps, with numerous quivers of arrows, war-clubs, battle-axes, and lances. We also killed a number of their horses, which doubtless was the reason of their leaving so many of their dead on the field of battle. The trappers had seven or eight men wounded, but none killed. Our allies lost eleven killed in battle, besides the five slain before; but none of those killed in battle were scalped.

Had this battle been fought in the open plain, but few of our foes could have escaped; and even as it was, had we continued to fight, not a dozen could have got away. But, considering that we were fighting for our allies, we did not exert ourselves.

As usual on all such occasions, our victory was celebrated in camp, and the exercises lasted several days, conformably to Indian custom.

General Ashley, having disposed of all his goods and completed his final arrangements, departed for St. Louis, taking with him nearly two hundred packs of beaver. Previous to his departure, he summoned all the men into his presence, and addressed them, as nearly as I can recollect, in the following words:

" Mountaineers and friends! When I first came to the mountains, I came a poor man. You, by your indefatigable exertions, toils, and privations, have procured me an independent fortune. With ordinary prudence in the management of what I have accumulated, I shall never want for any thing. For this, my friends, I feel myself under great obligations to you. Many of you have served with me personally, and I shall always be proud to testify to the fidelity with which you have stood by me through all danger, and the friendly and brotherly feeling which you have ever, one and all, evinced toward me. For these faithful and devoted services I wish you to accept my thanks; the gratitude that I express to you springs from my heart, and will ever retain a lively hold on my feelings.

" My friends! I am now about to leave you, to take up my abode in St. Louis. Whenever any of you return thither, your first duty must be to call at my house, to talk over the scenes of peril we have encountered, and partake of the best cheer my table can afford you.

" I now wash my hands of the toils of the Rocky Mountains. Farewell, mountaineers and friends! May God bless you all!"

We were all sorry to part with the general. He was a man of untiring energy and perseverance, cheerfully enduring every toil and privation with his men. When they were short of food, he likewise hungered; he bore full share in their sufferings, and divided his last morsel with them. There was always something encouraging in his manner; no difficulty dejected him; kind and generous in his disposition, he was loved equally by all. If, which was seldom, he had any disagreement with them, if he discovered himself in fault, he would freely acknowledge his error, and ask forgiveness.

Before he left he had a word of advice for me. "James," he commenced, "since I have been here I have heard much of your exploits. I like brave men, but I fear you are reckless in your bravery. Caution is always commendable, and especially is it necessary in encounters with Indians. I wish you to be careful of yourself, and pay attention to your health, for, with the powerful constitution you possess, you have many valuable years before you. It is my hearty desire to have you do well, and live to a good old age; correct your fault of encountering risks for the mere ostentatious display of your courage. Whenever you return home, come and see me, James; you will be a thousand times welcome; and, should you ever be in need of assistance, call on me first. Good-by."

He left the camp amid deafening cheers from the whole crowd. I did not see him again until the year 1836.

At the general's departure, we broke up our camp and marched on to the country of the Flat Heads, on the Snake River. On our arrival at the new rendezvous, we were rejoiced to learn that peace existed between the two nations—the Flat Heads and Black Feet, and that they were in friendly intercourse together. This was very favorable for our purpose; for it is with Indian tribes as with civilized nations, when at war, various branches of business are impoverished, and it becomes inconvenient for those engaged in them to make more than trifling purchases, just for the supply of their immediate wants. Hostilities are still more destructive to Indian commerce than to that of civilized nations, for the reason, that the time and resources of the whole community are engaged in their prosecution. The "sinews of war" with the Indian mean, literally, himself and his horse.

We spent the summer months at our leisure, trading with the Indians, hunting, sporting, and preparing for the fall harvest of beaver. We made acquaintance with several of the Black Feet, who came to the post to trade. One of their chiefs invited Mr. Sublet to establish a branch post in their country, telling him that they had many people and horses, and plenty of beaver, and if his goods were to be obtained they would trade considerably; his being so far off prevented his people coming to Mr. Sublet's camp.

The Indian appearing sincere, and there being a prospect of opening a profitable trade, Sublet proposed to establish a post among the Black Feet if any of the men were willing to risk their scalps in attending it. I offered to go, although I was well aware the tribe knew that I had contributed to the destruction of a number of their braves; but, to the Indian, the greater the brave, the higher their respect for him, even though an enemy. So, taking my boy Baptiste and one man with me, we packed up and started for Beaver River, which is a branch of the Missouri, and in the heart of the Black Foot country.

On our arrival, the Indians manifested great appearance of friendship, and were highly pleased at having a trading-post so conveniently at hand. I soon rose to be a great man among them, and the chief offered me his daughter for a wife. Considering this an alliance that would guarantee my life as well as enlarge my trade, I accepted his offer, and, without any superfluous ceremony, became son-in-law to *As-as-to*, the head chief of the Black Feet. *As-as-to*, interpreted, means heavy shield. To me the alliance was more *offensive* than defensive, but *thrift* was my object more than hymeneal enjoyments. Trade prospered greatly. I purchased beaver and horses at my own price. Many times I bought a fine beaver-skin for a butcher-knife or a plug of tobacco.

After a residence among them of a few days, I had slight difficulty in my family affairs. A party of Indians came into camp one day, bringing with them three white men's scalps. The sight of them made my blood boil with rage; but there was no help for it, so I determined to wait with patience my day of revenge. In accordance with their custom, a scalp-dance was held, at which there was much additional rejoicing.

My *wife* came to me with the information that her people were rejoicing, and that she wished to join them in the dance.

I replied, "No; these scalps belonged to my people; my heart is crying for their death; you must not rejoice when my heart cries; you must not dance when I mourn."

She then went out, as I supposed, satisfied. My two white friends, having a great curiosity to witness the performance, were looking out upon the scene. I reproved them for wishing to witness the savage re-

BECKWOURTH PUNISHES HIS DISOBEDIENT WIFE.

joicings over the fall of white men who had probably belonged to our own company.

One of them answered, "Well, your wife is the best dancer of the whole party; she out-dances them all."

This was a sting which pierced my very heart. Taking my battle-axe, and forcing myself into the ring, I watched my opportunity, and struck my disobedient wife a heavy blow in the head with the side of my battle-axe, which dropped her as if a ball had pierced her heart.

I dragged her through the crowd, and left her; I then went back to my tent.

This act was performed in such a bold manner, under the very noses of hundreds of them, that they were thunderstruck, and for a moment remained motionless with surprise. When I entered the tent, I said to my companions, "There, now, you had better prepare to hold on to your own scalps, since you take so much interest in a celebration over those of your murdered brethren." Their countenances turned ashy pale, expecting instant death.

By this time the whole Indian camp was in a blaze. "Kill him! kill him! burn him! burn him!" was shouted throughout the camp in their own language, which I plainly understood. I was collected, for I knew they could kill me but once.

Soon I heard the voice of my father-in-law crying, in a tone which sounded above all, "Stop! hold! hold! warriors! listen to your chief."

All was hushed in an instant, and he continued: "Warriors! I am the loser of a daughter, and her brothers have lost a sister; you have lost nothing. She was the wife of the trader; I gave her to him.

When your wives disobey your commands, you kill them; that is your right. That thing disobeyed her husband; he told her not to dance; she disobeyed him; she had no ears; he killed her, and he did right. He did as you all would have done, and you shall neither kill nor harm him for it. I promised the white chief that, if he would send a trader to my people, I would protect him and return him unharmed; this I must do, and he shall not be hurt here. Warriors! wait till you meet him in battle, or, perhaps, in his own camp, then kill him; but here his life is sacred. What if we kill them all, and take what they have? It will last but a few suns; we shall then want more. Whom do we get sach-o-pach (powder) from? We get it from the whites; and when we have expended what we have, we must do without, or go to them for more. When we have no powder, can we fight our enemies with plenty? If we kill these three men, whom I have given the word of a chief to protect, the white chief will send us no more, but his braves will revenge the death of their brothers. No, no; you shall not harm them here. They have eaten of our meat, and drunk of our water; they have also smoked with us. When they have sold their goods, let them return in peace."

At this time there were a great many Flat Heads at the Black Foot camp, as they were at peace with each other. After the speech of my father-in-law, a great brave of the Flat Heads, called Bad Hand, replied, " Hey! you are yourself again; you talk well; you talk like *As-as-to* again. We are now at peace; if you had killed these men, we should have made war on you again; we should have raised the battle-axe, never to have buried it. These whites are ours, and the Flat Heads would. have revenged their deaths if they had been killed in your camp."

The chief then made a loud and long harangue, after which all became quiet. *As-as-to* next came to my camp and said, " My son, you have done right; that woman I gave you had no sense; her ears were stopped up; she would not hearken to you, and you had a right to kill her. But I have another daughter, who is younger than she was. She is more beautiful; she has good sense and good ears. You may have her in the place of the bad one; she will hearken to all you say to her."

" Well," thought I, " this is getting married again before I have even had time to *mourn*."

But I replied, " Very well, my father, I will accept of your kind offer," well knowing, at the same time, that to refuse him would be to offend, as he would suppose that I disdained his generosity.

My second wife was brought to me. I found her, as her father had represented, far more intelligent and far prettier than her other sister, and I was really proud of the change. I now possessed one that many a warrior had performed deeds of bloody valor to obtain; for it is a high honor to get the daughter of a great chief to wife, and many a bold warrior has sacrificed his life in seeking to attain such a prize.

During the night, while I and my wife were quietly reposing, some person crawled into our couch, sobbing most bitterly. Angry at the intrusion, I asked who was there.

" Me," answered a voice, which, although well-nigh stifled with bitter sobs, I recognized as that of my other wife, whom every one had supposed dead. After lying outside the lodge senseless for some hours, she had recovered and groped her way to my bed.

"Go away," I said, "you have no business here; I have a new wife now, one who has sense."

"I will not go away," she replied; "my ears are open now. I was a fool not to hearken to my husband's words when his heart was crying, but now I have good sense, and will always hearken to your words."

It did really seem as if her heart was broken, and she kept her position until morning. I thought myself now well supplied with wives, having *two* more than I cared to have; but I deemed it hardly worth while to complain, as I should soon leave the camp, wives and all.

It is a universal adage, "When you are among Romans, do as the Romans do." I conformed to the customs of a people really pagan, but who regarded themselves both enlightened and powerful. I was risking my life for gold, that I might return one day with plenty, to share with her I tenderly loved. My body was among the Indians, but my mind was far away from them and their bloody deeds. Experience has revealed to me that civilized man can accustom himself to any mode of life when pelf is the governing principle—that power which dominates through all the ramifications of social life, and gives expression to the universal instinct of self-interest. By living with the savages, and becoming familiar with their deeds of injustice and cruelty — witnessing friends and companions struck down without a moment's warning—if a man has feeling, in a short time it becomes callous toward the relentless savage, who can mock the dying struggles of the white man, and indulge his inhuman joy as he sees his warm life-blood saturate the earth, on which, a few moments since, his victim stood erect in seeming security. Many a companion have I seen fall in the wild prairie or the mountain forest, dying with some dear name upon his lips, his body left as food for the wild beasts, or his bones to whiten in the trackless wilderness.

It will be said, " He might have staid at home, and not have hazarded his life amid such dangers." So it might be said of the hardy mariner, whose compass guides him through all parts of the pathless ocean. The same motive impels them both on their perilous career—self-interest, which, while it gratifies their individual desires, at the same time enriches and advances society, by adding its acquisitions to the mart of commerce.

We left the Black Foot country after a stay of twenty days, having purchased thirty-nine packs of beaver and several splendid horses at a sum trifling in real value, but what they considered as far exceeding the worth of their exchanges. The chief lent us an escort of two hundred and fifty mounted warriors, in addition to which nearly one hundred Flat Heads returned with us to our camp, whom we met the second day on our road (they having become alarmed for our safety, and being on the way to revenge our deaths, in the event of the Black Feet having proved treacherous). On our arrival we were greeted with the liveliest expressions of joy. Presents were made to our escort, and Mr. Sublet sent my father-in-law a valuable gift for his kindness to me, and as the assurance of his most distinguished consideration. I also sent some dress-patterns to my wives, in addition to the presents I had previously made them. The Black Feet, apparently well satisfied, returned to their homes.

CHAPTER XI.

Removal of our Rendezvous.—Battle with our Friends, the Black Feet.
—A Race for dear Life.—Great Victory over the Grovan Band of
Black Feet.

AFTER we had rested we departed for Snake River,
making the Black Foot buttes on our way, in order to
pass through the buffalo region. I received a severe
lecture from Mr. Sublet for my rashness while at the
trading-post. The second day of our march, one of
our men, while fishing, detected a party of Black Feet
in the act of stealing our horses in the open day. But
for the man, they would have succeeded in making off
with a great number. The alarm was given, and we
mounted and gave immediate chase. The Indians
were forty-four in number, and on foot; therefore they
became an easy prey. We ran them into a thicket of
dry bush, which we surrounded, and then fired in several places. It was quite dry, and, there being a good
breeze at the time, it burned like chaff. This driving
the Indians out, as fast as they made their appearance
we shot them with our rifles. Every one of them was
killed; those who escaped our bullets were consumed
in the fire; and as they were all more or less roasted,
we took no scalps. None of our party were hurt, except one, who was wounded by one of our men.

On the third day we found buffalo, and killed great
numbers of them by a " surround." At this place we
lost six horses, three of them belonging to myself, two
to a Swiss, and one to Baptiste. Not relishing the
idea of losing them (for they were splendid animals),

and seeing no signs of Indians, I and the Swiss started along the back track in pursuit, with the understanding that we would rejoin our company at the Buttes. We followed them to the last place of rendezvous; their tracks were fresh and plain, but we could gain no sight of our horses. We then gave up the chase, and encamped in a thicket. In the morning we started to return, and had not proceeded far, when, hearing a noise in our rear, I looked round, and saw between two and three hundred Indians within a few hundred yards of us. They soon discovered us, and, from their not making immediate pursuit, I inferred that they mistook us for two of their own party. However, they soon gave chase. They being also on foot, I said to my companion, "Now we have as good a chance of escaping as they have of overtaking us."

The Swiss (named Alexander) said, "It is of no use for me to try to get away: I can not run; save yourself, and never mind me."

"No," I replied, "I will not leave you; run as fast as you can until you reach the creek; there you can secrete yourself, for they will pursue me."

He followed my advice, and saved himself. I crossed the stream, and when I again appeared in sight of the Indians I was on the summit of a small hill two miles in advance. Giving a general yell, they came in pursuit of me. On I ran, not daring to indulge the hope that they would give up the chase, for some of the Indians are great runners, and would rather die than incur the ridicule of their brethren. On, on we tore; I to save my scalp, and my pursuers to win it. At length I reached the Buttes, where I had expected to find the camp, but, to my inconceivable horror and dismay, my comrades were not there. They had found no water on their route, and had proceeded to the river, forty-five miles distant.

My feelings at this disappointment transcended expression. A thousand ideas peopled my feverish brain at once. Home, friends, and my loved one presented themselves with one lightning-flash. The Indians were close at my heels; their bullets were whizzing past me; their yells sounded painfully in my ears; and I could almost feel the knife making a circuit round my skull. On I bounded, however, following the road which our whole company had made. I was scorching with thirst, having tasted neither sup nor bit since we commenced the race. Still on I went with the speed of an antelope. I kept safely in advance of the range of their bullets, when suddenly the glorious sight of the camp-smoke caught my eye. My companions perceived me at a mile from the camp, as well as my pursuers; and, mounting their horses to meet me, soon turned the tables on my pursuers. It was now the Indians' turn to be chased. They must have suffered as badly with thirst as I did, and our men cut them off from the river. Night had begun to close in, under the protection of which the Indians escaped; our men returned with only five scalps. According to the closest calculation, I ran that day ninety-five miles.*

My heels thus deprived the rascally Indians of their anticipated pleasure of dancing over my scalp. My limbs were so much swollen the next morning, that for

---

* Concerning this great race for life, it may appear impossible to some for a human being to accomplish such a feat. Those who survive of Sublet's company, and who know the distances from point to point of my celebrated race, will please to correct me publicly if I am in error in the distance. I have known instances of Indian runners accomplishing more than one hundred and ten miles in one day.— NARRATOR.

two or three days ensuing it was with great difficulty I got about. My whole system was also in great pain. In a few days, however, I was as well as ever, and ready to repay the Indians for their trouble.

The third day after my escape, my companion Aleck found his way into camp. He entered the lodge with dejection on his features.

"Oh!" he exclaimed, "I thank God for my escape, but the Indians have killed poor Jim. I saw his bones a few miles back. I will give any thing I have if a party will go with me and bury him. The wolves have almost picked his bones, but it must be he. Poor, poor Jim! gone at last!"

"Ha!" said some one present, "is Jim killed, then? Poor fellow! Well, Aleck, let us go back and give him a Christian burial."

He had seen a body nearly devoured on the way, most likely that of the wounded Indian who had chased me in his retreat from our camp.

I came limping into the crowd at this moment, and addressed him before he had perceived me: "Halloo, Aleck, are you safe?"

He looked at me for a moment in astonishment, and then embraced me so tight that I thought he would suffocate me. He burst into a flood of tears, which for a time prevented his articulation. He looked at me again and again, as if in doubt of my identity.

At length he said, "Oh, Jim, you are safe! And how did you escape? I made sure that you were killed, and that the body I saw on the road was yours. Pshaw! I stopped and shed tears on a confounded dead Indian's carcass!"

Aleck stated that the enemy had passed within ten feet without perceiving him; that his gun was cocked and well primed, so that if he had been discovered there would have been at least one red skin less to chase me. He had seen no Indians on his way to camp.

I was satisfied that some (if not all) of my pursuers knew me, for they were Black Feet, or they would not have taken such extraordinary pains to run me down. If they had succeeded in their endeavor, they would, in subsequent years, have saved their tribe many scalps.

From this encampment we moved on to Lewis's Fork, on the Columbia River, where we made a final halt to prepare for the fall trapping season. Some small parties, getting tired of inaction, would occasionally sally out to the small mountain streams, all of which contained plenty of beaver, and would frequently come in with several skins.

I prepared my traps one day, thinking to go out alone, and see what my luck might be. I mounted my horse, and, on approaching a small stream, dismounted to take a careful survey, to see if there were any signs of beaver. Carefully ascending the bank of the stream, I peered over, and saw, not a beaver, but an Indian. He had his robe spread on the grass, and was engaged in freeing himself from vermin, with which all Indians abound. He had not seen nor heard me; his face was toward me, but inclined, and he was intently pursuing his occupation.

"Here," thought I, "are a gun, a bow, a quiver full of arrows, a good robe, and a scalp."

I fired my rifle; the Indian fell over without uttering a sound. I not only took his scalp, but his head. I tied two locks of his long hair together, hung his head on the horn of my saddle, and, taking the spoils of the enemy, hurried back to camp.

The next morning our camp was invested by two thousand five hundred warriors of the Black Foot tribe. We had now something on our hands which demanded attention. We were encamped in the bend of a river— in the " horse-shoe." Our lodges were pitched at the entrance, or narrowest part of the shoe, while our animals were driven back into the bend. The lodges, four deep, extended nearly across the land, forming a kind of barricade in front; not a very safe one for the inmates, since, being covered with buffalo hides, they were penetrable to bullet and arrow.

The Indians made a furious charge. We immediately placed the women and children in the rear, sending them down the bend, where they were safe unless we were defeated. We suffered the Indians for a long time to act on the offensive, being content with defending ourselves and the camp. I advised Captain Sublet to let them weary themselves with charging, by which time we would mount and charge them with greater prospect of victory; whereas, should we tire ourselves while they were fresh, we should be overwhelmed by their numbers, and, if not defeated, inevitably lose a great many men.

All the mountaineers approved of my advice, and our plans were taken accordingly. They drove us from our first position twice, so that our lodges were between the contending ranks, but they never broke our lines. When they approached us very near we resorted to our arrows, which all our half-breeds used as skillfully as the Indians. Finally, perceiving they began to tire, I went and ordered the women to saddle the horses in haste. A horse was soon ready for each man, four hundred in number. Taking one hundred and thirty men, I passed out through the timber, keeping near the river until we could all emerge and form a line to charge them, unobserved, in the rear. While executing this diversion, the main body was to charge them in front. While defiling through the timber we came suddenly upon ten Indians who were resting from the fight, and were sitting on the ground unconcernedly smoking their pipes. We killed nine of them, the tenth one making good his retreat.

Our manœuvre succeeded admirably. The Indians were unconscious of our approach in their rear until they began to fall from their horses. Then charging on their main body simultaneously with Captain Sublet's charge in front, their whole force was thrown into irretrievable confusion, and they fled without farther resistance. We did not pursue them, feeling very well satisfied to have got rid of them as we had. They left one hundred and sixty-seven dead on the field. Our loss was also very severe; sixteen killed, mostly half-breeds, and fifty or sixty wounded. In this action I received a wound in my left side, although I did not perceive it until the battle was over.

As usual, there was a scalp-dance after the victory, in which I really feared that the fair sex would dance themselves to death. They had a crying spell afterward for the dead. After all, it was a victory rather dearly purchased.

A few days after our battle, one of our old trappers, named Le Blueux, who had spent twenty years in the mountains, came to me, and telling me he knew of a small stream full of beaver which ran into Lewis's Fork, about thirty miles from camp, wished me to accompany him there. We being free trappers at that time, the chance of obtaining a pack or two of beaver was rather a powerful incentive. Gain being my object, I readily acceded to his proposal. We put out from camp during the night, and traveled up Lewis's Fork, leisurely discussing our prospects and confidently enumerating our unhatched chickens, when suddenly a large party of Indians came in sight in our rear.

The banks of the river we were traveling along were precipitous and rocky, and skirted with a thick bush. We entered the bush without a moment's hesitation, for the Indians advanced on us as soon as they had caught sight of us. Le Blueux had a small bell attached to his horse's neck, which he took off, and, creeping to a large bush, fastened it with the end of his lariat, and returned holding the other end in his hand. This stratagem caused the Indians to expend a great amount of powder and shot in their effort to kill the bell; for, of course, they supposed the bell indicated the position of ourselves. When they approached near enough to be seen through the bushes, we fired one gun at a time, always keeping the other loaded. When we fired the bell would ring, as if the horse was started by the close proximity of the gun, but the smoke would not rise in the right place. They continued to shoot at random into the bushes without injuring us or our faithful animals, who were close by us, but entirely concealed from the sight of the Indians. My companion filled his pipe and commenced smoking with as much sang froid as if he had been in camp.

"This is the last smoke I expect to have between here and camp," said he.

"What are we to do?" I inquired, not feeling our position very secure in a brush fort manned with a company of two, and beleaguered by scores of Black Foot warriors.

In an instant, before I had time to think, crack went

his rifle, and down came an Indian, who, more bold than the rest, had approached too near to our garrison.

"Now," said Le Blueux, "bind your leggins and moccasins around your head."

I did so, while he obeyed the same order.

"Now follow me."

Wondering what bold project he was about to execute, I quietly obeyed him. He went noiselessly to the edge of the bluff, looked narrowly up and down the river, and then commenced to slide down the almost perpendicular bank, I closely following him. We safely reached the river, into which we dropped ourselves. We swam close under the bank for more than a mile, until they discovered us.

"Now," said my comrade, "strike across the stream in double quick time."

We soon reached the opposite bank, and found ourselves a good mile and a half ahead of the Indians. They commenced plunging into the river in pursuit, but they were too late. We ran across the open ground until we reached a mountain, where we could safely look back and laugh at our pursuers. We had lost our horses and guns, while they had sacrificed six or eight of their warriors, besides missing the two scalps they made so certain of getting hold of.

I had thought myself a pretty good match for the Indians, but I at once resigned all claims to merit. Le Blueux, in addition to all the acquired wiles of the Red Man, possessed his own superior art and cunning. He could be surrounded with no difficulties for which his inexhaustible brain could not devise some secure mode of escape.

We arrived safe at camp before the first guard was relieved. The following morning we received a severe

DESPERATE DEFENSE AGAINST FEARFUL ODDS.

reprimand from Captain Sublet for exposing ourselves on so hazardous an adventure.

As soon as the wounded were sufficiently recovered to be able to travel, we moved down the river to the junction of Salt River with Guy's Fork, about a mile from Snake River. The next day the captain resolved to pass up to Guy's Fork to a convenient camping-ground, where we were to spend the interval until it was time to separate into small parties, and commence trapping in good earnest for the season.

One day, while moving leisurely along, two men and myself proposed to the captain to proceed ahead of the main party to ascertain the best road, to reconnoitre the various streams—in short, to make it a trip of discovery. We were to encamp one night, and rejoin the main body the next morning. The captain consented, but gave us strict caution to take good care of ourselves.

Nothing of importance occurred that day; but the next morning, about sunrise, we were all thunderstruck at being roused from our sleep by the discharge of guns close at hand. Two of us rose in an instant, and gave the war-hoop as a challenge for them to come on. Poor Cotton, the third of our party, was killed at the first fire. When they saw us arise, rifle in hand, they drew back; whereas, had they rushed on with their battle-axes, they could have killed us in an instant. One of our horses was also killed, which, with the body of our dead comrade, we used for a breastwork, throwing up, at the same time, all the dirt we could to protect ourselves as far as we were able. The Indians, five hundred in number, showered their balls at us, but, being careful to keep at a safe distance, they did us no damage for some time. At length my com-

panion received a shot through the heel, while carelessly throwing up his feet in crawling to get a sight at the
Indians without exposing his body. 1 received some
slight scratches, but no injury that occasioned me any
real inconvenience.

Providence at last came to our relief. Our camp
was moving along slowly, shooting buffalo occasionally, when some of the women, hearing our guns, ran to
the captain, exclaiming, "There is a fight. Hark!
hear the guns!"

He, concluding that there was more distant fighting
than is common in killing buffalo, dispatched sixty
men in all possible haste in the direction of the reports.
We saw them as they appeared in sight on the brow
of a hill not far distant, and sent up a shout of triumph.
The Indians also caught sight of them, and immediately retreated, leaving seventeen warriors dead in front
of our little fort, whom we relieved of their scalps.

We returned to camp after burying our companion,
whose body was literally riddled with bullets. The
next day we made a very successful *surround* of buffalo, killing great numbers of them. In the evening,
several of our friends, the Snakes, came to us and told
us their village was only five miles farther up, wishing
us to move up near them to open a trade. After cur-
ing our meat, we moved on and encamped near the
friendly Snakes. We learned that there were one
hundred and eighty-five lodges of Pun-naks encamped
only two miles distant, a discarded band of the Snakes,
very bad Indians, and very great thieves. Captain Sublet informed the Snakes that if the Pun-naks should
steal any of his horses or any thing belonging to his
camp, he would *rub them all out*, and he wished the
friendly Snakes to tell them so.

EXTERMINATION OF THE PUN-NAKS.

Two of our men and one of the Snakes having strolled down to the Pun-nak lodges one evening, they were set upon, and the Snake was killed, and the two of our camp came home wounded. The morning volunteers were called to punish the Pun-naks for their outrage. Two hundred and fifteen immediately presented themselves at the call, and our captain appointed Bridger leader of the troop.

We started to inflict vengeance, but when we arrived at the site of the village, behold! there was no village there. They had packed up and left immediately after the perpetration of the outrage, they fearing, no doubt, that ample vengeance would be taken upon them.

We followed their trail forty-five miles, and came up with them on Green River. Seeing our approach, they all made across to a small island in the river.

"What shall we do now, Jim?" inquired our leader.

"I will cross to the other side with one half the men," I suggested, "and get abreast of the island. Their retreat will be thus cut off, and we can exterminate them in their trap."

"Go," said he; "I will take them if they attempt to make this shore."

I was soon in position, and the enfilading commenced, and was continued until there was not one left of either sex or any age. We carried back four hundred and eighty-eight scalps, and, as we then supposed, annihilated the Pun-nak band. On our return, however, we found six or eight of their squaws, who had been left behind in the flight, whom we carried back and gave to the Snakes.

On informing the Snakes of what had taken place, they expressed great delight. "Right!" they said.

" Pun-naks very bad Indians ;" and they joined in the scalp-dance.

We afterward learned that the Pun-naks, when they fled from our vengeance, had previously sent their old men, and a great proportion of their women and children, to the mountains, at which we were greatly pleased, as it spared the effusion of much unnecessary blood. They had a great "medicine chief" slain with the others on the island; his *medicine* was not good this time, at least.

We proceeded thence to a small creek, called Black Foot Creek, in .the heart of the Black Foot country.

It was always our custom, before turning out our horses in the morning, to send out spies to reconnoitre around, and see if any Indians were lurking about to steal them. When preparing to move one morning from the last-named creek, we sent out two men ; but they had not proceeded twenty yards from our *corral* before a dozen shots were fired at them by a party of Black Feet, bringing them from their horses severely wounded. In a moment the whole camp was in motion. The savages made a bold and desperate attempt to rush upon the wounded men and get their scalps, but we were on the ground in time to prevent them, and drove them back, killing four of their number.

The next day we were overtaken by the Snakes, who, hearing of our skirmish, expressed great regret that they were not present to have followed them and given them battle again. We seldom followed the Indians after having defeated them, unless they had stolen our horses. It was our policy always to act on the defensive, even to tribes that were known enemies.

When the Snakes were ready, we all moved on together for the head of Green River. The Indians numbered six or seven thousand, including women and children; our number was nearly eight hundred altogether, forming quite a formidable little army, or, more properly, a moving city. The number of horses belonging to the whole camp was immense.

We had no farther difficulty in reaching Green River, where we remained six days. During this short stay our numberless horses exhausted the grass in our vicinity, and it was imperative to change position.

It was now early in September, and it was time to break up our general encampment, and spread in all directions, as the hunting and trapping season was upon us. Before we formed our dispersing parties, a number of the Crows came to our camp, and were rejoiced to see us again. The Snakes and Crows were extremely amicable.

The Crows were questioning the Snakes about some scalps hanging on our lodge-poles. They gave them the particulars of our encounter with the Black Feet, how valiantly we had fought them, and how we had defeated them. The Crows were highly gratified to see so many scalps taken from their old and inveterate foes. They wished to see the braves who had fought so nobly. I was pointed out as the one who had taken the greatest number of scalps; they told them they had seen me fight, and that I was a very great brave. Upon this I became the object of the Crows' admiration; they were very anxious to talk to me and to cultivate my acquaintance; but I could speak very little of their language.

One of our men (named Greenwood), whose wife was a Crow, could speak their language fluently; he and his wife were generally resorted to by the Crows to afford full details of our recent victory. Greenwood, becoming tired of so much questioning, invented a fiction, which greatly amused me for its ingenuity. He informed them that White-handled Knife (as the Snakes called me) was a Crow.

They all started in astonishment at this information, and asked how that could be.

Said Greenwood in reply, " You know that so many winters ago the Cheyennes defeated the Crows, killing many hundreds of their warriors, and carrying off a great many of their women and children."

" Yes, we know it," they all exclaimed.

" Well, he was a little boy at that time, and the whites bought him of the Cheyennes, with whom he has staid ever since. He has become a great brave among them, and all your enemies fear him."

On hearing this astonishing revelation, they said that I must be given to them. Placing implicit faith in every word that they had heard, they hastened to their village to disseminate the joyful news that they had found one of their own people who had been taken by the Shi-ans when a *bar-car-ta* (child), who had been sold to the whites, and who had now become a great white chief, with his lodge-pole full of the scalps of the Black Feet, who had fallen beneath his gun and battle-axe. This excited a great commotion throughout their whole village. All the old women who remembered the defeat, when the Crows lost two thousand warriors and a host of women and children, with the ensuing captivity, were wondering if the great brave was not their own child; thereupon ensued the greatest anxiety to see me and claim me as a son.

I did not say a word impugning the authenticity of Greenwood's romance. I was greatly edified at the inordinate gullibility of the red man, and when they had gone to spread their tale of wonderment, we had a hearty laugh at their expense.

Our party now broke up; detachments were formed and leaders chosen. We issued from the camp, and started in all directions, receiving instructions to return within a certain day. There were a great many fur trappers with us, who hunted for their own profit, and disposed of their peltry to the mountain traders. The trappers were accompanied by a certain number of hired men, selected according to their individual preferences, the strength of their party being regulated by the danger of the country they were going to. If a party was going to the Black Foot country, it needed to be numerous and well armed. If going among the Crows or Snakes, where no danger was apprehended, there would go few or many, just as was agreed upon among themselves. But each party was in strict obedience to the will of its captain or leader: his word was supreme law.

My party started for the Crow country, at which I was well content; for, being a supposed Crow myself, I expected to fare well among them. It seemed a relief, also, to be in a place where we could rest from our unsleeping vigilance, and to feel, when we rose in the morning, there was some probability of our living till night.

CHAPTER XII.

Departure from the Rendezvous.—Trouble in Camp.—Leave the Party and Traps.—Arrival at the Crow Village.—Great Stir among the Crows.—Joyful Meeting with my Crow Parents, Brothers, and Sisters.—Three Years without seeing a White Man.

I NOW parted with very many of my friends for the last time. Most of the members of that large company now sleep in death, their waking ears no longer to be filled with the death-telling yell of the savage. The manly hearts that shrunk from no danger have ceased to beat; their bones whiten in the gloomy fastnesses of the Rocky Mountains, or moulder on the ever-flowering prairies of the far West. A cloven skull is all that remains of my once gallant friends to tell the bloody death that they died, and invoke vengeance on the merciless hand that struck them down in their ruddy youth.

Here I parted from the boy Baptiste, who had been my faithful companion so long. I never saw him again.

The party that I started with consisted of thirty-one men, most of them skillful trappers (Captain Bridger was in our party), and commanded by Robert Campbell. We started for Powder River, a fork of the Yellow Stone, and, arriving there without accident, were soon busied in our occupation.

A circumstance occurred in our encampment on this stream, trivial in itself (for trivial events sometimes determine the course of a man's life), but which led to unexpected results. I had set my six traps over night, and on going to them the following morning I found four beavers, but one of my traps was missing. I sought it in every direction, but without success, and on my return to camp mentioned the mystery. Captain Bridger (as skillful a hunter as ever lived in the mountains) offered to renew the search with me, expressing confidence that the trap could be found. We searched diligently along the river and the bank for a considerable distance, but the trap was among the missing. The float-pole also was gone—a pole ten or twelve feet long and four inches thick. We at length gave it up as lost.

The next morning the whole party moved farther up the river. To shorten our route, Bridger and myself crossed the stream at the spot where I had set my missing trap. It was a buffalo-crossing, and there was a good trail worn in the banks, so that we could easily cross with our horses. After passing and traveling on some two miles, I discovered what I supposed to be a badger, and we both made a rush for him. On closer inspection, however, it proved to be my beaver, with trap, chain, and float-pole. It was apparent that some buffalo, in crossing the river, had become entangled in the chain, and, as we conceived, had carried the trap on his shoulder, with the beaver pendent on one side and the pole on the other. We inferred that he had in some way got his head under the chain, between the trap and the pole, and, in his endeavors to extricate himself, had pushed his head through. The hump on his back would prevent it passing over his body, and away he would speed with his burden, probably urged forward by the four sharp teeth of the beaver, which would doubtless object to his sudden equestrian (or rather bovine) journey. We killed the beaver and took his skin, feeling much satisfaction at the solution of the mystery. When we arrived at camp we asked our companions to guess how and where we had found the trap. They all gave various guesses, but, failing to hit the truth, gave up the attempt.

"Well, gentlemen," said I, "it was stolen."

"Stolen!" exclaimed a dozen voices at once.

"Yes, it was stolen by a buffalo."

"Oh, come, now," said one of the party, "what is the use of coming here and telling such a lie?"

I saw in a moment that he was angry and in earnest, and I replied, "If you deny that a buffalo stole my trap, *you* tell the lie."

He rose and struck me a blow with his fist. It was my turn now, and the first pass I made brought my antagonist to the ground. On rising, he sprang for his gun; I assumed mine as quickly. The bystanders rushed between us, and, seizing our weapons, compelled us to discontinue our strife, which would have infallibly resulted in the death of one. My opponent mounted his horse and left the camp. I never saw him afterward. I could have taken his expression in jest, for we were very free in our sallies upon one another; but in this particular instance I saw his intention was to insult me, and I allowed my passion to overcome my reflection. My companions counseled me to leave camp for a few days until the ill feeling should have subsided.

The same evening Captain Bridger and myself started out with our traps, intending to be gone three or four days. We followed up a small stream until it forked, when Bridger proposed that I should take one fork and he the other, and the one who had set his traps first should cross the hill which separated the two streams and rejoin the other. Thus we parted, expecting to meet again in a few hours. I continued my course up the stream in pursuit of beaver villages until I found myself among an innumerable drove of horses, and I could plainly see they were not wild ones.

The horses were guarded by several of their Indian owners, or horse-guards, as they term them, who had discovered me long before I saw them. I could hear their signals to each other, and in a few moments I was surrounded by them, and escape was impossible. I resigned myself to my fate: if they were enemies, I knew they could kill me but once, and to attempt to defend myself would entail inevitable death. I took the chances between death and mercy; I surrendered my gun, traps, and what else I had, and was marched to camp under a strong escort of *horse-guards*. I felt very sure that my guards were Crows, therefore I did not feel greatly alarmed at my situation. On arriving at their village, I was ushered into the chief's lodge, where there were several old men and women, whom I conceived to be members of the family. My capture was known throughout the village in five minutes, and hundreds gathered around the lodge to get a sight of the prisoner. In the crowd were some who had talked to Greenwood a few weeks before. They at once exclaimed, "That is the lost Crow, the great brave who has killed so many of our enemies. He is our brother."

This threw the whole village into commotion; old and young were impatient to obtain a sight of the "great brave." Orders were immediately given to summon all the old women taken by the Shi-ans at the time of their captivity so many winters past, who had suffered the loss of a son at that time. The lodge was cleared for the *examining committee*, and the old women, breathless with excitement, their eyes wild and protruding, and their nostrils dilated, arrived in squads, until the lodge was filled to overflowing. I believe never was mortal gazed at with such intense and sustained interest as I was on that occasion. Arms and legs were critically scrutinized. My face next passed the ordeal; then my neck, back, breast, and all parts of my body, even down to my feet, which did not escape the examination of these anxious matrons, in their endeavors to discover some mark or peculiarity whereby to recognize their brave son.

At length one old woman, after having scanned my visage with the utmost intentness, came forward and said, " If this is my son, he has a mole over one of his eyes."

My eyelids were immediately pulled down to the utmost stretch of their elasticity, when, sure enough, she discovered a mole just over my left eye!

" Then, and oh then!" such shouts of joy as were uttered by that honest-hearted woman were seldom before heard, while all in the crowd took part in her rejoicing. It was uncultivated joy, but not the less heartfelt and intense. It was a joy which a mother can only experience when she recovers a son whom she had supposed dead in his earliest days. She has mourned him silently through weary nights and busy days for the long space of twenty years; suddenly he presents himself before her in robust manhood, and graced with the highest name an Indian can appreciate. It is but nature, either in the savage breast or civilized, that hails such a return with overwhelming joy, and feels the mother's undying affection awakened beyond all control.

All the other claimants resigning their pretensions, I was fairly carried along by the excited crowd to the lodge of the "Big Bowl," who was my father. The news of my having proved to be the son of Mrs. Big Bowl flew through the village with the speed of lightning, and, on my arrival at the paternal lodge, I found it filled with all degrees of my newly-discovered relatives, who welcomed me nearly to death. They seized me in their arms and hugged me, and my face positively burned with the enraptured kisses of my numerous fair sisters, with a long host of cousins, aunts, and other more remote kindred. All these welcoming ladies as firmly believed in my identity with the lost one as they believed in the existence of the Great Spirit.

My father knew me to be his son; told all the Crows that the dead was alive again, and the lost one was found. He knew it was fact; Greenwood had said so, and the words of Greenwood were true; his tongue was not crooked—he would not lie. He also had told him that his son was a great brave among the white men; that his arm was strong; that the Black Feet quailed before his rifle and battle-axe; that his lodge was full of their scalps which his knife had taken; that they must rally around me to support and protect me; and that his long-lost son would be a strong breastwork to their nation, and he would teach them how to defeat their enemies.

They all promised that they would do as his words had indicated.

My unmarried sisters were four in number, very pretty, intelligent young women. They, as soon as the departure of the crowd would admit, took off my old leggins, and moccasins, and other garments, and supplied

their place with new ones, most beautifully ornamented according to their very last fashion. My sisters
were very ingenious in such work, and they wellnigh
quarreled among themselves for the privilege of dressing me. When my toilet was finished to their satisfaction, I could compare in elegance with the most popular warrior of the tribe when in full costume. They
also prepared me a bed, not so high as Haman's gallows certainly, but just as high as the lodge would admit. This was also a token of their esteem and sisterly affection.

While conversing to the extent of my ability with
my father in the evening, and affording him full information respecting the white people, their great cities,
their numbers, their power, their opulence, he suddenly demanded of me if I wanted a wife; thinking, no
doubt, that, if he got me married, I should lose all dis-
content, and forego any wish of returning to the whites.

I assented, of course.

"Very well," said he, "you shall have a pretty wife
and a good one."

Away he strode to the lodge of one of the greatest
braves, and asked one of his daughters of him to bestow upon his son, who the chief must have heard
was also a great brave. The consent of the parent
was readily given. The name of my prospective father-in-law was Black-lodge. He had three very pretty daughters, whose names were Still-water, Black-
fish, and Three-roads.

Even the untutored daughters of the wild woods
need a little time to prepare for such an important
event, but long and tedious courtships are unknown
among them.

The ensuing day the three daughters were brought

to my father's lodge by their father, and I was requested to take my choice. "Still-water" was the eldest,
and I liked her name; if it was emblematic of her disposition, she was the woman I should prefer. "Still-
water," accordingly, was my choice. They were all
superbly attired in garments which must have cost
them months of labor, which garments the young wom-
en ever keep in readiness against such an interesting
occasion as the present.

The acceptance of my wife was the completion of the
ceremony, and I was again a married man, as sacredly
in their eyes as if the Holy Christian Church had fastened the irrevocable knot upon us.

Among the Indians, the daughter receives no patri-
mony on her wedding-day, and her mother and father
never pass a word with the son-in-law after—a custom
religiously observed among them, though for what reason I never learned. The other relatives are under no
such restraint.

My brothers made me a present of twenty as fine
horses as any in the nation—all trained war-horses.
I was also presented with all the arms and instruments
requisite for an Indian campaign.

My wife's deportment coincided with her name; she
would have reflected honor upon many a civilized
household. She was affectionate, obedient, gentle,
cheerful, and, apparently, quite happy. No domestic
thunder-storms, no curtain-lectures ever disturbed the
serenity of our connubial lodge. I speedily formed
acquaintance with all my immediate neighbors, and
the Morning Star (which was the name conferred upon
me on my recognition as the lost son) was soon a companion to all the young warriors in the village. No
power on earth could have shaken their faith in my

positive identity with the lost son. Nature seemed to prompt the old woman to recognize me as her missing child, and all my new relatives placed implicit faith in the genuineness of her discovery. Greenwood had spoken it, " and his tongue was not crooked." What could I do under the circumstances? Even if I should deny my Crow origin, they would not believe me. How could I dash with an unwelcome and incredible explanation all the joy that had been manifested on my return—the cordial welcome, the rapturous embraces of those who hailed me as a son and a brother, the exuberant joy of the whole nation for the return of a long-lost Crow, who, stolen when a child, had returned in the strength of maturity, graced with the name of a great brave, and the generous strife I had occasioned in their endeavors to accord me the warmest welcome? I could not find it in my heart to undeceive these unsuspecting people and tear myself away from their untutored caresses.

Thus I commenced my Indian life with the Crows. I said to myself, "I can trap in their streams unmolested, and derive more profit under their protection than if among my own men, exposed incessantly to assassination and alarm." I therefore resolved to abide with them, to guard my secret, to do my best in their company, and in assisting them to subdue their enemies.

There was but one recollection troubled me, and that was my lonely one in St. Louis. My thoughts were constantly filled with her. I knew my affection was reciprocated, and that her fond heart beat alone for me; that my promise was undoubtingly confided in, and that prayers were daily offered for my safety, thus distant in the mountains, exposed to every peril. Repeatedly I would appoint a day for my return, but some unexpected event would occur and thrust my resolution aside.   Still I hoped, for I had accumulated the means of wealth sufficient to render us comfortable through life; a fortunate return was all I awaited to consummate my ardent anticipation of happiness, and render me the most blessed of mortals.

Before proceeding farther with my Indian life, I will conduct the reader back to our camp the evening succeeding to my disappearance from Bridger.   He was on the hill, crossing over to me as agreed upon, when he saw me in the hands of the Indians, being conducted to their village, which was also in sight.   Seeing clearly that he could oppose no resistance to my captors, he made all speed to the camp, and communicated the painful news of my death.   He had seen me in the charge of a whole host of Shi-ans, who were conducting me to camp, there to sacrifice me in the most improved manner their savage propensities could suggest, and then abandon themselves to a general rejoicing over the fall of a white man.   With the few men he had in camp it was hopeless to attempt a rescue; for, judging by the size of the village, there must be a community of several thousand Indians.   All were plunged in gloom.   All pronounced my funeral eulogy; all my daring encounters were spoken of to my praise.   My fortunate escapes, my repeated victories were applauded in memory of me; the loss of their best hunter, of their kind and ever-obliging friend, was deeply deplored by all.

"Alas! had it not been for that lamentable quarrel," they exclaimed, " he would still have been among us. Poor Jim! peace to his ashes!"

Bridger lamented that he had advised me to leave

the camp, and again that he had separated from me at the Forks. " If we had kept together," he murmured, " his fate might have been prevented, for doubtless one of us would have seen the Indians in time to have escaped."

Thus, as I was afterward informed by some of the party, was my memory celebrated in that forlorn camp. Farther, having conceived a deep disgust at that vicinity, they moved their camp to the head waters of the Yellow Stone, leaving scores of beaver unmolested in the streams.

The faithful fellows little thought that, while they were lamenting my untimely fall, I was being hugged and kissed to death by a whole lodge full of near and dear Crow relatives, and that I was being welcomed with a public reception fully equal in intensity, though not in extravagance, to that accorded to the victor of Waterloo on his triumphal entry into Paris.

Bridger had never supposed that the Indians whom he saw leading me away were Crows, he being ignorant that he was so near their territory. His impression was that these were Cheyennes, hence I was given up for dead and reported so to others. My death was communicated to the rendezvous when the fall hunt was over, and there was a general time of mourning in mountain style.

I say "mountain style" in contradistinction to the manner of civilized circles, because, with them, when the death of a comrade is deplored, his good deeds alone are celebrated; his evil ones are interred with his bones. Modern politics have introduced the custom of perpetuating all that is derogatory to a man's fair fame, and burying in deep oblivion all that was honorable and praiseworthy. Hence I say, Give me the mountaineer, despite all the opprobrium that is cast upon his name, for in him you have a man of chivalrous feeling, ready to divide his last morsel with his distressed fellow—ay, and to yield the last drop of his blood to defend the life of his friend.

CHAPTER XIII.

War between the Crow Nation and other Indian Tribes.—My first Victory as a Crow Indian.—A Melancholy and Sentimental Indian.—Indian Masonry.—Return to Camp.—Great Rejoicing among my innumerable Relatives.—The Little Wife.

AFTER fêting for about ten days among my new neighbors, I joined a small war-party of about forty men, embodied for the ostensible purpose of capturing horses, but actually to kill their enemies. After advancing for three days, we fell in with a party of eleven of the Blood Indians, a band of the Black Foot tribe, immemorial enemies of the Crows. Our chief ordered a charge upon them. I advanced directly upon their line, and had struck down my man before the others came up. The others, after making a furious advance, that threatened annihilation to our few foes, curveted aside in Indian fashion, thus losing the effect of a first onset. I corrected this unwarlike custom. On this occasion, seeing me engaged hand to hand with the enemy's whole force, they immediately came to my assistance, and the opposing party were quickly dispatched. I despoiled my victim of his gun, lance, war-club, bow, and quiver of arrows. Now I was the greatest man in the party, for I had killed the first warrior. We then painted our faces black (their mode of announcing victory), and rode back to the village, bearing eleven scalps. We entered the village singing and shouting, the crowds blocking up our way so that it was with difficulty we could get along. My wife met me at some distance from our lodge, and to her I gave my greatest trophy, the gun. My pretty sisters next presenting themselves for some share of my spoils, I gave them what remained, and they returned to their lodge singing and dancing all the way. Their delight was unbounded in their new-found relative, who had drawn the first blood. My companions told how I had charged direct upon the enemy, how I struck down the first Indian at a blow, what strength there was in my arm, and a great deal more in my commendation. Again I was lionized and fêted. Relatives I had not seen before now advanced and made my acquaintance. I was feasted by all the sachems and great braves of the village until their kindness nearly fatigued me to death, and I was glad to retire to my lodge to seek a season of quietude.

It was a custom rigidly observed by the Crows, when a son had drawn the first blood of the enemy, for the father to distribute all his property among the village, always largely recollecting his own kin in the proposed distribution. I saw that my achievement had ruined my poor old father. He seemed contented, however, to sacrifice his worldly goods to the prowess of his illustrious son. It was the Crows' religion, and he was thoroughly orthodox. Another traditional memento was to paint a chief's coat with an image of the sun, and hang that, together with a scarlet blanket, in the top of a tree, as an offering to the Great Spirit, to propitiate him to continue his favorable regards.

Several small bands of the village had a grand dance after the victory, each band by itself. I watched them for some time, to see which band or clique contained the most active men. Having singled one, I broke into the ring, and joined the performance with great heartiness. Then their shouts arose, "The great brave, the Antelope, has joined our band!" and their dancing increased in vehemence, and their singing became more hilarious. By the act of joining their clique I became incorporated with their number.

For the next three weeks I staid at home, spending much of my time in trapping round the village. I was accompanied in these excursions by a fine and intelligent Indian, who was without a relative. He was very successful in trapping. One day we went to our traps as usual; he found eight fine beavers, but I had caught none. After flaying them, he offered me four of the skins. I looked at him in surprise, telling him they were caught in his traps—that they were his. "Take them," said he; "you are my friend: your traps have been unlucky to-day." Previous to this, our success had been about equal.

Then he wished me to sit down and have a talk with him. I sat down by him, and he began.

"My friend," said he, "I am alone in the world: all my kindred are gone to the land of the Great Spirit. I now want one good friend—a confidential bosom friend—who will be my brother. I am a warrior—a brave—and so are you. You have been far away to the villages of the white man; your eyes have seen much; you have now returned to your people. Will you be my friend and brother? be as one man with me as long as you live?"

I readily acceded to all his desires.

"It is well," said he, "and we must exchange traps."

I agreed to it.

"Now we must exchange guns."

It was done.

So we went on until we had exchanged all our personal effects, including horse, clothing, and war implements.

"Now," said he, "we are one while we live. What I know, you shall know; there must be no secret between us."

We then proceeded to my father's lodge, and acquainted him with the alliance we had entered into. He was much pleased at the occurrence, and ever after received my allied brother as his son; but the assumed relationship- debarred his ever entering the family as son-in-law, since the mutual adoption attached him as by ties of consanguinity.

Shortly after, another war party was levied for an excursion after the enemy, or their horses, as occasion might offer. The party consisted of eighty or ninety warriors. My adopted brother inquired of me if I was going with the party. I told him I was, and asked the same question of him.

"No," he said; "we are brothers; we must never both leave our village at once. When I go, you must stay; and when you go, I must stay; one of us must be here to see to the interests of the other. Should we both be killed, then who would mourn faithfully for the other?"

I was, as yet, but a private in the Crow army, no commission having been conferred upon me for what little service I had seen. We started in the night, as is their custom, leaving the village one or two at a time. My brother came to me in the evening, and expressed a wish to speak to me before I left, and pointed to a place where he wished me to meet him alone as we passed out of the village. I went as appointed, and found him there.

He first asked me if I had done any thing in the village.

I did not clearly see the import of his question, and I innocently answered " No."

" Why, have you not been to war ?"

" Yes."

" Did the warriors not impart to you the war-path secret ?"

" No."

"Ah! well, they will tell it you to-morrow. Go on, my brother."

We all assembled together and marched on. In the forenoon we killed a fine fat buffalo, and rested to take breakfast. The intestines were taken out, and a portion of them cleansed and roasted. A long one was then brought into our mess, which numbered ten warriors, who formed a circle, every man taking hold of the intestine with his thumb and finger. In this position, very solemnly regarded by all in the circle, certain questions were propounded to each in relation to certain conduct in the village, which is of a nature unfit to be entered into here. They are religiously committed to a full and categorical answer to each inquiry, no matter whom their confession may implicate. Every illicit action they have committed since they last went to war is here exposed, together with the name of the faithless accomplice, even to the very date of the occurrence. All this is divulged to the *medicine men* on the return of the party, and it is by them noted down in a manner that it is never erased while the guilty confessor lives. Every new warrior, at his initiation, is conjured by the most sacred oaths never to divulge the war-path secret to any woman, on pain of instant death. He swears by his gun, his pipe, knife, earth, and sun, which are the most sacred oaths to the Indian, and are ever strictly observed.

We marched on until we came to the Missouri River, and I was greatly edified at the novel manner in which we crossed the stream. A sufficient number of robes were brought to the river bank, and a *puckering-string* run around the entire edge of one, drawing it together until it assumed a globulated form. Five or six guns, with other articles necessary to be kept dry, were put into it, together with a stone for ballast. An Indian would then attach one end of a string to the *hide tub*, and, taking the other end in his teeth, swim across with the novel bark in tow. When unfreighted on the opposite shore, every thing would be as dry as when embarked. Thus all our freight was conveyed across in a very short time, and we recommenced our march.

We had not proceeded far when our spies returned, and reported that they had discovered a village of the As-ne-boines on Milk River, about forty miles distant. We started for the village, intending to relieve them of a few of their horses, of which we thought they had more than their share. We reached there, and succeeded in driving off nearly three hundred head; but, in re-crossing the Missouri, we lost about one third of them by drowning, in consequence of our crossing over a sand-bar, in which, though covered with water, the animals became involved and perished. We reached home in safety with the remainder without being pursued; indeed, on our whole route we did not see an Indian.

Although we brought no scalps, there was great rejoicing at our success. I received, in the distribution, seventeen horses, which I gave to my friends, taking care to give my father a liberal share, in the place of those he had previously parted with on my account.

I had a month's interval at home. Visiting at my father's lodge one day, he asked me why I did not head a party myself, and go on some expedition as leader. By so doing, he informed me, I stood a better chance of gaining promotion. "Your medicine is good," said he, " and the medicine of both will bring you great success."

I replied that I had been domiciliated there so short a time that I did not wish to be too precipitate in pushing myself forward, and that I preferred to fight a while longer as a brave, rather than risk the responsibility of being leader.

He replied, "Here is your brother-in-law, take him; also your brothers will go with you. If they all get killed, so be it; I will cheerfully submit to old age without them, and die alone."

I reflected that, in order to advance by promotion, I must risk every thing; so I consented to follow his advice.

"Black Panther," my brother-in-law, was anxious to follow me, and there were seven young striplings, from ten to eighteen years old, that my father called his sons, though, in fact, half of them were what I called nephews. I put myself forward as the leader, the party comprising only two men and the above-mentioned seven boys.

We departed from the village, and pressed on to the head-waters of the Arkansas, coming directly to the Arrap-a-ho and I-a-tan villages. At night we drove off one hundred and eighteen fine horses, with which we moved on in all possible haste toward home. We were then about three hundred miles from our village, and two hundred from the Crow country. In passing through the Park* we discovered three Indians coming toward us, driving a small drove of horses. We concealed ourselves from their view by dropping back over the brow of a small hill directly in their route, until they had approached within ten steps of us. We raised the war-hoop, and rushed out on them, killing two of the three; the third was at a greater distance, driving the cattle, and when he saw the fate of his companions he mounted one of the fleetest, and was soon beyond pursuit. My company had achieved a great victory, the spoils of which were fourteen horses, in addition to those already in our possession, two scalps, one gun, two battle-axes, one lance, bow, quiver, etc. This trivial affair exalted my young brothers in their own esteem higher than the greatest veteran their village contained. During their return home they were anticipating with untiring tongues the ovation that awaited them.

We fell in with no more enemies on our way to the village. The horses we had captured from the three Indians had been stolen by them from the Crows, and as a recovery of lost horses is a greater achievement in Indians' eyes than the original acquisition, our merit was in proportion. We entered singing, with our faces blackened, bearing two scalps and other trophies, and driving one hundred and thirty-two fine horses before us. The whole village resounded with the shouts with which our brethren and kindred welcomed us. I was

---

* Formerly one of the greatest places for beaver in North America, and well known to the mountaineers.

hailed bravest of the brave, and my promotion appeared certain.

My father and all his family rose greatly in popular favor. The Antelope's distinguished skill and bravery were reflected in lucent rays upon their names. "Great is the Antelope," was chanted on all sides, "the lost son of Big Bowl; their medicine is good and prosperous."

There is one trait in Indian character which civilized society would derive much profit by imitating. Envy is a quality unknown to the savages. When a warrior has performed any deed of daring, his merit is freely accorded by all his associate braves; his deeds are extolled in every public and private reunion, and his name is an incentive to generous emulation. I never witnessed any envious attempt to derogate from the merit of a brave's achievement. No damning with faint praise; none

"Willing to wound and yet afraid to strike;"

no faltering innuendoes that the man has not accomplished so much, after all. The same way with the women. When a woman's husband has distinguished himself, her neighbors, one and all, take a pride in rejoicing with her over her happiness. If a woman displays more ingenuity than common in ornamenting her husband's war-dress, or in adding any fancy work to her own habiliments, she at once becomes the pattern of the neighborhood. You see no flaws picked in her character because of her rising to note; no aspersions cast upon her birth or present standing. Such and such is her merit, and it is deserving of our praise; the fact perceived, it receives full acknowledgment. This leads to the natural conclusion that civilization, in introducing the ostentation of display which is too frequently affected without sufficient ground to stand upon, warps the mind from the charity that is natural to it, and leads to all the petty strifes, and scandalous tales, and heartburnings that imbitter the lives of so many in civilized life.

I now engaged in trapping until the latter part of December. I celebrated Christmas by myself, as the Indians knew nothing about the birth of our Savior, and it was hard to make them understand the nature of the event. At this time a trading-party started from our village for the Grovan and Mandan country, where there was a trading-post established, for the purpose of buying our winter supply of ammunition, and tobacco, and other necessary articles. I sent thirty beaver-skins, with directions what to purchase with their value, and had marked my initials on all of the skins. These letters were a mystery to the trader. He inquired of the Crows who had marked the skins with those letters. They told him it was a Crow, one of their braves, who had lived with the whites. Kipp, the trader, then sent an invitation to me to visit him at his fort.

While our party was away, our village was attacked by a combined party of the Siouxs and Re-ke-rahs, numbering two thousand five hundred. So sudden was the attack that they inflicted considerable mischief upon us before we had a chance to collect our forces. But when we at length charged on them, it was decisive. We penetrated their ranks, throwing them into the direst confusion, and they withdrew, leaving two hundred and fifty-three dead on the field. Our loss was thirty-one killed, and one hundred and sixty wounded. They had supposed that nearly all the warriors had left the village, when but a small party had gone, and they met with such a reception as they little expected. I had three horses killed under me, and my faithful battle-axe was red with the blood of the enemy to the end of the haft; fourteen of the Siouxs had fallen beneath it.

Although we had taken such a number of scalps, there was no dancing or rejoicing. All were busied in attending the wounded, or mourning their relatives slain. Their mourning consists in cutting and hacking themselves on every part of the body, and keeping up a dismal moaning or howling for hours together. Many cut off their fingers in order to mourn through life, or, at least, to wear the semblance of mourning; hence the reason of so many Western Indians having lost one or more of their fingers, and of the scars which disfigure their bodies.

The Crows fasten the remains of their dead in trees until their flesh is decayed; their skeletons are then taken down and inhumed in caves. Sometimes, but not frequently, they kill the favorite horse of the deceased, and bury him at the foot of the tree; but that custom is not followed so strictly with them as with most other tribes.

I was pacifically engaged in trapping during the ensuing winter, and the season being open and pleasant, I met with great success. Could I have disposed of my peltry in St. Louis, I should have been as rich as I coveted.

In the month of March (1826), a small war-party of twenty men left our village on an excursion, and not one of them ever came back, their pack-dogs (used for carrying extra moccasins when a party goes to war) alone returning to intimate their fate. Another party was quickly dispatched, of whom I was appointed lead-

er, and we soon came upon the remains of the massacred party, which yet bore the marks of the weapons
that had laid them low. There were also many fresh
Indian tracks about the place, which led us to the in-
ference that there were enemies near. We made immediate search for them, and had only marched about
six miles when we came upon a village of nine lodges,
which we instantly assaulted, killing every man but
two. These were on a hill near by, and as they made
off we did not follow them. My personal trophies in
this encounter were one scalp and the equipments of its
wearer; one young girl of about fourteen years, and a
little boy. We killed forty-eight of the enemy, and
took six women prisoners, together with a large drove
of horses, and a valuable stock of beaver, otter, and
other skins, with which we returned to the village.
There was great rejoicing again (not one of our party
was scratched), and the beaver-skins, to the number of
one hundred and sixty-three, were bestowed upon me
for my skill in command.

Before we made the assault we felt convinced that
this was the party who had killed our missing friends,
and our convictions were substantiated subsequently
by recognizing several weapons in their possession
which had formerly belonged to our braves; indeed,
some of our women prisoners acknowledged that our
departed brethren had killed many of their people.

The Crows treat the women whom they take prisoners much better than other tribes do. They do not
impose upon them a harder lot than their own women
endure, and they allow them to marry into the tribe,
after which they are in equal fellowship with them.
On finding themselves captives, they generally mourn
a day or two, but their grief quickly subsides, and they

seem to care no farther for their violent removal from their own people.

At this time the Crows were incessantly at war with all the tribes within their reach, with the exception of the Snakes and the Flat Heads; and they did not escape frequent ruptures with them, brought about by the Indians' universal obtuseness as to all law relating to the right of property in horses.

The Crows could raise an army of sixteen thousand warriors, and, although there were tribes much more numerous, there were none could match them in an open fight. The Camanches and Apaches have tilted lances with them repeatedly, and invariably to their discomfiture. If the Crows ever suffered defeat, it was when overwhelmed by numbers. One principal cause of their marked superiority was their plentiful supply of guns and ammunition, which the whites always more readily exchanged to them on account of their well-proved fidelity to the white man. When other tribes were constrained to leave their fire-arms in their lodges for want of ammunition, the Crows would have plenty, and could use their arms with great effect against an enemy which had only bow and arrows to shoot with. Farther, they were the most expert horsemen of any Indian tribe, notwithstanding the great name bestowed upon the Camanches and Apaches—those two great terrors of Northern Mexico. I have seen them all, and consider myself in a position to judge, although some, perhaps, will say that I am prejudiced in favor of the Crows, seeing that I am one *myself*.

Previous to my going among the Crows, the small-pox had been ravaging their camp, carrying them away in thousands, until, as I was informed by themselves, their number was reduced by that fatal Indian scourge to little better than one half. None of their medicine would arrest its course.

After our last-mentioned victory, the Crows met with numerous reverses, which were attended with severe loss of life. In their small war-parties going out on marauding expeditions I had never much confidence, although, individually, they were good warriors; therefore I never took part with them until six or eight of their parties would come back severely handled, and many of their braves slain. Thus their reverses accumulated until the whole village was one scene of mourning, numbers of them being self-mangled in the most shocking manner, and the blood trickling from their heads down to the ground. Some had lost a father, some a brother, some a sweetheart; in short, their appearance was too fearful to look upon, and their cries were too painful to hear.

When the last party came in, defeated with serious loss, I had just returned with a party from the pursuit of horse-thieves. We had brought in four scalps, and were performing the scalp-dance in honor of the event. On hearing the disastrous news of the return of the defeated party, we arrested the dance, and I retired into my lodge. Soon, however, a crowd of women came and lifted it directly from over me, leaving me in the open air. They then threw before me immense quantities of all kinds of goods, leggins, moccasins, and other things, until I was nearly covered with their miscellaneous offerings.

I called out, "Enough! I am aroused. I will go with your warriors and revenge the death of your friends." They were all satisfied, and stood still. The news then circulated through the village that the

Antelope was aroused, and himself going against the Cheyennes to revenge the death of their braves.

I had as yet met with no reverses since my translation. My *medicine* had always been good and true. I had never come home without scalps or spoils, and they began to associate my name with victory. The next day five hundred warriors rallied round me, among whom were some who had suffered recent defeat, and their minds were burning for revenge. I sent forward fifty spies, and moved cautiously on with the main body. My reputation was committed to my present success, and I took more than ordinary pains to vindicate the cause they had intrusted to my care. Every man was well armed and mounted, and I had full confidence in our ability to give a good account of double our number.

My command were very curious to learn my tactics. On one occasion, when they were completely harassing me with endless inquiries respecting my plan of attack, I told them, if they would bring me a silver-gray fox, unhurt, my medicine would be complete, and that we were sure of a great victory. In a moment they left me, and shortly returned with a live fox, which they had caught in a surround. I ordered them to choke it to death, and then flay it: it was done, and the beautiful skin was handed to me. I wrapped it round my medicine bow, and made a brief speech, informing them that the cunning of the fox had descended upon my head, and that my wiles would infallibly circumvent the enemy. Like another Alexander, I thus inspired confidence in the breasts of my soldiers, and the spirit I was infusing in others partly communicated itself to my own breast.

Some of the spies now returned and informed me

that they had discovered a village of Cheyennes containing thirty-seven lodges.

"Well," said I, after learning where it was, "now return and watch them strictly; if any thing happens, acquaint me with it promptly."

Away they went, but soon returned again to report that the enemy had moved down the creek (which was then called Antelope Creek, a small tributary of the Missouri), had passed through the *cañon*, and were encamped at its mouth. I ordered them to send in all the spies except ten, and to direct those ten to keep a sharp look-out. I then determined to follow them down the *cañon* and attack them at the mouth, thus cutting off their retreat into the *cañon;* but again I was informed that the enemy had moved farther down, and had encamped in the edge of the timber, with the evident intention of remaining there.

I approached their village with great caution, moving a few miles a day, until I occupied a position on a hill near it, where I had an almost bird's-eye view of the village underneath. I then sent all my extra horses, together with the boys and women, to the rear; I divided the warriors into three parties, reserving the smallest division of fifty men to myself. I placed the two chief divisions in juxtaposition, out of view of the enemy, and, with my small party, intended to descend upon the horses, thinking to draw them after me; my two concealed divisions would then inclose them as in a lane, and we, returning, would place them under a triple fire. I addressed them briefly, begging them to show the enemy they were Crows, and brave ones too, and that, if they would strictly obey my directions, we could retrieve all our recent reverses.

The two *corps d'armée* being in position, I was advancing with my small division, when we came suddenly upon two of the enemy, whom we instantly killed and scalped. We rode on, being in full sight of the enemy, but they made no offer to come out of their camp. We tried every means to provoke them to advance; we shook our two scalps at them, yet reeking with blood, and tantalized them all we could; but they would not move. To have charged them as they were situated would have entailed upon us severe loss. We had taken two scalps without loss of blood, more glorious in an Indian's estimation than to take one hundred if a single life was sacrificed. We had braved our foes; we had stamped them as cowards, which is almost equal to death; so, contenting myself with what was done, I concluded to draw off my forces and return home. We were received at the village with deafening applause. Every face was washed of its mourning-paint; gloom gave way to rejoicing; and the scalp-dance was performed with enthusiasm and hilarity. I was illustrated with the distinguished name of Big Bowl (Bat-te-sarsh), and hailed as a deliverer by all the women in the village.

A little girl, who had often asked me to marry her, came to me one day, and with every importunity insisted on my accepting her as my wife. I said, " You are a very pretty girl, but you are but a child; when you are older I will talk to you about it."

But she was not to be put off. " You are a great brave," she said, " and braves have a right to paint the faces of their wives when they have killed the enemies of the Crows. I am a little girl now, I know; but if I am your wife, you will paint my face when you return from the war, and I shall be proud that I am the wife of a great brave, and can rejoice with the other women

whose faces are painted by their brave husbands. You
will also give me fine things, fine clothes, and scarlet
cloth; and I can make you pretty leggins and moccasins, and take care of your war-horses and war implements."

The little innocent used such powerful appeals that,
notwithstanding I had already seven wives and a lodge
for each, I told her she might be my wife. I took her
to the lodge of one of my married sisters, told her that
the little girl was my wife, and that she would make
her a good wood-carrier, and that she must dress her
up finely as became the spouse of a brave. My sister
was much pleased, and cheerfully carried out all my
requests. As I shall have occasion to speak of this little girl again, in connection with the medicine lodge, I
shall say comparatively little of her at this time.

I spent the summer very agreeably, being engaged
most of the time in hunting buffalo and trapping beaver. I had now accumulated three full packs, worth in
market three thousand dollars.

One day I took a fancy to hunt mountain sheep, and
for company took my little wife with me. She was particularly intelligent, and I found by her conversation
that she surpassed my other wives in sense. She was
full of talk, and asked all manner of questions concerning my travels among the great lodges and villages of
the white man; if the white squaws were as pretty as
herself; and an endless variety of questions. I felt
greatly pleased with her piquant curiosity, and imparted much information to her. Fixing her deep black
eyes full upon mine, she at length said, "I intend, some
time in my life, to go into the medicine lodge." I looked
at her with astonishment. The dedication of a female
to the service of the Great Spirit is a dangerous at-

tempt. Like all forms of imposture, it requires a peculiar talent and fitness in the candidate who seeks to gain admission into the sacred lodge. The war-path secret is associated with the ministration, with many other fearful ceremonies. The woman who succeeds in her ambitious project is an honored participant in the sacred service of the Deity through life ; but where one succeeds numbers fail, and the failure entails instant death. Three years subsequent to this conversation, I shall have to relate how my little wife, in the breathless silence of ten thousand warriors, passed the fiery ordeal in safety, and went triumphantly into the lodge of the Great Spirit.

I had good success in hunting, killing a great number of sheep, and carried their skins with me to the village. On arriving, I called at the lodge of my allied brother, who insisted on my entering and taking a meal. I accepted his offer, while my little wife ran home to communicate my great success in hunting. Our meal consisted of strips of dried buffalo tongue, which, as the Indians did not half cook it, was a dish I never partook of. What was served me on this occasion, however, was well done, and I ate a hearty meal. Supper completed, I was praising the viands, and chanced to inquire what dish I had been eating. The woman replied that it was tongue, and expressed by her looks that I must have known what it was. My friend, knowing that I had departed from my rule, inferred that I had infringed my medicine, and he started up in horror, shouting, "Tongue! tongue! you have ruined his medicine! should our hero be slain in battle, you are a lost woman."

The poor woman was half dead with fear, her features expressing the utmost horror.

I issued from the lodge, bellowing in imitation of the buffalo, protruding my tongue, and pawing up the ground like a bear in fury. This was in order to remove the spell that had settled over me, and recover the strength of my medicine. I recovered at length, and proceeded toward my lodge, commiserated by a large crowd, who all deplored the taking of the food as a lamentable accident.

That same evening the village was notified by the crier that on the following day there would be a surround, and all were summoned to attend. I accompanied the party, and the surround was made, several hundred buffaloes being inclosed. On charging among them to dispatch them, we discovered seven Black Foot Indians, who, finding retreat cut off from them, had hastily provided themselves with a sand fort. I struck one of the victims with a willow I had in my hand, and retired thereupon, declaring I had wounded the first enemy. This, I believe I have before mentioned, is a greater honor than to slay any number in battle.

I had retired to a short distance, and was standing looking at the fight, when a bullet, discharged from the fort, struck the dagger in my belt, and laid me breathless on the ground. Recovering immediately, I arose, and found myself bleeding at the mouth. Imagining the ball had penetrated some vital place, I gave myself up for dead. I was carried to the village by scores of warriors, who, with me, supposed my wound to be mortal, and were already deploring their warrior's fall. The medicine men surrounded me, and searched for my wound; but, behold! there was only a small discoloration to be seen; the skin was not perforated. The ball was afterward found where I fell, flattened as if struck with a hammer. It was then declared that I

THE INDIAN POLICEMAN.

would recover. The enemy's bullets flattened in contact with my person—my medicine was infallible—I was impenetrable to wound! I did not afford them any light on the matter.

As soon as the poor woman who had entertained me at supper heard that I was wounded, she left for another village, and was not seen again for six months. Supposing herself to have been instrumental in destroying my medicine, and knowing that, if I died, her life would pay the forfeit of her carelessness, she did not dare to return. She chanced to see me unharmed at the village where she had taken refuge, and then she knew her life was redeemed.

While the doctor and medicine men were going through their spells and incantations previous to uncovering my wound, my relatives, in their solicitude for my life, offered profuse rewards if they would save me. Some offered twenty horses, some fifty, some more, in proportion as their wealth or liberality prompted. The doctors ransomed my life, and they received over five hundred horses for their achievement.

One day a slight dispute arose between one of the braves and myself about some trivial matter, and as both of us were equally obstinate in maintaining our views, we both became angry. My disputant remarked with great superciliousness, " Ugh! you pretend to be a brave, but you are no brave."

We drew our battle-axes at the same instant, and rushed at each other, but before either had an opportunity to strike, the pipe was thrust between us, compelling us to desist, to disobey which is instant death. This is the duty of certain Indians, who occupy the position of policemen in a city. They then said to my antagonist, " You said that ' Big Bowl' was no brave. You lied; we all know that he is brave; our enemies can testify to it, and you dare not deny it any more. Hereafter, if you wish to show which is the greatest brave, wait until you meet the enemy, then we can decide; but never again attempt to take each other's lives."

This interference procured peace. It was not long, however, before we both had a good opportunity to determine the question of our valor. A small party of thirty warriors was embodied, myself and my antagonist being of the number. After a short march we fell in with a war-party of eighteen Cheyennes, who, notwithstanding the disparity of numbers, accepted battle, well knowing that escape was impossible. I pointed out one of the enemy (who I could see by his dress and the peculiarity of his hair was a chief). "You see him?" I said. "Well, we can decide which is the best man now. You charge directly against him by my side."

This he readily assented to, but still I could detect in his countenance an expression which I deciphered, "I would rather not." I saw the Indian we were about to attack open the pan of his gun, and give it a slight tap with his hand to render its discharge certain. He presented his piece, and took the most deliberate aim as we advanced side by side to the attack. The death of one of us seemed inevitable, and I did not like the feeling of suspense. A few spurrings of our chargers, and we were upon him. I seized the muzzle of his gun at the very instant that it exploded, and cut him down with the battle-axe in my right hand. My left cheek was filled with the powder from the discharge, the stains of which remain to this day. My rival did not even strike at the Indian I had killed.

He then said to me, "You are truly a great warrior and a great brave; I was wrong in saying what I did. We are now good friends."

Our few enemies were quickly exterminated, the loss on our side being four wounded, including my powder-wound. My fame was still farther celebrated, for I had again struck down the first man, who was a great chief, and had actually charged up to the muzzle of his gun, what few Indians have the stamina to do. On our return with the spoils of victory we were warmly congratulated by the tribe, and I was still farther ennobled by the additional name of Bull's Robe, conferred on me by my father.

It was now the fall of the year. I had been a Crow for many moons. It was time to repair to the trading-post to obtain what articles we needed. I determined to accompany the party, and at least attend to the sale of my own effects. What peltry I had was worth three thousand dollars in St. Louis, and I was solicitous to obtain something like an equivalent in exchange for it.

We proceeded to Fort Clarke, on the Missouri. I waited until the Indians had nearly completed their exchanges, speaking nothing but Crow language, dressed like a Crow, my hair as long as a Crow's, and myself as black as a crow. No one at the post doubted my being a Crow. Toward the conclusion of the business, one of my tribe inquired in his own language for "be-has-i-pe-hish-a." The clerk could not understand his want, and there was none of the article in sight for the Indian to point out. He at length called Kipp to see if he could divine the Indian's meaning.

I then said in English, "Gentlemen, that Indian wants scarlet cloth."

If a bomb-shell had exploded in the fort they could not have been more astonished.

"Ah," said one of them, "you speak English! Where did you learn it?"

"With the white man."

"How long were you with the whites?"

"More than twenty years."

"Where did you live with them?"

"In St. Louis."

"In St. Louis! in St. Louis! You have lived twenty years in St. Louis!"

Then they scanned me closely from head to foot, and Kipp said, "If you have lived twenty years in St. Louis, I'll swear you are no Crow."

"No, I am not."

"Then what may be your name?"

"My name in English is James Beckwourth."

"Good heavens! why I have heard your name mentioned a thousand times. You were supposed dead, and were so reported by Captain Sublet."

"I am not dead, as you see; I still move and breathe."

"This explains the mystery," he added, turning to the clerk, "of those beaver-skins being marked 'J. B.' Well, well! if you are not a strange mortal!"

All this conversation was unintelligible to my Crow brethren, who were evidently proud to see a Crow talk so fluently to the white man.

"Now," I said, "I have seen you transact your business without interposing with a word. You have cleared two or three thousand per cent. of your exchanges. I do not grudge it you. Were I in your place I should do the same. But I want a little more liberal treatment. I have toiled hard for what I have obtained, and I want the worth of my earnings."

I set my own price upon my property, and, to the great astonishment of my Indian brethren, I returned with as large a bale of goods as theirs would all together amount to. But, as I have said, an Indian is in no wise envious, and, instead of considering themselves unfairly used, they rejoiced at the white man's profusion to me, and supposed the overplus he had given me was an indemnity for the captivity they had held me in.

On our return I made various presents to all my wives, some of whom I did not see for months together, and to many other relatives. I had still a good stock to trade upon, and could exchange with my brethren at any rate I offered. They placed implicit confidence in my integrity, and a beaver-skin exchanged with me for one plug of tobacco contented them better than to have exchanged it for two with the white man.

I had the fairest opportunity for the acquisition of an immense fortune that ever was placed in man's way. By saying one word to the tribe I could have kept the white trader forever out of their territory, and thus have gained the monopoly of the trade of the entire nation for any term of years. That I am not now in possession of a fortune equal to that of an Astor or a Girard is solely the fault of my own indolence, and I do not to this moment see how I came to neglect the golden opportunity.

While returning from the trading-post, we fell in with a party of about two hundred and fifty Cheyenne warriors, to oppose whom we numbered but two hundred warriors, besides being encumbered with a still greater number of women. As good fortune would have it, they attacked us in the daytime, while we were moving; whereas, had they but waited till we were encamped, and our horses turned out, I do not see how we could have escaped defeat. In traveling, every warrior led his war-horse by his side, with lance and shield attached to the saddle.

The enemy was first seen by one of our scouts at some little distance from the main body. On seeing they were discovered, they gave chase to him, and continued on until they came upon our whole party. Every man transferred himself to his war-horse, and was instantly ready to receive them. They advanced upon our line, were received without wavering, and finally driven back. It was now our turn to attack. We charged furiously with our whole force, completely sweeping every thing from before us, and killing or disabling at least fifty of the enemy. They rallied and returned, but the reception they met with soon put them to rout, and they fled precipitately into the timber, where we did not care to follow them.

Our loss was severe: nine warriors killed and thirteen wounded, including myself, who had received an arrow in the head—not so serious, however, as to prevent me doing duty. We also lost one pack-horse, laden with goods, but no scalps. We took eleven scalps upon the field, and the Cheyennes afterward confessed to the loss of fifty-six warriors. When we lost a horse in the action, the women would immediately supply its place with a fresh one. We were nearly two hundred miles from home, and we carried our dead all the way thither.

On arriving at home, I found my father greatly irritated. He had lost two hundred and fifty head of horses from his own herd, stolen by the Black Feet, who had raised a general contribution from the whole village. His voice was still for war, and he insisted on giving immediate chase. I dissuaded him from his intention, representing to him his advanced years, and promising to go myself and obtain satisfaction for his losses. He reluctantly consented to this arrangement; but, four or five days after my departure on the errand, his medicine became so strong that he started off with a party, taking an opposite direction to the one I had gone on. My party consisted of two hundred and twenty good warriors, and my course lay for the head-waters of the Arkansas, in the Arrap-a-ho country.

We fell in with no enemies on our way until we arrived at a village which contained upward of one hundred lodges. We formed our plans for assaulting the place the next day, when we discovered four white men, whom we surrounded. The poor fellows thought their last day was come, and I was amused to overhear their conversation.

" They will surely kill us all," said one.

" In what manner will they kill us ?" asked another.

" They may burn us," suggested a third.

Then they communed among themselves, little thinking there was one overhearing them who sympathized with every apprehension they expressed.

They summed up their consultation by one saying, " If they attempt to kill us, let us use our knives to the best advantage, and sell our lives as dearly as possible."

" Gentlemen," said I, " I will spare you that trouble."

" Great God !" they exclaimed, " Mr. Beckwourth, is that you ?"

" Yes," I replied, " that is my name. You are perfectly safe, but you must not leave our camp till to-morrow."

"For what reason?" they inquired.

"Because there is a village close by which we mean to assault at daybreak, and we do not wish our design to be known."

"Oh," said they, "we should not communicate your designs, and we did not even know of the village."

They then poured out before me a whole sea of misfortunes. They had been trapping—had met with very good success; the Indians had stolen their horses; in attempting to cross the river by means of a badly-constructed raft, the raft had fallen to pieces, and they had lost every thing—peltry, guns, and ammunition. They were now making their way to New Mexico, with nothing to eat and no gun to kill game with. They were among Indians, and were two or three hundred miles from the nearest settlements of New Mexico. I entertained them well while they staid, and, after our assault in the morning, I gave them two guns and twenty rounds of ammunition, and counseled them to take advantage of the surprise of the Indians to make good their escape. One of the four afterward informed me that they reached the settlements in safety, having killed a buffalo and a deer on the way.

We made the assault as appointed. We were mounted on horses we had taken from the village during the night, as Indians go on horse-stealing expeditions on foot. I divided my force into two bodies, giving my principal scout the command of one. I gave orders to run off their horses without risking a battle, if no opposition were offered; but, if they showed fight, to kill whatever came in their way. The Arrap-a-hos are very poor warriors, but on this occasion they defended themselves with commendable zeal and bravery. We were, however, compelled to kill fourteen of them, for our own security, before we could get their horses well started. On our side we had four wounded; and if they had not delayed to scalp the fallen Indians, that might have been avoided.

We succeeded in driving away over sixteen hundred horses, all well conditioned, with which we arrived safely at home. My father also returned about the same time with near three thousand head, all superior animals. The Bull's Robe family had certainly done wonders, and we were entertained to the greatest feast I had ever seen. The whole village was illuminated with numerous *feux de joie*, and such dancing was never known before.

I received another addition to my list of titles in commemoration of this event, Is-ko-chu-e-chu-re, the Enemy of Horses.

A feud now broke out, which had been long brewing, between two different parties in our village, one of which worshiped foxes, and the other worshiped dogs. The warriors of the latter party were called Dog Soldiers, of which I was the leader; the other party was led by Red Eyes. The quarrel originated about the prowess of the respective parties, and was fostered by Red Eyes, on the part of the rival company, and by Yellow Belly (in Indian A-re-she-res), a man in my company. This A-re-she-res was as brave an Indian as ever trod the plain, but he was also a very bad Indian—that is, he was disagreeable in his manners, and very insulting in his conversation.

Red Eyes was equally brave, but of a different disposition. His was a reserved pride; the braggadocio of A-re-she-res offended him. This rivalry developed into an open rupture, and the pipe-men were obliged to interfere to prevent open hostilities. At length it was proposed, in order to cement a final peace between the two warriors, that each should select from his own party a certain number of men, and go and wage common war against some enemy—the question of bravery to be decided by the number of scalps brought in on each side.

Red Eyes accordingly chose from his party eighteen of the best men, himself making the nineteenth—men who would suffer death rather than show their backs to the enemy. A-re-she-res, with his accustomed fanfaronade, said, "I can beat that party with less men; I will only take sixteen men, and bring in more scalps than they."

He came to me and said, "Enemy of Horses, I want you to go with me and die with me. It is of no use for you to stay with this people; they are not brave any longer. Come with me, and we will enter the spirit land together, where the inhabitants are all brave. There is better hunting ground in the country of the Great Spirit. Come!"

I replied I would rather not go on such an errand. I have women to live for, and defend against the enemies of the Crows; that when I fought I wished to destroy the enemy and preserve my own life. "That," said I, "is bravery and prudence combined."

"Ah!" answered he, "you a leader of the Dog Soldiers, and refuse to go! There are prettier women in the land of the Great Spirit than any of your squaws, and game in much greater abundance. I care nothing about my life: I am ready to go to the land of the Great Spirit. You must go with me; perhaps your medicine will save not only yourself, but all of us. If so, it will be so much the better."

I, not wishing to be thought cowardly, especially by

A-re-she-res, at length consented to accompany him, on the condition that he would stifle all harsh feeling against our brethren, and, let our expedition result as it would, accept the decision in good faith, and never refer to the past.

"It is well," he said; "let it be as your words speak."

The two parties started on different routes to the Cheyenne country. I regarded it as a foolhardy enterprise, but if it resulted in the establishment of peace, I was contented to take part in it, at whatever personal sacrifice. We used every precaution against a surprise, and A-re-she-res willingly adapted his movements to my counsel; for, though he was as brave as a lion, and fought with the utmost desperation, he was very inconsiderate of consequences, and had no power of calculating present combinations to come at a desired result.

After traveling about twenty days, we arrived at a considerable elevation, from whence we could see, at some distance on the prairie, about thirty of the enemy engaged in killing buffalo. We could also see their village at a distance of three miles.

"There is an opportunity," said A-re-she-res; "now let us charge these Indians in the open prairie."

"No, no," I replied; "there are too many of them; the Cheyennes are brave warriors; if you wish to carry home their scalps, we must get into their path and waylay them; by that means we shall kill many of them, and run less risk of our own lives. We shall gain more honor by preserving the lives of our warriors, and taking back the scalps of the enemy, than by sacrificing our lives in a rash and inconsiderate charge."

" Your words are true," said he, " and we will do as
you say."

" Then," added I, " turn your robes the hair side
out, and follow me."

We wound our way down the trail through which
they must necessarily pass to reach their village, and
kept on until we reached a place where there were three
gullies worn by the passage of the water. Through
the centre gully the trail passed, thus leaving a formidable position on each side, in which an ambuscade
had ample concealment. I divided my party, giving
the command of one division to A-re-she-res. We
took our stations in the ditches on each side the trail,
though not exactly opposite to each other. I directed
the opposite party not to fire a gun until they should
hear ours, and then each man to take the enemy in the
order of precedence. The unsuspecting Cheyennes,
as soon as they had finished butchering and dressing
the buffalo, began to approach us in parties of from
three to eight or ten, their horses loaded with meat,
which they were bearing to the village. When there
were about a dozen abreast of my party, I made a signal to fire, and nine Cheyennes fell before our balls, and
eight before those of A-re-she-res's party. Some few
of the enemy who had passed on, hearing the guns, returned to see what the matter was, and three of them
became victims to our bullets. We all rushed from
our hiding-places then, and some fell to scalping the
prostrate foe, and some to cutting the lashings of the
meat in order to secure the horses, the remainder keeping the surviving enemy at bay. Having taken twenty
scalps, we sprang upon the horses we had freed from
their packs, and retreated precipitately, for the enemy
was coming in sight in great numbers.

We made direct for the timber, and, leaving our horses, took refuge in a rocky place in the mountain, where we considered ourselves protected for a while from their attacks. To storm us in front they had to advance right in the face of our bullets, and to reach us in the rear they had to take a circuitous route of several miles round the base of the mountain. The enemy evinced the utmost bravery, as they made repeated assaults right up to the fortification that sheltered us. Their bullets showered around us without injury, but we could bring down one man at every discharge. To scalp them, however, was out of the question.

During the combat a great Cheyenne brave, named Leg-in-the-Water, charged directly into our midst, and aimed a deadly thrust with his lance at one of our braves. The warrior assailed instantly shivered the weapon with his battle-axe, and inflicted a ghastly wound in his assailant's shoulder with a second blow. He managed to escape, leaving his horse dead in our midst.

By this time we were encompassed with the enemy, which induced the belief in our minds that retreat would be the safest course. None of our party was wounded except A-re-she-res, who had his arm broken with a bullet between the shoulder and elbow. He made light of the wound, only regretting that he could no longer discharge his gun; but he wielded his battle-axe with his left hand as well as ever.

When night came on we evacuated our fortress, unperceived by our enemies. They, deeming our escape impossible, were quietly resting, intending to assault us with their whole force in the morning, and take our scalps at all hazards. Moving with the stealth of a cat, we proceeded along the summit of a rocky cliff until we came to a cleft or ravine, through which we descended from the bluff to the bottom, which was covered with a heavy growth of timber. We then hastened home, arriving there on the twenty-eighth day from the time we left.

They had given us over for lost; but when they saw us returning with twenty scalps, and only one of our party hurt, their grief gave way to admiration, and we were hailed with shouts of applause.

Our rival party, under Red Eyes, had returned five or six days previously, bringing with them seventeen scalps, obtained at the loss of one man. Our party was declared the victor, since we had taken the greater number of scalps, with the weaker party, and without loss of life, thus excelling our rivals in three several points. Red Eyes cheerfully acknowledged himself beaten, good feeling was restored, and the subject of each other's bravery was never after discussed.

We had still another advantage, inasmuch as we could dance, a celebration they were deprived of, as they had lost a warrior; they, however, joined our party, and wanted nothing in heartiness to render our dance sufficiently boisterous to suffice for the purpose of both.

All the dancing is performed in the open air, with the solid ground for a floor. It consists of jumping up and down, intermixed with violent gestures and stamping; they keep time with a drum or tambourine, composed of antelope-skin stretched over a hoop, the whole party singing during the performance.

CHAPTER XIV.

Great Loss of Horses in the Mountains.—Destructive Battle with the Black Feet.—Storming of their Natural Fort.—Trouble with the Cheyennes.

WE went along without noteworthy occurrence until the following March, when we moved from the western to the eastern side of what was at that time called Tongue River Mountain, one of the peaks of the Rocky Mountain chain. The buffaloes had receded from the environs of our old camping-ground, and had been attracted to the region whither we removed in consequence of the grass being in a more forward state.

Our community numbered ten thousand souls—men, women, and children—together with an immense number of horses. In crossing the mountain, we found the snow to be of so great depth, being farther increased with a three days' recent storm, that the mountain was impassable. In this severe journey, which occupied three days, we had twelve hundred horses perish in the snow. Previously, the Black Feet had stolen eight hundred head, and we were in no condition to follow them, as we were all engaged in packing up for removal. We reached the prairie, on the eastern side of the mountain, after a toilsome journey, and found good camping-ground on Box Elder Creek. The morning following our arrival we started on a surround, in parties of fifty and upward, as our whole population was without meat. I rode a pack-horse, and three of my wives were with me, each leading a saddle-horse. I had not proceeded far before I heard a noise that sounded very much like a war-hoop. I stopped my horse to listen. Those near me said it was a signal from one of the parties, who had discovered buffalo, and we proceeded on our journey. Soon, however, I heard the yell again, and I became satisfied there was something more than buffalo astir. I rode to a small eminence close by, and descried a party of our hunters at a distance making signals for others to succor them. I turned back to my wives, and dispatched two of them to the village for my war instruments, and then galloped on to ascertain the cause of the alarm. Not more than fifty of our warriors were then before me.

I then learned that they had before them a party of one hundred and sixty Black Foot warriors, who had thrown themselves into an apparently impregnable fortress. It was a stronghold manifestly thrown up in some of Nature's grand convulsions, it would seem, for the very purpose to which it was now applied. It was a huge mass of granite, forming a natural wall in front of a graduated height, varying from twenty-five feet to six feet, the lowest part; it was solid, and nearly perpendicular all round.

There was in our camp a young Kentuckian named Robert Mildrum, naturally a brave fellow, though he seldom went out in the war parties; but when the village was assaulted, he always fought like a tiger. He was a good trapper and a skillful blacksmith, and had been out in the employ of the American Fur Company. I met him while we were surveying the enemy's stronghold.

I said to him, " Mildrum, if the adage is true, there is policy in war. These Indians make no question of our bravery; had we not better resign to them the

GREAT BATTLE AT THE NATURAL FORT.

brunt of this encounter, and not expose our lives in a cause that we have no concern in? How do you intend to act?"

"As for me," said Mildrum, "I must be in the fray. If we are to see any fun, I want my share of the entertainment."

"Well," said I, "I shall endeavor to keep by you."

The Indians had by this time assembled to the number of from five to seven hundred, and were watching the fort indecisively, awaiting instructions from the chief. Many had succeeded in running and sheltering under the wall, while several had been shot in making the attempt. I ran to the wall to reconnoitre it, and soon saw there were two ways in which it could be taken; one was by bombardment, and the other was by storm. Bombardment was out of the question, as our heaviest calibre was a rifle-bore. I waited to see what steps would be taken.

Long Hair, the head chief of the nation, said, "Warriors, listen! Our marrow-bones are broken; the enemy has chosen a strong fort; we can not drive them from it without sacrificing too many men. Warriors, retreat!"

I replied, "No; hold! Warriors, listen! If these old men can not fight, let them retire with the women and children. We can kill every one of these Black Feet: then let us do it. If we attempt to run from here, we shall be shot in the back, and lose more warriors than to fight and kill them all. If we get killed, our friends who love us here will mourn our loss, while those in the spirit land will sing and rejoice to welcome us there, if we ascend to them dying like braves. The Great Spirit has sent these enemies here for us to slay; if we do not slay them, he will be angry with us, and will never suffer us to conquer our enemies again. He will drive off all our buffaloes, and will wither the grass on the prairies. No, warriors! we will fight as long as one of them survives. Come, follow me, and I will show you how the braves of the great white chief fight their enemies!"

" Enemy of Horses," exclaimed hundreds of the brave and impatient warriors who were crowded round me, "lead us, and we will follow you to the spirit land."

Accepting the charge, I stationed a large body of those who were never known to flinch on one side of the position, which I, with my followers, intended to scale. I thus thought to engage the attention of the enemy until we made good our entrance, when I felt no longer doubtful of success. I then told them as I threw up my shield the third time, and shouted "Hoo-ki-hi," they were to scale the wall as fast as possible, and beat down whatever resistance might be offered them.

I had divested myself of all my weapons except my battle-axe and scalping-knife, the latter being attached to my wrist with a string. I then made the signal, and when I raised the shout " Hoo-ki-hi," the party opposite began to hoist one another up. When I sprang for the summit of the wall, I found that my women were holding my belt; I cut it loose with my knife, and left it in their hands. I was the first on the wall, but was immediately followed by some scores of warriors. The enemy's whole attention, when we entered the arena, was directed to the opposite party, and we had time to cut numbers down before they were aware of our entrance. The carnage for some min-utes was fearful, and the Black Feet fought with desperation, knowing their inevitable doom if taken. The clash of battle-axes, and the yells of the opposing combatants were truly appalling. Many leaped the wall only to meet their certain doom below, where hundreds of battle-axes and lances were ready to drink their blood as soon as they touched ground. The interior surface of this huge rock was concave, and the blood all ran to the centre, where it formed a pool, which emitted a sickening smell as the warm vapor ascended to our nostrils. It was also a work of great difficulty to keep one's feet, as the mingled gore and brains were scattered every where round this fatal place. The blood of the Crow and the Black Foot mingled together in this common pool, for many of our warriors fell in this terrible strife.

All was silent within a few minutes after we had gained an entrance. Victims who were making away with their bowels ripped open were instantly felled with the battle-axe and stilled in death. The wounded were cared for by their friends, and the dead removed from sight. Upward of forty Crows were killed, and double the number wounded. There were engaged on the side of the Crows about twenty white men, and only one was wounded, though nearly all scaled the wall with the Indians. Mildrum was seriously injured by leaping from the heights after an Indian, but he soon recovered.

Our spoils were one hundred and sixty scalps, and an immense quantity' of guns and ammunition, a large amount of dried meats, with arrows, lances, knives, in great abundance.

Here an incident happened with my little wife and mother worth mentioning. They were seated outside, and under the wall, when Owl Bear, one of the chiefs, happening to pass, asked the girl if she was not the wife of the Enemy of Horses. She answered that she was.

"I thought so," he said, "because you are such a pretty little squaw; but you have no husband now; he was shot through the head in the fort, and instantly killed; and here you are playing with sticks!"

The poor thing, together with her mother, screamed out at the intelligence, and, seizing a battle-axe, each cut off a finger. The girl then stabbed her forehead with a knife, and was instantly dripping with blood. The chief came laughing to me, and said, "That little wife of yours loves you better than any of your other wives."

"How do you know?" I inquired.

"Because I told them all you were dead, and she was the only one that cut off a finger;" and he laughed aloud as he passed on.

Soon, however, she climbed the wall, and forced her way into the fort, and came directly to me. She presented a sickening spectacle, and was covered entirely with blood. Seeing me, she burst into tears, and as soon as she could articulate, said, "Why, you are not dead, after all! Owl Bear told me you were killed, and I came to seek your body."

"Who are you mourning for?" I asked; "is your brother or father scalped?"

"No; I mourned because I thought you were killed; Owl Bear told me you were."

"You must not believe all you hear," I said; "some Indians have crooked tongues. But come and spread your robe, and carry this gun and spoils of my first victim to the village, and there wash your face and bind up your finger."

She did as I directed her, and departed.

As soon as we had collected all the trophies bequeathed us by our fallen foes, and gathered all our own dead, we moved back to the new camp. On our way, I exerted myself to the utmost to console the afflicted mourners. I told them that their friends were happy in the spirit land, where there were no enemies to fight, where all was everlasting contentment, and where they were happy in endless amusement. I said that in a few days I would avenge the fall of our warriors, and depart for that peaceful land myself.

I could plainly see that this last promise afforded them more satisfaction than all my other consoling remarks; but I disliked to see their horrid fashion of mourning, and my promise of future victory speedily washed their faces of their present grief; for a promise from me was confided in by all the tribe. There was, of course, no dancing, for we had lost too many warriors; but in the evening there was great visiting throughout the village, to talk over the events of the day, and hear the statements of those who had taken part in the battle. Long Hair came to the lodge of my father to congratulate me on my great feat in scaling the wall, and to talk of the victory of his people achieved through my valor. All who were present related the deeds they had performed. As each narrated his exploits, all listened with profound attention.

While this was going on, my little wife, who sat near by, crawled behind me, and, whispering in my ear, inquired if I had obtained any *coos*. These *coos* she inquired after are the same as counts in a game of billiards: the death of one warrior counts as one; of two warriors counts as two; every battle-axe or gun taken counts one to the victor's merit. I said I had not, at which she looked aghast. But when the question was put to me by the chief shortly after, I answered "Eleven." On this she administered eleven taps on my back with her finger, and again whispered, "Ah! I thought your tongue was crooked when you told me you had no *coos*." All the *coos* are registered in the great medicine lodge in favor of the brave who wins them.

I trust that the reader does not suppose that I waded through these scenes of carnage and desolation without some serious reflections on the matter. Disgusted at the repeated acts of cruelty I witnessed, I often resolved to leave these wild children of the forest and return to civilized life; but before I could act upon my decision, another scene of strife would occur, and the Enemy of Horses was always the first sought for by the tribe. I had been uniformly successful so far; and how I had escaped, while scores of warriors had been stricken down at my side, was more than I could understand. I was well aware that many of my friends knew of the life I was leading, and I almost feared to think of the opinions they must form of my character. But, in justification, it may be urged that the Crows had never shed the blood of the white man during my stay in their camp, and I did not intend they ever should, if I could raise a voice to prevent it. They were constantly at war with tribes who coveted the scalps of the white man, but the Crows were uniformly faithful in their obligations to my race, and would rather serve than injure their white brethren without any consideration of profit.

In addition to this, Self-interest would whisper her counsel. I knew I could acquire the riches of Crœsus if I could but dispose of the valuable stock of peltry I had the means of accumulating. I required but an object in view to turn the attention of the Indians to the thousands of traps that were laid by to rust. I would occasionally use arguments to turn them from their unprofitable life, and engage them in peaceful industry. But I found the Indian would be Indian still, in spite of my efforts to improve him.

They would answer, "Our enemies steal our horses; we must fight and get them back again, or steal in turn. Without horses we can make no *surrounds*, nor could we, to protect our lives, fight our foes when they attack our villages."

Of course these arguments were unanswerable. So long as they were surrounded with enemies, they must be prepared to defend themselves. The large majority of Indian troubles arise from their unrestrained appropriation of each other's horses. It is their only branch of wealth; like the miser with his gold, their greed for horses can not be satisfied. All their other wants are merely attended to from day to day; their need supplied, they look no farther; but their appetite for horses is insatiable: they are ever demanding more.

Mildrum and myself had a long conversation on the subject while he was smarting with the injury he received in leaping from the fort. He would say, "Beckwourth, I am pretty well used to this Indian life; there is a great deal in it that charms me. But when I think of my old Kentucky home—of father, mother, and other friends whom I tenderly love, and with whom I could be so happy, I wonder at the vagabond spirit that holds me here among these savages, fighting their battles, and risking my life and scalp, which I fairly suppose exceeds in value ten thousand of these blood-thirsty heathen. How, in the name of all that is sacred, can we reconcile ourselves to it ?   Why don't we leave them ?"

The medicine men held a council, and resolved to remove the village ; the Great Spirit was displeased with the spot, and had therefore suffered all our warriors to be killed.   We accordingly pulled up stakes and moved a short distance farther.

While we were busy moving, my little squaw angered me, and I drove her away.   She not daring to disobey me, I saw no more of her until she supposed my anger was appeased.   She then came to the lodge while I was conversing with my brothers, and, putting her childish head into the door, said humbly, " I know you are angry with me, but I want you to come and stay at our lodge to-night ; we are outside the village, and my father and mother are afraid."

" Yes," said my brother, " she has no ears now ; she is but a child ; she will have ears when she grows older ; you had better go and protect the old people."

I told her to run home, and I would soon follow.

I went to the lodge accordingly.   In the night I heard the snorting of horses, which were tied near the lodge door.   I crept softly out and looked carefully around.   I then crawled, without the least noise, out of the lodge, and caught sight of an Indian, who I knew was there for no good purpose.   He was using the utmost precaution ; he had a sharp-pointed stick, with which he raised the leaves that lay in his way, so that his feet might not crush them, and thus alarm the inmates of the lodge.   Every step brought him nearer to the animals, who, with necks curved and ears erect, gave an occasional snort at the approach of the Indian. This would bring him to a halt.   Then again he would bring his stick into action, and prepare a place for another step, not mistrusting that he was approaching the threshold of death. The ropes were tied close to the lodge door, and to untie them he must approach within six feet of where I lay on the ground. I let him advance as near as I thought safe, when, with one bound, I grappled him, and gave the war-hoop. He was the hardest to hold that ever I had my arms around, but I had both his arms pinned in my embrace round his lithe and nimble body, and he could not release one so as to draw his knife. Instantly we were surrounded with fifty armed warriors; and when I saw a sufficient breastwork round about, I released my hold and stepped back. He was riddled with bullets in an instant, and fell without a cry.

His scalp sufficed to wash off the mourning-paint from every face in the village, and all was turned into mirth, although this general change in feeling did not restore the dismembered fingers or heal their voluntary wounds. Greater than ever was the Enemy of Horses, and I received a still more ennobling appellation, *Shas-ka-o-hush-a*, the Bobtail Horse. The village exhausted itself in showing its admiration of my exploit; and my single scalp was greeted with as much honor as if I had slaughtered a hundred of the enemy.

CHAPTER XV.

Short Account of Pine Leaf, the Crow Heroine.—Twenty Days' Battle with the Cheyennes.—Return of the Village to the west Side of the Mountains.—Letter from M'Kenzie.—Visit to his Trading-post at the Mouth of the Yellow Stone.

IN connection with my Indian experience, I conceive it to be my duty to devote a few lines to one of the bravest women that ever lived, namely, Pine Leaf—in Indian, Bar-chee-am-pe. For an Indian, she possessed great intellectual powers. She was endowed with extraordinary muscular strength, with the activity of the cat and the speed of the antelope. Her features were pleasing, and her form symmetrical. She had lost a brother in the attack on our village before mentioned—a great brave, and her twin brother. He was a fine specimen of the race of red men, and bade fair to rise to distinction ; but he was struck down in his strength, and Pine Leaf was left to avenge his death. She was at that time twelve years of age, and she solemnly vowed that she would never marry until she had killed a hundred of the enemy with her own hand. Whenever a war-party started, Pine Leaf was the first to volunteer to accompany them. Her presence among them caused much amusement to the old veterans; but if she lacked physical strength, she always rode the fleetest horses, and none of the warriors could outstrip her. All admired her for her ambition, and as she advanced in years, many of the braves grew anxious for the speedy accomplishment of her vow. She had chosen my party to serve in, and when I engaged in the fiercest struggles, no one was more promptly at my side than the young heroine. She seemed incapable of fear; and when she arrived at womanhood, could fire a gun without flinching, and use the Indian weapons with as great dexterity as the most accomplished warrior.

I began to feel more than a common attachment toward her. Her intelligence charmed me, and her modest and becoming demeanor singled her out from her sex. One day, while riding leisurely along, I asked her to marry me provided we both returned safe. She

"PINE LEAF," THE INDIAN HEROINE, MOUNTED ON HER WAR-HORSE.

flashed her dark eye upon mine, "You have too many already," she said. "Do you suppose I would break my vow to the Great Spirit? He sees and knows all things; he would be angry with me, and would not suffer me to live to avenge my brother's death."

I told her that my medicine said that I must marry her, and then I could never be vanquished or killed in battle. She laughed and said, "Well, I will marry you."

"When we return?"

"No; but when the pine-leaves turn yellow."

I reflected that it would soon be autumn, and regarded her promise as valid. A few days afterward it occurred to my mind that pine-leaves do not turn yellow, and I saw I had been practiced upon.

When I again spoke to her on the subject, I said, "Pine Leaf, you promised to marry me when the pine-leaves should turn yellow: it has occurred to me that they never grow yellow."

She returned no answer except a hearty laugh.

"Am I to understand that you never intend to marry me?" I inquired.

"Yes, I will marry you," she said, with a coquettish smile.

"But when?"

"When you shall find a red-headed Indian."

I saw I advanced nothing by importuning her, and I let the matter rest. However, to help her on with her vow, I never killed an Indian if she was by to perform it for me, thinking that when her number were immolated there might be better chance of pressing my suit.

We frequently shifted our camping-ground, in order to keep up with the buffalo and furnish our horses with sufficient grass, for we had such an immense number that the prairie round our lodges in a few days had the appearance of a closely-mown meadow. Finally, we removed to the western side of the mountain again, and encamped on Little Horn River, one of the sources of the Yellow Stone. Shortly after our encampment, we found there was a village of Cheyennes about twelve miles distant, and an incessant warfare was maintained between the two villages for twenty days. Sometimes they would take three or four Crow scalps; in return, our party would retaliate by taking as many of theirs. Thus they went on, with varying fortune, during the whole twenty days.

I had never been engaged in these skirmishes; but one evening, I, with three others, among whom was Yellow Belly, resolved to go on an adventure. Accordingly, we started for the Cheyenne, arriving there the next morning, and unhesitatingly entered their village while the inmates were quietly reposing. After passing through one quarter of their village, we saw an Indian approaching, who, on perceiving us, wheeled his horse to escape. I shot an arrow into his back, but, before he fell, I rode up, cut him down with my battle-axe, and rode on. One of our party, not wishing to lose his scalp, dismounted to take it. In doing so he lost his horse, which followed us, leaving his rider on foot close to the enemy's village, whence the aroused warriors were issuing like hornets. Perceiving his danger, I rode back, and took him up behind me. We had to run for it; but we made good our escape, driving home before us seven horses captured from the enemy. This was considered a great achievement by our Crow brethren, and they again washed their faces.

The enemy now charged on our village, killing six

Crows, among whom was a brother-in-law of mine. His relatives appealed to me to avenge them. Supposing that the enemy would renew the attack the next day, I selected one hundred and thirty warriors, all well mounted, to waylay them. We posted ourselves midway between the belligerent villages, but the Cheyennes had passed within a few hundred yards before we were in ambush. Being there, the idea occurred to me to await their return. On their repulse from the village we would spring up and cut off their retreat, and, I made no doubt, succeed in killing a great number of their warriors.

It fell out as I had expected. The Crows drove them back with a loss to the enemy of four; and when they neared us, their horses were badly jaded, and our friends hotly in pursuit. We sprung up, cutting off their retreat, and they, sorely pressed in their rear, seeing our party in front cutting down right and left, became panic-struck, and fled in all directions.

We took sixteen scalps, with the horses and equipments of the fallen warriors, and returned home in triumph. This made twenty scalps taken in one day, which was considered by the Crows a glorious victory, and the scalp-dance was performed with unusual vivacity. In this battle the heroine was by my side, and fought with her accustomed audacity. I counted five *coos*, and she three, for three enemies killed with her lance. The Cheyennes, disconcerted with their misadventure, moved their village away from the Crow territory.

We also took up our line of march, and moved on to Clarke's Fork, a branch of the Yellow Stone, where we found abundance of buffalo and good grass. While encamped here I received a letter from Mr. M'Kenzie,

written at Fort Union, at the mouth of the Yellow
Stone, where he desired me to see him. It was delivered to me by Mr. Winters, who, in company with one
man, had found his way unharmed. M'Kenzie wished
me to see him immediately on business of importance,
as he wished, through my influence, to establish a trade
with the Crows.

On communicating my intention of performing the
journey, all expostulated at my going. I gave them
my positive word that I would return in eighteen suns,
if not killed on the way. It was a long and hazardous journey to undertake, having to traverse a distance
of seven hundred and sixty miles, exposed to numerous bands of hostile Indians. I succeeded in reaching the fort in safety, where I found M'Kenzie with a
great stock of miscellaneous goods. I arrived late in
the afternoon, dispatched my business with him hastily, and started on my return in the morning. I took
ten pack-horses laden with goods to trade with the Indians, in addition to which several boats were freighted and sent to me up the Yellow Stone. Two men
accompanied me to the Crow country. We had no
trouble on our way until we arrived within a few miles
of our village (as I supposed it), when, as we were
marching on, I remarked something unfamiliar in the
appearance of the place. I ordered the two men to
turn their animals up a little valley close by, while I
took a nearer look at the village. A closer inspection
confirmed my mistake; I saw the lodges were painted
a different color from our own. I followed the pack-
horses, and found a trail which led to the Crow village,
and concealed from the observation of the village we
had approached. Soon after entering the trail, I discovered the fresh tracks of five Indians, going the di-

rection that we were. I halted the pack-horses, and rode on to get a sight of them. At a short distance I perceived the five men, and, unobserved by them, I rode on and entered a low place until I approached within a few rods of them. I took a short survey of them, and concluded that they must be enemies belonging to the village we had just left. They were on foot, and I conceived myself a match for the whole five. I leveled my rifle, and was taking aim, when my horse moved his head and disconcerted my sight. I tried again, with precisely the same result. I then dismounted, and advanced two or three steps nearer my object. As I was about to fire, having the rein on my arm, the horse made another motion, thus spoiling my aim for the third time. At that moment one of them made a yawning expression in the Crow language, and I was so terrified at his narrow escape that the rifle dropped from my hand. I called to them, telling them the danger they had escaped.

" Why," said they, " you would not have attacked five of us ?"

" Yes," I said, " and would have killed every one of you, had you been enemies."

They then informed me that they had lost two men that day near the village of the Black Feet, who were now, beyond doubt, dancing over their scalps. I did not wait to hear more, but directed them to return to my horses and assist the men in getting on to the Crow village as soon as possible. I rode forward to make my arrival known.

My return was welcomed with the liveliest demonstrations of joy by the whole tribe. But I delayed no time in ceremonial. I called a council forthwith, and informed them that the Black Feet were encamped ten miles distant, that two of our warriors had that day fallen by their hands, and that we must go and avenge their death. The chief assented; but, as a preliminary, directed me and another to count their lodges that night. I undertook the dangerous task, although extremely fatigued with my long journey. We succeeded in the object of our expedition, and found their lodges outnumbered ours by one. There are, as a general thing, from four to six warriors to a lodge; the Black Foot village comprised two hundred and thirty-three lodges; hence we could form a pretty accurate estimate of the number of warriors we had to contend with.

Their village was closely watched by our spies; every movement made by the enemy was promptly reported to our chief. During the night they appeared to sleep soundly, probably fatigued with a late dance. But in the morning they were astir betimes, and having packed up, started forward in our direction, apparently unaware of our presence. On they came — men, women, and children — utterly unconscious of the terrible shock that awaited them. Our warriors were never better prepared for a conflict, and never more certain of victory. We were drawn up on a high table prairie, our whole force concealed from view at no greater distance than half pistol-shot.

Their chief led the van, and with him were several young squaws, who were laughing and dancing around him, evidently to his great amusement. They were near enough to launch the thunders of war upon them, and our chief gave orders to charge. The order was instantly carried into effect. The chief who, a moment before, was so joyous, surrounded by his tawny young squaws, was the first to fall beneath my battle-axe, and his attendants scattered like chaff before the wind. We were upon the warriors so unexpectedly that they had hardly time to draw their weapons before they were overthrown and put to flight. They were encumbered with women, children, and baggage. Our attention was directed solely to the men; the women were unharmed, except those who were overturned by our horses.

During the engagement, a powerful Black Foot aimed a blow at me with his battle-axe, which Pine Leaf deprived of its effect by piercing his body through with her lance. In a few moments the fighting was over, and after pursuing the flying enemy through the timber, we returned to collect the spoils of victory. We took one hundred and seventy scalps, over one hundred and fifty women and children, besides abundance of weapons, baggage, and horses. The Crows had twenty-nine wounded.

This was a severe blow to the Black Feet; such a slaughter is of rare occurrence in Indian warfare. Notwithstanding this sad defeat, they rallied their broken band, and attacked us again in the afternoon; but it amounted to nothing, and they fled in gloomy confusion beyond the Crow territory.

Pine Leaf never signalized herself more than on this occasion. She counted six *coos*, having killed four of the enemy with her own hand. She had but few superiors in wielding the battle-axe. My horse was killed by the blow which was aimed at my head by the Indian whom the heroine killed. I wore a superb head-dress, ornamented with eagles' feathers and weasels' tails—the labor of many days. Early in the action, three of these tails were severed by a bullet which grazed my head. "These Black Feet shoot close," said the heroine, as she saw the ornaments fall; "but never fear; the Great Spirit will not let them harm us."

I took a very pretty young woman prisoner, but was obliged to give her up to one of the braves, who had my promise before the battle that if I took one I would give her to him, and if he took one he should give her to me. When a warrior (of the Crow tribe) takes a woman prisoner, she is considered his sister, and he can never marry her. If she marries, her husband is brother-in-law to her captor. Our prisoners soon forgot their captivity; they even seemed pleased with the change, for they joined with great alacrity in our scalp-dance over the scalps of their own people.

All Indian women are considered by the stronger sex as menials : they are thoroughly reconciled to their degradation, and the superiority of their "lords and masters" is their chiefest subject of boast. They are patient, plodding, and unambitious, although there are instances in savage life of a woman manifesting superior talent, and making her influence felt upon the community.

During my visit at Fort Union I engaged to build a fort for M'Kenzie to store his goods in safety at the mouth of the Big Horn River, one of the branches of the Yellow Stone. Accordingly, I repaired to the place to select a good site and commence operations. On arriving at the spot, I found the boats close by, but as there was no secure quay at the junction of the streams, I selected a site about a mile below. There were fifty men, who had arrived with the boats, hired to assist me in erecting the fort. The stipulated dimensions were one hundred and twenty yards for each front, the building to be a solid square, with a block-house at opposite corners. The fort was erected of hewn logs planted perpendicularly in the ground; the walls were eighteen feet high. As soon as the pickets were up, we built our houses inside, in order to be prepared for the approach of winter. When I had been engaged about six weeks upon its construction, four hundred lodges of Crows moved into our immediate vicinity, thus affording us plenty of company, and a sufficient force to protect us against the attacks of hostile tribes.

When we had completed our building we unloaded the boats, and commenced trading with the Indians. During the first year the company was very unsuccessful, sinking over seventeen thousand dollars in the undertaking. This, however, was principally attributable to the outlay upon the fort (the wages of the fifty men engaged in constructing it ran for twelve months), and to the number of presents which it is customary, on such occasions, to distribute among the Indians.

After the Crows had removed to the fort, they were repeatedly annoyed with attacks from different hostile tribes. I was engaged in two small encounters during the winter, in both of which we were completely victorious. The Crows were fully occupied in protecting their own horses, or levying contributions upon their neighbors.

During the winter we accumulated a large amount of peltry, which in the spring I sent down to Fort Union in five Mackinaw boats, built by ourselves for the purpose. I sent a sufficient number of men to take good care of the boats, and to return up stream with a fresh supply of goods. I then left the fort in charge of Winters, leaving him thirty men for a guard. I also had provided an ample stock of dried meat, so that they might avoid the risk of hunting for provisions.

Early in May we commenced our march in search of summer quarters. We traveled by easy stages, and on a circuitous route, so that when we finally arrived at Rosebud Creek, a branch of the Yellow Stone, we found ourselves but twenty miles distant from the fort.

After we had remained about a week at our encampment, our village was invested by a large war-party of Black Feet. It happened very fortunately we were building a medicine lodge at the time, and our whole force was at home, which circumstance most probably preserved us from a disastrous defeat. Our enemies numbered about four thousand warriors, to oppose whom we had two thousand eight hundred practiced warriors, besides the old men, who always acted as village guards. At daybreak the enemy advanced upon our village with great impetuosity. Our war-horses being tied to our lodge doors, the first alarm found our defenders ready mounted to meet the assailants. We did not allow them to enter the village, but advanced on to the plain to meet them. The contest was severe for several minutes, and the clash of battle-axes and the fierce yells of the opposing forces made the whole prairie tremble. The two parties charged alternately, according to the Indian mode of warfare; but the Crows gained ground at every attack, for they fought with every thing at stake. The fight lasted for several hours. Early in the action we discovered a manœuvre of the enemy which would probably have resulted seriously for us had we not perceived it in time. About half their force was detached to attack us in the rear, and take possession of the village. I formed from fifteen to eighteen hundred warriors into a body, and rode down to meet their detachment as it wound around the foot of a small hill. They were in quick march to gain their position, and approached in seeming security. My warriors being formed upon the brow of a hill under which the enemy was passing, I gave the order for a rush down the hill upon them. The attack was made with such irresistible force that every thing in our way was overthrown, and warriors and horses were knocked into promiscuous piles. We happened to burst upon their centre, thus severing them in two, and the confusion they became involved in was so irremediable that their only hope was to get back to their main body with as little delay as possible.

In the attack, a lance thrown by a Black Foot perforated my leggin, just grazing the calf of my leg, and entered the body of my horse, killing him on the spot. My ever-present friend, Pine Leaf, instantly withdrew it, releasing me from a very precarious situation, as I was pinned close to the horse, and his dying struggles rendered such proximity extremely unsafe. I sprang upon the horse of a young warrior who was wounded, and called to some of our women to convey the wounded man to a place of safety; the heroine then joined me, and we dashed into the conflict. Her horse was immediately after killed, and I discovered her in a hand-to-hand encounter with a dismounted Black Foot, her lance in one hand and her battle-axe in the other. Three or four springs of my steed brought me upon her antagonist, and, striking him with the breast of my horse when at full speed, I knocked him to the earth senseless, and before he could recover, she pinned him to the ground with her lance and scalped him. When I had overturned the warrior, Pine Leaf called to me, " Ride on ; I have him safe now."

I rode on accordingly, but she was soon mounted again and at my side. The surviving Black Feet speedily dispersed, and they all retreated together, leaving the Crows master of the field. They left behind ninety-one killed, besides carrying off many dead with their wounded. We lost thirty-one killed, and a large number wounded. I had five horses killed under me, but received no wound. Our enemies, in their retreat, drove off sixteen hundred horses, among which were eighty of my own, but we had plenty left, and we considered these only lent to them. We had no dance, and the relatives of the slain went through their usual mourning.

A few days after this battle a messenger arrived from the fort with a request for me to return as quickly as possible, as the Black Feet were continually harassing the men, and they were in fear of a general attack. Accordingly, I returned in the latter part of June, and found affairs in a very serious condition. The Indians had grown very bold, and it was hazardous to venture outside the fort.

One morning seven men were sent about one mile away to cut house-logs, it being supposed there were no Indians in the vicinity. Some time in the forenoon I heard the report of a rifle close to our gate. I ran out, and just caught sight of the retreating Indians as they entered the bushes. They had shot and scalped one of our men as he was chopping only a few paces from the gate. The danger that the other men might be placed in then occurred to me, and, ordering the men to follow me, I mounted my horse and hastened to their rescue. I was followed by about one half the men, the remainder preferring the protection of the wooden walls. I soon discovered our men;

they were surrounded by forty Indians, the chief of whom appeared to be addressing the sun, and was gesticulating with his battle-axe. On his raising his arm, I sent a ball through his body, and then shouted to the men to run to me. They started, but one of them was shot down before they reached me. The survivors were so terrified that they did not dare to stop when they reached me, but continued their course unslackened until they gained the fort. My followers, seeing their alarm, became fugitives in turn, and I was left alone within gunshot of the remaining thirty-nine Indians. Uttering deafening yells, they made a rush for me; my horse became frightened, and I could scarcely mount him. However, by running by his side a few paces, I managed to leap on his back, and retreated at full speed, while their bullets and arrows flew around me like hail. When I approached the fort, a voice near me cried, " Oh, Jim! don't leave me here to be killed."

I wheeled round, and, with my double-barreled gun in my hand, made a charge toward the whole approaching party, who, seeing my resolute bearing, turned and scampered off. I rode up to the person who had called me, and found him an old man, who was unable to run, and had been abandoned by his valorous companions to the mercy of the savages. I assisted him on to my horse, and was about to spring on behind him, when the horse sprang forward, leaving the old man's gun behind, and carried him safely to the fort. By this time the Indians had returned upon me. I ran wherever a shelter offered itself; and, when closely pressed, would face round and menace them with my guns. Within a few hundred yards of the fort I came to a small covering which had been used as a shelter by the horse-guards, and I sprang into it, with the Indians at my heels. After expending the contents of my guns, I plied them with arrows to their hearts' content, until they gave up the fray and retired. This took place in fair view of the fort, when not one of its doughty inmates dare come to my assistance, and who even refused to resign their fire-arms to the women, who were anxious to come to my rescue.

When at length I succeeded in reaching the fort, I favored the men with my unreserved opinion of them. I had been the means of saving their lives even after the chief of the savages had returned thanks to the sun for their scalps, which he had already deemed secure. I really believe that with Pine Leaf and three other squaws I could have stormed and taken the fort from their possession.

These men were not mountaineers; they were nearly all Canadians, and had been hired in the East; they were unused to savage warfare, and only two of them had seen an Indian battle. If they had come out like men, we might have killed one half the Indians, and I should have been spared a great deal of hard feeling. They acknowledged, however, that I had flogged the Indians alone, and that six of them were indebted to me for their lives.

In July, after the arrival of the boats, the Crows again returned to the fort. They came to make purchases with what small means they possessed, as they had disposed of all their peltry on their previous visit. They, however, brought in a great quantity of roots, cherries, berries, etc., which they traded for articles of necessity; they also sold sixty horses, which we sent to M'Kenzie at the lower fort (Clarke).

It greatly charms the Indians to see new goods;

when they have the means to buy there is no end to their purchases. When the lances, battle-axes, and guns are spread before their eyes, glittering with their burnished steel, notwithstanding they may have a dozen serviceable weapons at home, they must infallibly purchase a new one. If one purchases, all must follow; hence there is no limit to their demand but the very important one imposed by the extent of their exchangeable commodities.

The newly-arrived boats were manned with Canadians, all strangers in the country, nearly all having been imported for boating, as they were willing to submit to the hardships of such a life for a smaller remuneration than men hired in the States. On their arrival, their brethren related a thousand tales about the Indians, and what feats I had performed against them single-handed. They listened to the marvelous tales, and gazed at me in wondering admiration.

When Canadians are fairly broken in, and have become familiar with Indian character, they make the best of Indian fighters, especially when put to it in defense of their own lives. They become superior trappers too, being constituted, like their native ponies, with a capacity to endure the extremest hardships and privations, and to endure starvation for an incredibly long period.

CHAPTER XVI.

Departure from Fort Cass.—Capture of Squaws.—Battle with the Black
Feet ; with the Cheyennes.—Great Success of the Crows in stealing
Horses.—A successful Fall for Beaver.—Return to the Fort with
Peltry.

AFTER having arranged every thing in the fort
(which I have forgotten to mention we named after
Mr. Cass), and given all needful instructions to Winters, who was in charge, I again left. My intention was to induce the Crows to devote their undivided attention to trapping, not alone for their own
benefit, but for the interest of the company in whose
service I was engaged. I well knew that if I was with
them they would capture five beavers to one if left to
themselves. I had obtained great influence in the
medicine lodge, and could often exert it to prevent a
war-party from making a useless excursion against
their enemies. I would tell them in their council that
my medicine told me not to go to war ; that it was to
their interest to employ their warriors in trapping all
the beavers possible, so that they might have the
means of purchasing ammunition and weapons for
themselves, as well as beads, scarlet cloth, and blankets for the women ; that by-and-by we should be attacked by the enemy, and be unprovided with the
means of defense ; that they would then kill all our
warriors, and make captives of our women and children, as the Cheyennes had captured my mother when
I was an infant, many winters gone ; that they should
save all their warriors against a time of need, and only

engage in war when the safety of their village was at stake.

These representations would frequently dissuade them from their belligerent purpose, and beaver-skins would be brought into the village by the pack; but they would soon tire of their pacific occupation, and their enemies' horses would offer them temptations which they could not resist.

Nearly all the Crows having left the fort before I did, only a few warriors remained to bear me company. I engaged to meet them at the mouth of the Little Horn within a given number of nights, and I knew I should be expected. We arrived in safety at the place appointed, and within the time I had specified.

Soon after our arrival, it was proposed to send out a war-party, not so much to fight as to reconnoitre; to see where horses could with least difficulty be procured, and gain a general intelligence of how matters stood. We set out, and had traveled slowly along for nearly two weeks, when our scouts returned to apprise us that there was a large crowd of women approaching toward us. We were then in a forest of plum-trees, bearing large red plums, which were fully ripe, and were very delicious. Feeling satisfied that the women were coming to gather fruit, we secreted ourselves, intending, at a given signal, to surround them while they were busily employed. Accordingly, we waited until they all set themselves about their task, they keeping up an incessant jabber among themselves like so many blackbirds or bob-o-links, and having no suspicion that the Crows would so soon come in for their share. At a sound from the whistle, they were entirely surrounded, and their merry chatter was hushed in an instant. We marched them to an open piece of ground, made them form a line, and proceeded to make a selection. The aged, the ill-favored, and the matrons we withdrew from the body, telling them to return to the village, and depart without clamor. They went away in sullenness, with their eyes flashing fire. The remainder, to the number of fifty-nine, very attractive looking young women, we carried along with us ; and as we were but three miles distant from their village, and could plainly see the smoke of their lodges, we deemed it prudent to lose no time in making our way home. There were three warriors in the company of the women when first descried, but they were not inclosed in our surround, and we could find no traces of them in any direction.

On our return toward home the captives were, as usual, gloomy for an hour or two; but they very quickly brightened, and amused us with their smiles and conversation during the whole of the journey. In four days we reached the village, and were received with "thunders of applause." Four of the prisoners were adjudged my prizes, who, according to Indian customs, became my sisters. For my services in this expedition I was honored with the name of Boah-hish-a (Red Fish). Our prisoners were kindly received, and treated with becoming attention. I carried my four sisters to my lodge, and distributed them among my relatives. They were all married to Crow braves, and added materially to the strength of my band of relatives ; for it is esteemed a great honor to marry the sister of a great brave, which appellation I had long borne.

Pine Leaf had captured two prisoners, and offered me one of them to wife. I answered, " You once told me I had already wives enough. I will not add to their number until I marry the heroine of the Crow nation."

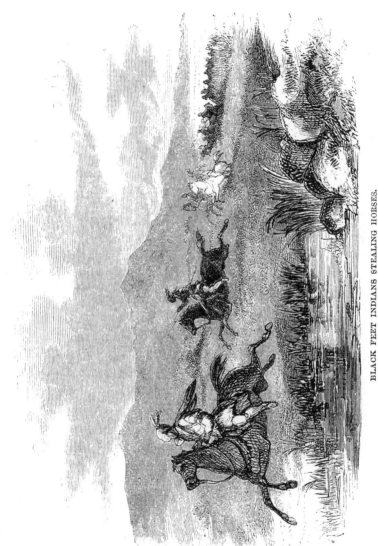

BLACK FEET INDIANS STEALING HORSES.

"Ah, you have found the red-handed Indian, then," she said, laughing mockingly.

She always received my advances with this unsatisfactory nonchalance, that it was with some unpleasantness of feeling I approached the subject. But the more I saw of her lofty bearing, and witnessed the heroic deeds that she performed, the more ardent became my attachment to her. When she was by my side in battle, it seemed as if I had increased strength and courage; when she was away, which happened rarely, I felt a vacancy which no other warrior could supply. There was none bolder than herself, and she knew it; there were others of greater strength, but her deficiency in muscular power was more than indemnified by her cat-like agility, and she would kill her man while others where preparing to attack.

There was one thing that irritated the noble girl's curiosity, and that was the war-path secret. Having killed many in battle, having followed where any dared to lead, "Why am I debarred from that important communication?" she would ask. "Why am I sent off with the women and children, when that secret is told the warriors of but one battle?"

I would tell her that the misfortune of her sex rendered it impossible that she could ever have the secret unveiled to her; that, should she break her trust, she would surely pay the forfeit with her life. She would become angry at such representations, and her black eyes would glow like fire.

Soon after this capture, a band of Black Feet made reprisals by breaking our inclosure and taking seven hundred horses. I immediately collected a small party and went in pursuit. We speedily overtook them, and recovered all the horses except sixty, bearing the enemy, who precipitately fled, leaving two of their party dead. On our return we were received with the usual demonstrations of joy, and the horse-dance was performed by the village, together with the scalp-dance, which lasted nearly all night.

About this time my allied friend raised a war-party, and went in quest of the enemy; the heroine, ever active and prepared, accompanying him. I staid behind. They returned in a few days, bringing eight scalps of the Coutnees—one of the bands of the Black Feet. They had lost two of their warriors, much to the annoyance of the heroine, as she was prevented from dancing, although she had counted two *coos.* She then declared that she would go to war no more, except in my company ; but she had to break her word, and the next time she engaged in fight she received a severe wound. She wished me to raise a force immediately, and go and kill an enemy, so that she could wash her face. I declined, however, on the ground that I was soon to go to the fort, and that I would engage in no hostile encounters until my return.

When a war party loses one of its members, the survivors are compelled to wear their mourning-paint, until that same party, or an individual member of it, has wiped out the blot by killing one of the enemy without incurring loss of life. Thus it not unfrequently happens, when no opportunity of avenging a loss occurs, that the mourners wear paint for months, regularly renewing it as it wears off.

Small parties were continually going out and returning with varying success. The grand total of horses stolen by the Crows from all other tribes during that year amounted to near six thousand head. During the same period, however, they lost a great number stolen from them.

I visited the fort again in October, with three hundred lodges of the Indians, the remainder following us in a few days. A great number of the Indians had been busy with their traps for about two months, and we took into the fort a great quantity of peltry, which procured for the Indians every thing they needed, besides finery for the women.

When I arrived, I was informed that the head-hunter of the fort had been killed during my absence.

" Now," said Pine Leaf, " you will go to war for one of your people, and I will go with you, so that I can wash my face."

The fort had been subject to alarms during the whole time of my absence, but had only lost the man here referred to.

As soon as the Indians had finished their trading, I directed them to move to the Yellow Stone, as far up as " Pompey's Tower," telling them that I would join them in four nights. Then, as soon as I could get ready, I loaded twelve pack-horses with goods for retail, and, taking two Canadians with me, I went on and joined the village at the appointed place.

This much performed, I then attended to the frequent solicitations of the heroine, by leading a party, and going in pursuit of the Black Feet to chastise them, as I told the Crows, for killing the white hunter. We were absent eleven days, and returned with only four scalps and seventy-four horses. I received an arrow in my head; and there were three other warriors wounded, but none killed. The heroine then washed her face of the mourning-paint, which she had been grieving about so long.

At this time I was third counselor of the nation, having been fifth and fourth previously. In the Crow nation there are six counselors, and by them the nation is ruled. There are also two head chiefs, who sit with the counsel whenever it is in session. The office of first counselor is the highest in the nation, next to the head chiefs, whose authority is equal. If in any of these divisions, when a matter is brought to the vote, the suffrages are equal, one of the old pipe-men is summoned before the council, and the subject under discussion is stated to him, with the substance of the arguments advanced on both sides ; after hearing this he gives his casting vote, and the question is finally settled.

When war is declared on any tribe, it is done by the council. If any party goes out without the authority of the council, they are all severely whipped ; and their whipping is no light matter, as I can personally testify. It makes no difference how high the offender ranks, or how great his popularity with the nation— there is no favor shown ; the man who disobeys orders is bound to be lashed, and if he resists or resents the punishment, he suffers death.

We raised a war-party of three hundred men to act against the Cheyennes, having one of the head chiefs as leader. We moved on foot toward their country, which was about two hundred and fifty miles from our village. In this expedition I acted in the capacity of head spy, and was of necessity continually in advance of the main party. Being near the enemy, according to our calculations, I was some distance ahead, with four other spies, when we discovered five of the Cheyenne warriors in the act of dressing a buffalo, which they had just killed. We crept slyly up within gunshot of them, and each singled out his man and fired. Four fell at the discharge ; the other mounted his horse and fled. I mounted one of the other horses, and pursued him within sight of his village, when I wheeled and returned to the camp, well knowing that we should be pursued immediately after the fugitive communicated his news. I found the camp readily, and acquainted the chief with what had happened, although it is against orders for spies to commence any attack. I told him that we were compelled to fight them to save our own lives, as the enemy had discovered us. "That is all right," he said, "but they will be soon after us, and we must retreat as fast as we can."

We returned on our steps without losing a moment, and traveled all night. It was very cold, with considerable snow on the ground. In the morning we built a fire, and as soon as we had warmed ourselves we moved on. One man, who was lame, lingered by the fire after we had left, and he rejoined us in great alarm, telling us that the Cheyennes were on our trail in great force, and were but a short distance behind us. We then put our boys and horses into a deep gully close by, and also stepped in ourselves, as soon as we had discharged one volley at our pursuers, who were then within short gunshot distance. They numbered from fifteen hundred to two thousand warriors, all mounted, while we were but a very few warriors, and had not more than a dozen horses in all. We were in a strong position, however, one which they dared not to storm, even with their whole force. Frequently a few more daring cavaliers would advance to the edge of the bank, and hurl their lances into our midst; but they rarely escaped our bullets. We had killed and wounded a great number in this manner, which taught our foe to be more cautious in his approaches; when our chief, losing heart, declared there was no hope for us, and that we infallibly should be all "rubbed out."

He addressed his son, a lad about sixteen years of age, in the following strain: "My son, we shall be all killed here. The Cheyennes are very brave, and they have a cloud of warriors before us. It must never be said that my son was killed by them, therefore I must kill you myself before I die. Die, my son, first!"

In an instant his son was a corpse, prostrate at the feet of his savage father. This, thought I, is the first time I ever saw a person killed to save his life. The actions of the old chief were wild throughout the whole proceeding. After killing his son, he rushed upon the top of the bank, and addressed himself to the enemy, an exposed mark to their arrows, as follows:

"Ho, Cheyennes! here I am! come and kill me! I am the great chief of the Crows. Come and kill me first, and then you can easily kill my warriors. Many of your braves have fallen by my hand; their scalps darken my lodge. Come! come and kill me!"

I was astonished at such rashness, and still more astonished at the enemy, who, on seeing him a fair mark for their bullets, even withdrew to a greater distance, and appeared to be perfectly paralyzed. After a while, our head chief descended, and took a long smoke at his pipe. The enemy retired without troubling us farther. In the night we decamped, and made all possible haste to our village, where we arrived in safety without any molestation from the enemy. The chief attributed our escape to the interposition of the Great Spirit, whom the sacrifice of his son had propitiated in our behalf.

We killed fourteen of the enemy while in our intrenchment, making eighteen, and wounded a great number. We had eight killed, including the chief's son, and ten or eleven slightly wounded.

When we arrived at home there was great mourning, and we all assumed paint on our faces as usual. But we wore it only a short time before we took ample revenge. Pine Leaf did not accompany us on this expedition.

CHAPTER XVII.

Victory over the Cheyennes.—Treachery of the Snake Indians.—Loss of six Crow Warriors.—Victory over the Snakes and Utahs.—A Mountaineer killed.—Trouble in the Wigwam.—I am disgraced.— Great Sacrifice of my Father's Property.—Three Whippings for violating Crow Morals.—Great Battle with the Re-ka-ras.

FOUR days after our return, our chief, still smarting at the sacrifice he had made for the salvation of his people, burned for revenge. He selected a body of over two hundred warriors, and started forthwith in search of the enemy.

The night following his departure, I also raised two hundred men, and started in a contrary direction. We proceeded on until we came to Laramie Forks, where Fort Laramie has since been built, and were in sight of a Cheyenne village. While we were surveying the village, eleven of their men, laden with meat, came up and encamped within a few hundred yards of where we were. We immediately threw ourselves flat upon the ground, resolved to wait until the coming of night, in order to make secure work of our attack on them, and prevent any of their number escaping to alarm the village. At a late hour we silently approached their camp when they were all sound asleep; a dozen guns were discharged at them in a moment, and we rushed in with our battle-axes to complete the work. We took their scalps, and were soon on the retreat, bearing away all the meat we needed, besides nineteen horses, and the slain warriors' equipments. We returned to the village, and washed off the mourning-paint, making the whole village ring with our dancing and rejoicing. The additional name of Ar-ra-e-dish (the Bloody Arm) was conferred upon me.

The old chief came in three days subsequently, bringing fourteen scalps and equipments, without having lost a single man.

Many of my readers will doubtless wonder how a man who had been reared in civilized life could ever participate in such scenes of carnage and rapine. I have already related that I was brought up where similar outrages were committed upon the defenseless inhabitants of the new settlements. Impressed with the recollection of these early scenes, I hardly ever struck down an Indian but my mind reverted to the mangled bodies of my childish play-fellows, which I discovered on my way to the mill, barbarously murdered by the savages. In after years I have experienced the natural ferocity of the savage, who thirsts for the blood of the white man for no other purpose than to gratify the vindictive spirit that animates him. I have seen the paths of the trappers dyed with their blood, drawn from their hearts by the ambushed savage, who never knew mercy, but remorsely butchered all who came in his way. Such is Indian nature. When I fought with the Crow nation, I fought in their behalf against the most relentless enemies of the white man. If I chose to become an Indian while living among them, it concerned no person but myself; and by doing so, I saved more life and property for the white man than a whole regiment of United States regulars could have done in the same time.

Before I close this narrative, I shall take the liberty to express my opinions, and afford those having control of the War Department some counsel about the cheapest, most expeditious, and most certain method of quelling their Indian troubles, on which the newspapers are harping so much. I know that with five hundred men of my selection I could exterminate any Indian tribe in North America in a very few months. But so long as our government continues to enlist the offscouring of European cities into our army, and intrusts the command to inexperienced officers fresh from West Point, just so long will they afford food for the Indians in and about the Rocky Mountains. Encumbered as our army is with baggage-wagons and artillery, an Indian chief can move his whole community farther in one day than our soldiers can follow them in three.

When our victorious celebration was over, I started on a small trading expedition to the Snake Indians. I had received an invitation from their chief to trade among them, and I selected eight warriors to accompany me. On arriving at their village, I found that the Utahs had joined them, and a great number of them were thronging the village. Knowing that the Utahs and Crows were deadly enemies, I sedulously watched their movements, and very speedily felt distrust for the safety of myself and party, as the whole camp savored strongly of treachery. I mustered my little party around me, and found them without guns. On inquiring the cause, they informed me they had traded them away for horses. I suppose my looks expressed my disapprobation. Mistaking me, they said there was yet one fine horse left, which I could have at the price of my gun.

I had finished my traffic, and had disposed of every thing except my gun, when the Snakes came to me and offered to trade for that. I said, "No; I never sell my gun, except when at home and among my own people." The Snakes then told us to go, that things were bad in their camp. We sprang upon our horses, and struck out at full speed; but we soon discovered a large party of Indians were in close pursuit. We then found they had not sold us their fastest horses, as they gained on some of my party, and shot and scalped them without our ability to defend them. I succeeded in reaching the mountain with two of my men, having lost six noble young warriors in my flight. I knew there would be terrible mourning and loss of fingers, until I could teach the Snakes a lesson which would serve them to remember for a long time.

After devoting a short space to bewailing my misfortune, I requested a council to be called, and never did I enlarge with such wrathful vehemence as I then fulminated against the Snakes, holding them up to the abhorrence of the fathers for their treachery in decoying our unsuspecting warriors into their camp, and then letting loose a pack of murderous savages at our heels, after we had, through their complicity, parted with our only means of defense. I demanded five hundred warriors to go and wipe out the stain, and inflict summary chastisement on the village for their duplicity.

My argument was listened to with the profoundest attention, and all I proposed was readily acceded to. "Let the Red Arm have all that he asks," was the unanimous voice of the assembly.

My warriors rallied around me almost at a moment's

notice, and we mounted our horses and sped in the direction of the Snake country, on Green River. On the eighth day our scouts came in and reported that they had found a large number of the Snakes, scattered in small parties, who were engaged in killing buffalo. We held on until we came in sight of them. I distributed my warriors as the occasion suggested, ordering them to attack the various small camps, while I, with my party, should attack their main body. They were overthrown and dispersed by my brave warriors, with severe loss. We took over one hundred scalps, and a great quantity of guns and other warlike implements. We had sixteen men wounded, including myself (I received two slight wounds from arrows), but none of them dangerously. This blow brought the Snakes to their senses, and they immediately sent a deputation to our village to sue for peace.

A circumstance happened on the evening preceding our attack which caused me the deepest regret. While the spies were reconnoitring, they perceived two Indians, as they supposed, leave the enemy's camp, and proceed down the *cañon*. This circumstance they reported to me. I ordered them to return, and kill them if they could find them. They went in pursuit of the two stragglers, and when they came in sight of them they had their robes over their heads, and were kneeling down over a fire. They fired, and one of the two fell mortally wounded; the other sprang out of his robe, when, to their surprise, they saw he was a white man. They, however, took him prisoner, and brought him to my camp. I was absent at their return; but on the following morning I remarked a very dejected look on their countenances, and I asked them what was the matter.

"We have done very bad," said one; "we have reddened our hands with the blood of the white man."

"Well, how did it occur?" I inquired.

"Ask that white man, and he will tell you all."

I walked up to the unhappy prisoner, whose looks betrayed the keenest anguish, and addressed him in English.

"How are you, my friend?"

He started as if electrified, and looked me closely in the face.

"What brought you here?" I continued.

"I was brought here by these Indians, who killed my companion while we were building a fire to warm ourselves. I suppose I am brought here to be killed also?"

"No, my friend," I said, "you are safe. The Crows never kill white men."

"Are these Crows?"

"Yes."

"Well, well! Then you must be Mr. Beckwourth?"

"Yes, that is my name. And now, without the least fear of danger, relate the occurrence fairly: if my warriors have killed a white man intentionally, they shall be punished."

He then related how he and his companion went into the *cañon*, and how they made a fire to render themselves comfortable away from the Indian camp; how that their robes were over their heads, entirely concealing their faces from view, and that he felt fully confident that my warriors, in firing upon them, had mistaken them for Indians.

"Well," I said, "since the mistake is so apparent, you will greatly serve me to make the same statement to your companions when you return to your camp;

for the Crows are entirely innocent of any design to shed the blood of the white man, and it would be deplorable for any misunderstanding to arise in consequence of this lamentable occurrence."

"I shall make a fair statement of the fact," he said, "and should be very sorry to be the means of any trouble."

He then informed me that he and his late companion were trappers; that his party were in winter-quarters, and encamped with the main body of the Snakes; and that they had come out with this party after meat. I then gave him my reasons for attacking the Snakes, and begged him to commend me to all the old mountaineers.

"There is not a day passes," he said, "but some one mentions you, to wonder where you are, and what you are now doing. I can tell them all that I have seen you, and conversed with you."

I then told him he was at liberty to go at any time; that he could take all the horses belonging to him, and all else that he needed. We assisted him with the body of his unhappy friend upon the back of a horse, and, bidding me adieu, he departed.

The Snakes dispatched a deputation of forty warriors and a medicine chief to the Crows to negotiate peace. They attached all the blame of the late rupture to the Utahs, whom, they said, they could not control, and that the death of our six young warriors was entirely against their wish.

This we knew was false, for there were ten Snakes to one Utah in the camp at the time of the outrage. They also pleaded that they had tried for a long time to induce the Utahs to return home, knowing that they were enemies to the Crows. We at length adjusted the conditions of peace, smoked the calumet, and, after an exchange of presents, they returned to their home.

About this time a brave, named Big Rain, was elected chief of the village for the term of six moons. His duties were to superintend all the village removals, to select sites for camps, order surrounds; in short, he was a kind of mayor, and alone subject to the head chief. Big Rain possessed the most beautiful squaw in the whole village; she was the admiration of every young brave, and all were plotting (myself among the rest) to win her away from her proud lord. I had spoken to her on several occasions, and, whenever opportunity offered, would tender her my most ceremonious obeisance; but she never favored me with any return. Not only was she beautiful, but she was very intelligent, and as proud as Lucifer; and the gorgeous dyes of the peacock were not more variegated or more showy than her attire. Since the elevation of her husband, I fancied that she assumed rather haughtier airs; and I determined to steal her from her lord, be the consequences what they might.

I went one evening to her brother's lodge, and acquainted him that there was a woman in our village that I loved, and that I must have her at all hazards.

"Well, warrior," said he, "if it is any of my relatives, I will assist you all in my power. You are a great brave, and have gained many victories for us, and it is but right that your desires should be gratified."

"Thank you," said I; "but I will try alone first, and if I do not succeed, then I shall be very glad of your assistance."

As an acknowledgment for the prompt tender of his services, I presented him with a quantity of tobacco. "Now," added I, "I want you to call in all your neighbors to-night, and let them smoke as long as they please. After they are assembled, bar the door of your lodge, and amuse them as long as you can with the rehearsal of your adventures. In the mean time, I will be engaged."

I then went to my bosom friend and brother, and made part to him of what I had in hand, which revelation greatly amused him. I requested him to act as sentry over the lodge where they were all smoking—Big Rain with the rest, for I had seen him enter—and remain there until he was satisfied they had filled their pipes for the last time, and then to call out to me, but to mislead them in the place where he was addressing me. This he promised to perform, and we both started on our errands.

I went to Big Rain's lodge, dressed and painted in the extreme of the fashion, and saw the lady reclining, half asleep, upon her couch, and several of her female relatives asleep about the room. Nothing daunted, I strode to the couch of Mrs. Big Rain, and laid my hand gently on her brow.

She started up, saying, " Who is here ?"

" Hush !" I replied ; " it is I."

" What do you want here ?"

" I have come to see you, because I love you."

" Don't you know that I am the chief's wife ?"

" Yes, I know it ; but he does not love you as I do. He never goes to war, but stays idly in the village. I am a great brave, and always go to war. I can paint your face, and bring you fine horses ; but so long as you are the wife of Big Rain, he will never paint your face with new *coos.*"

" My husband will kill you."

" Well, then the Crows will talk of you for many

winters, and say that the great brave, 'The Bloody Arm,' died for a pretty woman."

"Your father," she said, "will lose all his horses, and all his other property, and will become poor in his old age. I respect your father, and all your relatives, and my heart would cry to see them poor."

"If my father loses his horses, I can steal more from our enemies. He would be proud to lose his horses if his son could get a wife as handsome as you are. You can go to war with me, and carry my shield. With you by my side, I could kill a great many enemies, and bring home many scalps. Then we could often dance, and our hearts would be made merry and glad."

"Go now," she pleaded; "for if my husband should return, and find you here, he would be very angry, and I fear he would kill you. Go! go! for your own sake, and for mine, and for the love you have for the Crows, go!"

"No," said I, "I will not go until you give me a pledge that you will be mine when an opportunity offers for me to take you away."

She hesitated for a moment, and then slipped a ring off her finger and placed it on mine. All I now had to do was to watch for a favorable chance to take her away with me on some of my excursions. Just as I was about to leave, my friend called me as though I had been three miles away. I went out and joined him.

"What luck?" inquired he.

"Good," said I.

"Prove it to me, I will believe," said my friend.

I held out my finger to him, displaying the ring.

"Enough," said he; "but I could not otherwise have believed it."

The following day, with six warriors in full cos-tume, I visited Big Rain at his lodge.

" Ah!" said he, " you are going on a war-excursion, my friend ?"

" No," I answered. " We came to see which way you are going to move, how many days you will trav-el, and how far each day ; so that we may find good places to encamp, and know where to find the village in case we should encounter the enemy."

" You are very kind," said he ; " then you intend to be my spy. I have many brothers and other rela-tives among the braves, but not one has ever made me that offer."

" No," thought I, " they don't care as much about your wife as I do."

" Go," said he, " and the Great Spirit will protect you."

I then left, accompanied by my six warriors. The second day out, in the afternoon, as we were traveling slowly along, I discovered, at about a mile distance, a party of twenty-seven Black Foot warriors, just emerg-ing from the Bad Pass. We immediately retraced our steps toward home, and traveled all night, until we ar-rived within three miles of the village. When within sight, we telegraphed with the aid of a small looking-glass, which the Crow scouts usually carry, and every motion of which is understood in the village. I made a signal that I had discovered the enemy, and a second that they were approaching. In a moment I could discover a great stir in the village. When we arrived, I reported to his honor, Big Rain, how many we had seen, what tribe they were, where they had passed the previous night, and where they could then be found. The chief then ordered his madam to bring us some

water, an order she complied with, smiling coquettish-
ly at me the while.

I then retired to my lodge to change my dress, as
portions of it were stained with our travel through the
mountains. While I was in my lodge, madam came
over with a splendid war-horse, which her husband had
sent me, on which to return and fight the Black Feet
I had just discovered. She said, " My husband has
sent this war-horse to the Bloody Arm, and requests
him to lead the Crows to the enemy."

I was soon on the road, with enough mounted warriors to eat the whole party of the enemy; for they
were only a short distance from our village, and, desirous of excitement, every one wished to go. Judging
where the enemy would encamp that night, we traveled on until we arrived near the anticipated encampment.

Previous to starting, my little wife, who, by being
the wife of a great brave, was as good as any woman,
wished to bear me company and carry my shield. But
I refused her, alleging that the danger was too great,
and promising to paint her face when I returned. One
of my sisters then volunteered, and I accepted her offer, taking her with me to carry my shield and lead
my war-horse.

As soon as it was light enough in the morning, I
sent out small parties in all directions to look for their
trail, that we might track them to their den. In ten
or fifteen minutes after the parties left, we heard the report of a gun, and the war-hoop raised. The Crows
assembled in the direction of the report, all drawing
toward a centre. When I arrived, I saw that the
Black Feet had chosen a strong position, and that we
had another fort to storm. It was built partly by na-

ture, but human industry had improved the stronghold. It was low water, and there was a pile of drift on a naked sand-bar, and trees had been felled from the bank upon the drift-pile, forming quite a shelter. Over this position the enemy was placed, protected with a breast-work formed of timber taken from the drift. When I reached the ground, I saw two of our reckless braves talking carelessly under the enemy in this inclosed space, as if they had been in a secure lodge. I regarded them for a moment, and, thinking to display as much bravery as they had, I dismounted and ran to the place, although several shots were fired at me from the fort, none of which took effect.

"What are you here for?" inquired one of them of me.

"In the first place," I said, "tell me what you are here for."

"Why we are old warriors, and you are not."

"If I am not an old warrior," I answered, "I will be one."

I then regarded the rough flooring over head, which separated us from our foes, and perceived an aperture hardly large enough to admit my fist. I stood under it a moment, and as the warriors were moving about, one of them stepped over the aperture and remained there. I thrust my lance up with my whole force, and drew it back reeking with blood.

"There, old warriors," said I to my two companions, "who has drawn the first blood now? Who struck them first? Old warriors, or a young brave? How do you like the look of my lance? Do you see it?"

"Yes, yes, we see it. You have done well, young brave!"

"Well," said I, "you can stay here out of danger;

but I am going out to my warriors, and then to storm the fort."

I ran back with the same success that I had entered it, brandishing my dripping lance, and ordered a charge, which was obeyed as soon as given. In five minutes there was not a Black Foot left within alive. They made scarcely any defense, so sudden and overwhelming was the shock.

We had one warrior killed by the first discharge of the enemy, and six wounded. We then returned home, and, notwithstanding our slain warrior, we celebrated a dance, and devoted the next day to mourning our loss. In robing his remains for the spirit land, we dressed him in the most costly manner, using trinkets, seam-embroidered cloth, and the most costly articles, to show the inhabitants of the spirit land that he was a great brave, and much respected on earth. Over all was wrapped the best of scarlet blankets, and his arms were enfolded therein.

> Oh shroud him in his hunting-shirt,
>   And lay him in the glen,
> Away, away from jealous foes,
>   Away from sight of men—
>
> With bow and painted arrow,
>   That never failed its aim,
> When by his fleet and favorite steed
>   The bounding bison came.
>
> Go, kill the warrior's favorite horse,
>   His crouching, lonely hound;
> To shield so brave a warrior
>   In the happy hunting-ground.

While the villagers were crying and putting on a coat of mourning-paint for the departed warrior, I was busied in my domestic affairs. I sent my sister to madam with a large quantity of service-berries, which had been finely dried the preceding summer, together with some sweet potatoes, telling her to request madam to send me her extra moccasins, in order to lash them together with my own on my pack-dog, and to appoint a place to meet me that evening. My sister was astonished, and said, "Is it possible that you intend to take Ba-chua-hish-a (Red Cherry) with you? Why, we shall all become poor! We shall not have a horse to ride! But I don't care; she is a pretty woman, and will make a good robe-dresser."

Away she hied, and soon returned with my lady's moccasins. Ah, ah! thought I, I am all right now! I expected that the course of true love would not run very smooth with me in the end, but would, on the contrary, carry me over breakers which would most probably break my neck; but I fortified myself with the old adage, "Faint heart never won fair lady," and I determined to hazard all consequences.

The appointed time had arrived, and, on going to the place of assignation, I found my lady true to her word—in fact, she was there first. We joined the party, thirty-four in number, and traveled all night in the direction of the Black Foot country. On the sixth day, at nightfall, we arrived at the Mussel Shell River, a little below the mouth of the Judith, and in sight of a village of the enemy. I looked out a good place for a reserve camp, and then, selecting eighteen of the most expert horse-thieves, we started for the village. We succeeded in capturing one hundred and seventeen horses without being discovered, and arrived safe with them at the camp. We all started immediately back for the village. The warriors took but two horses each, giving the rest to me and my new wife.

Meanwhile, Big Rain made discovery of the loss of

his wife, and was greatly disturbed in mind. My father, knowing the aggressor, commenced giving away to his near relatives all his choicest stock and other valuable property, until the storm should blow over.

When we rode in, the people came out to meet us, rejoicing at our success. Big Rain was out likewise; he took no part in the rejoicing, however, but ordered his wife and me to be surrounded. I was seized by Big Rain, together with half a dozen of his sisters, all armed with scourges, and they administered a most unmerciful whipping. I lay down to it, and received it with true Indian fortitude, though I certainly did think they would beat me to death. If I had resisted, they would have been justified in killing me; also, if they had drawn one drop of blood from me, I should have been justified in taking their lives. They laid it on so unmercifully, that I became angry, and hoped they would draw blood. After the flagellation was performed, the next penalty was, to strip my father and myself of all our horses and other effects (our war-implements excepted). My father was stripped of five hundred horses. I lost about eighty.

"Pretty dear for a very pretty woman," thought I. However, I soon had my horses made up to me by presents from my friends.

We performed the horse-dance that night, though I danced without owning one. During the amusement I conveyed word to the wife of Big Rain that I should go out again the next night, and should expect her company, appointing her to meet me at the same place as before. She returned a favorable answer. My little wife hauled me over the coals for stealing a *married* woman, when there were enough maidens in the village that I could select. I told her that I wished to have the handsomest woman in the village for my lodge.

The appointed hour arrived, and Big Rain's wife was faithful to her promise. We started off with only seventeen warriors. We were gone four days, and returned with three scalps. We met a war-party of nine warriors, six of whom outstripped us and escaped.

On my return I was again seized, and received another such a flogging as the first, laid on with equal good-will.

After my dressing, I retired to my lodge, when a woman approached me bearing some burden in her arms. She addressed me: "Here is something will gladden your heart; he will make as great a brave as his father: his name is Black Panther. Here, look at your child."

Sure enough, my little wife had presented me with a son, who is at this present time (1855) first counselor of the Crow nation.

Two nights afterward, I started on a third expedition with a party of sixty-three warriors, my new wife accompanying me for the third time. We took a southerly course toward the country of the Black Feet, and captured near two hundred head of horses, with which we returned home by way of the fort. On arriving at the fort, I found that my services were required, and that they were about to dispatch a courier after me on business of great importance. I told the commander that I must go home with my party, but that I would return to the fort with the least possible delay. Accordingly we started on. On the road we fell in with a small party of trappers, who were under the conduct of an old schoolmate of mine, David Adams. They seemed greatly dejected, and I inquired of them the cause. Adams then related that he had been robbed of every thing he possessed by some of his men confederated with a number of my Indians, and that they had sent him off in the forlorn condition in which I now saw him. I asked him to describe the appearance of the Indians who took part in robbing him.

"One of the party," said he, "was not an Indian, but a mulatto."

"There was no mulatto when I left," I answered, "and you must be mistaken."

"No," he replied, "I am not. You will find him there on your return."

"Well," said I, "get up and return to the village with me; I will sift this matter to the bottom."

He declined to accompany me. "They told me, if I returned," he urged, "that they would kill us all; and I dare not go back."

"Come with me," I said. "If there is any killing to be done, I will have a hand in it."

He at length consented to return with me. On gaining the village, I rode up to my father's lodge, and said, "How is this? You allow white men to be robbed in the village, directly under your eyes! Do you wish to call down the vengeance of the great white chief upon the Crows? Do you wish them to be made poor and miserable, like the other tribes? Have I not often told you of the immense number of white warriors; that they were like the sand of the prairie—as the leaves of the forest?"

"Hold, my son! I had nothing to do in the matter. My heart was sorrowful when I heard of the crime. It was High Lance who committed it."

"Then I will go and kill him, or be killed myself," said I; and away I sped to the lodge of High Lance.

"Go with him—go with him!" exclaimed my father to all my brothers and relatives around. "He is mad; go and protect him."

I advanced to High Lance, who was standing at his lodge, who, on seeing me approach, stepped in and shut his door. I dismounted, and tore his door down in an instant, and demanded of him what he had been doing. I remarked that his lodge was extremely well supplied with goods.

"High Lance," said I, in an authoritative tone, "restore to these men their horses without one moment's delay."

"I have taken no horses," said he, sullenly.

"Send for them in an instant," said I.

By this time my Dog Soldiers, the bravest men in the nation, were surrounding me.

"What does our chief want?" demanded they.

I told them that I wanted all the goods taken out of the lodge of High Lance, for that he had assisted to steal them from a white man, who was my friend. Instantly the lodge was hoisted, and torn into a thousand pieces, and High Lance, the mulatto, and eleven white men, were exposed to plain view.

I then accosted the mulatto: "What are you doing here, you black velvet-headed scoundrel? You come here in my absence to put the devil into the heads of the Indians, who are bad enough already? I will have your scalp torn off, you consummate villain!"

The poor fellow was frightened almost to death, and trembled in every joint. He replied, "The Crows gave me liberty to stay here and trap in their country, and—"

"Not another word," interrupted I; "though I will hang you, at any rate."

Then, turning to the eleven renegade white men, I said, "I give you just five minutes to leave the village; if you are longer in going, I will order my warriors to scalp every one of you. You assume to be white men, and yet think no more of yourselves than to enter an Indian village and set such an example to the savages; whereas, if they were to treat you in such a manner, you would think death too light a punishment. You rob your own race, and forbid their return to the village under pain of death, allying yourselves with the worst Indian in the tribe. After stripping your victim, you forcibly deprive him of his few trusty followers, and bid him go through these trackless wilds, filled with murderous savages, who, had they come across him, would have murdered him before he reached the fort."

I rated them thus soundly, but not one offered to lift his hand. The stolen horses were very quickly forthcoming, and the purloined property was readily produced. I restored it to my friend before them.

"Now," I said, addressing the gang, "you can return to the fort with Mr. Adams; but if I hear that you offer to molest him in any way, your scalps shall pay for it."

Then, turning to the mulatto, I said, "You have instigated all this mischief, and I should only be doing my duty to put my threat into execution, and hang you as I promised. However, you can go to the fort with these men. I shall be there about as soon as you will, and I will attend to your case then. I'll see if I can not teach you better than to come among the Crows again."

Mr. Adams belonged to Captain Bonneville's company, and was leader of a party of about twenty men; he had come into the Crow country for the purpose of trading and trapping. The mulatto had arrived previously, and had brought a Canadian with him: the mulatto could speak the Crow language tolerably well. He had become acquainted with High Lance, who was a bad Indian, and had relations as bad as himself; and through this clique he had obtained permission to stay and trap in the country. On the arrival of Mr. Adams, the mulatto made himself very familiar with his men, representing to them that they were fools to travel for hire, when they could stay among the Crows with him and do so much better. By these arguments he induced eleven of Mr. Adams's party to desert him, when, with the participation of High Lance and other bad Indians, they stripped him of all his goods. Mr. Adams expressed his warmest thanks to me for my interference. I told him I had only done my duty, as I always had done in like cases, and should continue to do as long as I remained with the Crows.

This business settled, I received a third sound thrashing from my new wife's husband and relatives for again making free with his wife.

After the lapse of three days I left for the fort, again taking my friend's lady. Her husband, finding that I was incorrigible, grew furious, and declared he only wished to have me in his power once more. My Dog Soldiers said to him, " You have whipped him three times, and you shall whip him no more, neither shall you do him any farther harm. Red Cherry loves him, and she does not love you; she will always go with him. You might as well try to turn Big Horn back to its mountain sources as to attempt to separate them, unless you kill them. You would not be so cowardly as to spill the blood of the pretty Red Cherry because she loves our chief. If you should fight him, he will kill you; and if you should assassinate him, we would avenge his death. No, no! Big Rain must not hurt our chief. But we will buy your claim to the Red Cherry, and give her to Red Arm for his own. You, a great chief, should despise to want a woman who loves another warrior better than you!"

Big Rain drooped his head on finding the Dog Soldiers were against him, and gave way to deep reverie. He loved the Red Cherry as children love the delicious fruit bearing the same name. After weighing the matter well, he reluctantly acceded to the offer, and consented to resign all interest and title in Mrs. Big Rain for the consideration of one war-horse, ten guns, ten chiefs' coats, scarlet cloth, ten pairs of new leggins, and the same number of moccasins.

The stipulation was forthwith produced by my faithful Dog Soldiers, and I had the exclusive right to the Red Cherry, without the fear of a drubbing every time I returned.

Such acts are as common among the Rocky Mountain tribes as they have been among the whites in California since the discovery of gold there, though in the latter place, the penalty is frequently more severe than among the wild tribes of the mountains and prairies.

My new wife was the perfection of symmetry. Few of the Caucasian race could boast of handsomer features, and nothing but the rich olive color of the skin betrayed her Indian origin. Big Rain always regarded me with an evil eye after the transaction, and sev-

eral times attempted to induce the lady to return to
him. Many warriors, whose wives had played truant,
had cut off their noses to deprive them of their attractions. I told Red Cherry that if ever she should return to Big Rain, he would surely serve her so. She
never manifested any disposition to leave me; and my
engagement to the American Fur Company enabled
me to dress my wives better than any other woman in
the whole nation.

It was now early spring, and I started for the fort.
Before I left, I told the Crows what time I wished
them to follow me with their peltry.

On my arrival, I was informed that a Mr. Johnson
Gardner had bought quite a large lot of goods, which
he had taken to his camp, eighteen miles down the
river. The morning after my arrival, three men were
dispatched from the fort to acquaint him that I had
come. I had two hundred warriors with me; and on
the night of our arrival we formed a camp and turned
out the horses, not apprehending any danger. Early
in the morning one of my followers went out to fetch
up the horses, when he found them all missing, and
the trail visible on which they had been taken away.
The alarm was instantly given, and I ran to the top
of the hill to take a general survey. I saw two objects
on the ice, which appeared to me to be men; and this
excited my apprehensions that they were two of the
men dispatched from the fort, as they lay in the direction which they had taken. I collected my warriors
instantly for the pursuit, placing all our women and
children in the fort. I ordered some of the white men
down on the ice to bring in the supposed bodies.
Alas! my suspicions proved too true! All three men
had been butchered, and when we rode up their bod-

ies were scarcely cold. The eyes of the warriors flashed fire, and, without delaying a moment, on we swept
in pursuit of revenge. We traveled about thirty miles
(each man leading his war-horse), and our saddle-horses
were beginning to tire, and we saw nothing of the enemy. Darkness would close over us, we feared, before
we could overtake them. We then mounted our war-
horses, which were as swift as the wind, and, leaving
the saddle-horses behind, on we went faster than ever.
Darkness was already upon us, when we came in sight
of a large fire in the distance.

" Now, boys, we have them!" cried I.

We rode on until we neared the camp of the enemy,
as we supposed, and then I examined their position
previous to the onset. Just as I was about to give
the order to charge, I heard a voice from the camp
saying, " Throw them in! D—n them, throw them
in!"

I then saluted the camp, shouting at the top of my
voice, " Halloo the camp! Don't shoot, boys; we are
Crows! I am Jim Beckwourth!"

I then rode up with my whole party, and found that
they had taken two prisoners from the very party we
were in pursuit of, and under the following circumstances: The pursued party rode up to the camp, and
several of them dismounted, among whom was Antoine
Garro (a Canadian half-breed), well known in St.
Louis. Garro could speak tolerably good English.

He accosted Gardner with " How d'do ? You have
got a good fire."

" Who are you," inquired Gardner, " that you speak
English ?"

" My name is Garro."

" What Indians are those with you?"

"Oh, they are good Indians; they will not hurt you."

Gardner discovered that too many were dismounting and crowding round his camp; and he perceived that many of them rode in the direction of his horses, and he became alarmed, as he well might be at his situation.

"Garro," said he, again, "tell me, what Indians are these?"

"They are Re-ka-ras," said he; "they have borrowed your horses, but they will bring them back again." He said this as he saw Gardner look in the direction of his horses.

"Re-ka-ras!" repeated Gardner. "To your guns, men; seize them!"

Old Garro stepped away with an accelerated pace, and two only of the Indians were arrested.

Garro stood off at a safe distance, and demanded the two Indians.

"You can not have them until you bring me my horses," said Gardner.

"Then we will have the tops of your heads," threatened the old rascal.

"Yes, you would have the tops of our heads; but come and take them, if you can."

They rode off, taking every horse that Gardner possessed; and if he had not been on the alert, they would have taken a few scalps as well.

These were the two prisoners that were in question when we rode up. They had bound them with trap-chains, and were in the act of throwing them into a tremendous log fire that was burning in the camp. They opened the logs on the top of the fire, and, swinging the two victims into the flames, rolled back the burning logs. There was a terrible struggle for a moment; then all was still. A blue flame towered high above the pile, and quickly subsided. My Indians begged the privilege of scalping them before they were burned; but Gardner told them he wished to burn them up clean. " You are going after their companions," he said, " and you can get plenty more scalps."

" Yes," they replied, " we will get plenty, and bring your horses back besides."

I really felt proud of my warriors in seeing them animated with so true a spirit. We breathed our horses for a few minutes, for they were in a perfect foam, and then started after them again in hot pursuit.

By next morning, we came within two gunshots' distance of the enemy without being perceived, as a roll in the prairie hid us from their view. We rested for a few moments, to refresh our horses and prepare them for the charge. We heard a continual firing, as if kept up by the enemy, and then a terrific explosion, which made the earth tremble; yells of the savages succeeded to this, and I then learned that there had been a battle between the Indians and traders, and that the whole stock of the traders' powder had exploded.

Now, thought I, is the time to charge; and I gave the word to my impatient warriors. We were among them like a thunder-bolt, even before they had time to mount their horses; for they had not yet recovered from the fright of the explosion. We cut down one hundred and seventy-two of them before they had time to fire twenty shots. The whole force of the enemy amounted to four hundred men, and those who remained unhurt scattered in all directions. We did not pursue them, as our horses were so badly jaded.

Pine Leaf, who charged gallantly by my side, was

wounded with a bullet, which broke her left arm just below the elbow. Placing her wounded arm in her bosom, she grew more desperate than ever, and three of the enemy met their death from the point of her lance after she received her wound. Becoming faint from loss of blood, she was constrained to retire.* We had twelve others wounded.

We recovered all our own horses, and recaptured those belonging to Gardner, besides a great number in the possession of the enemy. For spoils we gathered near two hundred scalps, and a vast amount of fire-arms and other equipments. After this signal victory we returned to Gardner's camp, reaching there the same evening.

Before leaving, however, we took three blackened and disfigured bodies, the remains of the trappers who had so heroically defended themselves, and who, to all appearance, had blown themselves up rather than fall into the hands of the enemy. This supposition was warranted by the appearance of the ground. Evidently the savages had set fire to the grass all round, thinking to burn them out; but it had not reached them. I surmised that the Indians had charged on them in a body, and, when near to the trappers, had been scattered with the ignition of three kegs of powder in the possession of the trappers, for some of the carcasses of the Indians were badly scorched.

Our reception at the camp of Gardner was enthusiastic. "Beckwourth and his brave warriors forever!" rent the air in acclamations. They joined us, and went

---

* The heroine's arm was set in good style by Dr. Walton, at Gardner's camp, and in a few weeks it was sound again. The Indians have no bone-setters ; when their bones get broken, they tie them up as well as possible, and trust in Providence for the result.

on to the fort with us. When we came in sight of the place we formed all in line, and displayed our scalps on the ends of sticks, and discharged our guns, and sung at the top of our voices. This brought every person out of the fort to look at us. We then opened our column, and I requested Gardner to drive all the horses with full speed to the fort. Just before he reached there we spurred our horses on to the front, and encircled the fort several times, still displaying our scalps, and singing the scalp-dance burden louder and louder, while all the occupants of the post joined in. There were hilarious times round the fort that night.

We had sent word to the village to summon the Crows to the trading-post, to help us mourn for the three white men who had recently been killed on the ice, and who were yet unburied. I omitted to mention in proper place that Glass's body was found near the fort—probably on his retreat after he had discovered the Indians. The whole village, accordingly, started to join us, while I and my party went out to meet them and acquaint them with our success. In consideration of my distinguished services, I was elevated to second counselor of the nation.

We met them about a day's ride from the fort, and had a great celebration over the communication of our victory. We returned together and buried the three men, amid the most terrible scenes that I had ever witnessed. The crying was truly appalling. The three men were well known, and highly esteemed by the Crows. When their bodies were lowered to their last resting-place, numberless fingers were voluntarily chopped off and thrown into the graves; hair and trinkets of every description were also contributed, and the graves were finally filled up.

JAMES P. BECKWOURTH. 259

I then set the men to work in building boats, to carry our peltry down to Fort Union, at the mouth of the Yellow Stone, whither I intended going as soon as the river was free from ice. When completed, I put on board seven hundred packs of buffalo robes—ten robes in each pack—and forty-five packs of beaver. I forwarded orders for such goods as were wanted, and also word for another clerk in the place of poor Rose, who had lost his life in the service of the company.

CHAPTER XVIII.

Departure from the Fort with the Crows.—I am elected First Counselor of the Nation.—Death of the head Chief.—I am appointed Successor.—Last Moments of the Chief.

THE Indians having made all their requisite purchases, moved on to the Little Horn River, six or eight days' travel from the fort. We encamped here for the purpose of planting tobacco, which is done by the prophets and medicine men; after which a great feast is provided, and a general time of dancing and rejoicing follows.

The tobacco-plant grows spontaneously in the Snake country, but it is cultivated by the Crows and several other tribes. It is a tolerably good substitute for the cultivated species, for the purpose of smoking, but it is unfit to chew. The plant very closely resembles garden sage, and forms into heads similar to the domestic flax.

At this camp the First Counselor made a speech to the warriors, and spoke in substance as follows: "Warriors! Red Bird has served you faithfully many winters. He is now old. He can be young no more.

His body has been made weak by the numerous wounds he has received in fighting the enemies of the Crows. He now wishes for repose, and not to be disturbed in his slumbers by being called into the council at all hours of the night, when his body, once so powerful, now requires rest. He is desirous of joining the medicine men, that he will not be compelled to go to war; but he will always be ready to defend his own village, the women and the helpless, and to give up his life for them. Red Bird's medicine in the war-path has grown weak; let the younger warriors, who are brave and active, have an opportunity to try their medicine. We have plenty who deserve to be promoted, who are as brave as the she-bear, and as swift as the antelope. Warriors, I now give up my position as first counselor. I have done."

Long Hair replied as follows:

"Red Bird, we feel that our hearts are sorry that you have seen fit to cease to be our first counselor. You have served our people long and faithfully. Your counsel has been good: under your wise direction we have prospered. We would rather that you had still directed us; but you say it is your desire to have repose. Be it so. We know that your body is weak. We know that you have received numerous wounds from the weapons of our enemies. We know that you never turned your back upon the foe. Now we need a sixth counselor, and must select one from the braves here present. Will you name him for us?"

"No," said the old man; "I have never had any enemies among my braves, and I do not wish to make them now. I should not know which to choose, were I to attempt it. They are all brave."

It was at length resolved that one of the medicine

men should be blindfolded, and go among the most
distinguished braves, and whoever he first placed his
hand upon should take his seat as sixth counselor.
The distinguished braves then gathered promiscuous-
ly together; a close bandage was placed over the eyes
of the medicine man, and away he went among the
crowd.   The five counselors being among the braves,
he placed his hand on one of them, and cried out,
"Here is your sixth counselor."

"You are wrong," said Long Hair; "he is counselor
already."

He then went through the crowd, and laid his hand
upon another brave, crying out as before.   Long Bow
was therefore declared to be the choice of the people
for sixth counselor of the nation.   When the seat of
the first counselor falls vacant, the others are elevated
one degree, thus leaving the lowest station vacant.

The village now crossed the Big Horn on their way
to Sun River Creek, a small tributary of the Yellow
Stone.   At Big Horn I took forty warriors, and started in quest of Black Feet and horses.   After traveling
two days, I was overtaken by the head chief, A-ra-poo-
ash, with one hundred and seventy-five warriors.   He
was evidently chagrined about something.   Not wishing him to go to war, as I expected nothing less than
that he would rush in and throw away his life, I told
him that I should avoid the war-path, that my medicine told me my war-path was bad, and I intended to
return to the village.   I started forthwith, and he followed me.   On coming in sight of the village, we halted and encamped for the night.

I stole away in the night with seventy-five warriors,
and made for the enemy's country, hoping that the old
chief would return to the village.   But he took my

trail the next morning, and overtook me with his remaining followers.

He advanced to me, and said, "Bloody Arm, you are a great warrior; you do not wish me to go to war, but I will. I shall never return to the village. I am going to die. The Crows are fools. I have given them good counsel, and they would not listen to my words. I have fought for them during many years. I have shed much blood for them. I have tried to make them a great people, but they have closed their ears. I am going to the big village of the Great Spirit. If you do not wish to go in the path with me, you can go in another path; I will find the enemy alone, and die."

When he had finished speaking, he dismounted. Then, placing the edge of his shield on some buffalo chips, he said, "Warriors, you see my shield. If it rises, I shall die before I return to the village; if not, I shall return." He then addressed the sun for some minutes, after which he took his lance and made several motions with it. Then, giving a bound, the shield was raised as high as his head, and not a warrior saw him touch it. Then every one present believed his words, namely, that he would never return alive to the village. I knew that the shield must have some elevating agency, but it was concealed: my attention was so riveted upon the chief, that I did not discover the power that produced the seeming miracle.

The scouts now ran in to report that there were fourteen Black Feet but a short distance off, who were approaching us on foot. All was then bustle of preparation for a moment, and the trick of the shield was forgotten. Away we sped to find the enemy. We speedily found them, and they, perceiving escape was impossible, prepared to sell their lives as dearly as they could.

The old chief was the first to charge impetuously upon the scanty foe; as his steed plunged through them, he cut down one with his battle-axe; then, wheeling and again passing their line, he clove a second. Again turning to pass the enemy's line a third time, he had already raised his arm to strike, when an arrow entered his body just below the hip, and passed clean through, showing itself near the shoulder.

Every warrior paused in astonishment at seeing their chief thus furiously engaged; but when he fell a demon seemed suddenly to possess them, and the few surviving Black Feet were hewed to pieces in a moment. Every warrior gathered round the dying chief; his life-blood was fast draining from his mortal stroke.

"Warriors," he said, "I came here to die. My wish will soon be gratified. A-ra-poo-ash will lead you no more to war. My home will soon be in the Spirit Land. My people were fools, and would not listen to my counsel. Bloody Arm, come to me. You must now take the place of A-ra-poo-ash. You are brave and wise. You fight the enemy, and vanquish them without losing our own warriors. Your medicine is powerful. Warriors, listen to your dying chief! You, Bloody Arm, are the only brave who can keep the nation together. The Crows disobeyed my orders, and I did not like to punish them for it. I loved my people too well; I was too kind to them for their own good. I was too indulgent. They all fear you, and will obey your words. If they obey you, they will increase and become a powerful people, as I have wished them to be; but if they disobey you, they will not be a nation two winters more. Their enemies are numerous and powerful, and they will rub out all the Crows unless they hearken to what you say. My eyes grow dim. Red Arm, are you listening? I can not see."

"I am listening to all you say," I replied.

"It is well. Then take this shield and this medal; they both belong to you. The medal was brought from our great white father many winters ago by the red-headed chief. When you die, it belongs to him who succeeds you. Listen. Tell Nam-i-ne-dishee, the wife that I have always loved, that if our child, yet unborn, shall be a son, to tell him who his father was. Red Arm, listen."

"I hear you," I said.

"Let my body be buried under this spot. Suffer no warrior to make a track on this war-ground for one season. Then come and seek my bones, and I will have something good for you.

"I can hear the voice of the Great Spirit. It sounds like the moaning of the mighty wind through the dark, gloomy forest. He calls for A-ra-poo-ash to come to the spirit land. I must go. Re—mem—ber!"

The word "remember" expired on his lips as his soul winged its flight to the spirit land. Every warrior (except Yellow Belly, who was a brother of the old chief) immediately set up the most dismal cryings that I have ever heard in my life. I dispatched a herald to the village to inform them of the head chief's death, and then burying him according to his directions we slowly proceeded homeward. My very soul sickened at the contemplation of the scenes that would be enacted at my arrival. When we drew in sight of the village, we found every lodge laid prostrate. We entered amid shrieks, cries, and yells. Blood was

DEATH OF A-RA-POO-ASH.

streaming from every conceivable part of the bodies of all who were old enough to comprehend their loss. Hundreds of fingers were dismembered; hair, torn from the head, lay in profusion about the paths; wails and moans in every direction assailed the ear, where unrestrained joy had a few hours before prevailed. This fearful mourning lasted until evening of the next day.

The morning following I ordered the removal of the village in the direction of the Rose Bud. We there built a council-lodge, and all the prophets and medicine men in the village were assembled in it on its completion. The national records were read over, and, after a lengthy ceremony performed by the great men, it was unanimously declared that they had elected me First Counselor, and that, conjointly with Long Hair, I was head chief of the nation. Which *pronunciamiento* was recorded.

It then devolved upon me to deliver my inaugural address. As nearly as I can recollect, I spoke as follows:

" Brothers and warriors! The great A-ra-poo-ash is no more. He has met his fathers and kindred who preceded him to the Spirit Land. He has told all concerning you that yet survive on earth. He has related your deeds of bravery, which makes the spirits rejoice; he has also told of your disobedience to your chief, which has made them cry and become dark. The Great Spirit becomes angry at you when he sees his heroes mourn. But, although you displeased A-rapoo-ash by disobedience, and made his heart to mourn, he intercedes for you there, that, if you now obey the chiefs you have chosen to lead you, your war-paths may constantly be prosperous; your buffalo and beaver shall always abound, and you may become a great and powerful people.

"I am now your great chief. If you obey what I say to you, I can make you all you wish to be. By my long stay with the whites, I possess advantages which the chiefs of no other tribe possess. I can get twice as much for our robes and beavers as you ever got before. I came back to you. I can talk to our white brethren, and they understand all my words. They know that if they cheat my people I shall find it out.

"My medicine tells me that we must not make war on our enemies, unless they first kill our people or steal our horses : we must then attack them with many warriors, so that we may run no danger of being rubbed out. I shall never consent for our nation to have more than two villages at one time. Let those two villages keep their warriors, their wives, and their children together, and not subdivide, when they are sure to be attacked by the enemies. When our village is united, no enemy will ever dare to attack it.

"My brother, Long Hair, is a very great brave, a wise chief. He will guide one village, and it will be my duty to guide the council and direct the other. I want all my warriors to lay aside the battle-axe and lance for a season, and turn their attention to hunting and trapping. Our streams are full of beaver, as also are our prairies with buffalo. Our squaws excel all others in dressing robes, for which the whites pay us a great price. Then let us get all the robes they can dress, and not keep them in idleness as mere playthings. If we keep them at work, they will be healthy, and strong, and brave, when they become warriors. They can also buy every thing they require, both for themselves and their children, while the beavers of the warriors will also supply our wants.

"Warriors! How can we do all this, if we scatter over the country in numerous little villages, subject to continual attacks from our enemies, who will cut us off, a few at a time, until we are all rubbed out? No; obey me, and keep yourselves undivided; and if enemies attack us, we can kill ten of them when they kill one Crow: thus my medicine says. But if you disobey me, and will not hearken to my words, then I shall surely leave you, and return to my white friends, not enduring to see the nation become weak, and flying before their enemies, and our women and children carried into captivity. Obey and assist me, then, and I will do my best in your behalf. Warriors, I have done."

This oration was received with undisguised approval, and I received the name of Good War Road.

A herald having been dispatched to our other village to acquaint them with the death of our head chief, and request them to assemble at the Rose Bud, in order to meet our village and devote themselves to a general time of mourning, there met, in conformity with this summons, over ten thousand Crows at the place indicated. Such a scene of disorderly, vociferous mourning no imagination can conceive, nor any pen portray. Long Hair cut off a large roll of his hair, a thing he was never known to do before. The cutting and hacking of human flesh exceeded all my previous experience; fingers were dismembered as readily as twigs, and blood was poured out like water. Many of the warriors would cut two gashes nearly the entire length of their arm; then, separating the skin from the flesh at one end, would grasp it in their other hand, and rip it asunder to the shoulder. Others would carve various devices upon their breasts and shoulders,

and raise the skin in the same manner, to make the
scars show to advantage after the wound was healed.
Some of their mutilations were ghastly, and my heart
sickened to look at them; but they would not appear
to receive any pain from them.

It was frequently asked of me why I did not mourn.
I told them that my medicine forbade me to mourn in
their manner, but that I mourned in my heart, and in
painting my face. I would frequently represent to
them the folly of maiming themselves, and appearing
before the eyes of the Great Spirit so greatly disfigured; but I lost my labor. By torturing themselves
their pagan minds supposed they were rendering ac-
ceptable sacrifices to the Great Spirit, and performing
penance for offenses against his will. It was religion;
and to interfere with their received opinions would
have subjected me to the imputation of infidel, and
perhaps have entailed upon me expulsion from my
high office.

The mourning over, I selected seventy young warriors, and started out in search of feats of arms (according to their custom), to prove my fortune in my
new office. I crossed the Missouri into the As-ne-boine
country, where we fell in with fifteen Indians and four
old women. We killed them all, and returned home
with their scalps. There was but slight rejoicing on
my return, on account of our recent affliction.

I should have mentioned that at the assembly of
our two villages a grand council was held, wherein
certain principles of action were deliberated and adjusted. On the death of a chief all his plans die with
him, and it devolves upon his successor to come to
an understanding with his confederate head chief. In
this deliberation it is determined upon what rules the

villages shall move, which direction each shall take, and what shall be the relations existing between them. There is generally a harmony preserved between the chiefs, and much method is shown in the preliminary adjustment of details. Long Hair and myself were the best of friends, and my allied brother was the elect to the office of Sixth Counselor, so that there was a promising indication of unanimity in our administration.

The villages then separated, with an understanding that they should again assemble at the fort in one moon. The attention of the nation was turned to trapping and killing buffalo, and the stock of accumulated peltry that fall was prodigious.

When I started on my excursion to the As-ne-boines, Pine Leaf begged to accompany me. Her arm was far from sound, and I refused to take her. However, soon after I had left, one of my leaders invaded the Cheyenne country, and, regardless of my wishes, she accompanied the expedition. She was brought home, as all supposed, mortally wounded. A ball had penetrated her left breast, just escaping the heart; it had passed through her body, coming out at the shoulder-blade, and tearing away a portion of it in its exit. On seeing her in this pitiable condition, I resigned all hope of her recovery. "So much," said I, "for disregarding my counsel. I would not allow you to go with me, in consideration of your wound; but you took advantage of my absence, and now you are done for."

"Well," she replied, "I am sorry that I did not listen to my chief; but I gained two *coos*."

The party accompanying her lost four warriors, wounded in rescuing her, and saving her scalp. She eventually recovered, but it was a long while before she could again go to war. The Cheyennes were defeated in the end, with the loss of three scalps, which were brought into camp.

The two villages met at the time appointed at the fort, and disposed of all their peltry. A Mr. Tulleck was sent up as clerk, and to him I intrusted full charge of the fort, promising him the protection of the Crows for the winter, as I intended that one of our villages should take up their winter quarters in his vicinity. I was at this time salaried by the American Fur Company at three thousand dollars per annum, to reside with the Crows and procure their trade for the company.

Our whole nation then crossed the Yellow Stone, and moved on to Mussel Shell River, whence we purposed to go and gather the remains of our late head chief, as the time he had specified for their removal had arrived. The Indians count four seasons in the year; namely, green grass, yellow grass, leaf falling, and snow falling. Our party destined to collect the bones consisted of seven or eight hundred persons of both sexes. On arriving at the grave, we discovered a new Indian trail passing directly over the spot, and we started in immediate pursuit. After a march of six miles, we came upon a Black Foot village of twenty-seven lodges, who were returning from the trading-post, having made extensive purchases. At sight of them, every warrior's breast kindled with revenge, they remembering the fall of their chief. We charged furiously upon them, killing and taking prisoners about one hundred and fifty of their party. While the warriors were engaged in the attack, our women attacked the Black Foot women, and killed many of them and their children before we could interfere to stop it. We captured quite a number of young women and little boys, with an abundance of horses, weapons, ammunition, scarlet cloth, beads, and sundries. We did not receive a scratch, as we attacked them with such over-whelming numbers that they offered trifling resistance, their chief endeavor being to save themselves by flight.

We took up the body of our chief and returned with it to the camp. Then there was another ceremony of cutting and maiming, and a body of two hundred lodges was sent to deposit the remains in the burial-ground of the chief's ancestors. While this party were away on their mission, those who remained with us busied themselves in collecting the various sorts of fruit with which the country abounded.

I now received my last name—for I was on the pinnacle of my fame, and they could ennoble me no farther—Nan-kup-bah-pah (Medicine Calf).

After tarrying about three weeks, we returned to the fort, where we again spent a short time, and then proceeded to the Big Horn, where we had engaged to meet Bear's Tooth, who had the conduct of the burial party.

While we were resting at the fort, a small party of twenty-three warriors, led by Little Gray Bull, stole from our camp at night, unknown to the chiefs, and when at a safe distance sent us word that they were going to the Cheyenne country in pursuit of spoils. They were the *élite* of our party, the *braves des braves*. Not one of that devoted band ever returned. What fate befell them remains to be shown.

CHAPTER XIX.

Departure from the Fort.—Arrival of Fitzpatrick and Party at the Crow Village.—Hair-breadth Escape from a Massacre.—Rescue and Restoration of Property to the Owners.—Departure of the Party.— My Return to the Fort.—Escape from Black Feet.—Defeat of the Crows.

WHILE staying at our camp on the Big Horn, a messenger arrived with the intelligence that Thomas Fitzpatrick was back upon the mountain, and that he wished me to visit him without loss of time. My affairs were in such a position that I could not possibly leave, but I sent my father and two of my best warriors to escort him into the village. The next morning they returned with Fitzpatrick and party, to the number of thirty-five men, and over two hundred horses. They encamped a short distance out. I visited the camp, and was received with a cordial welcome. I was introduced to a Captain Stuart, an English officer, who had figured conspicuously, as I was informed, under the Iron Duke, and was now traveling the Far West in pursuit of adventure; also to a Dr. Harrison, a son of the hero of Tippecanoe, and to a Mr. Brotherton, with several other gentlemen, who were all taking a pleasure excursion.

While sitting in their quarters, I observed some of the Crows looking very wistfully at the horses belonging to our new friends. Knowing that the most incorruptible of Indians have a moral weakness for horses, I ordered some of my faithful Dog Soldiers to watch them. I then invited the gentlemen to the village, which invitation they readily accepted. The visitors left at an early hour, but Fitzpatrick remained to talk matters over until quite late in the evening. I offered him a bed in my lodge, but he preferred sleeping in his own quarters.

Shortly after his arrival, Fitzpatrick incidentally mentioned that the Cheyennes had killed an entire party of Crows (but he omitted all mention of the part his men had taken in the massacre), and that one of his men had been wounded in the affair. He had also a horse that had belonged to one of the fallen heroes, purchased by him of the Cheyennes. Had he acquainted me with this circumstance when he first saw me, the very unpleasant sequel that I am about to relate would have been avoided.

One of the Crow braves was son to a member of the party massacred, and he recognized his late father's horse. This discovery had occasioned the scrutiny which I had remarked early in the evening, but the cause of which I was in utter ignorance. On the retiring of Fitzpatrick I lay down for the night. I had not fallen asleep, when the murdered brave's son entered my lodge, and addressed me: "Medicine Calf, what must we do with these white men?"

"What must you do with them?" repeated I, not apprehending his meaning.

"Yes, I say so."

"Why, take them into your lodges and feast them, and give them beds to sleep on, if they wish it."

"No, no, that is not what I mean," he said; "you know these are the white men who killed my father. They have his horse here with them, and a wounded man—wounded in their fight with the Crows."

He then left me to go, as I supposed, to his lodge,

and I thought no more of the matter. I soon fell
asleep, and woke no more till morning. On awaking,
I heard a great rush or trampling of horses, and, springing out of bed, I inquired of a squaw what was the
matter in the village.

" Why, don't you know the whites are all dead?"
she made reply.

" The whites are all dead!" repeated I, thunderstruck.

I ran out and ordered my war-horse to be got ready
in a moment. I next ran to the lodge where Winters
slept, and found it filled with Crows. I asked what
all this uproar meant.

" I don't know," said he ; " I have wished to go to
your lodge to see you, but they would not let me leave.
They have been clamoring about Thomas—Thomas—
Thomas, all night."

At this moment Fitzpatrick rode up, with an Indian
behind him.

" Fitz," said I, " what in the name of God does all
this mean? Where are your men?"

" They are all dead, I expect, by this time," said he,
blankly ; " and I presume you have sent for me to
murder me at your own discretion."

" When did you leave them? Were they alive when
you left them?"

" They were going down the river, and a thousand
Indians in hot pursuit after them," he said.

" Go over to my father's lodge," I said to him, " and
stay till I return."

I then mounted my war-horse, being well armed,
and addressed my father : " I am mad," I said ; " I
am going to die."

He gave the war-hoop so loud that my ears fairly

tingled, as a signal for my relatives to follow me. They gathered round. " Go," said he, " and die with the Medicine Calf."

On I dashed, in mad career, for six or seven miles along the bank of the river, until I came in sight of the men. I seemed to have traveled the space in the same number of minutes, for the horse flew with lightning speed upon his errand. He dropped dead beneath me; in his prodigious exertions he had burst a blood-vessel.

I ran forward on foot, shouting to Fitzpatrick's men, " Run to me! Run to me quickly!"

They heard me, and hesitated at my summons. At length one started, and the others followed, running at their utmost speed toward me. A hill rose on each side the river, closing together and arching over the stream, at a short distance in advance of the party when I arrested their steps. In this pass the Crows had taken their position, intending to massacre the party as they attempted to force their passage.

As they reached me, I serried them around me, the Crows charging from the hills upon us at the same time. I now saw my band of relatives and friends approaching us from the village. As the exasperated Indians came surging on toward us, I advanced toward them, and ordered them to desist.

They arrested their course: " What do you want?" they asked; " do you wish those whites to live?"

" After you have killed me," I said, " you can march over my dead body and kill them, but not before."

They then wheeled, and fell in with my party of relatives, who were fast arriving and encircling the whites. I then requested each man to mount horse behind my

relatives, and return with us to the village. All did
so except Stuart. I requested him also to mount.
"No," said he, "I will get on behind no d—d rascal;
and any man that will live with such wretches is a
d—d rascal."

"I thank you for your compliment," I returned;
"but I have no time to attend to it here."

"Captain Stuart," said Charles A. Wharfield, afterward colonel in the United States army, "that's very
unbecoming language to use at such a time."

"Come, come, boys," interposed Dr. Harrison, "let
us not be bandying words here. We will return with
them, whether for better or for worse."

After I had mounted the party, I borrowed a horse
of one of my warriors, and led them back to the village. For temporary safety, I deposited the party in
my father's lodge.

Fitzpatrick inquired of me, "Jim, what in the name
of God are you going to do with us?"

"I don't know yet," I said; "but I will do the best
possible for you."

I then called the Dog Soldiers to me, and commanded them, together with the Little Wolves, to surround
the village, and not suffer a single person to go out.
They all repaired to their stations. I next took fifty
faithful men, and made a thorough search throughout
the village, beginning at the extreme row of lodges.
By this means I recovered all the goods, once in the
possession of Fitzpatrick, in good condition, except his
scarlet and blue cloths, which had been torn up for
blankets and wearing apparel, but still not much injured for the Indian trade. I also recovered all his
horses, with the exception of five, which had been
taken to Bear's Tooth's camp. I had the goods well

secured, and a strong guard of my relatives placed over them.

The reader may perhaps inquire what restrained the infuriated Crows from molesting the rescued party on their way to the village. Simply this: when an Indian has another one mounted behind him, the supposition is that he has taken him prisoner, and is conducting him to head-quarters. While thus placed, the Indian having him in charge is responsible with his life for his security; if he fails to protect him, himself and all his kindred are disgraced; an outrage upon the prisoner is construed into pusillanimity on the part of the custodian. Prisoners are also safe while in custody in the village; their inviolability is then transferred to the responsibility of the chief. This is Indian morals.

I was informed subsequently that the Englishman, as soon as he approached me, cocked his gun, intending to shoot me. It was well for him, as well as his party, that he altered his mind; for, if he had harmed me, there would not have been a piece of him left the size of a five-penny bit. I was doing all that lay in my power to save the lives of the party from a parcel of ferocious and exasperated savages; his life depended by the slightest thread over the yawning abyss of death; the slightest misadventure would have proved fatal. At that moment he insulted me in the grossest manner. The language that he addressed to me extorted a look of contempt from me, but I had not time for anger. I was suspected of complicity with the Indians, or, rather, of having instigated the fiendish plot. No man of common sense could entertain such a suspicion, when he sees the part I took in the affair. Had I conspired the tragedy, I had but to rest in my bed until the deed was consummated. Every man would have been killed, and no one but the conspirators have known their fate. To be sure, I was in the service of the American Fur Company, and Fitzpatrick was trading upon his own account; but that could afford no motive to conspire his death. I had not the faintest objection to his selling every thing he had to the Crows. But they had nothing to buy with; they had disposed of all their exchangeable commodities but a short time since at the fort. Further, I was personally acquainted with Fitzpatrick, with whom I never had an ill word; and some of his party stood high in my regard. Dr. Harrison, if only for his noble father's sake, I would have defended at the risk of my own life. They were all bound to me with the ties of hospitality, and I have yet to hear of any action committed by me that would warrant the assumption of such deep perfidy. I have been informed that Captain Stuart offered one thousand dollars to a certain individual to take my life. I can hardly think the charge is true, for the individual thus said to be bribed has had many opportunities of earning his reward, and still I am alive.

After the goods were secured and the horses brought up, it was discovered that Captain Stuart's horse, a fine iron-gray, was missing. It was traced to the possession of High Bull, a very bad Indian, and I was informed that he had declared he would kill the first man that should come after him. Stuart valued his horse highly, as well he might, for he was a noble animal; he was, therefore, very anxious to obtain him. Fitzpatrick had acquainted Stuart that I was the only person in the nation that could procure the horse's restitution.

Accordingly, he visited me, and said, " *Mr.* Beckwourth" (he mistered me that time), "can you get my horse for me?"

I replied, " Captain Stuart, I am a poor man in the service of the American Fur Company, to sell their goods and receive the peltry of these Indians. The Indian who has your horse is my best customer; he has a great many relatives, and a host of friends, whose trade I shall surely lose if I attempt to take the horse from him. Should the agent hear of it, I should be discharged at once, and, of course, lose my salary."

" Well," said he, " if the company discharge you for that, I pledge you my word that I will give you six thousand dollars a year for ten years."

" Captain Stuart is a man of his word, and able to perform all he promises," said Fitzpatrick.

" Well," replied I, " I will see what I can do."

I then dispatched an Indian boy to High Bull with the message that I wanted the gray horse he had in his possession. The boy delivered his message, and the Indian retorted with a " Ugh!" which startled the boy almost out of his skin, and he came bounding back again, saying the Indian was mad.

In a short time High Bull came riding his horse, and said, " Medicine Calf, did you send for this horse?"

" I did."

" Well, here he is."

" Take him back," I said, " and keep him safe until I send for him."

Stuart was wonder-stricken at this proceeding, as our discourse was unintelligible to him.

" If I could get my hand on that horse's neck," he said, " the whole village should not get him away from me."

I was annoyed at this braggadocio, and was glad the Indians did not understand him.

Fitzpatrick requested Captain Stuart to remain quiet, saying, " Beckwourth has passed his word to you that you shall have your horse. He will be forthcoming when you want him."

The next morning they prepared to leave the village. The horses were all packed, and every thing in readiness.

" Am I to have my horse ?" said Captain Stuart.

" He will be here in a moment, sir," said I.

High Bull then rode the horse up to the party and dismounted, giving me the reins.

" Now, sir, you can mount your horse," said I, delivering him into his owner's possession.

He mounted, and the party started. I took one hundred and fifty of my choice Dog Soldiers, and escorted them a distance of fifteen miles. Before leaving them, I cautioned Fitzpatrick to keep on his journey for three days without stopping to encamp. I told him that the Indians were exasperated, and the two villages were together, and it was not in my power to keep them from following them. I was apprehensive they would dog them a considerable distance, but that a three days' journey would place them in safety.

Instead of following my advice, he encamped the following afternoon. Within an hour after his delay, almost all his horses were taken by the Indians, not leaving him enough to pack his goods. I afterward learned that Stuart saved his gray horse. I saw the Crows had made free with my friends' horses, for I saw several of them about the village subsequently. However, I was satisfied I had done my duty ; I could not have done more to my own father or brother. Still my life was sought after, and my character basely assailed.

The fate of the Crow warriors I will mention episodically here, as I gathered it from Fitzpatrick, and afterward from the Cheyennes.

The party had encamped between two villages, having the Cheyennes on one side and the Siouxs on the other. They were in utter ignorance of their dangerous proximity. Being quickly discovered by one of the enemy, he returned and alarmed his village, and dispatched a messenger to the neighboring village; and in a few moments our small band was surrounded by a force of fifty times their number. Their position was a strong one, being chosen in a deep hollow or gully. They received the assault with unflinching intrepidity, and fought until they were all exterminated except their chief—they killing thirty-four of their foes. The chief seemed to wear a charmed life; neither lead nor arrows could harm him. He advanced from his position and tantalized his foes. He invited them to come and kill him, saying that the scalps of his enemies made his lodge dark, and that he had ridden their horses till he was tired of riding. They were filled with admiration of his daring. They told him he was too great a brave to be killed; that he might go, and they would not hurt him.

"No," said he, pointing to his dead companions; "you have killed all my warriors; they have gone to the land of the Great Spirit; now kill me, so that I may go with them. I am the Little Gray Bull; come and kill me. I ask not to live. My heart disdains your offers of mercy. My brothers and friends will avenge my death."

He would frequently advance toward his swarming enemies; as he approached, they retired. He then returned toward his dead companions, and again defied them to come and kill him. He was eventually shot down, probably by a bullet fired by one of Fitzpatrick's men, who, being encamped with the Cheyennes, had joined them for the sport of shooting Indians. There were two small boys in the party of Crows, who went as moccasin-carriers. They were taken prisoners, and placed behind two warriors to be conveyed to the village. While on the way thither, each drew his knife and plunged it into the body of his custodian, each killing his man. The little fellows were cut to pieces in an instant, which was their own choice, rather than to be captive to the enemy.

When I returned from escorting Fitzpatrick, I informed the Crows of the fate of their party; but I withheld all mention of the participation of the whites. Thereupon ensued another dreadful time of mourning.

When I parted from Fitzpatrick and party, they all appeared very grateful for their deliverance, and, if they had not lost their horses when they encamped, I presume they never would have entertained other but friendly feelings toward me.

Shortly after this occurrence we held a grand council relative to certain national affairs. I then again proceeded, taking Winters and four warriors with me. When we had approached within a mile of the fort, I happening to be considerably in advance of the party, in ascending a small hill, when near the summit, I peered carefully over, and discovered a party of Black Feet, not more than three hundred yards distant, sitting by the roadside, smoking their pipes. I drew back my head, for I saw one Indian coming directly upon me, and motioned my men to a ravine close by. Then, dismounting, I crept back to the brow of the hill, and lay down flat until the Indian's head came within sight. I sprang instantly to my feet, and shot him dead. In less than a minute I had his scalp; ran back and mounted my horse; then, riding to the summit of the hill, I displayed the scalp to the Indians, who were advancing at their topmost speed. As soon as they saw me they turned and fled, thinking, no doubt, that I had a strong force lying in wait. I rode on and overtook my party, and we reached the fort without molestation or pursuit. About two hours after, the Indians presented themselves before the fort, and challenged us to come out and fight. We hoisted the scalp I had just taken in answer to the invitation. I consider we may thank my acquired habit of caution for our escape, for, had the Indian surprised us instead of my surprising him, it is more than probable that every one of us would have been killed.

We were detained at the fort for the space of eight days, on account of the numbers of the Black Feet prowling about. They finally left, and as soon as we were satisfied that the way was clear, we loaded ten pack-horses with goods, and Winters and myself— taking two men each—returned to the Crow village. The villages had separated during our absence; Long Hair and his village having taken one direction, and mine having taken another. Winters took Long Hair's trail, with the goods; I followed my village through the Bad Pass, and overtook it at Black Panther Creek. I then went on to Wind River, trapping and hunting very successfully all the way, the journey occupying about a month. We went into winter quarters under Wind River Mountain, at the mouth of Po-po-on-che (Long Grass Creek). Here, after gathering a sufficient quantity of buffalo and elk horns, we supplied ourselves with a large outfit of fine new bows. The horns are thrown into hot springs which abound in that region, where they are kept until they are perfectly mallable; they are then taken out and straightened, and cut into strips of suitable width. It takes two buffalo horns to make a bow of sufficient length. They are pieced in the centre, and riveted; then they are bound strongly at the splice with sinew. Bows made of this material are equaled by none other except those made from the horn of the mountain sheep.

While we were encamped here, numerous small parties of Crows went to war without leave, and in almost every instance were defeated; on some excursions they were entirely destroyed. One party, consisting of thirty-nine warriors, led by the Constant Bird, a great war-chief, went to the Black Foot country, and every one of them was killed. They had killed and scalped one of the enemy, whom they met alone, and again journeyed on, when they came suddenly upon a whole village of Black Feet, and were themselves instantly discovered. To save themselves they resorted to an ingenious device, which certainly offered fair to save them. On being discovered, instead of retreating, they kept on and entered the enemy's village, pretending they came with authority to conclude a peace. The Indians, putting faith in their mission, concluded peace accordingly. While thus engaged proposing terms and smoking cozily, one of the Black Foot squaws stole a sack belonging to them. After the departure of the Crows, the sack was examined, and among its contents was found the identical scalp they had taken a short time previously. Raising the war-hoop, the Black Feet assembled in great numbers, and, making immediate pursuit after the Crows, they overtook them, and massacred every one. This intelligence was brought by express from Fort Maria, the Black Foot trading-post, to Fort Cass, the Crow trading-post. On receipt of this intelligence, there was another general scene of mourning and vowing vengeance. I used all the arguments that I could frame to prevent these mischievous guerilla expeditions, but they would steal off in the night in spite of my entreaties or my denunciations, and I did not like to resort to punishments.

Several of the high functionaries inquired of me to what cause I attributed such repeated disasters. I answered as follows: "Warriors! the causes are clear enough. My medicine tells me the causes. Firstly, you robbed my white friends, stealing their horses away, and even attempting to take their lives when they were under my protection, and when you knew it grieved my heart to have wrong done to them. A second cause: you are continually acting contrary to the wishes of A-ra-poo-ash, who went to the Spirit Land on account of your disobedience. I have also expressed the same wishes to you, telling you to apply yourselves to collecting skins, in order to have the wherewith to purchase the things that you need. These, my orders, are openly disobeyed, and the Great Spirit is very angry with the nation for their thieving, and disregard of the orders of their head chief."

They then inquired what they should do to appease the wrath of the Great Spirit. I answered again: "Warriors! to appease the just anger of the Great Spirit, you must discontinue your war-parties, and remain peaceably at home for one moon. You can then prepare a great sacrifice, and do penance for that time, and let the Great Spirit see that you really repent the evil you have committed. By so acting, you may recover the favor which the Great Spirit has evidently withdrawn from you; by continuing in your obstinate ways, you will assuredly be rubbed out as a nation."

The sacrifices that they offer on such occasions are curious. One sacrifice is made by shaving the manes and tails of some of their best war-horses, and painting on their bodies a rude delineation of the sun. They then turn them out, but never drive them away; and if they follow the other horses, it is a sure sign that the Great Spirit is following them also.

I had become so sickened with their constant mourning, which was kept up through the whole village day and night, that I determined to take a small party and see if I could not change the face of affairs. Accordingly, I raised fifty warriors, and started for the Cheyenne village, near the site of the present Fort Laramie. The first night we encamped on the Sweet Water River. The morning ensuing was clear and cold, and we started across a plain twenty miles wide, with neither trees nor bushes in the whole distance. Across this plain was a mountain, which I wished to reach that night, in order to provide ourselves with fire-wood and have a warm camp. When we had traversed this desert about midway, a storm came on, which is called by the mountaineers a Poo-der-ee. These storms have proved fatal to great numbers of trappers and Indians in and about the Rocky Mountains. They are composed of a violent descent of snow, hail, and rain, attended with high and piercing wind, and frequently last three or four days. The storm prevented our seeing the object for which we were directing our course. We all became saturated with the driving rain and hail, and our clothing and robes were frozen stiff; still we kept moving, as we knew it would be certain death to pause on our weary course. The winds swept with irresistible violence across the desert prairie, and we could see no shelter to protect us from the freezing blast. Eventually we came to a large hole or gully, from eighteen to twenty feet deep, which had been made by the action of water. Into this place we all huddled, and were greatly protected from the wind. Being exhausted with our exertions, we wrapped ourselves as well as we could in our frozen robes, and lay down. How long we lay there I could form no idea. When I attempted to stir, it required the exercise of all my strength to free myself from the mass of snow that had fallen upon me while asleep. I saw that if we tarried there it would be inevitable death to us all, and it was still storming furiously. I aroused my second in command, named "A Heap of Dogs," and told him that we must arouse ourselves and bestir our warriors, or we should all perish.

"No," said he; "it is too painful; let us stay here and all die together."

I told him that I should go at all risks, and made a spring thereupon, he laying himself down again. I had not proceeded much more than three hundred yards when I came upon a gulch, or dry creek, in which was a drift pile composed of a large accumulation of dry wood. I made an opening and crawled in; then striking fire, I got it well burning, and returned to my perishing warriors to relate my discovery. They arose and shook off the loose snow from their robes, and essayed to proceed. But many of them were so weak and stiffened that they could but crawl along. After getting thawed and comfortably warmed before a blazing fire, I found there were two of our party missing. I returned with two or three others to search for them, and we had to dig away the snow to arrive at them;

but the vital spark had fled—they were stiff in death. We staid by our fire, which increased in body and warmth, for two days, by which time the storm having subsided, we returned home. The relatives of the lost warriors made a great mourning for them, while the friends of those who returned with me showered presents and blessings upon me for having been instrumental in saving their kinsmen's lives.

It was a time of intense cold. Our whole party were more or less frostbitten; my face and ears were severely frozen, and were sore for a long time. The wild buffalo approached so near to our fire that we could shoot them without stirring from our seats. As an excuse for my ill success, I informed the Crows that the wrath of the Great Spirit was not yet appeased.

Soon after this catastrophe, I informed my people that I wished to wander solitary for a space, to mourn for my two warriors who had perished in the snow. My real intention was to get to the fort, and thus have a respite from the unceasing crying and howling that was kept up throughout the village. On making my intention known, two white men, named Mildrum and Cross, who were staying in our village, desired to accompany me. We started accordingly, taking one squaw with us as servant. On our second day out, we were surprised by a party of two hundred and fifty Black Feet. We took shelter in a thicket of willows, resolved to make a brave stand, and sell our lives for all they were worth. The squaw showed herself a valuable auxiliary by taking good care of our horses, six in number, and building us a little fort of sand, behind which we stood in great security, watching our enemies as they ever and anon made their appearance. We were thus invested for thirty-six hours, the Indians hovering about, and losing one of their number at every discharge, without daring to rush in upon us, which had they ventured upon would have proved our inevitable destruction. We were situated so close to the river that we could be supplied with water at all times by the squaw without incurring danger.

The second night, our besiegers, having wearied of their exertions, gave us comparative repose. Availing ourselves of the lull, we muffled our horses' feet with our capotes, cut to pieces for the purpose, and, stealing gently down the slope of the bank, we forded the shallow stream, and made the best of our way home. We went whooping and galloping at full speed into the village, displaying nineteen scalps on various parts of our horses. Our victorious return created the most thrilling sensation throughout the village. Every face was washed, the scalp-dance was performed (the first time for two months), and the hilarity was universally indulged in. The Great Spirit's wrath was appeased, the tide had turned in favor of the Crows, and a continuation of victory was predicted from this brilliant achievement.

CHAPTER XX.

Excursion to the Fort.—Arrival of Long Hair's Village.—Building of a new Medicine Lodge.—Triumphant Entrance of my little Wife into the Lodge.—Attack on the Crow Village by the Siouxs.—Meeting of the two Crow Villages.—Visit of the Grovans.—Visit to the Grovans and Fort Clarke.

A PARTY of nine trappers happening to call at the village on their way to the fort, among whom was my old friend Harris, I proposed to accompany them. We started, and reached the fort without accident, except sustaining another siege from the Black Feet. After our departure, the whole village followed to purchase their spring supply of necessaries at the fort. They brought an immense stock of peltry, with which they purchased every thing that they stood in need of.

About a week after our arrival, the other Crow village, under Long Hair, encamped without the fort, all of them deep in mourning. The same ill luck had attended them in their excursions as we had suffered, and eighty warriors had fallen without one gleam of success. I availed myself of this opportunity to impress upon the minds of Long Hair and his followers that the cause of their misfortune was owing to the conduct of the Crows toward Fitzpatrick and his party, which representation they all firmly believed.

When the two villages had finished their trading, we all moved back to the Big Horn, where we constructed a new medicine lodge for the medicine men, prophets, and dreamers to prophesy and hold their deliberations in. These lodges are erected every year—the first moon in May; the whole tribe is assembled at the festival, and the ceremonies are continued for seven days. Before the poles are raised, the medicine men select from the assembled multitude a warrior whom they deem qualified to assume the functions of a medicine chief. The man they select is compelled to serve; no excuse that he can frame is accepted as valid. He is then taken to a lodge-pole and lashed to one end; an eagle's wing is placed in each hand, and a whistle (similar to a boatswain's) placed between his lips. Thus equipped, he is hoisted a distance of forty feet, until the pole assumes its perpendicularity and is adjusted in its proper place. Raising the first pole is analogous to laying the first stone. The first one being hoisted, abundance of others are raised into their places, until the whole space is inclosed. They are then covered with green buffalo hides, descending to within six feet of the ground, the inclosure being left open at the top. About one hundred and twenty hides are generally required for the purpose, and a space is thus obtained capable of holding from seven to eight hundred persons.

I was the subject selected on this occasion; and when I was raised upon the pole in the manner I have just described, the officials declared that I was raised solely by the elevating power of my wings, whence they inferred that my medicine was very powerful.

When the lodge is completed, the medicine men and other functionaries assemble the most distinguished braves within the building for a rehearsal of their achievements and an enumeration of their *coos*. Each brave then gives an account of his exploits thus: "I killed one or more Cheyennes (as the case may be) on such a day, in such a place, and took such and such spoils. You know it, Crows." The medicine chief then exhibits his marks, pronounces the warrior's statement correct, and confirms it by his record. This ratification each warrior passes through, and there is seldom any discrepancy between his statement and the record. Sham battles are then fought in illustration of the manner in which the different trophies were acquired, the rehearsal reminding the *civilized* spectator of a theatrical representation, only that in this case the performance is more in earnest.

This examination gone through with, the lodge is then prepared for the medicine men, prophets, and dreamers to go through the ceremony of initiating a virtuous woman. The members of the conclave endure a total abstinence from food and water for seven days previous to the ceremony, unless any one faints from exhaustion, in which case some slight nourishment is afforded him.

The warriors are then drawn up in two lines, "inward face," a few feet apart, and the female candidate for "holy orders" presents herself at the lodge door. She harangues them when she first presents herself, and then marches between the extended lines of the dusky warriors. Here is the fearful ordeal. If she has ever been guilty of any illicit action, her declaration of innocence is refuted by a dozen voices, a thousand bullets riddle her body in a moment, and her flesh is hacked into morsels.

This is the fearful war-path secret. It will be remembered that my little wife had resolved to dedicate herself to this service; when only a child she had determined upon entering the medicine lodge. On this occasion she was candidate for admission. She came to me to be dressed for the ceremony; she was robed in her best attire, and I painted her as the custom prescribes.

The warriors are in line, and the Sanhedrim in readiness. The herald announces that Nom-ne-dit-chee (The One that Strikes Three), wife of the head chief, Medicine Calf, offers herself for election. Intense excitement prevails through the assembly as her name is pronounced, and it is re-echoed through the lines of the warriors. She presented herself at the door of the lodge, and calmly met the concentrated gaze of thousands. A breathless silence prevailed.

She commenced her address. "Can it be said that there are no virtuous women among the Crows? Can it be true that our medicine men can not make medicine, nor our prophets prophesy, nor our dreamers dream, because so few of you are virtuous? Oh women! it is shameful to you to be so faithless. Our nation is disgraced because of your conduct, and the Crows will soon cease to be a people. The Great Spirit is angry with you, and has brought disgrace upon our warriors on account of your evil practices. Our prairies will become wastes like yourselves, producing no good thing; and our buffalo will bellow at you, and leave the hunting-grounds of the Crows, and go to the country of a more virtuous people."

Then addressing the warriors, she continued:

"Warriors! I have this day volunteered to carry the sand, the wood, and the elk-chips into the lodge. You are brave warriors, and I hope your tongues are not crooked. I have seen our women attempt to do it, and they have been cut to pieces. I am now about to try it myself. Before I start for the materials at the other end of your extended lines, if there be a warrior, or any other man under the sun, who knows any thing wrong in me, or injurious to my virtue, let him speak. I, too, am ready to go to the spirit land, for there is one there who knows me innocent of the bad deeds which disgrace the women of our country."

She then passed with a firm step between the lines of the warriors to the sand. Taking the bowl, she dipped a small quantity, and returned with it to the lodge, and then made two other trips for the wood and elk-chips. Returning for the third time, she received the vociferations of the assembled multitude. The functionaries came forth to meet her, and passed their hands over her head, shoulders, and arms, extolling her to the skies, and proclaiming there was one virtuous woman in the Crow nation. She was then presented with my medicine shield by the great medicine chief, to preserve and carry for me, no one but myself having authority to take it from her.

I trembled while she was passing this perilous ordeal, and its triumphant termination filled me with delight. She was a girl of superior endowments, and, if they had been fostered by a Christian education, I know no woman who would surpass her in worth, elegance, or attainments. Had she ever failed in her conduct, it would have been thundered in her ears when she stooped to gather the sand, and a cry would have arisen that she was polluting the medicine of the nation. If the candidate is killed during the inauguration ceremonies, nothing more is done in the same medicine lodge: it is immediately torn down, and the tribe moves to some other place, where it builds another lodge, and the same observances are again gone through with.

In the mean while, women are engaged cooking and preparing a sumptuous feast of every thing in season. All kinds of meats and dried berries, variously cooked, are spread before the partakers, which includes all who can obtain seats, except the medicine men, prophets, and dreamers. Their fast continues for seven days, during which time their inspiration is continually moving them. There are plenty of warriors in attendance to convey messages and execute orders, like deputy sheriffs in a justice's court; and as fast as an ordinance is dreamed out, prophesied upon, and medicined, the instructions are delivered to the messengers, and away they start, one party in this direction, and one party in another, to communicate the instructions and execute orders.

While we were yet at the lodge, a deputation of

about a dozen Grovan warriors came to solicit our assistance against the Cheyennes and Siouxs, who had made a combined attack upon them, killing about four hundred of their warriors. In reply to the application, we told them that we had lost many warriors during the past winter, and that we must avenge our own men first; but that we would go and see them in the course of the summer, and hold a conference with them on the subject.

There are two bands of the Grovans: the Grovans of the Missouri, which the Crows sprung from, and whose language they speak, and the Grovans of the prairie, who form a band of the Black Feet. The Grovans of the Missouri were then a weak tribe or band, having, by their incessant wars with the surrounding tribes, been reduced to a very insignificant number of warriors. When the Crows separated from them, the nation was deemed too numerous. This separation was effected, according to their reckoning, above a century since. Those Grovans and the Crows have always been on very friendly terms, and even to this day consider themselves descendants of the same family. They do not move about, like many wandering tribes, but remain stationary and cultivate the ground. Their lodges are built of poles, filled in with earth; they are spacious, and are kept comparatively neat.

I would here remark that the name " Crow" is not the correct appellation of the tribe. They have never yet acknowledged the name, and never call themselves Crows. The name was conferred upon them many years ago by the interpreters, either through their ignorance of the language, or for the purpose of ridiculing them. The name which they acknowledge themselves by, and they recognize no other, is in their language Ap-sah-ro-kee, which signifies the Sparrowhawk people.

The villages separated at this time. Long Hair went up the Yellow Stone, to Clarke's Fort, in order to kill buffalo and gather fruit when ripe, while I went with my village on a circuit, and finally rested on the banks of Powder River, a branch of the Yellow Stone. While busy killing buffalo, we were suddenly attacked by the Cheyennes to the number of two thousand warriors. I had been advised by my scouts of their contemplated attack, and was consequently prepared to receive them. They were seriously disappointed in charging upon our empty lodges; and, while they were in confusion, we thundered upon them from our concealment, driving them before us in all directions for upward of two miles. Our victory was complete. We took sixty-three scalps, besides horses and weapons in abundance. We had eighty warriors wounded, principally with lances and arrows, but every one recovered. The heroine did good service, having thoroughly recovered from her terrible wound. She had two horses killed under her, but escaped unhurt herself, using her lance as adroitly as ever.

The village moved on, directly after the battle, in the direction of our friends the Grovans; but, before we arrived, we rubbed out a party of eleven Cheyennes, who had been to the Grovan village on a war excursion, and we carried their scalps and presented them to the Grovans. When we arrived in sight of their villages —five in number—and halted with our whole force on a small hill which overlooked their towns, on perceiving us they were filled with alarm, believing us to be the Cheyennes, returned with a force sufficient to exterminate them. But they discovered us to be Crow friends, and their joy was now proportionate to their

former despondency. We passed through their villages two abreast, and all were out upon the tops of
their lodges to welcome us as we rode through. The
acclamations resounded on every side. They looked
upon us as their deliverers and friends, who had come
to protect the weak against the strong, that their wrongs
might be avenged, and their faces be washed once more.
From their villages we rode on to Fort Clarke through
the Mandan villages, defiling before the fort in double
columns. Every man in the fort was on the battle-
ments, gazing at our long lines of mounted warriors.
While defiling past, we were correctly counted by Mr.
Kipp. Several alighted and visited the fort, and Mr.
Kipp inquired for the Crow who spoke English. No
one understood him until he came across a Mandan
who spoke the Crow language fluently. They inquired
of him for me. I replied he was somewhere about. I
was dressed in full costume, and painted as black as a
Crow, and neither the Mandan nor Kipp recognized me.
The Mandan informed Kipp that I was present.

" Yes," said I, " Beckwourth is present."

" Well, well!" exclaimed Kipp, in astonishment;
" is that you, Beckwourth ?"

I replied that it was, indisputably.

" Then why did you not declare yourself when I
was inquiring for you? I certainly should never have
distinguished you from any other Indian."

At this moment my wife entered, carrying my boy
in her arms. A great interest was taken in him by all
the inmates of the fort, greatly to the delight of his
proud mother, and by the time the child had passed
through all their hands he had received presents enough
to load a pack-mule.

We staid with our friends ten days, part of which

time was occupied in arranging a combined plan of defense against the Black Feet. When we departed, Long Hair presented us with an ample stock of corn and pumpkins. We passed the Yellow Stone, and traveled on by easy marches to the Mussel Shell River, killing and dressing buffalo during our whole journey. Here we encamped to await the arrival of Long Hair. Our spies kept us advised of the movements of the enemy, and intelligence was brought us that he was manifestly concentrating his forces at the Three Forks of the Missouri for a grand attack. I knew that we were also vigilantly watched by the enemy's spies, and I determined to make no movement that would warrant the suspicion that their movements were known to us. Long Hair shortly joined us with his whole force, and I felt perfectly at ease now, notwithstanding the most strategical movements of our enemy.

After various demonstrations on either side, we feigned a division of our forces, and marched one half of them to a spot which concealed them from the table-land, thus leading the enemy to the belief that we were still ignorant of his intentions and his numbers.

At daybreak the following morning we heard the noise of their innumerable horse-hoofs, and shortly after they burst upon our tenantless lodges like a thunder-cloud. I suffered about one third of their warriors to become entangled in the village, and I then gave the order to charge. The shock was irresistible; their advancing division was attacked on all sides, and the appearance of my concealed warriors sent a panic through the tribe. They fled precipitately without venturing to look round to see if they were pursued. It was a complete rout, and purchased at but slight cost to ourselves. We gathered over four hundred scalps, and took fifty women prisoners; we captured five hundred horses, one hundred guns, and weapons, blankets, and camp equipage beyond enumeration. Our loss was four killed and three hundred wounded, some of whom afterward died of their wounds.

Our wounded warriors attended to, and our spoils gathered, we moved on without delay to our tobacco plantation, as it was now time to gather our crop. We journeyed by way of the fort, and on our road fell in with a party of fifteen Black Foot warriors, who were driving a large drove of horses they had stolen from the Snakes. We entrapped the enemy into a ditch and killed the whole party, and their recent acquisition came in very serviceably, as our stock of horses was greatly diminished. We found our crop excellent, and, as our numerous hands made light work, our harvest was soon gathered.

We then passed on at our leisure, killing more or less buffalo daily, until we arrived at Tongue River, about the new moon of Leaf Fall. On our way we lost nearly three hundred head of horses, which were stolen by the Black Feet. We did not trouble ourselves to pursue them, as we felt confident they were but lent them, and that they would shortly be returned with good interest. At Tongue River we confederated with our friends, the Grovans, in an attack upon the Cheyenne village; from thence we returned to the Yellow Stone, when I detached a party of one hundred and sixty warriors on an excursion to the Black Foot village, and they returned bringing six hundred fine horses with them. We then passed on to Fort Cass, where we witnessed much dejection and gloom, occasioned by a serious reverse which they had experienced since our last visit.

CHAPTER XXI.

Attacks of the Black Feet on the Fort.—Six White Men killed.—
Abandonment of Fort Cass.—Fort constructed at the Mouth of the
" Rose Bud."—Removal of the Village.—Peace concluded with the
As-ne-boines.—Hair-breadth Escape.—Death of Mr. Hunter, of Ken-
tucky.

WHILE we were indulging in a display of our captured horses while encamped outside the fort, the Spotted Antelope, one of my relatives, came to me, and in-
timated that I had better visit the fort, as they had lost
six men by the Black Feet. He was in mourning-paint
for the victims, because the whites were his friends.
I dismounted, and passed through the encampment on
my way to the gate. As usual, I found my father's
lodge, in which my little wife resided, pitched nearest
to the fort, with the other lodges of my various relatives grouped in a row, their contiguity to my parent's
lodge being graduated by their propinquity of kin. I
found Pine Leaf seated by my wife, amusing herself
with the Black Panther (whose civilized patronymic
was *Little Jim*), while almost all the other women
were dancing. I delayed a moment to inquire why
these two women were not dancing with the others.
Pine Leaf, with solemn air and quivering lip, said,
" Your heart is crying, and I never dance when your
heart cries."

" Neither do I," said the little woman.

This was a greater concession than the heroine had
ever made to me before. She had told me that she
would marry me, and she had frequently informed my

sisters and my little wife of a similar intention; but this promise was always modified with a proviso—a contumacious "if," which could never be avoided. "I will marry the Medicine Calf," she would say, "*if* I marry any man." A great many moons had waxed and waned since she first spoke of the pine leaves turning yellow, but they had not yet lost their verdure, and I had failed to discover a red-handed Indian.

In conversation with Mr. Tulleck, the commandant of the fort, I learned that they had been incessantly harassed by the Black Feet ever since our last visit, who had invested them on all sides, rendering it extremely dangerous for any of the inmates to venture outside the gate. He further informed me that he had had six men massacred and fifty-four horses stolen. He had sent for me, he said, to come and select a new site, where they would be liable to less molestation, and be less in fear of their lives.

I consulted with our chiefs and braves upon the selection of a more secure location for a new fort, and it was unanimously agreed upon that the mouth of the Rose Bud, thirty miles lower down the river, offered the best situation, as the country was fair and open all round, and afforded the hostile Indians no good places of concealment. There was also a fine grazing country there, and plenty of buffalo, so that a village of the Crows could winter under the fort, and afford them the protection of their presence.

As soon as the Crows had completed their purchases, I started them up the Big Horn on their way back, with the promise that I would rejoin them in a few days. I then took a boat filled with goods, and twenty men, and dropped down the river until we came across a beautiful location for the new fort. We then returned, and removed the effects of the present fort to the new site, and then immediately set about constructing a new post. We measured off one hundred and eighty yards square, which we inclosed as quickly as possible with hewn timber eighteen feet high, and of sufficient thickness to resist a rifle ball: all the houses required for the accommodation of the inmates were commodiously constructed inside.

Having finished the construction of the fort, I gave full instructions for the management of its affairs, and then departed for the village, where my presence was required to incite the Indians to devote themselves to trapping and hunting buffalo, for which service I was paid by the American Fur Company.

As I was about starting, a deputation of fifty As-ne-boines came to the post, leaving a letter from Mr. M'Kenzie at the lower fort addressed to me, requesting me to constrain the As-ne-boines into a treaty of peace with the Crows, in order that their incessant wars might be brought to a close, and the interests of the company less interfered with. Had they arrived earlier, while the village was present at the old fort, I would have immediately called a council of the nation, and had the business settled. I seriously regretted their inopportune arrival, as it not only delayed the conclusion of the proposed peace, which was in every way desirable, but it would have saved me a very hazardous and anxious journey with the whole deputation of hostile Indians on our way to the village, where I had but one companion as a guarantee for my security. I was aware that the Indians remembered many a horse-*borrowing* adventure wherein I had taken an active part, and I had had too much experience of Indian character not to appreciate to the full the imminent danger I incurred in trusting myself with this band of savages in our intended journey across the wilderness.

Mr. Kean, a native of Massachusetts, was my' companion on this excursion. We started on foot, in company with the party of As-ne-boines. Every thing went well until our fourth day out. We were traveling leisurely along, the Indians in close conversation among themselves, of which I understood but little—not enough to make out the subject of their consultation, though I mistrusted I formed the matter of their discourse. One of the chiefs and his son were a few rods in advance, in close conversation. The party at length halted, and sat down on the grass to smoke. My companion, unsuspicious of evil, started on to kill buffalo while the party rested. The chief and his son, who were in advance, returned, and passed one on each side of me. I instantly heard a gun-click, which I felt certain was the sound of cocking it. I turned my head, and saw the chief's son with his piece leveled ready to shoot. I sprang to my feet, and grasped the barrel of his gun just as he discharged it, the load passing into the air. I drew my battle-axe, and raised it to strike the treacherous rascal down; but a chief arrested my arm, saying, as nearly as I could understand him, "Hold! Don't strike him: he is a fool!"

A general melee then ensued among the party; high words were bandied, and there seemed an equal division among them on the propriety of taking my life. By this time I had withdrawn a few yards, and stood facing them, with my rifle ready cocked. On hearing the report, my companion ran back, and, seeing how matters stood, exclaimed, "There is a fort just ahead, let us run and get into it; we can then fight the whole parcel of the treacherous devils."

We started for it, but the Indians were ahead of us; they arrived there first, and took possession of it, and again had a long confab, while we remained at their mercy outside. The party opposed to killing me appeared greatly to predominate, and we were not again molested, though neither I nor Mr. Kean slept one moment during the ensuing night. In the morning we started on our way, but we kept strict watch on their movements. The following afternoon I discovered two Indians on the hill-side, and, although they were at a great distance, I conceived them to be Crows, most likely spies from the village, which proved to be the case. No one had seen them but myself, and I imparted my discovery to my friend. I then told the head chief, who well understood the Crow language, that we were near the Crow village, and that if any of them should visit our camp during the night, he must be sure to call me before he suffered any of his people to speak to them, or they would be all inevitably massacred. He accordingly issued orders to that purport to all his men, and erected his lodge in front of the party, so as to be the first inquired of by the Crows. I and my partner then lay down, and soon were sound asleep.

About midnight the chief shook me, and informed me the Crows were coming. A host of warriors swarmed around our encampment, and, pointing their guns at the camp, said, "What people are you? Budda-ap-sa-ro-kee" (we are Sparrowhawks).

"Go back," I replied; "I have other people with me, who are come to make peace."

On hearing my voice, which they readily recognized, they retired.

The next morning we moved on and met the village, who were approaching toward us. The As-ne-boines, on seeing such a host, began to tremble. Our soldiers came driving along, my brave Dog Soldiers ineffectually striving to keep them back; for, as they restrained them in one place, they broke through in another, until the warriors rode almost upon the toes of their guests. A council was shortly called to listen to the arguments of the *envoyé extraordinaire* from the As-ne-boine nation. Several of the council applied to me for my sentiments on the subject, but I deferred it to the collective wisdom of the nation.

When I had at first arrived, like many another foolish man, I mentioned to my wife the narrow escape of my life I had just made, and she, like many another foolish woman, unable to contain herself, related the information to Pine Leaf, who was her bosom friend. While the council were busy deliberating, and some explanatory statements had been listened to regarding a matter which I supposed would have afforded no food for discussion, the heroine entered the assembly.

"Warriors!" she said, "you are assembled here, I believe, to deliberate on peace or war with the As-ne-boines. In coming to our village with the Medicine Calf, they attempted to take his life, and came very near accomplishing their end. Will you conclude peace with a people who possess such base hearts? I do not believe you will."

Such an instantaneous change of countenance in an assembly was never before seen. Pine Leaf, the nation's favorite, had spoken, and, as usual, had spoken to the purpose. Though a woman, her influence was every where strongly felt, even in council. She had a gift of speech which the bravest warriors might well envy; she was ever listened to with admiration, and in truth, though young, her judgment on all important matters was generally guided by sound sense.

Every eye in the assembly flashed fire at the intelligence of this contemplated treachery, and was directed first upon me and then upon the As-ne-boines. I immediately arose and said,

"Warriors! I conducted these people to our village because they said they were anxious to make peace with us. While on the road, one young As-ne-boine, whom they declared to be a fool, attempted to shoot me, but the others interfered to prevent him, and were sorry for what he had done. This was no deliberate treachery; it was the folly of the young man, and the party showed their friendly intention by their prompt interference. Do not allow this to make any difficulty in the way of a peace with the As-ne-boines."

My obligation to the Fur Company made it my duty to smooth the matter over, for at this moment the slightest whisper from me would have sufficed to hack the whole deputation to pieces in a moment.

The council held a short consultation together, and the first councilor arose and thus addressed himself to the chief of the As-ne-boines:

"As-ne-boines! you behold that chief (pointing to me)? Our women and all our warriors carry him here (holding out his left hand, and indicating the palm with a finger of his right hand); he is our chief; he is our great chief; he and his brother (Long Hair), who sits by him, are the two great chiefs of our nation. It is he who has made us great and powerful; it is he who has rendered us the terror of other nations; it is he who, by living with his white friends for many winters, and knowing them all, has brought us guns and ammunition, and taught our young men how to use them. It is he who has built us a fort, where we can at all times go and buy every thing we require. He loves the white man, and has made all the whites to love us. We fight for the whites, and kill their enemies, because they are the friends of our chief. If you had killed him, our nation would have mourned in blood.

"Listen, As-ne-boines! If you had killed our chief, our whole nation would have made war on you, and we would have put out your last fire, and have killed the last man of your nation. We would have taken possession of your hunting-grounds; our women would have become warriors against you; we would have hunted you as we hunt the wild beasts. Now go! we will not harm you. Go! We will sleep to-night; but we will not make peace until we sleep, and our hearts have considered upon it. Come to us again when your hearts are clean: they are foul now; and when you come, you must have your tongues straight. You are poor; you have no horses. We have plenty, and will give you horses. I have done. Go!"

They made no reply, but went straightway out of the lodge. A horse was furnished to each man; those who were without guns received one, and several articles were presented to them by our women. "Go! go! go!" was dinned in their ears from all present; and, accordingly, they went.

They proceeded immediately to the trading-post, where they gave a stirring narrative of what they had seen. They told them they had seen many chiefs, but never one approaching to the great Crow chief; that all his people loved him; that when he entered the village, all the children ran up to him, and shook him by the hand; and that they had never seen a chief so much respected by his warriors and all his people.

They told how, when I arrived, I was presented with the best war-horse they had ever seen; that he had two panther-skins on his saddle, and a collar about his neck trimmed with bears' claws, and a bridle surpassing all they had ever heard of. They said that they would all have been killed on their approach to the village, as the Crows came to the camp during the night; but that the great chief only spoke one word, and the tribe was stilled, and departed in a moment. Not a word did they mention about their attempt on my life. They merely said that the Crows would not make peace with them, but had wished to treat again with them at some future time. I suspect they must have told marvelous tales when they reached home, for we were not troubled with them any more for a long time.

The Crows have something of the Gallic temperament: they must have excitement, no matter whence derived, although the excitement of war suits them by far the best. They were again clamorous for war, they did not care against whom, and I alone must lead them, as my presence was a guarantee of success. Many of my friends opposed my going. My father's medicine told him that I should meet with a great disaster. My wife pleaded with me to remain. Even the heroine, who never before showed reluctance to engage in war, had forebodings of disaster, and earnestly entreated me to stay. But I had previously given my word to my warriors, and had selected one hundred and fifty-four of my best followers to engage in an expedition. I must confess that if I had obeyed my own feelings, or, rather, if I had attended to my own misgivings, I should certainly have staid at home. What motive prompted me to go? and what gain could possibly accrue to mixing with savages in their intestine broils with other savages?

However, we started. Little White Bear, as brave a warrior as ever drew bow-string, was my second in command, and Pine Leaf was one of the number. We started for the Black Foot territory, traveling by way of the fort, where we staid three days. They had already finished their pickets, and the work was progressing finely. There were fifty men employed upon it.

Mr. Tulleck inquired where I was going. I told him that my warriors wanted employment, and, to gratify them, I was going to the Black Foot country in quest of scalps or horses. He said, " For God's sake, do not go, Jim! I have a presentiment that a great calamity awaits you—that I shall never see you again. For your own safety, turn back to the village, or rest here."

Many of my friends, who were working at the fort, expressed the same sentiments; all mentioned a foreboding that, if I should venture into the Black Foot country with my little force, I should infallibly be cut to pieces. I thought such despondency only natural, since they had been so badly harassed with the enemy that their fears magnified the danger. Still it was singular that both civilized and savage should give way to such forebodings.

The morning for our departure came; my warriors were impatient to get on. Some had galloped on ahead, and were prancing and curveting, awaiting my departure. I prepared my going with a heavy heart, which ill fortified me against the representations of my friends. I started, Mr. Tulleck and several of my friends accompanying me a few rods. I bade them good-by: my friend Tulleck's eyes filled with tears. I was seized with momentary hesitation: what did all this portend? I looked round for my moccasin-bearer; he had gone on: this determined me; I dashed off to my warriors, resolved to listen to no such idle fears.

There was a young gentleman with me named Hunter, a Kentuckian, who, having a great curiosity to witness an Indian battle, insisted on joining in the expedition. The first night that we were encamped, being influenced by what I had heard all around me, and fearing some disaster might happen to him among us, I begged of him to go back to the fort and await our return there. He refused to listen to me. We then offered him as many of our best horses as he might wish to select after our return, as an inducement for him to be hired to go back. But all in vain. "I have started with you," he said, "and I will go; if I am to lose my life, there is no help for it."

My warriors did not wish him to go, as they feared a white man might bring us bad luck. Some expressed a fear that he might be killed with us, and that I should then cry. He was a free trapper in the country, and much respected at the fort.

We continued our course until we arrived at Little Box Elder Creek. Here our spies discovered a Black Foot village, which, from a cursory examination, we concluded consisted of but few lodges. At midnight we abstracted a large drove of about seven hundred horses, and started directly upon our return. We did not drive so fast as is customary on such occasions, for we thought that the few Black Feet that the village contained could be easily disposed of, should they venture to molest us.

About ten the next morning, our spies, being about six hundred yards in advance of us, signaled to us to hasten, as they had discovered some men. We accelerated our speed, thinking there might be a chance of adding a few scalps to our present booty. Having advanced a few hundred yards, we discovered more Black Feet than we had bargained for, and I became aware that a terrible battle must ensue. The whole scene appeared alive with them, outnumbering us ten to one. There was not a moment to lose. I directed all the boys to drive on the horses with the utmost speed possible, and to await us two days at the fort; if we should not arrive during that time, to go home and report to the village that we were all slain. I also requested Mr. Hunter to select the best horse in the herd, and go with the boys. But he refused, saying, if there was any fighting in the wind, he wanted to have his hand in it. I then endeavored to persuade the heroine to go, but was answered with an emphatic " No !"

The boys started with the horses, but only succeeded in reaching the fort with about two hundred. We had a very poor chance for defending ourselves against such an overwhelming force as was then before us in an open field-fight. There was no fort, nor breast-work, nor rocks, nor bushes to protect us, but we were exposed to the storm of bullets and arrows that they poured upon us without ceasing. At last we discovered a large hole in front of a hill, and we all leaped into it for shelter. The enemy, confident of an easy victory, displayed great bravery for Black Feet. They charged up to the very brink of our intrenchment, discharging their volleys at us in lines, which, considering the advantage of their position, produced comparatively little effect. One of my warriors repeatedly ran out of the intrenchment alone, and drove all before him. Exasperated at my cursed misadventure, and absolutely sickening at the scene of mourning we should occasion at the village, I grew desperate, and lost all consideration of safety. I sprang from the gully, and rushed singly among a crowd of besiegers; wherever I advanced the enemy drew back. It was truly astonishing to see three or four hundred recede, and many of them fairly run, as often as two or three of us showed ourselves at the top of the bank, when they might have burned us to death with the powder from the muzzles of their guns. They seemed to be panic-struck or bewildered. The warrior who had charged so often among them had his thigh broken; he then sat down and tantalized them. He told them who he was, how many of their warriors' scalps he had taken, and at what times; how many of their squaws and horses he had captured; and then desired them to come and finish him, and take his scalp, for it had long been forfeit to them. He reminded me of the words of the poet, which I had read when at home:

> " Remember the wood where in ambush we lay,
> And the scalps which we bore from your nation away;
> Remember the arrows I shot from my bow,
> And remember your chiefs by my hatchet laid low."

He was soon killed, being pierced with numerous arrows and bullets.

An old brave in the pit exclaimed, "Let us not stay in this hole to be shot like dogs; let us go out and break through the ranks of the Black Feet. They can not kill us all; some will get away. I will go foremost; I can break through their ranks alone."

Some hundreds of the enemy had climbed the hill, as they could not half of them get to the side of the pit, and thence they showered volleys of stones upon us, which annoyed us more than their bullets. At length, Little White Bear desired the old brave to lead, and we would follow and break through their line. I requested Hunter to keep as near the front as possible when we made the charge, as he would incur less danger of being cut down. He took his place accordingly. Out we rushed from the pit, the old warrior leading the way, and hewing down right and left, until the enemy finally opened their column and suffered us to pass through. We left twenty-four of our party behind, either killed in the pit, or cut down in forcing their column. I was near the rear, and, after passing a short distance from their line, I came upon poor Hunter, who had his back broken by a ball, and was in a dying condition. I asked him if he was badly hurt; he answered, " Yes, I am dying; go on and save yourself: you can do me no good."

When the Little Bear came up to him, he sat down by his side and refused to leave him. He said, " I will die with my white friend, and go with him to the spirit land."

I looked and saw him fall over upon the body of poor Hunter; he was also killed.

Pine Leaf had cut her way through in advance of me, and was dodging first one way and then the other, as she awaited for me to cut up.

"Why do you wait to be killed?" she inquired. "If you wish to die, let us return together; I will die with you."

We continued our retreat for a few miles, but the enemy no longer molested us; he had not followed us more than two hundred yards. We had left all our robes behind us in the pit, that we might not be burdened with them in our charge. The weather was extremely cold, and we halted to build a large fire, which we rested by all night, warming one side at a time.

The old brave who led the assault lost a son in the strife; he continued to sing all the way until he became hoarse, and he could sing no more. He prayed to the Great Spirit to give him an opportunity to avenge his loss, which prayer was accorded several times over during the ensuing winter. The heroine lost one joint off the little finger of her right hand, amputated with a bullet; the little finger of her other hand she had cut off at the death of her twin-brother. Fortunately, I had saved my capote, and I gave it to her to wear, as she was suffering severely with the cold. We also killed several buffaloes on our way to the fort, and made wrappers of the raw hides for many of the men; still a number were badly frozen in their bodies and limbs.

This was my Russian campaign. I lost more men, and suffered more from the cold on this expedition, than in any other in which I had command either before or since.

The boys reached the fort with the horses before we did. They had more than enough to mount us all on our way home. There was great joy at the fort at our return in such numbers, as they had supposed it impossible for one of us to escape.

When I left the lamented Hunter upon the field, he said, " Jim, when you pass this way, I ask you to take my bones to the fort, and have them buried. Write home to my friends, and inform them of my fate. Goodby! Now go and save yourself."

" It shall be done," I said; and the following spring it was done as I had promised.

We rested at the fort four or five days to recruit ourselves. While staying there, a party of thirty warriors from Long Hair's village came to see how they were progressing with the fort. There were some in

my party who belonged to that village, and they returned with them. They also informed us where our
village was, as it had been removed during our absence. Having provided ourselves with robes in the
place of those we had left behind, we started onward
with dejected feelings, and in deep mourning.

On our arrival we found the village likewise in
mourning. They had lost four warriors by the Black
Feet while resisting an attempt to steal our horses.
When informed of our disaster, there was a general renewal of their lamentations; more fingers were lopped,
and heads again scarified. The Medicine Calf had
been defeated, and for some hidden cause the Great
Spirit was again wroth with the Crows.

CHAPTER XXII.

Meteoric Shower.—Its Effect upon the Indians.—Their Sacrifice to
the Great Spirit.—Continued Hostilities with the Black Feet.—A
Black Foot burned in the Crow Village.—Visit to the Fort.

IN case any captious "elders of the congregation"
had been inclined to throw the blame of my recent disaster upon my shoulders, I was provided with a sufficient portent to screen me from consequences. After
quitting the fort on our way to Little Box Elder (as before related), and while exhausting all my powers of
persuasion to induce Mr. Hunter to return, we observed
a remarkable meteoric shower, which filled us all (more
particularly my followers) with wonder and admiration.
This was at our first encampment after leaving the fort
in the latter end of October, 1832. Although my warriors were ready to face death in any form, this singular phenomenon appalled them. It was the wrath of

the Great Spirit showered visibly upon them, and they looked to me, in quality of medicine chief, to interpret the wonder. I was as much struck with the prodigious occurrence, and was equally at a loss with my untutored followers to account for the spectacle. Evidently I must augur some result therefrom, and my dejected spirits did not prompt me to deduce a very encouraging one. I thought of all the impostures that are practiced upon the credulous, and my imagination suggested some brilliant figures to my mind. I thought of declaring to them that the Great Spirit was pleased with our expedition, and was lighting us on our way with spirit lamps ; or that these meteors were the spirits of our departed braves, coming to assist us in our forthcoming fight. But I was not sanguine enough to indulge in any attractive oratory. I merely informed them I had not time to consult my medicine, but that on our return to the village I would interpret the miracle to them in full.

On our arrival, I found the people's minds still agitated with the prodigy. All were speaking of it in wonder and amazement, and my opinion was demanded respecting the consequences it portended. Admonished by my defeat, I had no trouble in reading the stars. I informed them that our people had evidently offended the Great Spirit ; that it was because of his wrath I had suffered defeat in my excursion, and returned with the loss of twenty-three warriors. I thence inferred that a sacrifice must be made to appease the wrath of the Great Spirit, and recommended that a solemn assembly be convened, and a national oblation offered up.

I was fully confident that by thus countenancing such pagan superstitions I was doing very wrong, but, like many a more prominent statesman in civilized governments, I had found that I must go with the current, and I recommended a measure, not because it was of a nature to benefit the country, but simply because it was popular with the mass.

The camp in which we then were was a mourning-camp, in which medicine would have no effect. Therefore we moved to Sulphur River, ten miles distant, in order to offer up our sacrifice. All the leading men and braves assembled, and I was consulted as to the kind of offering proper to make for the purpose of averting the wrath that was consuming us. I ordered them to bring the great medicine kettle, which was of brass, and capable of holding ten gallons, and was purchased at a cost of twenty fine robes, and to polish it as bright as the sun's face. This done, I ordered them to throw in all their most costly and most highly-prized trinkets, and whatsoever they cherished the most dearly. It was soon filled with their choicest treasures. Keepsakes, fancy work on which months of incessant and patient toil had been expended, trinkets, jewels, rings so highly prized by them that the costliest gems of emperors seemed poor by their side— all these were thrown into the kettle, along with a bountiful contribution of fingers, until it would hold no more. I then had weights attached to it, and had it carried to an air-hole in the ice where the river was very deep, and there it was sunk with becoming ceremony. Three young maidens, habited like May queens, carried the burden.

This great sacrifice completed, the minds of the people were relieved, and the result of the next war-party was anxiously looked forward to to see if our oblation was accepted. Their crying, however, continued unabated, so much to the derangement of my nervous system that I was fain to retire from the village and seek some less dolorous companionship. My bosom friend and myself therefore started off unnoticed, and traveled on without stopping until we came to a hill some seven or eight miles distant. He was pre-eminently a great brave, at all times self-possessed and unobtrusive. I always considered him as endowed with the most solid sense, and possessing the clearest views of any Indian in the nation. His spirits were generally somewhat dejected, but that I attributed to the loss of all his relatives. When I wished to enjoy a little converse or sober meditation, he always was my chosen companion, as there were qualities in his character which interested me and assimilated with my own. He never craved popularity, never envied the elevation of others, but seemed rather to rejoice at another person's success. He would listen to me for an entire day when I spoke of my residence with the whites, and told of their great battles, where thousands were slain on both sides; when I described their ships carrying immense guns capable of sweeping hundreds of men away at a discharge; and when I depicted to him their forts, to which our forts for size or strength were but as ant-hills. I then would tell him of the great Atlantic Ocean, and the millions of white men living beyond it; of countries where there was no summer, and others where there was no winter, and a thousand other marvels, of which I never spoke to other warriors, as their minds were too limited to comprehend me.

After listening to me with the deepest attention until I would grow tired of talking, he would seem to be perfectly amazed, and would be lost in a deep reverie for some time, as though endeavoring to raise his ideas to a level with the vast matters he had been listening to. Occasionally he would tell me of the traditions handed down from generation to generation in the Indian race, in which he was " elegantly learned." He told me of the mighty tribes of men who had once inhabited this vast continent, but were now exterminated by internecine wars; that their fathers had told them of a great flood, which had covered all the land, except the highest peaks of the mountains, where some of the inhabitants and the buffaloes resorted, and saved themselves from destruction.

We were on a hill, as before mentioned, some seven or eight miles from the village, engaged in one of these long cosmographical discussions, when my companion, chancing to turn his head, descried some object at a great distance. Pointing it out to me with his finger, " There is a people," he exclaimed. I looked in the direction indicated, and saw a small party of Black Feet approaching.

" Sit still," said I, " and let us see where they encamp; we will have every one of them to-night."

We watched them until they halted at a couple of small Indian forts, with which the country abounds, and we saw they were soon joined by four or five others who came from another direction, and who were evidently scouts. From the direction which they came, I saw they had not discovered our village.

" Now," said I, " let us return; we will have that party. We will collect a few trusty warriors, and not mention our discovery to a living soul, not even telling our warriors the errand we are upon until we get within sight of the camp-fires of the enemy. Then we will return with their scalps, and put an end to this howling that deafens my ears."

We started on our way to the village. I desired
him to select from his friends, and I would assemble
my own.

"No," said he, "my friends are fools. I don't want
them. But you collect your warriors, and I will be
one of them."

Accordingly, I went to my father, and desired him
to send for about seventy-five of my brothers and relatives, and tell them the Medicine Calf wished to see
them; but I charged him not to tell them they were
going away from the village. As they mustered one
at a time, I acquainted them that I wanted them to
leave the village singly and with the utmost secrecy,
to meet me with their guns and battle-axes at a certain hour and in such a place, and in the mean time to
answer no word to whatever question might be asked
them.

At the appointed hour I repaired to the post, and
found them all in readiness. I then marched them to
the place of attack. When we arrived within sight of
our foes we found them all very merry; they were singing the Wolf Song, or Song of the Spies, they having
no suspicion that they were so near to the Crow village. We went cautiously up to the forts, which were
but a few yards apart; and while they were yet singing we pointed our guns, and, at a signal given by me,
all fired. The whole party were slain; their notes
were cut short in death. Taking their scalps (nineteen
in number) and guns, we reached our village by daylight, and entered it singing, dancing, and shouting.

The village was aroused, and men, women, and children came running from all directions to learn the cause
of the disturbance. We displayed our nineteen scalps,
and I took to myself full credit for the force of my

medicine in divining where to find the foe, and cognizance was taken of the fact in the medicine lodge. We had five days' dancing to do full justice to this brilliant achievement, and I had become so tired of their continual mourning that their savage yells of delight seemed quite a luxury.

One night a party of Black Feet came to borrow some of our horses, and happened to be caught in the fact. The alarm was given, the marauders fired upon, and one of them had his leg broken by a ball. He was found the next morning, unable to get away; but he sat up and defended himself until he had shot his last arrow. He was then brought into the village, and it was decided to burn him. A large fire was built, which was surrounded by hundreds, and when the fire was well burnt up the poor fellow was thrown in. This was the first act of the kind I had ever known the Crows to commit; but there was no preventing it. It is an appalling sight to behold a human being, or even an inferior animal, perish in the flames; I trust my eyes may never witness such another scene. To see the writhing agony of the suffering wretch when cast into the darting flames, and hear his piercing shrieks as the blaze gradually envelops his whole body, until the life is scorched out of the victim, and he falls prostrate among the logs, soon to become a charred mass of cinders undistinguishable from the element that consumed it—it is indeed a sight only fit for savages to look at.

I learned this one truth while I was with the Indians, namely, that a white man can easily become an Indian, but that an Indian could never become a white man. Some of the very worst savages I ever saw in the Rocky Mountains were white men, and I could mention their names and expose some of their deeds, but they have most probably gone to their final account before this.

Our village now moved on toward the fort to purchase our spring supplies. Both villages could only raise forty packs of beaver and nineteen hundred packs of robes; but for their continual wars, they could as easily have had ten packs for one. But it is impossible to confine an Indian to a steady pursuit—not even fighting; after a while he will even tire of that. It is impossible to control his wayward impulses; application to profitable industry is foreign to his nature. He is a vagrant, and he must wander; he has no associations to attach him to one spot; he has no engendered habits of thrift or productiveness to give him a constant aim or concentration of purpose.

Both villages at length assembled at the new fort, and our spring trading was briskly entered into. We rested for over a week, and I then proposed moving, as the time was approaching for our building a new medicine lodge. The night preceding our proposed departure, thieves were discovered among our horses; the alarm was given, and a party went in pursuit. They returned with six Sioux scalps, and two of our own men wounded. The remainder of the rascals succeeded in getting away with sixteen of our animals, we not considering them worth following after.

We then postponed our departure four days, and devoted ourselves to noise and festivity. The welkin rung with our shouts, and the fort shook with the thunder of our earthquake step.

CHAPTER XXIII.

Removal to our Tobacco-ground.—Expedition to the Arrap-a-hos for Horses. — Discovered, and the Party scattered. — Wanderings for fourteen Months.—Return at last amid tremendous Rejoicing.

WE left the fort, and proceeded toward our tobacco-ground. We planted the seed, and spent a short time in festivity. It was deemed inexpedient to build a medicine lodge this season, as all the business could be transacted in a temporary one.

Our stock of horses being greatly diminished, we deemed this a fitting time to try and replenish it, and various small parties sallied out for that purpose. I left with only seventeen warriors for the country of the Arrap-a-hos, situated on the head-waters of the Arkansas. On arriving at their village we found a great number of horses, upon which we made a descent; but we were discovered before we could lay our hands on any, and had to scatter in all directions in our effort to escape. One of our party had his leg broken with a rifle ball, but he did not fall into the enemy's hands, as he crawled away and secreted himself. Two months subsequently he found his way home, with his leg nearly healed. He stated that, after receiving his wound, he plunged into the river, which flowed close by, and swam to an island, there concealing himself in a thick brush. The enemy moved away the next day, and he swam back to their camping-ground, where he found an abundance of meat, which he carried over to his quarters; upon this he fared sumptuously until he was strong enough to walk; then he made his way home.

I saw the village move the next morning, and, gathering four of my scattered companions, I followed the enemy at a respectful distance until they encamped for the next night. We then made another descent upon their fold, and succeeded in obtaining each man a horse. We saw no more of the remains of our party until we returned to our village upward of a year subsequently.

We came to the resolution to quit the Arrap-a-hos, and pay the Snakes a visit. On reaching them we found horses in abundance, and could have levied upon them for any number; but, being at peace with the tribe, we contented ourselves with exchanging our jaded and foot-sore animals for five fresh ones from their drove. Here we dropped an arrow, and they recognized it for a Crow arrow readily; we also put on new moccasins, and left our old ones behind us. When the Snakes fell in with the Crows some time after, they charged them with stealing their horses, which charge the Crows strenuously denied. The Snakes persisted, and, to confirm their accusation, produced the arrow and the abandoned moccasins. This satisfied the Crows that it must be some of the Arrap-a-ho expedition, and hopes of our safety were revived.

From the Snakes we passed on to the Flat Head territory, where we found thousands of horses, but felt ourselves under the same moral restrictions as with the Snakes. Accordingly, we merely exchanged again, and again left five pairs of moccasins. Subsequently they made the same charge against the Crows, and accused them of infringing the treaty. The Crows again pleaded innocence, and again the moccasins convicted them of their guilt. They, however, resorted to diplomatic *finesse*, and an appeal to arms was averted. Again their hopes were rekindled of seeing us once more.

We then took a notion to pay the Coutnees a flying visit, where we made another exchange. We could have taken all the horses we wanted, but, to get home with them, we must have taken a wide circuit, or have passed through the territory of two hostile nations. We next moved to the As-ne-boine River, which empties into Hudson's Bay. Here we borrowed one hundred and fifty head of fine horses from the Blood Indians, and started on our way home. We arrived, without accident, at the Mussel Shell River, within one day's ride of our own people, where we encamped, intending to reach home the next day; but that night the Crows swept away every horse we had, not even leaving us one for our own use. We must have slept very soundly during the night; indeed, we were all greatly fatigued, for we did not hear a single movement. In getting our horses, they glorified themselves over having made a glorious haul from the Black Feet.

Not liking to be foiled in our resolution to return home with a respectable accompaniment of horses, we retraced our steps to the As-ne-boine River, intending to start another drove. On our return we found our friends had left, and had crossed to the other side of the mountain. We followed on, but delayed so long on the western slope, that the heavy snow-storms now falling cut off all possibility of returning home before spring; therefore we built a comfortable lodge in what was called Sweet Mountain, in a *cañon*, where we could kill a buffalo every day, the skins of which, covered entirely over our lodge, made a very agreeable abode for the winter. We also killed several large wolves, and dressed their skins in the nicest manner.

We likewise took three Black Foot scalps. The Indians whose horses we had been in pursuit of, after having roamed about considerably, had gone into winter quarters only twelve or fifteen miles distant; their smoke was visible from our lodge. On the return of spring we visited our neighbors' camp, and selected one hundred and twenty head of such horses as we thought would stand the journey. We then returned over the mountain, and reached as far as the Judith in safety, which was within three days' ride of the village. We were greatly fatigued, and halted to encamp for the night and rest our jaded horses. Again the Crows stripped us of every horse, leaving us on foot once more. Resolved not to be beat, we determined to try our luck a third time before we returned to our village. I told my four companions that my medicine promised me success, and that when we did eventually get home we should be able to see what amount of affection was felt toward us by our people, by ascertaining how much crying had been done for us.

I had no doubt we had been mourned as dead, for we had been absent above a year. During this time, we subsequently learned, there had been great mourning for us, and many had cut off their hair. My father, however, still persisted that I was alive, and would some day return, and he would allow none of his family to cut off their fingers for me. At the time the Flat Heads went in with their complaint, they were about to elect another chief to fill my place; but when they saw the five pairs of moccasins produced, they knew they must have had Crow wearers, and their hopes were revived of again seeing us, and the election ceremony was postponed. My father would have no steps taken toward filling my vacant place before the erection of the next medicine lodge. He said he did not know where his Calf had rambled, and it was his firm belief that in the course of time he would ramble home again.

When we reached the As-ne-boine for the third time, we found that our friends who had accommodated us with the two previous droves of horses had gone over the mountain, and passed down that river to Fort Row, one of the Hudson's Bay trading-posts. By the appearance of their trail we judged that they had been joined by other villages, probably from the Coutnees and Pa-gans, all on their way to the trading-post for the purchase of their spring supply of goods. We followed their trail for several days, which grew fresher and fresher, until one afternoon we came suddenly upon a horse. We were at that time in thick timber, with a dense growth of underbrush, and thousands of wild pea-vines about.

On seeing the horse we halted suddenly. On looking farther around, we discovered horses of all colors and stripes, ring-streaked and speckled. Shortly the sound of voices reached our ears. In an instant we stooped down and crept under the almost impenetrable vines, nor did we venture to move from our hiding-place until night. We could distinctly hear the chatter of men, women, and children around us, and some of the squaws came most dangerously near when gathering fire-wood for their camp-fires. We could occasionally peep out, and we saw in those glimpses that they had beautiful horses, and, besides, that they were in good traveling condition. We then felt no doubt that the Coutnees were in company, since they always prided themselves in spotted horses, as Jacob of old took pride in spotted cattle. In that encampment it so little entered into their heads to anticipate molestation that they had placed no horse-guards to keep watch.

The noise of the horses in tearing through the pea-vines assisted us materially in our nocturnal enterprise. We selected two hundred and eighty of their largest, strongest, and handsomest cattle, with which we lost no time in making direct for Crow-land; nor did we venture to give rest to their hoofs until a journey, continued through three days and nights, placed what we considered a safe distance between us. We then ventured to encamp for the night, to afford to the poor tired-out animals an opportunity to rest for a while, but starting off at early dawn to preclude all possibility of recapture.

On the fifth day we discovered an Indian a short distance from our trail, who was coming in an oblique direction toward us. He stopped on the hill-side at some little distance off, and motioned for us to approach him. Supposing him to be a Crow, I desired my companions to drive on, while I went to see what he wanted. When I had approached within a few yards of him, he put on an air of surprise, and placed his hand to his shoulder with the intention of drawing his bow. I sprang upon him instantly and cut him down, and despoiled him of his scalp and quiver. When about to leave to overtake my companions, I perceived the distant smoke of a Black Foot village situated immediately in the direction that we were journeying, and it was beyond doubt that the Indian I had just killed was a spy belonging to that village. He must have mistaken us for some of his own tribe, and only discovered his mistake when I approached near enough for him to distinguish my features.

My companions returning to me, we altered our course, and passed over a mountain covered with deep snow, so hard, however, that we passed it without losing a horse. This was one of the spurs of the Rocky Mountains, and covered with perpetual snows.

After sixteen days of almost incessant travel day and night, we came in sight of our village just as the sun was sinking behind the distant mountains. We approached within a mile of the village, and encamped under a small hill, as yet unperceived by our people, for the hill in the shelter of which we lay was between ourselves and the village. It was now the latter end of June (I think), in the year 1834.

After resting a while, I thought to get some tobacco, to indulge in a smoke before making our grand *entrée*, at the same time requesting my companions to keep a sharp look-out, and see that the Crows did not steal our horses again. Finally, three of us entered *incog.*, and smoked with several of the old men, not one of whom recognized us or once thought of us. We passed all through the village, looking leisurely about us; the streets were full of people, yet not one bestowed a thought on us. When it became somewhat late, and the inhabitants had principally retired, I dismissed my two companions to the camp, telling them I would get some tobacco, and rejoin them in a short time. I then entered the lodge of one of my wives, who was asleep in bed. I shook her by the arm, and aroused her.

Waking, she inquired, " Who is this in the lodge ?"

I answered, " It is your husband."

" I never had but one husband," she replied, " and he is dead."

" No," said I, " I am he."

" You are not dead, then, as we have believed ?"

"No," I said; " I have been wandering a long while, and have only just returned."

" We all mourned you," she continued, " many moons ago, and we all mourn you now every day. We believed that the enemy had killed you."

" No," I said, " I escaped. I have now brought home a large drove of beautiful spotted horses, and if you will do as I wish you, you shall have your choice of the whole drove, and you will become a medicine woman also."

" I will do what you wish me," she replied.

" Well, I want you, when you get up in the morning, to request the village to refrain from crying for one sun. Tell them that you dreamed that I came home riding a large and spotted horse, having the other four men with me; that we had nearly three hundred of the most beautiful horses you ever saw, and that we rode with large wolf-skins spread on our horses' backs, mine being as white as the drifted snow."

She agreed to do all as I had bidden her; I then left her lodge; but, before quitting the village, I called in at my father's lodge. All was still around, and, entering on tip-toe, I reached down the medicine shield, which no one but his wife or eldest son is privileged to handle, and, opening it, I took out all his medicine tobacco, carrying it back to the camp with me, and then replaced the shield upon its peg. I then returned to our camp, and enjoyed a good smoke with my companions, our spirits waxing elate at the surprise we had in store.

Early the next morning, the woman, true to her word, narrated her dream to the astonished inhabitants, with whatever additions her own fancy suggested. My father and mother listened attentively to her revelation ; and, before she had got through with her narrative, she had quite a numerous auditory. We were watching the occurrence from the brow of the hill; and, knowing she would have to rehearse her vision several times before it was generally known throughout the village, we did not hurry to show ourselves.

My father and mother, having heard her through, turned and entered their lodge. Suddenly the medicine shield caught my mother's eye—it had evidently been moved. My father took it down and opened it —the tobacco was gone. This opened the "old gentleman's" eyes. "It is well," he said; "my son lives!" and he believed the substance of the dream as fervently as the prophetess who uttered it. The bystanders, seeing his medicine so strong, and he beginning to sing and dance, they all joined in, until the noise of their revelry reached us on our distant eminence.

Now was our time. We mounted our caparisoned steeds, and, forming ourselves in procession, we commenced our grand *entrée*, singing and shouting at the top of our voices. Our tones are heard, and the villagers gaze around in surprise. " Hark!" they exclaimed; "look yonder! there are five men mounted on large spotted steeds. Who are they ?"

All was hushed as the grave in the village, each striving to catch the sound of our distant strains. The five horsemen disappeared as if by magic, and reappeared driving a large drove of horses before them of all colors. The horsemen again pause on the summit. " Hark! listen! they sing again! Who can they be?"

Not a soul yet stirred from the village. We drove

our horses down toward them, and left them there, while we took a circuit around, displaying our scalps, but still keeping over gunshot distance. The old men came out to us, carrying drums; each of us took one, and then we bounded away to the rear of our horses. We raised a well-known song, and all listened to the tones of the returning Medicine Calf. At length our wives and relatives broke away from the throng, and darted over the plain to meet us. They fairly flew over the intervening space to welcome us in their arms. A tall sister of mine outstripped the rest, and arrived first, and immediately after my little wife was also by my side. After a warm greeting exchanged with these, the warriors came up, and saluted us with a shout that would have aroused Napoleon's Old Guard from their graves. We were lifted from our horses, and almost denuded of our clothing, and carried by the impetuous throng into the village. My father had painted his face into an exact resemblance of Satan, in token of his joy at my happy return. I was kissed and caressed by my mother, sisters, and wives until I fairly gasped for breath.

Any person who has never beheld a real downright rejoicing among savages can form but a faint conception of their unrestrained manifestations; words can convey no adequate idea of it. Being untutored and natural, and not restricted by any considerations of grace or propriety, they abandon themselves to their emotions, and no gesture is too exaggerated, no demonstration too violent for them to resort to.

My friend, with many others, had given me up for dead, and had adopted another in my place; so that there were now three of us who all knew one another's secrets. Pine Leaf was overjoyed at my return.

She had become confident of my death, and was only waiting to ascertain the nation that had killed me in order to revenge my loss, or be sacrificed to my manes. Couriers were immediately dispatched to the other village to acquaint them with our return, and to invite them to participate in the celebrations of the event. Long Hair returned for answer, " Tell my brother I will fly to see him." They lost six warriors on their way to our village, through carelessly straggling in detached parties, consequently they came to us in mourning for their loss.

The two droves of horses which the Crows had released us of were all religiously returned. Those that the captors had given away were promptly delivered up, so that we were now in possession of a very numerous drove. I distributed my share among my relatives, friends, wives, and wives' relatives, until I had only just enough for my own use. I gave my father an elegant steed, the largest in the whole drove. To the heroine I gave a spotted four-year-old, a perfect beauty, one that I had intended for her as we were driving them home. He proved to be a superior warhorse, and there were but few among the thousands that we possessed that could distance him with her upon his back. She was very proud of him, and would suffer no one but herself to ride him.

It took me a long time to rehearse all our adventures while away. I was required to do it very minutely and circumstantially—even to describe all our camping-grounds, and relate every minute occurrence that transpired during our long pilgrimage.

We had certainly incurred exceeding risk in the route we had traveled; in recurring to it I marveled at our escape. Any five men might start upon such an adventure, and not one party in ten would ever return. I reflected, however, that I was a little more sagacious than the Indians, and that I had my physical faculties as well developed as theirs. I could see fully as quick as they could, and ride as fast, if they undertook to chase me in the mountains.

I now found that I had thousands of friends, whether attracted by my fancy horses or not, and that I was the idol of my proud parents. The mother of Black Panther always lived with my father, and if both survive, I presume she does to this day. I gave him the child when it was quite young, to adopt as his son, in obedience to his reiterated solicitations.

CHAPTER XXIV.

Excursion to the Fort.—Great Battle with the Cheyennes on the Way.—Rejoicing on my Arrival at the Fort.—Horses stolen by the Cheyennes.—Pursuit and Battle with the Thieves.—Battle with the Black Feet.—Return to our Village.

WHEN the rejoicings were over, a council was called to deliberate on the future operations of the nation, wherein the resolution was taken to keep united until Leaf Fall. About the latter end of August I started for the fort, taking with me three hundred and fifty warriors, with as many women and children, among whom was my little wife. While on our way thither, we encamped one night on Fallen Creek, and lost upward of fifty horses, stolen by the Cheyennes. We pursued them with our whole force, and, soon overtaking them, a fight ensued between numbers about equal. I had charged in advance of the line, and, as I was always dressed in full costume when on these excursions, I offered an excellent mark to any one skilled in shooting. I was proceeding at an easy canter, when my horse was shot through the head, the ball entering near the ear, and he fell, his last spring hurling me head foremost against a huge rock, which I struck with such force that I saw another dense meteoric shower, and the blood gushed from my mouth, nose, and ears. When I recovered my senses I found both parties over me, each struggling to obtain me. The Crows prevailed eventually, and my scalp was saved. My warriors were fully convinced of my death, as I lay so long motionless; but they were determined to preserve my scalp. The enemy, seeing our women and children approach, mistook them for a re-enforcement of Crow warriors, and they gave up the contest and fled precipitately, leaving us masters of the field, with all the horses they had just stolen from us, besides a great number of their own, which they had not time to drive off. We only obtained three scalps from the enemy, losing none ourselves, though we had several warriors wounded.

We then resumed our journey to the fort, reaching there without farther trouble. When we arrived within sight and hearing, we, as usual, struck up a song. All the women from the fort ran out, exclaiming, "Here comes a war-party of the Crows; they are singing! Look at their scalps: they come from the country of the Cheyennes; they have conquered our enemies. See, they are all painted!"

I had long been supposed dead at the fort. It was conjectured that Big Bowl (my father) had the conduct of the party, and there was no inquiry made for me. We entered amid a thousand How d'ye do's, and my wife and "Little Jim" were comfortably provided with the best quarters in the fort. I was standing among the busy throng, who had already fallen to admire the new goods, still feeling the effects of my severe shake, when I saw one of the female inmates eye me very inquiringly. She inquired of my wife who that Indian was. She answered, " He is my husband."

" What! are you married again ?" the woman exclaimed, in astonishment.

" No, not *again*," she replied, in her very modest manner; " did you not know that the Medicine Calf was alive and had returned ?"

" Then that surely is the Medicine Calf," the woman exclaimed, "now standing in the fort !" and ran to Mr. Tulleck to acquaint him with the news.

"Where is he ? where is the Medicine Calf?" Mr. Tulleck called aloud, and looking among the throng without perceiving me.

I addressed him in English, calling him by name. I thought at first that he would fall to the ground ; it was some seconds before he could speak, his astonishment was so overwhelming. At last he found tongue, and broke out in all kinds of expressions of joy and welcome. The men, too, attached to the fort, on hearing of my arrival, came running in with their utmost speed to welcome one whom they had all long since supposed dead. So heartfelt a welcome I could not have expected. Little Jim had been taken from his mother's hand before it was known that I was present. He was a general pet at the fort, and it usually took one good horse to carry all the presents bestowed upon mother and child. He was then near three years old, running every where, and was already looked upon by the Crows as their future chief.

We tarried at the fort a few days, engaged in hunting buffalo for its men and our own family. Our consumption was several carcasses a day. During my long absence the Crows had neglected their traps, and they had not dressed more than half the usual number of robes, which caused a sensible falling off in the trade of the fort, and diminished very materially the profits derived by the company from Fort Cass. No reduction, however, was made in my salary on account of my absence, which I considered very liberal conduct on the part of the company.

My warriors, becoming uneasy at their inactive life, desired to be led against the Black Feet. To gratify them, I selected one hundred and six warriors, and sent the others back to the village with the women and children, except my wife, whom I requested to stay at the fort to await my return. We marched into the enemy's country, and in the daytime came suddenly upon one of their villages. There were lodges enough to contain three hundred warriors, but they were probably gone upon an expedition, for there were but few present to receive us. We unhesitatingly assaulted it, although we had but little fighting to do. We took upward of twenty scalps, and eighteen women and children prisoners. We captured two hundred and sixty horses, besides weapons, clothing, and other spoils.

Here I succeeded in having a good joke at the heroine's expense, with which I plagued her for a long time. She was swifter on foot than any warrior, and we were on foot during this excursion. On seeing us advance, a young Indian, about sixteen, took to his heels, running like a deer. The heroine made after him with her antelope speed, certain to catch him. The Indian did his best, frequently turning his head, like a negro with an alligator at his heels. Seeing that his pursuer must overtake him, and not relishing the idea of having her lance transfix his body—for she was preparing to hurl it—he suddenly stopped and faced about, at the same time throwing his bow down and holding up both hands to beg for his life. She did what no other warrior in our party would have done— her woman's heart took pity on the poor fellow's pitiable condition—she spared his life, and marched him back captive.

He being her prisoner, no one had authority over his life but herself. He was a fine-looking young man, but when he was brought among the Crow warriors he trembled in every joint, expecting nothing less than to be killed.

I thought this too good an opportunity for a joke not to make use of it.

"I see," said I, addressing myself to Pine Leaf, "you have refused all our braves that you might win a husband from the enemy."

All the warriors shouted at the sally; but the poor girl was sorely perplexed, and knew not what to do or say. We rallied her so much on her conquest that she finally became quite spunky, and I did not know whether she would run her prize through with her lance or not. One day I told her I had talked with her prisoner about his capture. "Well," said she, "and what has he to say about it?"

"Why," I answered, "he says he could have killed you as well as not, but that you promised to marry him if he would spare your life."

She was fully practiced upon, and she flushed with anger. "He lies!" she exclaimed. "You know I can not speak to these Black Feet, or I would make him tell a different tale. I have often told you, as well as other warriors, that I do not wish to marry ; my tongue was straight when I said so. I have told you often, and I have told your sisters and your wives, that, if ever I did marry, I would have you, and none other. So why do you trifle with my feelings ?"

What she said was a genuine ebullition of feeling; for, although an Indian girl, her heart was as proud, as sensitive, and as delicate as ever beat in the breast of civilized woman. To soothe her ruffled temper, I told her I would intrust a secret to her. I had undertaken my prolonged journeying, when all supposed me dead, and she along with the rest, solely to search through the Rocky Mountains for a " red-headed Indian." I had been unsuccessful in my search, and had returned with spotted horses.

She laughed immoderately at my invention.

We now returned to the fort with our trophies, where we had a joyous time. My warriors gave a horse to each man at the fort, about fifty in number, and every woman staying there also received one. I selected the best one I had, and made Little Jim present it to Mr. Tulleck, with which delicate attention he was greatly delighted. My boy could now speak quite plain. The men at the fort had taught him to swear quite fluently both in French and English, much more to their satisfaction than to mine. But I trusted he would soon forget his schooling, as the Crows never drink whisky, nor use profane language.

We left the fort, and reached our village without accident. On our arrival we found the people in mourning for the loss of two warriors, killed in the village by an attack of the Cheyennes; and, notwithstanding my recent success, we had to take part in the crying, in obedience to their forms.

The Cheyennes, in their late attack, used very good generalship; but the result was not so good as their design would seem to promise. They started with a force of three thousand warriors, and, dividing their army, five hundred marched directly over the Tongue River Mountain, where they were safe from molestation, while their main body passed round in another direction, placing themselves in ambush in a place agreed upon, so as to fall upon the Crows should they pursue their flying division. But the Crows were too wary for them, and their bright design failed.

The division of five hundred made a descent upon the horses, killing the two Crows that were among them, and unable to escape in time. It was in open day, and our stock was so immense that they actually did succeed in driving off about twelve hundred, of which our family owned about eighty. Many of our choice mares, with their foals, and a great number of our war-horses, seemed to have intelligence of the business in hand, and ran with full speed to the village, where the enemy did not care to follow them. Hundreds of our warriors were ready for the conflict, and were impatiently awaiting the order to attack; but their chiefs strictly forbade their advance, and even charged my faithful Dog Soldiers with the duty of enforcing their orders. There were in the village over four thousand warriors, a force sufficient to repel any attack; but the old heads seemed to suspect something at the bottom of their foes' audacity, and thus escaped the trap that was prepared for them. The horses we cared but little about, as it was easy to replace them at any time, without risking the lives of so many brave warriors.

On my return, all this was related to me by the

council. They inquired my opinion of the policy they had acted upon, and I assented to the wisdom of all they had done. I further recommended that no war-party should leave the village for at least two weeks, but that all should devote themselves to trapping beaver, as a means better calculated to please the Great Spirit, and after that it was likely he would reward our excursions with more constant success.

My advice was approved of, and my medicine was pronounced powerful. Every trap in the village was accordingly brought to light, and a general preparation made for an active season of trapping: peltry-parties scattered for every stream containing beaver. My old friend and myself, with each a wife, composed one party; we took twelve traps, and in ten days collected fifty-five beaver-skins. All who went out had excellent success, as the streams had been but little disturbed for several months. Our two weeks' combined industry produced quite a number of packs.

It was now about the 1st of October. I had promised, after our two weeks' trapping, to lead a party in a foray upon the Cheyennes. I selected over four hundred warriors, and started in pursuit of something—whether horses or scalps was a matter of indifference. After an easy travel of twenty days, our spies keeping a vigilant look-out on the way, a large village was reported some few miles in advance. Knowing whom we had to deal with, I used my utmost caution, for we were beyond the reach of re-enforcement if I should fall into any difficulties. We ascended a hill which overlooked their village. We saw their cheerful-looking fires, and would have liked to warm ourselves by similar ones; but, although firewood was abundant, it seemed barely advisable to indulge in such a luxury.   By the size of the village, it was evident we had a powerful enemy before us, and that he was brave we had learned by previous experience.   After surveying it as well as we could by the gleam of the stars, I determined to go down into their village, and obtain a closer observation.   I took three braves with me, and, turning our robes the hair side out, we descended the hill and entered the village.

We found they had recently built a new medicine lodge, and the national council was in session that night.   We walked up to the lodge, where there were a number of Cheyennes smoking and conversing, but we could not understand a word they said.   I passed my hand inside to reach for a pipe.   One was handed to me ; and after all four of us had taken a few whiffs, I handed it back to my accommodating lender.   We then strolled leisurely through their town, and returned to our own camp somewhat late in the evening.

About midnight we visited their herd, and started out quite a large drove, which we found at daylight consisted of eight hundred head ; with these we moved with all possible speed toward home, taking the directest route possible.   We drove at full speed, wherever practicable, until the next day at noon ; we then turned short round the point of a mountain, and awaited the arrival of our pursuers.   Our animals were well rested when the enemy came up, and we had just transferred ourselves to the backs of some that we had borrowed from them.   As soon as they had rounded the point—about two hundred and fifty in number—we issued out to attack them ; and, although they were somewhat surprised to behold so large a force, they quickly formed and awaited the onset.   We were soon upon them, killing several, and having a few of our own wounded. We withdrew to form another charge; but, before we were ready to fall on them again, they divided their line, and one half made a daring attempt to surround our horses, but we defeated their aim. They then retreated toward their village, they finding it necessary to re-enforce their numbers before they could either recover their animals or fight our party with any show of success.

I afterward learned, when a trader in the Cheyenne nation for Sublet, that their main body, consisting of two thousand warriors, had started with them, but turned back when within four miles of our temporary resting-place. The smaller division traveled back as fast as possible in the endeavor to reach them, and bring them back to the attack. After proceeding two or three hours in their trail, they suddenly came in sight of them as they were resting to dress some buffalo. By means of couriers and signals, they soon had the whole army on the march again; but by this time we were "over the hills and far away," having resumed our retreat immediately our pursuers left us.

Those who are driving horses in a chase such as this have a great advantage over their pursuers, since the pursuer must necessarily ride one horse all the time, but those that are driving can change as often as they please, taking a fresh horse every half hour even, if occasion requires. In case there is great urgency with a drove, a number of warriors are sent in advance to lead them, while others are whooping and yelling behind. Under this pressure, the animals generally get over the ground at a pretty good rate.

On our arrival at home with thirteen scalps, over eight hundred horses, and none of our party killed, it may be judged that we made much noise and shouting.

The trip we had just accomplished was a severe one, especially for the wounded, and none but Indians could have lived through such torment; but they all finally recovered. They begged to be left upon the road, urging that they must inevitably die, and it was a folly to impede our flight and jeopardize our lives; but I was determined, if possible, to get them in alive; for, had I lost but one, the village would again have gone into mourning, and that I was desirous to avoid.

CHAPTER XXV.

Visit of the whole Crow Nation to the Fort.—Seven Days' Trading and Rejoicing.—Separation of the Villages.—Expedition to the Camanches. — Narrow Escape from their Village. — Battle with the Black Feet.—The Whites assist us with their Cannon.—Captured by the Black Feet.—Recaptured by the Crows.—Final Victory.

HAVING now quite a respectable amount of peltry on hand, both of our villages started for the fort to purchase winter supplies. We carried upward of forty packs of beaver, and two thousand four hundred packs of robes, with which we were enabled to make quite an extensive trading. We loitered seven days in the vicinity of the fort; then the villages separated, for the purpose of driving the buffalo back to the Yellow Stone, where they would keep in good condition all winter. This required a considerable force of men, as those animals abounded by the thousand at that time where they are now comparatively scarce, and it is a conclusion forced upon my mind that within half a century the race of buffaloes will be extinguished on this continent. Then farewell to the Red Man! for he must also become extinct, unless he applies himself to the cultivation of the soil, which is beyond the bound of probability. The incessant demand for robes has slain thousands of those noble beasts of the prairie, until the Indians themselves begin to grow uneasy at the manifest diminution, and, as a means of conservation, each nation has adopted the policy of confining to itself the right of hunting on its own ground. They consider that the buffalo belongs to them as their exclusive property; that he was sent to them by the Great Spirit for their subsistence; and when he fails them, what shall they resort to? Doubtless, when that time arrives, much of the land which they now roam over will be under the white man's cultivation, which will extend inland from both oceans. Where then shall the Indian betake himself? There are no more Mississippis to drive him beyond. Unquestionably he will be taken in a surround, as he now surrounds the buffalo; and as he can not assimilate with civilization, the Red Man's doom is apparent. It is a question of time, and no very long time either; but the result, as I view it, is a matter of certainty.

The territory claimed by the Crows would make a larger state than Illinois. Portions of it form the choicest land in the world, capable of producing any thing that will grow in the Western and Middle States. Innumerable streams, now the homes of the skillful beaver, and clear as the springs of the Rocky Mountains, irrigate the plains, and would afford power for any amount of machinery. Mineral springs of every degree of temperature abound in the land. The country also produces an inconceivable amount of wild fruit of every variety, namely, currants, of every kind; raspberries, black and red; strawberries, blackberries, cherries; plums, of delicious flavor and in great abundance; grapes, and numberless other varieties proper to the latitude and fertile nature of the soil.

I am fully convinced that this territory contains vast mineral wealth; but, as I was unacquainted with the properties of minerals during my residence with the Crows, I did not pay much attention to the investigation of the subject. One thing, however, I am convinced of, that no part of the United States contains richer deposits of anthracite coal than the territory I am speaking of, and my conviction is thus founded. I one night surrounded a small mountain with a large force of warriors, thinking I had observed the fires of the enemy, and that I should catch them in a trap. But, to my great surprise, it proved to be a mountain of coal on fire, which had, I suppose, spontaneously ignited. I immediately drew off my forces, as I was fearful of an explosion. I could readily point out the place again.

It would be extremely hazardous to attempt any scientific explorations without first gaining the consent of the Crows. They have been uniformly friendly with the whites; still, they would be jealous of any engineering operations, as they would be ignorant of their nature. The Crows are a very reserved people, and it would be difficult to negotiate a treaty with them for the cession of any portion of their land. They have always refused to send a deputation to Washington, although repeatedly invited. Indeed, when I was their chief, I always opposed the proposition, as I foresaw very clearly what effect such a visit would produce upon their minds. The Crows, as a nation, had never credited any of the representations of the great wealth, and power, and numbers of their white brethren. In the event of a deputation being sent to Washington, the perceptions of the savages would be dazzled with the display and glitter around them. They would return home dejected and humiliated; they would confound the ears of their people with the rehearsal of the predominance and magnificence of the whites; feeling their own comparative insignificance, they would lose that pride in themselves that now sustains them, and, so far from being the terror of their enemies, they would grow despondent and lethargic; they would addict themselves to the vices of the weaker nations, and in a short time their land would be ingulfed in the insatiable government vortex, and, like hundreds of other once powerful tribes, they would be quickly exterminated by the battle-axes of their enemies. These are the considerations that influenced me while I administered their affairs.

From the fort I started on foot with two hundred and sixty trusty warriors for the Camanche territory. We had reached their ground, and were traveling leisurely along upon a high, open prairie, when our spies suddenly telegraphed to us to lie flat down—an order which we promptly obeyed. We soon learned that there was a number of Indians, some distance beyond, engaged in running buffalo and antelope as far as we could see. There appeared to be an outlet to the prairie, through which we could see them emerging and disappearing like bees passing in and out of a hive. We found at night that it was a wide *cañon*, in which their village was encamped, extending over three miles, and must have contained several thousand warriors. They had just driven a host of horses into it, to have them ready, most probably, for the next day's chase. There were still thousands of horses scattered in every direction over the prairie, but I preferred to take those

already collected. The Camanches, being seldom troubled by the incursions of their neighbors (as most of the
tribes hold them in dread), take no precaution for the
safety of their animals, for which reason they fell an
easy prey to us.

At the usual time of night we paid a visit to their
immense herd, and started an innumerable drove ; we
found it larger than we could successfully drive, and
were therefore obliged to leave several hundreds of
them on the prairie. We then placed a sufficient number of horse-guides ahead, and, whipping up our rear,
we soon had an immense drove under full speed for our
own country, making the very earth tremble beneath
their hoofs. We continued this pace for three days
and nights, closely followed by our enemies, who, having discovered their loss the next morning, started
after us in pursuit. They kept in sight of us each
day, but we had the advantage of them, as we could
change horses and they could not, unless they happened to pick up a few stragglers on the road.

On the third day I happened to be leading, and just
as I rose to look over the summit of a hill on the Arkansas, I discovered a large village of the Cheyennes
not far in advance, and lying directly in our course.
In an instant we turned to the left, and continued on
through a hollow with all our drove, the Camanches
not more than two or three miles in our rear.

On our pursuers arriving at the spot where we had
diverged to the left, they held their course right on,
and, pouncing upon the astonished Cheyennes, conceived they were the party they were in pursuit of.
We could distinctly hear the report of the guns of the
contending parties, but did not slacken our pace, as
our desire to get home in safety outweighed all curios-

ity to see the issue of the conflict. We afterward learned that the Cheyennes inflicted a severe beating upon their deluded assailants, and chased them back, with the loss of many of their warriors, to their own country. This was fine fun for us, and Fortune aided us more than our own skill, for we were saved any farther trouble of defending our conquest, and eventually reached home without the loss of a single life.

Our pursuers being disposed of, we allowed ourselves a little more ease. On the fifth day of our retreat we crossed the Arkansas, and, arriving on the bank of the Powder River (a branch of the south fork of the Platte), we afforded ourselves a rest. We drove all our horses into a *cañon*, and fortified the entrance, so that, in case of molestation, we could have repulsed five times our number. There was excellent pasture, affording our wearied and famishing horses the means of satisfying their hunger, and refreshing themselves with rest. We also needed repose, for we had eaten nothing on the way except what we happened to have with us, in the same manner as our horses would crop an occasional mouthful of grass while pursuing their flight.

After refreshing ourselves we resumed our journey, and, striking the Laramie River, we passed on through the Park, and then crossed the Sweet Water River into our own territory, where we were safe. We fell in with Long Hair's village before we entered our own, with whom we had a good time. Before parting we gave them five hundred horses. From thence we went down to the fort in quest of our own village, but learned they were about twenty miles out, encamped on the Rose Bud. The inmates of the fort thought it must have rained horses, for such a prodigious drove they never saw driven in before. We made them a present of a Camanche horse all round, and, having staid one night with them, the next morning we journeyed on to our village.

We found them all dancing and rejoicing over the success of the other war-parties, who had reached home before us, and our arrival increased their joy to such an extreme that there was no limit to their extravagant manifestations.

We had not parted from the fort more than two or three hours when Big Bowl called there, also in quest of the village, bringing two thousand seven hundred horses, which he had taken from the Coutnees.

Tulleck informed him that his son had but just left for the village with a large drove.

"Yes," said the old man, "but I can laugh at him this time."

"No, no," replied Tulleck, "he has beat you; he has twice as many as you."

"Ugh!" exclaimed the old brave; "his medicine is always powerful."

We must have started with five thousand horses, for many gave out on the way and were left behind, besides a number that must have straggled off, for the Cheyennes afterward informed me that they picked up a considerable number which had undoubtedly belonged to our drove.

My father, after presenting them with a horse all round at the fort, whipped his drove up, saying that he would yet overtake the Medicine Calf before he reached the village.

He arrived just before sunset, when the joy was at its height.

We had horses enough now to eat us out of house and

home, about eight thousand head having been brought in during the last ten days.

When the rejoicing was through, I divided my village, sending two hundred lodges round to start the buffalo toward the mountain, while I took one hundred and seventy lodges, and made a circuit in the direction of the fort, encamping in the bottom close by. I had with me eight or nine hundred warriors, besides my division of the women and children.

While staying in the vicinity of the fort we were usually very careless, never apprehending any attack; but on the third day of our encampment here we were suddenly assailed by nearly fifteen hundred Black Foot warriors, who were probably aware that we had divided our village, and had followed us as the smallest party. Myself and several other warriors were in the fort when the attack was made, but we soon hastened to join our warriors. The contest became severe. The Black Feet fought better than I had ever seen them fight before. The Crows, being outnumbered by their enemies, were sorely pressed, and every man had to exert himself to the utmost to withstand the assault. The men at the fort, seeing our situation, brought out to our aid a small cannon on a cart. The enemy, seeing them bring it up, charged on it and carried it, the Frenchmen who had it in charge running back to the fort with all possible speed. The Crows, seeing what had happened, made a furious charge on the captors of the cannon, and succeeded in retaking it, though not without the loss of several killed and wounded in the conflict. The gun was loaded with musket-balls, and, when finally discharged, did no damage to the enemy.

I was in another quarter, encouraging my warriors

to protect our lodges, and we at length succeeded in beating them off, although they drove away over twelve hundred head of our horses with them, without any possibility of our wresting them from them, at least at that time. We lost thirteen warriors killed, twelve of whom were scalped, and about thirty wounded. It is a wonder we did not suffer a loss three times more severe. But the Black Feet are not steady warriors; they become too much excited in action, and lose many opportunities of inflicting mischief. If bluster would defeat a foe, their battles would be a succession of victories. Had we in the least mistrusted an attack, by being in readiness we could have repulsed them without the least effort. But they caught us totally unprepared; there was not a man at his post until they were about to fall upon us. The enemy lost forty-eight scalps in the encounter, besides a number of dead and wounded they carried away with them without our being able to lay hands upon them. They had also over one hundred horses shot under them.

We suffered a severe loss in the death of the veteran brave Red Child, the hero of a hundred fights, who was killed and scalped at his lodge door. His wife, who was by, struck the Indian who scalped him with a club, but she did not strike him hard enough to disable him. The loss of the old brave was severely felt by the whole nation. The crying and mourning which ensued pained me more than the loss of our horses. After spending the night in mourning, we moved on to the other division, to carry the woful tidings of our reverse. When we rejoined them there was a general time of crying. I took a great share of the blame to myself, as it was upon my proposition that the village had been divided and the disaster sustained. I suggested it with a view to facilitate business, never dreaming of an attack by such an overwhelming force.

When the excitement had subsided, I determined to wash their faces or perish in the attempt. I ordered every one that could work to engage in the erection of a fort in the timber, sufficiently large to hold all our lodges, laying out the work myself, and seeing it well under way. I directed them, when they had finished the construction, to move their lodges into it, and remain there till my return, for, thus protected, they could beat off ten times their number.

I then took nearly seven hundred of our best warriors, and started for the Black Feet, resolved upon revenge, and careless how many I fell in with.

A small party had recently come in with two scalps, which they had obtained near the head of Lewis's Fork, Columbia River. They reported a large village of eight hundred lodges, from which numerous war-parties had departed, as they had crossed their trails in coming home. They knew the direct road to the village, how it was situated, and all about it, which was of great service to me. I therefore took them with me, and employed them as scouts. Every warrior was well provided for hard service; each man had a riding-horse, and led his war-horse by his side.

On the seventh day we came in view of their village, but we deferred our attack till the next day. The enemy had chosen a very good position; they were encamped on a large bend of the river, at that time shallow and fordable every where. I detached fifty of my warriors for a feint, while I stole round with the main body to the high ground, taking care to keep out of sight of the enemy. Having gained my position, I signaled to the light division to feign an attack, while my men were so excited I could hardly restrain them from rushing out and defeating my purpose. My plan succeeded admirably. The Black Feet, having suffered themselves to be decoyed from their position by the flight of the fifty warriors, I sounded a charge, and my men rushed upon the unprotected village like a thunderbolt. We swept every thing before us; the women took to the bush like partridges; the warriors fled in every direction. They were so paralyzed at our unexpected descent that no defense was attempted. I threw myself among the thickest group I could see, and positively hacked down seventeen who pretended to be warriors without receiving a scratch, although my shield was pretty well cut with arrows. If my warriors had all come to their work according to the example that even the heroine set them, not one of the Black Feet who ventured to show fight would have escaped. The heroine killed three warriors with her lance, and took two fine little boys prisoners. We found but about a thousand warriors to oppose us, while there were lodges enough to contain three times the number. We only took sixty-eight scalps after all our trouble—a thing I could not account for. We took thirty women and children prisoners, and drove home near two thousand head of horses, among which were many of our own.

As I had never seen the Black Feet fight so well as at the fort, I expected an equal display of valor on this occasion, but they offered nothing worthy the name of defense. I learned from my prisoners that my old father-in-law was in that village, whose daughter I had nearly killed for dancing over the scalps of the white men. We had only one warrior wounded, who was shot through the thigh; but it was not broken, and, like all Indian wounds, it soon got well. We reached home in less than four days; and, after our arrival, singing and dancing were kept up for a week.

In taking prisoners from an enemy we gain much useful information, as there are always more or less of their tribe domiciliated with us, to whom the captives impart confidence; these relate all that they hear to the chiefs, thus affording much serviceable information that could not otherwise be obtained. The women seem to care but little for their captivity, more particularly the young women, who have neither husbands nor children to attach them to their own tribe. They like Crow husbands, because they keep them painted most of the time with the emblems of triumph, and do not whip them like their Black Foot husbands. Certain it is that, when once captured by us, none of them ever wished to return to their own nation. In our numerous campaigns that winter we also took an unusual number of boys, all of whom make excellent Crow warriors, so that our numbers considerably increased from our prisoners alone. Some of the best warriors in the Crow nation had been boys taken from the surrounding tribes. They had been brought up with us, had played with our children, and fought their miniature sham-battles together, had grown into men, become warriors, braves, and so on to the council, until they were far enough advanced to become expert horse-thieves.

That winter was an exceedingly fortunate one for the Crow nation; success crowned almost every expedition. Long Hair's warriors achieved some great triumphs over the Black Feet, and in one battle took nearly a hundred scalps.

When Long Hair heard of our misfortune at the

fort, he sent a messenger to our village to offer some of his warriors to assist us in retrieving our reverse. But before the arrival of the messenger we had been and returned, and were all in the height of rejoicing. He hastened back to his village to impart the glad tidings, in order that they might rejoice with us.

We then engaged in trapping beaver and hunting buffalo for the next three weeks, during which time we suffered no molestation from any of our enemies.

CHAPTER XXVI.

Deputation from the As-ne-boines.—Characteristic Speech of Yellow Belly.—Visit to the Fort.—Visit to Fort Union.—Rescue of Five White Men from Starvation.—Arrival at Fort Cass.—Departure for the Village.—Visit of the Snakes to the Crows.

WE received another deputation from the As-ne-boines to sue for a renewal of peace. We had lost a warrior and two women, who had been massacred when away from the village, and on discovery of the bodies we followed the trail of the perpetrators in the direction of the Black Foot country. We eventually discovered that many petty outrages, which we had charged upon the Black Feet, were in reality committed by the treacherous As-ne-boines. On their return from their thievish inroads they were in the habit of proceeding very near to a Black Foot village, with which they were at peace, and then, turning obliquely, would cross the Missouri into their own country. Becoming acquainted with this oft-repeated *ruse*, we determined to chastise them. I accordingly crossed the Missouri with a force of eight hundred and fifty men, and invaded their territory with the determination to inflict upon them such a chastisement as should recall them to a sense of decency. We encountered a small village, only numbering forty lodges, on their way to Fort Union, and within a few hundred yards of the fort. Seeing our approach, they intrenched themselves in a hollow, rendering our assault a work of danger. But we stormed their position, and killed twenty-six warriors (all of whom we scalped); the remainder we could not get at, as we found their position impregnable.

Admonished by this chastisement, they sent another deputation to us to treat for the re-establishment of peace. But their propositions were unfavorably received, and Yellow Belly favored them with his sentiments in the following rather unpalatable and characteristic strain:

"No," said he, in answer to their representations, "we make peace with you no more. You are dogs—you are women-slayers—you are unworthy of the confidence or notice of our people. You lie when you come and say that you want peace. You have crooked and forked tongues: they are subtle like the tongue of the serpent. Your hearts are corrupt: they are offensive in our nostrils. We made peace with you before because we pitied you; we looked upon you with contempt, as not even worthy to be killed by the Sparrowhawks. We did not wish for your scalps: they disgrace our others; we never mix them even with those of the Black Feet. When we are compelled to take them from you on account of your treachery, we give them to our pack-dogs, and even they howl at them. Before, we gave you horses to carry you home, and guns to kill your buffalo; we gave you meat and drink; you ate, and drank, and smoked with us. After all this, you considered yourselves great braves in scalping two of our women.   Our women would rub out your nation and put out all your fires if we should let them loose at you.   Come and steal our horses when you think best, and get caught at it if you want to feel the weight of our tomahawks.   Go! we will not make peace with you; go!"

After this very cordial reception, we had no more intercourse with the As-ne-boines for some time.

Shortly after the departure of this delegation, we set out for the fort to trade away our peltry, which amounted to a considerable number of packs.   On arriving there, I found a letter from a Mr. Halsey, who then had charge of Fort Union, the head-quarters of the American Fur Company.   The letter was couched in rather strong terms, and was evidently written when he was under the influence of temper.   The company had their trading-posts among every tribe with which the Crows were at war, and for many months past there had been a great falling off in trade.   The Indians had brought in but little peltry, and the universal complaint among all was that it took all their time to defend themselves against the Crows.   The Crows had killed scores of their warriors; the Crows had stolen all their horses; the Crows had captured their women and children; the Crows had kept them mourning and crying; their trappers dare not go out to trap for fear of the Crows; their hunters dare not, and could not, kill buffalo for fear of the Crows; in short, by this letter it appeared that the poor Crows were the constant terror of all the surrounding tribes.

He concluded his epistle, "For ——'s sake, do keep your d—d Indians at home, so that the other tribes may have a chance to work a little, and the company may drive a more profitable business."

I knew perfectly well that these incessant wars were very prejudicial to the company's interest, but it was impossible for me to remedy the evil. Other tribes were continually attacking the Crows, killing their braves, and stealing their horses, and, of course, they were bound to make reprisals. In justice to the Crows I must say, that other tribes were generally the aggressors, until the policy was forced upon me of endeavoring to "conquer a peace." I thought, if I could make the Crow nation a terror to all their neighbors, that their antagonists would be reduced to petition for peace, and then turn their battle-axes into beaver-traps, and their lances into hunting-knives.

Our villages, having made their purchases, left the fort, but staid in the vicinity, engaged in trapping and making robes. The letter I had just received from Halsey requested my attendance on him that spring. I left my people, and went down the river to Fort Union. On arriving, I found a large body of the As-ne-boines encamped near the fort. Their chiefs immediately came to me, wishing me to conclude peace with them as representative of the Crow nation. They attempted to palliate their late misdeeds by throwing the blame on a few As-ne-boine desperadoes, who had acted without the authority or the cognizance of the national council, and that they had been severely punished by the tribe for their excesses.

In answer, I told them that I had no authority to conclude peace; that, even if I had, they would not observe a peace longer than one moon; that I thought the Crows would throw difficulties in the way of entertaining their propositions, but that they could apply to the council again, and learn how they were inclined.

Mr. Halsey and all the sub-traders present interceded with me to exert myself in establishing a peace between the two nations, which request I promised to comply with. The chiefs inquired whether we would take their lives in the event of their visiting us on such a mission. I assured them that the Crows would hold their lives sacred; that they were not dogs, as many nations were, but that they were a great and magnanimous nation, whose power was predominant, and who killed no enemies but in battle.

I remained at the fort about three weeks, and, as most of the sub-traders, clerks, and interpreters were in, we had a glorious time. It was at least three or four years since I had last visited there; for, though I fought a battle outside its walls lately, I did not see fit at that time to make them a call.

The boats being ready to return, I started with them, but their progress was so slow and wearisome on their way up to the Yellow Stone that I leaped ashore, intending to make my way over dry land. I have always rejoiced that I was prompted to take that step, for I became instrumental thereby in performing a merciful deed among so many that might be termed unmerciful.

I had not traveled more than three miles when I came across a white man, named Fuller, in a famishing condition. I had a companion with me, whom I started off to the boats to bid them prepare something suitable to recover the poor fellow, and to order them to touch on shore when they came to where he lay. Fuller was quite delirious. I had discovered him just in the nick of time, as he could not have survived many hours longer. My companion was not long in performing his errand, and, when the boat touched for him, we carried him on board, and gave him tea and warm restoratives. He shortly revived, and then gave me to understand, in a very incoherent manner, that he had four companions in a similar condition near to where I had found him.

At this intelligence we went on shore again to succor them also. We had a long hunt before we succeeded in finding them, and when we at last discovered them, we found them picking and eating rosebuds, or, rather, the pods containing seed of last year's growth. When they saw us approaching they attempted to run, supposing us to be Indians; but, their strength failing them, they sought to conceal themselves in the bushes. We made known our errand to them, and invited them on board the boat. Our opportune offer of service seemed so providential, that the fortitude of the poor famishing fellows could not sustain them, and they all gave way to a plentiful flood of tears. We conveyed them on board the boat, and furnished them with food adapted to their emaciated condition.

When in some measure restored, they informed us that they had been trapping in the mountains, their party originally consisting of eleven men; that they were on their road to Fort Cass, with their pack-horses and four packs of beaver, when they were set upon by the Black Feet, who killed six of their party, and despoiled them of every article they had, and it was by a miracle that they escaped from their hands. When they had supposed themselves near the fort, they saw a great number of Indians, whom they took for Black Feet; to avoid them, they took a wide circuit through the prairie. The Indians whom they mistook for Black Feet were a party of Crows, and if they had gone up to them and made their case known, the Crows would have escorted them to the fort, and probably have pursued the Black Feet, and have retaken their property. On returning from their circuit, they struck the river a great distance below the fort, and were still traveling down the river in search of it. They had nothing to eat, and nothing to kill game with to relieve their wants. They went on with the boats, while I and my companion resumed our "over-land route."

We reached the fort several days in advance of the boats. I only rested one night there, and then proceeded directly on to my Indian home. Shortly after my arrival there, the villages moved on up the river, proceeding leisurely, and killing buffalo and dressing robes on the way. We finally reached the mountain streams, and, as it was now near September, the beaver were getting to be in fine condition for trapping.

We had at this time a visit from eight hundred lodges of the Snakes, who came for the purpose of trading, as they had no trading-post of their own. They remained with us several weeks, and ·we had a very agreeable time together. This furnished me with an opportunity of enlarging to the Crows upon the superior delights of peace. We could visit the lodges of our Snake friends, and they could visit ours without cutting each other's throats. Our women could chatter together, our children gambol and have their sham-battles together, while the old veterans could talk over their achievements, and smile at the mimic war-hoops of their children. They could also trade together, and derive mutual benefit from the fair exchange of commodities. I contrasted this with the incessant butcheries that distinguished their intercourse with some tribes, and asked them which relation was the more desirable.

The Crows had many things to trade away which they had no need for, or, if they had needed them, they could replace them with a fresh supply from the fort. The nation was desirous that their guests should see the trading-post, where all their goods were stored beyond the reach of their enemies, and whence they drew their supplies as often as they had need of them; for the simple Crows supposed that the posts, with their contents, were the property of the nation, and that the whites who were in charge there were their own agents. To gratify their natural pride, I led a party to the fort, among whom were two hundred of our Snake visitors. On entering the fort, and looking over the store-house, they were struck dumb with astonishment; they could not comprehend the vastness of the wealth that was displayed before them. They had never before seen a depôt of goods, and this exceeded all they had any previous experience of. The rows of guns highly polished, the battle-axes, lance-blades, scarlet cloth, beads, and many curiosities they had never seen before, filled them with admiration; they could not gaze sufficiently at these indications of our wealth.

They inquired of the Crows whether our nation made all those articles there. They told them that they did not; that they were made at our great fort below, in comparison with which this was but a small lodge; that all our supplies were manufactured there, and brought up the river in great boats by our white friends.

They then inquired by what means they had gained the alliance of the whites; that, instead of killing them and banishing them from their hunting-ground, as they did to many nations, they should give themselves the great trouble to serve them with their boats, and bring them such immense supplies.

The Crows informed them that their great chief, the Medicine Calf, had been instrumental in accomplishing all this. By his long residence with the whites, after his sale to them by the Cheyennes when he had become a great brave, he had gained surprising influence with the great white chief, who loved the Medicine Calf, and had taught him to make forts, and had suffered him to come back to his people in order to teach them to become great, and overcome all their enemies.

The Snakes were wonder-stricken at such marvels. The unassailable fort (which a single bomb-shell would have blown to atoms), filled with an inexhaustible store of rich goods; our great fort down the river, in comparison with which this was but a small lodge, and where all these marvelous products of our ingenuity were manufactured; our mysterious connection with the whites, which procured us the advantage of their unremunerated services, and shielded us with the irresistible succor of the great white chief—all this overpowered their imagination. The wealth and power of the Crow nation exceeded all conception, and to oppose them in war was to incur unavoidable destruction.

After the Snakes had traded off their stock of peltry, obtaining large supplies in exchange, we returned to the village. They had wonderful narratives of the big fort and wealth of the Crow nation to spin to their fellow-villagers. In fact, they were so impressed with the idea of our superiority that two hundred lodges of the Snakes joined our nation, and never separated from them. They had a chief of their own, but conformed to our laws and regulations, proving themselves faithful *fellow-citizens*, and emulating our best warriors in battle. This coalition increased our force to the number of five hundred warriors—more than we had lost in battle for four years preceding. They intermarried with our women, and in a few years were so completely transformed that they had quite forgotten their Snake origin. On our return, the remainder of our friends left us.

During our absence the Black Feet had invaded our dominion, and made off with upward of three thousand of our horses, very greatly to our detriment. The Snakes were anxious to pursue them, or, at least, to assist their hosts in recapturing their stolen property, but Long Hair declined their proffered service. He said, "No, I am too old to run after them, and the warriors must have some one to direct them. Should any accident befall my people, the medicine chief would be grieved. We must wait his return from the fort; if he then deems it proper to punish them, he will not be long without the means."

Our villages still remained together, and we moved on to the head-waters of the Yellow Stone. We had several war-parties out, and some endeavoring to retrieve our equine losses, while those who remained in the village applied themselves to trapping and hunting. The Snake women were very skillful in dressing robes —far superior to our own, as they had been more engaged in it.

My warriors were again burning with the desire for war and horse-raids, although our prairies were alive with animals. Inaction seemed to consume them. In spite of my prohibition, they would steal away in parties during the night. When convicted, I would inflict severe floggings upon them by my Dog Soldiers (who did not spare the lash); but it was to little purpose. In fact, they took it as honorable distinction to receive a lashing, inasmuch as it indicated their overruling ardor for war; and the culprit who received a flogging this morning for disobedience of orders, was sure to be off at night again.   An old warrior despises the sight of a trap; hunting buffalo, even, does not afford him excitement enough.   Nothing but war or a horse-raid is a business worth their attending to, and the chief who seeks to control this predilection too far loses popularity.

Accordingly, I gave way to the general desire of my warriors.   I selected one hundred and sixty trusty braves, intending "to lay alongside" my old friends the Black Feet, and wipe out one or two old scores I had marked against them.   I invaded their territory with my little force, and marched on, admonishing my spies to extreme vigilance.   We came in sight of a village, and secreted ourselves till the proper hour of night. On our march we discovered a single Indian.   Some of the party called him to them, and clubbed him down and scalped him.   He had mistaken us for his own people.

At midnight we visited their herd, and drove out six hundred and forty head.   A number of their best cattle were tied at the doors of their lodges and in their corrals.   I arrived home safe with my booty, and, as I had taken one scalp, we had a great dance.   All our other parties were very successful, excepting one.   That was one that had gone on an expedition against the Arrap-a-hos.   Pine Leaf was in the number.   They had taken about a thousand horses, and, having reached a distance that they supposed safe, they slackened their pace, and were proceeding carelessly along.   Suddenly their pursuers came in sight—a strong posse comitatus—and retook all their animals except those that bore the fugitives, and killed three of their comrades. The heroine came back in mourning, looking like the last of her race.

One of our victorious parties brought back fifty boys and girls whom they had captured while gathering fruit. Since the loss of our three thousand horses to the Black Feet we had captured six thousand, two thousand five hundred of which had been recovered from the Black Feet.

We now moved on to the Yellow Stone, and crossed it, the villages still keeping together. We then journeyed on slowly in the direction of the fort, trapping and hunting all the way. We kept a vigilant eye upon our prisoners, for fear they might attempt an escape to their own tribes, and thus bring upon us a foe when we had no time to attend to him.

This was a very productive fall for peltry, and we sent in great quantities to the fort in advance of our arrival. I remained at the trading-post nearly the whole of the winter. In the early spring the Crows sent for me to rejoin them. I went, accordingly, and found that their long-continued good fortune had suffered a reverse. They had grown careless in their expeditions, and had lost some of their warriors. They wished my aid to revenge their deaths and wash their faces.

I required them to defer their retaliation until their robes were dressed and sent to the fort. They took hold of the business in good earnest, and every robe was soon ready for market.

It was now time to plant our tobacco, and we all moved in the direction of our planting-ground. The seed was put in, and the attending ceremonial gone through with. Our pacific business thus completed, the warriors began to prepare for war. Our horses had been but little used during the winter, and they were all fat and in high condition.

I took three hundred and sixty warriors and went against the Cheyennes. We discovered a moving village of sixty lodges, charged on it, and bore away nine scalps, with considerable booty, without losing one drop of blood. Pine Leaf was in my party, and being so unfortunate as not to count one *coo*, she was greatly out of humor, and blamed me for depriving her of the opportunity of killing an enemy. The truth is, we had no time to favor her, as I was desirous to secure our booty and get off without endangering the loss of a man.

Her young Black Foot prisoner had become quite a warrior; he went to war constantly, and bid fair to equal his captor in valor. He was already a match for an ordinary Sioux warrior, and took great pride in his sister Pine Leaf.

All our war-parties returned without loss, and the nation resumed its customary good spirits. I then returned to the fort, where I rested all the summer.

My thoughts had for a long time past reverted to home. Year after year had rolled away, and now that I had attained middle life, they seemed to pass me with accelerated pace, and the question would intrude upon my mind, What had I done? When I abandoned myself seriously to reflection, it seemed as if I had slumbered away the last twelve years. Others had accomplished the same toils as myself, and were now enjoying the fruits of their labor, and living in luxury and ease.

But what had been my career? and what advance had I made toward this desirable consummation? I had just visited the Indian territory to gratify a youthful thirst for adventure; I had narrowly escaped starvation in a service in which I had no interest; I had traversed the fastnesses of the far Rocky Mountains in summer heats and winter frosts; I had encountered savage beasts and wild men, until my deliverance was a prevailing miracle. By the mere *badinage* of a fellow-trapper I had been adopted among the savages, and had conformed my superior habits to their ruthless and untutored ways; I had accompanied them in their mutual slaughters, and dyed my hand crimson with the blood of victims who had never injured me; I had distinguished myself in my barbarian seclusion, and had risen to supreme command in the nation I had devoted myself to. And what had I to show for so much wasted energy, and such a catalogue of ruthless deeds?

I had been the means of saving many a fellow-creature's life. Did they still owe me gratitude? Possibly some few did, while others had forgotten my name. In good truth, when I sought the results of my prolonged labors, I found I had simply wasted my time. I had bestowed years upon others, and only moments upon myself.

However, I still lived, and there was yet time to take more heed unto my ways. I resolved to go home and see my friends, and deliver myself from this present vagabond life. The attachments I had formed during my savage chieftainship still retained some hold upon my affections, and it was barely possible I might return to them, and end my days among my trusty braves. There at least was fidelity; and, when my soul should depart for the spirit land, their rude faith would prompt them to paint my bones, and treasure them until I should visit them from my ever-flowering hunting-ground, and demand them at their hands.

Such sober thoughts as these occupied my mind during my summer residence at the fort. I had brought with me all the peltry we had accumulated, in order to be in season for the boats, which were soon to start for the lower fort. I had directed the village to follow along with whatever peltry they might collect before the departure of the boats.

In obedience to this instruction, about two hundred and fifty warriors came down, bringing their commodities with them; but the boats had gone, and I still was waiting at the fort.

One day a party of my men were out to hunt buffalo for our own use, when they accidentally scared up eleven Black Feet, who were lurking about on the look-out for horses. They chased them into our old camping-ground, and the fugitives had taken refuge in our old temporary fort. I was sitting at the fort the while, busily conversing with persons present; I heard the report of their guns, and supposed, if the affair proved serious, I should be promptly sent for. Bad Hand, one of my leaders, finally said, "They are fighting out yonder, and I don't suppose they can do any thing without we are with them. Let us go."

We each threw on a chief's coat, and went down to see how matters stood. I found the Black Feet fortified in their position, and our men ineffectually firing upon them. I ordered an immediate assault, placing myself at their head. We advanced a few paces at a rapid rate, when I fell senseless, with the blood gushing from my mouth in a stream. All supposed me mortally wounded, and I was carried into the fort to breathe my last.

The boats had left, and Tulleck happened to be starting after them just as I was carried in. Seeing my wounded condition, and every one pronouncing me in a dying state, he reported me as being dead at the lower fort, whence the news traveled to my friends in St. Louis that I had been killed in a fight with the Indians.

In an hour or two it was discovered that there was still life in me, and that I was reviving. I was examined: there was no bullet-wound on my body, and again it was proved that my broad-bladed hunting-knife (though not the same one) had averted the blow. It had been struck with an ounce of lead impelled with the full force of gunpowder. I speedily recovered, but continued sore for a long time.

Every Black Foot was killed by my men, who scaled their defense and leaped upon them in such numbers that they almost smothered them. Only four of my warriors were wounded. Intelligence of my injury was sent to the village, which was three weeks in reaching them. One thousand warriors instantly set out for the fort, all my wives accompanying them; but I had recovered before their arrival.

Our party had scarcely encamped outside the fort, when the Black Feet, who were always haunting us, stole about eight hundred head of horses. On discovering the theft, a large party started on their trail up the river. The depredators would have to cross the river to get home, and there was no crossing for horses nearer than fifteen miles, after which they had to go on to the Mussel Shell, a distance of twenty miles farther, and only ten from the fort. I knew that this would be the route of the fugitives, because it was their regular beat. I had had no thought of going until it suddenly occurred to me that the party in pursuit would most likely fail to overtake the thieves, while

I had so admirable an opportunity to catch them on the Mussel Shell. I took a party, therefore, forded the river near the fort, and went on straight to the Mussel Shell, where I posted my men. Our unsuspecting victims came up, singing in great merriment, and driving our horses before them, all of which were jaded. I suffered them to approach close upon us, and then gave the word to charge. Never was a party taken more by surprise; they were too dumbfoundered to offer resistance, and all we had to do was to chop them down. We had their twenty-four scalps in little more than the same number of seconds.

When the other party came up and found the work done, they thought we had been rained down there. They knew they had left us at the fort, and we had not passed them on the way, and where did we come from?

Pine Leaf was with the party, and she was ready to blow me off my horse. It was unfair to take the job out of their hands, after they had almost run their horses off their legs in the chase. I expressed my regret at the fortunate turn affairs had taken, and promised never to offend in the same manner again; but it was a long while before I could banter her into good humor.

I remained at the fort all the summer (as before stated), intending to go down the river on my way to St. Louis with the last boats in the fall. While idling there, I found the five men whom I had rescued from starvation in a penniless condition, and unable to go to work again. It seemed the company had issued orders to their agents to furnish no more outfits to free trappers on their personal credit, as the risk was too great, from their extreme liability to be killed by the Indians. To engage to work for the company at the price they were paying hands was only perpetuating their poverty; for they were running the same risk of their lives as if trapping for themselves, and their remuneration was but as one to ten. They were downhearted, and knew not what to do. Considering their sad condition, I determined to befriend them, and risk the chances. I therefore offered to give them an excellent outfit, and direct them to the best beaver-ground in the Crow nation, where they would be protected from all harm by my Crow warriors as my friends, my interest to be one half of the proceeds.

This offer was cheerfully accepted by the five men, and they were highly elated at the prospect. I then acquainted the Crows that those men were my friends; that they were the remains of a party of eleven, of whom six had been killed by the Black Feet, who had despoiled them of every thing they had, and that I had found these in the prairie almost famished to death. I had engaged them to stay in the nation and trap for me, and I wished my faithful Crow braves to protect them in their pursuit, and suffer none to offer them molestation. This they all readily promised to do, and were even pleased with the trust; for it was a belief with the Crows that the beavers in their streams were too numerous ever to be diminished. My bosom friend offered to remain with them, to show them the best streams, and render them all the assistance in his power. He was a most valuable auxiliary, as his skill in trapping I never saw excelled. They went to work, and met with extraordinary success; my share of their labors of less than three months amounted to five thousand dollars.

CHAPTER XXVII.

Departure for St. Louis.—Visit Fort Union.—Fort Clarke.—Descend
to the A-rick-a-ra Country.—Am taken Prisoner.—Extraordinary
Means of Release.—Reach St. Louis.—Scarcely recognized by my
Sisters.—Changes.—Estrangement of Friends.—Sigh for my Indian Home.

THE Sparrowhawk nation was all assembled at the
fort, to take leave of the Medicine Calf for several moons.
The boats had arrived filled with a fresh stock of goods,
and the nation made purchases to the amount of many
thousands of dollars.   The boats being now ready to
return again, I made a short address to my people before I bade them adieu.

" Sparrowhawks !" I said, "I am going to leave you
for a few moons, to visit my friends among the white
men.   I shall return to you by Green Grass, when the
boats come back from the country of the whites.   While
I am away, I desire you to remember the counsel I
have often given you.   I wish you to send out no war-
parties, because you want for nothing, and your nation
is feared by all the neighboring tribes.   Keep a good
look-out over your horses, so as to afford the enemy no
opportunity of stealing them.   It is through carelessness in the horse-guards that one half the horses are
lost, and it is the loss of horses that leads to half the
battles that you fight.   It is better not to have your
horses stolen in the first place, than to steal more in
the place of those you have lost.

" I also commend Mr. Tulleck to your care, as well
as all the inmates of the fort.   Visit them often, and

see that they are not besieged or starved out by their enemies. Do not let the Black Feet or any other bad Indians harm them. Behave yourselves as becomes my faithful Crows. Adieu!"

They all promised obedience to my instructions, and I was soon on board. The boats were cast loose, and we were borne rapidly down stream by the swift current of the Yellow Stone.

We called at Fort Union, and I staid there three days. Here I had a fine canoe built, and two oarsmen furnished me to carry me to St. Louis. I was bearer of a large package of letters; and when my little craft was finished, I stepped on board and launched out upon the swift-rolling current of the Missouri. After the brilliant opportunities I had had of realizing a princely fortune, my only wealth consisted of an order upon the company for seven thousand eight hundred dollars.

Arriving at Fort Clarke, we made another short stay. The A-rick-a-ras, whose country was some hundred and fifty miles farther down, had just stolen nearly all the horses belonging to the fort. Bellemaire, the interpreter of the fort, proposed to me to go after them, and see if we could recover some of the horses. I consented, and we went down to their village in my canoe, and on our arrival there found them all dancing. Antoine Garro, with two relatives, were in the number. On seeing our approach, one shouted, "Here come white men!" and Garro and his brother instantly sprang toward us and pushed us into a lodge, where we were apparently prisoners. A council was summoned to decide upon our fate, and I had but slight hopes of ever seeing St. Louis. A young Indian came at that moment, and mentioned in a whisper to Peter that there was a large boat approaching. He made a long harangue before the others, in which he earnestly and energetically declaimed against taking the lives of white men. He concluded his oration by saying, "You have now my opinion, and remember, if you decide upon taking these white men's lives, I stay with you no longer." He then left the council and went down to the boat, where he advised the occupants to cross to the other side of the river, as the Indians were at that moment deliberating upon the fate of Bellemaire and three others. Garro's father happened to be on board, who was a great man among the Indians, and, on learning what business was in hand, he provided himself with a club, and entered the village with his son Peter. He then set about the council, and administered to all the members such a hearty thrashing, laying about him as if fighting wild bulls, that I thought he must surely slay some of them.

"There!" exclaimed the old man, after having belabored them till he was out of breath, "I'll teach you to deliberate on the lives of white men, dogs as ye are!"

The Indians offered no resistance, and said not a word. We remained all night with old Garro's company, and returned to the fort in the morning. Bellemaire recovered his own horses, but could obtain none belonging to the fort. We called at all the forts that lay in our way, to collect what dispatches they had to send, making but brief stay, however, as I was impatient to be getting on. At Fort Canaille I obtained a passenger, a son of Mr. Pappen, who was going to St. Louis, and I received reiterated charges to be very careful of him.

Soon after our departure from the fort there came on a cold rain-storm, which lasted several hours; the storm raged fiercely, and we had to make fast to a snag in the middle of the river to save ourselves from driving ashore. I had my Indian fire-striker, and, amid all the wind and rain, I repeatedly lit my pipe. My young passenger was astonished at the performance. "If you can strike a fire," he exclaimed, "in such a storm as this, I do not fear perishing."

When the storm had somewhat abated, we landed to encamp. I shot two fat wild turkeys, which were quite a rarity to me, after having lived so many years on buffalo-meat, there being no turkeys in the Crow country. On arriving at Jefferson City I felt quite sick, and showed symptoms of fever; but I was anxious to reach home without laying up. A steamboat coming down the river, I went on board, canoe and all, and was soon landed on the dock of St. Louis.

It was fourteen years since I had last seen the city, and what a difference was observable in those few years! But I was too sick to take much notice of things, and hastened to my sister's house, accompanied by the carpenter of the boat.

He rapped; the door was opened by my younger sister; I was supporting myself against the wall. Greetings passed between them, for my companion was acquainted with my family; and he then informed her that he was the bearer of sad news—her brother James was dead.

My sister Louise began to cry, and informed him they had learned the news some weeks since.

Then turning to me, he said, "Come in, Jim, and see your sister cry for you."

I advanced, and addressed her in my old familiar manner, "How do you do, Lou?"

I must have been a curious looking object for an affectionate sister to recognize. All my clothing consisted of dressed antelope, deer, and the skins of mountain sheep, highly ornamented by my Indian wives. My long hair, as black as the raven's wing, descended to my hips, and I presented more the appearance of a Crow than that of a civilized being.

She gazed at me for a moment with a searching look, and then exclaiming, "My God, it is my brother!" she flew into my arms, and was for some time unable to speak.

At length she said, "We received a letter informing us of your death, and that Mr. Tulleck had seen you borne into Fort Cass dead."

My elder sister, Matilda, was up stairs, entertaining a few female friends, and Lou bounded up stairs to acquaint her that her brother James wished to speak to her.

Thinking her to be jesting, she said, "Are you not ashamed of yourself to jest on such a subject?" and she shed tears at thus having me recalled to remembrance.

Louise asseverated her earnestness, and Matilda reproved her for her wantonness, but would not budge to go and see for herself. At length a Mrs. Le Fèvre said, "Matilda, I believe she is in earnest, and if you do not go and see, I will."

She had been a child with me, and we used to repeat our catechism together; now she was married, and the mother of several children.

She came tripping down stairs into my sister's apartment, making a ceremonious courtesy as she entered. My sister introduced her to me, asking me if I did not recollect my *commère* (for we were baptized together). I had forgotten her, but the mention of this circumstance recalled her to my mind, and there was another embracing.

Her faith being thus confirmed, my sister Matilda was called down, and my reception from her was even more cordial than from the preceding friends. She was a woman of great warmth of feeling, and her heart was full to overflowing with the emotions my name had called up. She was the eldest of the family, and since our mother's death she had been at once mother and sister to us all. Although I was the vagrant of the family, I still lived in her sisterly heart, and the supposition that my earthly career was closed had only hallowed my memory in her affections.

This was my second reception by my relatives after I had been supposed dead. One by my savage friends, who, in welcoming me as their long-lost child, exhibited all the genuine emotions of untutored nature; and this second by my civilized friends, who, if less energetic in their demonstrations of attachment, showed equal heartfelt joy, equal sincerity, and far superior decorum.

The following morning I visited the company's office and delivered my letters. I became too weak to walk home, and Mr. Chouteau very obligingly drove me back in his carriage. I was compelled to take to my bed, where I was confined for several days, under good medical attendance, and most assiduously attended by my relatives.

Their answers to my many inquiries confounded me entirely.

" Where is my father ?"

" He went back to Virginia, and died there many years ago."

" Where are my brothers ?"

" They are scattered about the country."

" Where is such and such a friend ?"

"In his grave."

"Where is Eliza?"

"She was married a month ago, after receiving intelligence of your certain death."

I ceased my querying, and averted my eyes from my sister's gaze.

And this, I mused, is my return home after years of bright anticipations of welcome! This is my secure and sunshiny haven, after so long and dangerous a voyage! My father dead, my brothers dispersed, my friends in their graves, and my loved one married! She did well—I have no right to complain—she is lost to me forever! If a man's home exists in the heart of his friends, with the death and alienation of those friends his cherished home fades away, and he is again a wanderer upon the earth.

I do not know whether it was disappointment at so much death, mutation, and estrangement, or whether I bore the disease immediately in my own heart, but I was disappointed in my return home; the anticipations I had formed were not realized—a feeling of cynicism passed over me. I thought of my Indian home, and of the unsophisticated hearts I had left behind me. Their lives were savage, and their perpetual animosities repulsive, but with this dark background there was much vivid coloring in relief. If the Indian was unrelenting, and murdered with his lance, his battle-axe, and his knife, his white brother was equally unfeeling, and had ways of torturing his victim, if less violent, not the less certain. The savage is artless, and when you win his admiration there is no envious reservation to prompt him to do injustice to your name. You live among them honored; and on your death, your bones are stored religiously in their great cave along with

others of preceding generations, to be each year visited, and painted, and reflected on by a host of devoted
companions. There is not the elegance there, the luxury, the refined breeding, but there is rude plenty,
prairies studded with horses, and room to wander without any man to call your steps in question. My child
was there, and his mother, whom I loved; a return
there was in no way unnatural. I had acquired their
habits, and was in some manner useful to them. I had
no tie to hold me here, and I already almost determined upon returning to my Indian home.

Such thoughts as these, as I lay on my sick-bed,
passed continuously through my mind. A few of my
early friends, as they heard of my return, came one
after the other to visit me; but they were all changed.
The flight of time had wrought furrows upon their
smooth brows, and the shadow of the wings of Time
was resting upon the few fair cheeks I had known in
my younger days.

CHAPTER XXVIII.

Disagreeable Rencounters in St. Louis.—Messenger arrives from Fort
Cass.—Imminent Peril of the Whites from the Infuriated Crows.—
The Cause.—Immediate Return.—Incidents of my Arrival.—Pine
Leaf substituted for Eliza.—Last Battle with the Black Feet.—
Final Adieu to the Crows.

IT now comes in the order of relation to describe two
or three unpleasant rencounters I had with various parties in St. Louis, growing out of the misunderstanding
(already related) between the Crows and Mr. Fitzpatrick's party. I had already heard reports in the mountains detrimental to my character for my supposed ac-

tion in the matter, but I had never paid much attention to them. Friends had cautioned me that there were large sums of money offered for my life, and that several men had even undertaken to earn the rewards. I could not credit such friendly intimations; still I thought, on the principle that there is never smoke but there is fire, that it would be as well to keep myself a little on my guard.

I had recovered from my sickness, and I spent much of my time about town. My friends repeatedly inquired of me if I had seen Fitzpatrick. Wondering how so much interest could attach to my meeting with that man, I asked one day what reason there was for making the inquiry. My friend answered, "I don't wish you to adduce me as authority; but there are strong threats of taking your life for an alleged robbery of Fitzpatrick by the Crow nation, in which you were deeply concerned."

I saw now what to prepare for, although I still inclined to doubt that any man, possessed of ordinary perceptions, could charge me with an offense of which I was so manifestly innocent. True, I had met Fitzpatrick several times, and, instead of his former cordial salutation, it was with difficulty he addressed a civil word to me.

Shortly after this conversation with my friend I went to the St. Louis Theatre. Between the pieces I had stepped to the saloon to obtain some refreshments, and I saw Fitzpatrick enter, with four other not very respectable citizens. They advanced directly toward me. Fitzpatrick then pointed me out to them, saying, "There's the Crow."

"Then," said the others, "we are Black Feet, and let us have his scalp."

They immediately drew their knives and rushed on me.

I then thought of my friend's salutary counsel to be on my guard, but I had no weapon about me. With the agility of a cat I sprung over the counter, and commenced passing tumblers faster than they had been in the habit of receiving them. I had felled one or two of my assailants, and I saw I was in for a serious disturbance.

A friend (and he is still living in St. Louis, wealthy and influential) stepped behind the bar, and, slapping me on the shoulder, said, " Look out, Beckwourth, you will hurt some of your friends."

I replied that my friends did not appear to be very numerous just then.

" You have friends present," he added; and, passing an enormous bowie-knife into my hand, stepped out again.

Now I was all right, and felt myself a match for the five ruffians. My practice with the battle-axe, in a case where the quickness of thought required a corresponding rapidity of action, then came into play.

I made a sortie from my position on to the open floor, and challenged the five bullies to come on; at the same time (which, in my excited state, was natural enough) calling them by the hardest names.

My mind was fully made up to kill them if they had only come at me; my arm was nervous; and my friends, who knew me at that time, can tell whether I was quick-motioned or not. I had been in situations where I had to ply my battle-axe with rapidity and precision to redeem my own skull. I was still in full possession of my belligerent powers, and I had the feeling of justice to sustain me.

I stood at bay, with my huge bowie-knife drawn, momentarily hesitating whether to give the Crow warhoop or not, when Sheriff Buzby laid hands on me, and requested me to be quiet. Although boiling with rage, I respected the officer's presence, and the assassins marched off to the body of the theatre. I followed them to the door, and defied them to descend to the street with me; but the sheriff becoming angry, and threatening me with the calaboose, I straightway left the theatre.

I stood upon the steps, and a friend coming up, I borrowed a well-loaded pistol of him, and moved slowly away, thinking that five men would surely never allow themselves to be cowed by one man. Shortly after, I perceived the whole party approaching, and, stepping back on the side-walk in front of a high wall, I waited their coming up. On they came, swaggering along, assuming the appearance of intoxication, and talking with drunken incoherency.

When they had approached near enough to suit me, I ordered them to halt, and cross over to the other side of the street.

" Who are you?" inquired one of them.

" I am he whom you are after, Jim Beckwourth; and if you advance one step farther, I will blow the tops of your heads off."

" You are drunk, ar'n't you?" said one of the party.

" No, I am not drunk," I replied; " I never drink any thing to make a dog of me like yourselves."

I stood during this short colloquy in the middle of the side-walk, with my pistol ready cocked in one hand and my huge bowie-knife in the other; one step forward would have been fatal to any one of them.

" Oh, he's drunk," said one; " let's cross over to the other side." And all five actually did pass over, which, if any of them is still living and has any regard for truth, he must admit to this day.

I then proceeded home. My sister had been informed of the rencounter, and on my return home I found her frightened almost to death ; for Forsyth (one of the party) had long been the terror of St. Louis, having badly maimed many men, and the information that he was after me led her to the conclusion that I would surely be killed.

A few days after I met two of the party (Forsyth and Kinney), when Forsyth accosted me, "Your name is Beckwourth, I believe ?"

I answered, "That is my name."

"I understand that you have been circulating the report that I attempted to assassinate you ?"

"I have told that you and your gang have been endeavoring to murder me," I replied, "and I repeat it here."

"I will teach you to repeat such tales about me," he said, fiercely, and drew his knife, which he called his Arkansas tooth-pick, from his pocket.

The knife I had provided myself with against any emergency was too large to carry about me conveniently, so I carried it at my back, having the handle within reach of my finger and thumb. Seeing his motion, I whipped it out in a second.

"Now," said I, "you miserable ruffian, draw your knife and come on ! I will not leave a piece of you big enough to choke a dog."

"Come," interposed Kinney, "let us not make blackguards of ourselves ; let us be going." And they actually did pass on without drawing a weapon.

I was much pleased that this happened in a public part of the city, and in open day ; for the bully, whom it was believed the law could not humble, was visibly cowed, and in the presence of a large concourse of men. I had no more trouble from the party afterward.

In connection with this affair, it is but justice to myself to mention that, when Captain Sublet, Fitzpatrick, and myself happened to meet in the office of Mr. Chouteau, Captain Sublet interrogated Fitzpatrick upon the cause of his hostility toward me, and represented to him at length the open absurdity of his trumping up a charge of robbery of his party in the mountains against me.

Being thus pressed, Fitzpatrick used the following words: " I never believed the truth of the charge myself; but when I am in the company of sundry persons, they try to persuade me into the belief of it, in order to raise trouble. I repeat, it is not my belief at this present moment, and I will not be persuaded into believing it again." Then turning to me, he said, " Beckwourth, I have done you a great injustice by ever harboring such a thought. I acknowledge it freely, and I ask your forgiveness for the same. Let us be as we formerly were, friends, and think no more about it."

Friends we therefore mutually pledged ourselves, and friends we have since remained up to this day.

While in town I called on General Ashley, but he happened to be away from home. I was about leaving the house, when a melodious voice invited me in to await the general's return.

" My husband will soon be back," the lady said, " and will be, doubtless, pleased to see you."

I turned, and really thought I was looking on an angel's face. She moved toward me with such grace, and uttered such dulcet and harmonious sounds, that I was riveted to the spot. It was the first time I had seen the lady of General Ashley.

I accepted her invitation, and was shown into a neat little parlor, the lady taking a seat at the window to act as my entertainer until the return of the general.

"If I mistake not," she said, "you are a mountaineer?"

I put on all the airs possible, and replied, "Yes, madam, I was with General Ashley when he first went to the mountains."

Her grace and affability so charmed me that I could not fix my ideas upon all the remarks she addressed to me. I was conscious I was not showing myself off to advantage, and she kept me saying "Yes, madam" and "No, madam," without any correct understanding of the appropriateness, until she espied the general approaching.

"Here comes the general," the lady said; "I knew he would not be long away."

Shortly the general entered the lodge, and fixed his eye upon me in an instant, at the same time whipping his pantaloons playfully with his riding-whip.

Rising from a better chair than the whole Crow nation possessed, I said, without ceremony, "How do you do, general?"

"Gracious heavens! is this you, Beckwourth?" and he seized my hand with the grip of a vice, and nearly shook off my scalp, while his lady laughed heartily at the rough salutation of two old mountaineers.

"My dear," said the general, "let me introduce you to Mr. Beckwourth, of whom you have heard me so often make mention. This is the man that saved my life on three different occasions in the Rocky Mountains; had it not been for our visitor, you would not have been Mrs. Ashley at this moment. But you look sickly, James; what is the matter?"

I replied, "I had been confined to my bed since my arrival in St. Louis."

We had a long conversation about the mountains and my residence with the Crow nation. I was very hospitably entertained by my former commander and his amiable lady, and when I left, the promise was extorted from me to make repeated calls upon them so long as I remained in the city.

About the latter end of March a courier arrived from Fort Cass, bringing tidings of a most alarming character. He had come alone through all that vast extent of Indian territory without being molested. It seemed as though a special providence had shielded him.

He found me in the theatre, and gave me a hasty rehearsal of the business. It seems that a party of trappers, who had heard of my departure for St. Louis, having fallen in with a number of Crows, had practiced upon them in regard to me.

" Your great chief is gone to the white nation," said the trapper spokesman.

" Yes, he has gone to see his friend, the great white chief."

"And you will never see him again."

" Yes, he will come back in the season of green grass."

" No, the great white chief has killed him."

" Killed him!"

" Yes."

" What had he done that he should kill him?"

" He was angry because he left the whites and came to live with the Indians—because he fought for them."

It is the greatest wonder in the world that every one

of the trapper party did not lose their scalps on the spot. If the Indians had had any prominent leader among them, they infallibly would have been all killed, and have paid the penalty of their mischievous lying. Unfortunately for the Crows, they believe all the words of a white man, thinking that his tongue is always straight. These trappers, by their idle invention, had jeopardized the lives of all the white men in the mountains.

The Indians said no more, but dashed off to the village, and carried the news of my death.

" How do you know that he is dead?" they inquired.

" Because the whites told us so, and their tongues are not forked. The great white chief was angry because he staid with our people, and he killed him."

A council was immediately held to decide upon measures of vengeance. It was determined to proceed to the fort and kill every white man there, and divide all the goods, guns, and ammunition among themselves; then to send out parties in every direction, and make a general massacre of every white man. Innumerable fingers were cut off, and hair without measure, in mourning for me; a costly sacrifice was then made to the Great Spirit, and the nation next set about carrying out their plans of vengeance.

The village moved toward the fort. Many were opposed to being too hasty, but all agreed that their decisions should be acted upon. The night before the village reached the fort, four women ran on in advance of the village to acquaint Mr. Tulleck of the sanguinary intention of the Crows. Every precaution was taken to withstand them—every gun was loaded. The village arrived, and, contrary to all precedent, the gates of the fort were closed.

The savages were infuriated. The whites had heard of the death of the Medicine Calf, and had closed the gates to prevent the anticipated vengeance. The inmates of the fort were in imminent peril; horror was visible on their countenances. They might hold their position for a while, but an investment by from ten to fifteen thousand savages must reduce it eventually. Tulleck was seated on the fort in great perplexity. Many of the veteran Crow warriors were pacing to and fro outside the inclosure. Yellow Belly was provisional head chief during my absence. Tulleck called him to him.

He rode up and inquired, "What is the matter? Why are your gates shut against us?"

"I had a dream last night," replied Tulleck, "and my medicine told me I had to fight my own people to-day."

"Yes, your bird told you truth; he did not lie. Your chief has killed the Medicine Calf, and we are going to kill you all."

"But the Medicine Calf is not dead; he will certainly come back again."

"Yes, he is dead. The whites told us so, and they never lie. You need not try to escape by saying he is not dead, for we will not believe your words. You can not escape us; you can neither dig into the ground, nor fly into the air; if you attempt to run, I will put five thousand warriors upon your trail, and follow you to the white chief: even there you shall not escape us. We have loved the whites, but we now hate them, and we are all angry. You have but little meat in the fort, and I know it; when that is gone, you die."

My son, "little Jim," was standing near the fort, and Mr. Tulleck called him to him. The child's answer was, "Away! you smell bloody!"

Mr. Tulleck, however, induced him to approach, and said, "Black Panther, I have always loved your father, and you, and all the warriors. Have I ever told you a lie?"

"No."

"They have told you that your father is dead, but they have lied; he lives, and will come back to you. The white chief has not killed him. My words are true. Do you believe your friend, and the friend of your father?"

"Yes. I love my father; he is a great chief. When he is here, I feel happy—I feel strong; but if he is dead, I shall never feel happy any more. My mother has cried four suns for him, and tells me I shall see him no more, which makes me cry."

"Your father shall come back, my son, if you will listen to what I now say to you."

"I will listen."

"Go, then, and ask Yellow Belly to grant me time to send for your father to the country of the white men, and if he be not here by the time the cherries shall have turned red, I will then lay down my head, and you may cut it off, and the warriors may kill us all, for we will not fight against them. Go and tell the chief that he must grant what I have told you for your sake, and if he does not listen to you, you will never see your father any more. Go!"

The child accordingly went to Yellow Belly, and begged him to grant one request. The chief, supposing that he was about to request permission to kill a particular man at the fort, said, "Certainly, my son; any request you make shall be granted. Speak! what is it?"

The child then informed Yellow Belly what the

Crane had said—that he would have his father back by the time the cherries turned red, or that he would suffer his head to be cut off, and deliver up his whites to the Crows, and would not fight.

"It shall be so, my son," Yellow Belly assented; "go and tell the Crane to send for your father, for not a warrior shall follow the trail of the white runner, or even look upon it. If he does as he says, the whites shall all live; if he fails, they shall all die. Now go and harangue the people, and tell all the warriors that the Crane is going to send for your father, and the warrior who follows the runner's trail shall die. Yellow Belly has said it."

He mounted a horse, and did as the chief had directed.

Joseph Pappen volunteered to deliver the message to me: it was encountering a fearful hazard. His inducement was a bonus of one thousand dollars.

The morning following the receipt of this intelligence I saw Mr. Chouteau, who was in receipt of a letter from Mr. Tulleck by the same messenger. He was in great uneasiness of mind. There was over one hundred thousand dollars' worth of goods in the fort, and he urged me to start without delay. The distance from St. Louis was estimated at two thousand seven hundred and fifty miles, and the safety of the men rendered the greatest expedition necessary. Any sum I might ask would be willingly paid me.

"Go!" said he; "engage as many men as you wish; purchase all the horses you require: we will pay the bills." He also furnished me with instructions to all the agents on the way to provide me with whatever I inquired for. The price I demanded for my services was five thousand dollars, which was, without scruple, allowed me. I hired two men to accompany me (Pappen being one), to whom I gave fifteen hundred and one thousand dollars respectively.

Our horses being procured, and every necessary supplied us, away we started upon our journey, which occupied us fifty-three days, as the traveling was bad. Our last resting-place was Fort Clarke. Thence we struck directly across through a hostile Indian country, arriving in safety within hailing distance of the fort before the cherries were ripe, although they were very near it.

I rested on a gentle rise of ground to contemplate the mass of people I saw before me. There they lay, in their absorbing devotedness to their absent chief; day and night, for long months, they had staid by that wooden inclosure, watching for my return, or to take fearful vengeance upon their prey. They had loved the whites, but those whites had now killed their chief because he had returned to his own people to fight for his kindred and nation—the chief who had loved them much, and made them rich and strong. They were now feared by their enemies, and respected by all; their prairies were covered with thousands of horses, and their lodges were full of the wealth derived from the whites. For this the white chief had killed him, and a war of extermination was denounced against them. The fort and its inmates were within their grasp; if the Crane would redeem his pledge and produce their missing chief, all were well; but if the appointed time passed by, and he were not forthcoming, it was fearful to contemplate the vengeance they would inflict.

When I thought of those contemptible wretches, who, merely to wanton with the faith that the artless savages reposed in them, could fabricate a lie, and arouse all this impending danger, I felt that a death at the stake would not transcend their deserts.

I put my horse into speed, and rode in among the Indians. I made the usual salutation on arriving before them, and, riding through their ranks sullenly, I repeated two or three times, "I am angry!" Every eye was turned on me, but not a warrior stirred; the women seized their children and ran into lodges. The Medicine Calf had arrived, but he was angry.

I advanced to the strong and well-secured gate of the fort, and struck it a heavy blow with my battle-axe. "Halloo, boys!" I shouted; "open your gate, and admit a friend."

"Jim Beckwourth! By heavens, Jim Beckwourth!" was repeated from tongue to tongue. The gates flew open upon their massive hinges, and, as I rode through, I said, "Leave the gates open, boys; there is no longer danger."

I exchanged but a few words with Mr. Tulleck, as I had a difficult business before me. The people I had to mollify were subject to strange caprices, and I had not resolved what policy to adopt toward them.

I went and sat down sullenly, hanging my head so low that my chin rested upon my breast: this was a token of my great displeasure. The braves came round me slowly. My wives all formed themselves in a circular line, and marched round me, each one pausing as she passed to place her hand on the back of my neck.

The brave old Yellow Belly was the first one to speak, and what he said was to the purpose.

"What is the matter with our chief?" he inquired; "who has angered the Medicine Calf?"

"Did I not tell you," I said, "that I left you in

charge of the Crane and these other whites during my absence? And what do I behold on my return?"

"Yes, I told you I would take care of the Crane and these other whites while you were gone, and I have done so. My warriors have killed buffalo for them to eat, and our women have brought them wood and water for their use, and they are all alive. Look! Yonder is the Crane; and his white people are all with him—are they dead?"

"No; but you intended to kill them."

"Yes; but listen: if you had not returned before the cherries turned red, we should have killed them all, and every other white man besides that we could have found in the Am-ma-ha-bas (Rocky Mountains). Now hear what I have to say:

"Suppose I am now going to war, or I am going to die. I come to you and say, 'My friend, I am going to die yonder; I want you to be a kind friend to my children, and protect them after I depart for the land of the Great Spirit.' I go out and die. My wives come to you with their fingers cut off, their hair gone, and the warm blood pouring from their bodies. They are crying mournfully, and your heart pities them. Among the children is a son in whom you behold the image of your friend who is no more. The mother of that child you know to be good and virtuous. You have seen her triumphant entry into the medicine lodge, where you have beheld so many cut to pieces in attempting the same. You say, Here is the virtuous wife of my friend; she is beloved and respected by the whole nation. She asks you to revenge her loss —the loss that has deprived her of her husband and the child of its father. In such a case, what would you do?· Speak!"

"I should certainly take my warriors," I replied, "and go and avenge your loss."

"That is just what I was going to do for your relatives, friends, and nation.   Now punish me if I have done wrong."

I had nothing to say in answer, and my head again fell—the spell was not yet broken.   The Crow Belt, an old and crafty brave, whispered to a young warrior, who rose in silence, and immediately left the fort.

Mrs. Tulleck shortly presented herself, and commenced tantalizing the Crows.

"What are your warriors waiting for, who have been thirsting so many suns to kill the whites ?   You have been brave for a long while ; where is all your bravery now ?   The gates are set wide open, and only three have joined the few whites whom you thirsted to kill ; why don't you begin ?   What are you afraid of ?"

She continued in this aggravating strain, the warriors hearing it all, although they did not appear to notice her.   The woman's voice was agreeably relieved by tones uttered outside the gate, which at that moment fell upon my ear, and which I readily recognized as the voice of Pine Leaf.   She was haranguing her warriors in an animated manner, and delivering what, in civilized life, would be called her valedictory address.

"Warriors !" she said, "I am now about to make a great sacrifice for my people.   For many winters I have been on the war-path with you ; I shall tread that path no more ; you have now to fight the enemy without me.   When I laid down my needle and my beads, and took up the battle-axe and the lance, my arm was weak ; but few winters had passed over my head.   My brother had been killed by the enemy, and was gone to the hunting-ground of the Great Spirit. I saw him in my dreams. He would beckon for his sister to come to him. It was my heart's desire to go to him, but I wished first to become a warrior, that I might avenge his death upon his foes before I went away.

"I said I would kill one hundred foes before I married any living man. I have more than kept my word, as our great chief and medicine men can tell you. As my arm increased in strength, the enemy learned to fear me. I have accomplished the task I set before me; henceforward I leave the war-paths of my people; I have fought my last battle, and hurled my last lance; I am a warrior no more.

"To-day the Medicine Calf has returned. He has returned angry at the follies of his people, and they fear that he will again leave them. They believe that he loves me, and that my devotion to him will attach him to the nation. I therefore bestow myself upon him; perhaps he will be contented with me, and will leave us no more. Warriors, farewell!"

She then entered the fort, and said, "Sparrowhawks, one who has followed you for many winters is about to leave your war-path forever. When have you seen Bar-chee-am-pe shrink from the charge? You have seen her lance red with the blood of the enemy more than ten times ten. You know what her vow was, and you know she has kept her word. Many of you have tried to make her break her word, which you knew she had passed to the Great Spirit when she lost her brother. But you found that, though a woman, she had the heart of a warrior.

"Do not turn your heads, but listen. You have seen that a woman can keep her word. During the many winters that I have followed you faithfully in the war-path, you have refused to let me into the war-path secret, although you tell it to striplings on their second excursion. It was unfair that I could not know it; that I must be sent away with the women and children, when the secret was made known to those one-battle braves. If you had seen fit to tell it to me, it would have been secret until my death. But let it go; I care no farther for it.

"I am about to sacrifice what I have always chosen to preserve—my liberty. The back of my steed has been my lodge and my home. On his back, armed with my lance and battle-axe, I knew no fear. The medicine chief, when fighting by my side, has displayed a noble courage and a lofty spirit, and he won from my heart, what no other warrior has ever won, the promise to marry him when my vow was fulfilled. He has done much for our people; he has fought their enemies, and spilled his blood for them. When I shall become his wife, I shall be fond and faithful to him. My heart feels pure before the Great Spirit and the sun. When I shall be no more on the war-path, obey the voice of the Medicine Calf, and you will grow stronger and stronger; we shall continue a great and a happy people, and he will leave us no more. I have done."

She then approached me, every eye being intently fixed upon her. She placed her hand under my chin, and lifted my head forcibly up. "Look at me," she said; "I know that your heart is crying for the follies of the people. But let it cry no more. I know you have ridden day and night to keep us from evil. You have made us strong, and your desire is to preserve us strong. Now stay at home with us; you will not be obliged to go to war more than twice in twelve moons. And now, my friend, I am yours after you have so long been seeking me. I believe you love me, for you have often told me you did, and I believe you have not a forked tongue. Our lodge shall be a happy one; and when you depart to the happy hunting-ground, I will be already there to welcome you. This day I become your wife—Bar-chee-am-pe is a warrior no more."

This relieved me of my melancholy. I shook the braves by the hand all round, and narrated much of my recent adventures to them. When I came to my danger in the A-rick-a-ra country, they were almost boiling with wrath, and asked my permission to go and exterminate them.

Pine Leaf left the fort with my sisters to go and dress for the short marriage ceremony. She had so long worn the war costume that female apparel seemed hardly to become her; she returned so transformed in appearance that the beholder could scarcely recognize her for the same person.

When I visited her lodge in the evening I found her dressed like a queen, with a lodge full of her own and my relatives to witness the nuptials. She was naturally a pensive, deep-thinking girl; her mind seemed absorbed in some other object than worldly matters. It might be that her continual remembrance of her brother's early fall had tinged her mind with melancholy, or it might be constitutional to her; but for an Indian girl she had more of that winning grace, more of those feminine blandishments—in short, she approached nearer to our *ideal* of a woman than her savage birth and breed would seem to render possible.

This was my last marriage in the Crow nation. Pine Leaf, the pride and admiration of her people, was no longer the dauntless and victorious warrior, the aveng-

er of the fall of her brother.   She retired from the field
of her glory, and became the affectionate wife of the
Medicine Calf.

The difficulty being now entirely removed, we quitted our encampment, and went on a hunting excursion.
We were away but a few days, and then returned to
the fort.   One morning it was discovered a large drove
of horses was missing.   A party was dispatched along
the trail, which conducted them precisely the same route
they took before.   I raised a party, and again struck
across the Mussel Shell, and, finding I was before the
fugitives, I secreted my warriors as before.   We had
waited but a few moments, when I saw the enemy
emerge from the pines, not more than a mile distant.
Pine Leaf and my little wife were with me.   My new
bride, as she saw the enemy approach, lost all recollection of her new character; her eye assumed its former
martial fire, and, had she had her former war equipments, beyond all doubt she would have joined in the
dash upon the foe.

The pursued, which was a party of Black Feet, were
hard pressed by their pursuers in the rear, but very
shortly they were harder pushed in the van.   When
within proper distance, I gave the word Hoo-ki-hi
(charge), and every Black Foot instantly perished.   So
sudden was our attack, they had not time to fire a gun.
I struck down one man, and, looking round for another
to ride at, I found they were all dead.   The pursuers
did not arrive in time to participate in the fight.   We
took thirty-eight scalps, and recovered one thousand
horses, with which we returned to the fort.   This was
my last battle in the Crow nation; the scalp I relieved
the Black Foot of was the last I ever took for them.

Before my sudden recall from St. Louis I had entered into negotiations which I now felt I would like to complete. I had informed the Crows, after my marriage with Pine Leaf, that I must return to the country of the whites, as they had called me away before I had had time to finish my business. When the boats were ready to go down stream I stepped on board, and proceeded as far as Fort Union. Previous to departing, I informed the Crows that I should be back in four seasons, as I at that time supposed I should. I told them to credit no reports of my death, for they were all false; the whites would never kill me. Pine Leaf inquired if I would certainly come back. I assured her that, if life was preserved to me, I would. I had been married but five weeks when I left, and I have never seen her since.

I was disappointed in my expectation of entering into a satisfactory engagement to the agent of the company, so I kept on to St. Louis. In good truth, I was tired of savage life under any aspect. I knew that, if I remained with them, it would be war and carnage to the end of the chapter, and my mind sickened at the repetition of such scenes. Savage life admits of no repose to the man who desires to retain the character of a great brave; there is no retiring upon your laurels. I could have become a pipe-man, but I did not like to descend to that; and, farther, I could not reconcile myself to a life of inactivity. Pine Leaf and my little wife would have excited their powers of pleasing to procure me happiness; but I felt I was not doing justice to myself to relapse irretrievably into barbarism.

It certainly grieved me to leave a people who reposed so much trust in me, and with whom I had been associated so long; and, indeed, could I have made an engagement with the American Fur Company, as I had hoped to do, I should have redeemed my promise to the Crows, and possibly have finished my days with them. But, being mistaken in my calculations, I was led on to scenes wilder and still more various, yet dignified with the name of greater utility, because associated with the interests of civilization.

CHAPTER XXIX.

Return to St. Louis.—Interview with General Gaines.—The Muleteers' Company.—Departure for Florida.—Wreck of the "Maid of New York."—Arrival at Fort Brooke.—Tampa Bay.—Bearer of Dispatches to General Jessup.—Battle of O-ke-cho-be.—Anecdotes and Incidents.

I HAD speedy passage to St. Louis, and arrived there after an absence of five months. I mentioned that I had left some business unsettled at the time of my sudden leave. This was none other than an affair matrimonial; but on my return I had some misunderstanding with my fair dulcinea, and the courtship dropped through.

At this time the Florida war was unfinished. General Gaines was in St. Louis for the purpose of raising a company of men familiar with Indian habits. Mr. Sublet had spoken to him about me, and had recommended me as being particularly well acquainted with Indian life. The general sent a request that I would call upon him at his quarters. I went accordingly, and was introduced by Sublet.

The general inquired of me how I would like to go to Florida to fight the Indians. I replied that I had seen so much of Indian warfare during the last sixteen years that I was about tired of it, and did not want to engage in it again, at least for the present. He remarked that there was a good opportunity there for *renown*. He wished, he said, to raise a company which would go down as muleteers ; that their duties would be light, and so on through the stereotyped benefits peculiar to a soldier's life.

Sublet recommended me to engage. Florida, he said, was a delightful country, and I should find a wide difference between the cold region of the Rocky Mountains and the genial and salubrious South.

The general then inquired if I could not raise a company of mountain-boys to go with me. I replied that I thought I could, or that, at any rate, I would make the effort.

The trapping business was unusually dull at that time, and there were plenty of unoccupied men in the city ready to engage in any enterprise. I went among my acquaintance, and soon collected a company of sixty-four men. I went and reported my success to the general. He wished to see the men. I brought them all forward, and had their names enrolled. I was appointed captain of the company, with three lieutenants elected from the men.

On the ninth day of my stay in St. Louis, we went on board a steamer going down stream, and were quickly on our way to the Seminole country. We had a delightful journey to New Orleans, where we were detained five days in waiting for a vessel to transport us to the fields of "renown." While waiting in New Orleans I fell in with several old acquaintances, who gave me an elegant parting dinner. I then sported the commission of captain in the service of Uncle Sam.

Our vessel, the Maid of New York, Captain Carr, being at length ready for sea, my soldiers, with their horses, were taken on board, and we set sail for Tampa Bay. I now, for the first time in my life, saw salt water, and the sickness it produced in me led me to curse General Gaines, and the trappings of war to boot. Our vessel stranded on a reef, and there she remained snug enough, all efforts to dislodge her proving fruitless. There was one small island in sight to leeward; in every other direction there was nothing visible but the heaving ocean. Wreckers, who seemed to rise from the sea-foam, flocked instantly around us, and were received by our captain with a ready volley of nautical compliment. The vessel had settled deeply into a bed of sand and rock; the water was rapidly gaining in her hold, and my commission, together with my gallant companions in arms, seemed, at that moment, to have a slim chance of ever serving our respected uncle in the "fields of renown." I ascended the rigging to take a survey of the country. Many a time an elevated prospect had delivered me from difficulties, if dissimilar, yet not less imminent, than those that now menaced me. Still I felt that, could those ratlines I was now ascending be transformed into the back of my Indian war-steed, this ocean be replaced with a prairie, and that distant speck which they called an island be transmuted into a buffalo, I would give my chance of a major-generalship in purchase of the change; for the sensations of hunger I began to feel were uncomfortably acute, and I saw no immediate prospect of alleviating the pain. Suddenly I saw a long line of black smoke, which I thought must be from a prairie fire. I reported my discovery to the captain, and he hoisted our colors at half-mast, to signal for assistance. A small steamer came in sight, and made toward us, and finally ranged up under our stern. She took off all my men except myself and twelve others.

I wrote to the commandant at Tampa Bay to inform him of our situation, and asking him for immediate assistance. After twelve days' stay on the reef, two small brigs came out to us, and received on board ourselves, with our horses and forage, conveying us to Tampa Bay, where they cast anchor. Major Bryant sent for me to his quarters, and I forthwith presented myself before him.

This officer gave me a very cordial welcome, congratulating the service on having an experienced mountaineer, and saying several other very complimentary things. At length he said, " Captain Beckwourth, I wish to open a communication between this port and the head-quarters of Colonel Jessup, distant about one hundred miles. I have received no dispatches from there, although nine couriers have been dispatched by Colonel Taylor."

I replied, " Sir, I have no knowledge of the country ; I know nothing of its roads or trails, the situation of its posts, nor do I so much as know the position of Colonel Jessup's command. To attempt to convey dispatches while so little prepared to keep out of harm's way, I very much fear, would be to again disappoint the service in the delivery of its messages, and to afford the Seminoles an additional scalp to those they have already taken."

He pooh-poohed my objections. " A man," said Major Bryant, " who has fought the Indians in the Rocky Mountains the number of years that you have, will find no difficulty here in Florida."

" Well," I assented, " furnish me with the bearings of the country, and direct me to the colonel's camp, and I will do my best to reach there."

Accordingly, the major furnished me with all the

necessary instructions, and I started alone on my errand.

It was my acquired habit never to travel along any beaten path or open trail, but rather to give such road a wide berth, and take the chances of the open country. I observed my invariable custom on this occasion, merely keeping in view the bearings of the position I was steering for. I started from Major Bryant's post about sunrise, and reached the colonel's head-quarters at nightfall the following day. I passed through the camp without seeing it ; but the sound of a bugle falling on my ear, I tacked about, and finally alighted upon it.

As I rode up I was hailed by a sentinel,

" Who come dere ?"

" An express."

" Vat you vant in dish camp ?"

" I wish to see Colonel Jessup. Call the officer of the guard."

" Vat for you come from dat way vere ish de Schimynoles ?"

" Call your officer of the guard," said I, impatiently. The officer of the guard at length appeared.

" What are you here again for ?" he inquired of me.

" I wish to see the commanding officer," I replied.

" Yes, you are always wishing to see the commanding officer," he said ; " but he will not be troubled with you much longer ; he will soon commence hanging you all."

" I demand to be shown to the commanding officer, sir," I reiterated.

" Who are you, then ?"

" I am a bearer of dispatches."

" Give them to me."

"I was not instructed to give them to you. I shall not do it, sir."

"I believe you came from the Seminoles; you came from that direction."

"You believe wrong, sir. Will you show me to Colonel Jessup, or will you not?"

This very cautious officer of the guard then went to the marquee of the colonel, and addressed him: "Here is another of those Seminoles, sir, who says he has dispatches for you. What shall I do with him?"

The colonel came out, and eyed me scrutinizingly.

"Have you brought dispatches for me?" he inquired.

"I have, sir."

"From where?"

"From Tampa Bay, sir."

"He came from the Seminoles, colonel," interposed the officer of the guard.

"You are mistaken again, sir," I said, giving him the look of a Crow in the midst of a battle; for I was not yet hireling enough not to feel aggravated at being called by implication a liar.

"Let me see your dispatches," said the colonel.

I handed him the documents; he took them, and passed into his tent.

This did not suit me. I resolved to return instantly. I had not been treated with common civility; no inquiries had been made about my appetite; I was not even invited to alight from my horse. I had neither eaten nor slept since I left Tampa Bay. I was on the point of turning my horse's head, secretly resolving that these were the last dispatches I would bear in that direction, when the colonel called,

"Captain Beckwourth, alight! alight, sir, and come into my quarters. Orderly, have Captain Beckwourth's horse taken immediate care of. You must be hungry, captain."

"What I need most now is sleep," I said; "let me have a little repose, and then I shall feel refreshed, and will not refuse to sit down to a meal."

The colonel bowed assent, and, raising a canvas door, pointed out to me a place for repose, at the same time promising me I should not be disturbed. When I awoke, I presented myself, and was regaled with a good substantial supper. This recruited me, and I was again fit for service.

The colonel made many inquiries of my past service. Major Bryant had made very favorable mention of me in his dispatches, which seemed to have inspired quite an interest in the colonel's mind. He asked me if I was a native of Florida, where I had spent my early days, and my reason for entering the army. I answered all his questions as briefly as possible, mentioning that I had been tempted among the Seminoles by the promise held out by General Gaines of my gaining "renown." The colonel thought my company of mountaineers a valuable acquisition to the service, and he made no doubt we should achieve great credit in ferreting out the hiding-places of the Indians.

He soon had his papers ready; they were delivered to me, and I departed. On the way I stopped at a fort, the name of which I forget, and took a fresh horse. I finally arrived at the Bay without seeing an Indian.

I staid with my company for two or three weeks at Fort Brooke, during which time we were engaged in breaking-in mules. We were then placed under the command of Colonel Taylor, afterward General, and President of the United States, whose force was composed of United States troops and volunteers, some of the latter being from Missouri. The colonel advanced southward with sixteen hundred men, erecting, as we advanced, a fort at the interval of every twenty-five miles.

On the morning of Christmas-day (1837) our camp was beleaguered by a large force of Indians, and Colonel Taylor ordered an advance upon them. The spot was thickly grown with trees, and numbers of our assailants were concealed among the branches; as our line advanced, therefore, many were singled out by the enemy, and we lost fearfully in killed and wounded. The yelling was the most deafening I ever heard, for there were many negroes among the enemy, and their yells drowned those of the Red Men. I soon found we had a different enemy from the Black Feet to fight, and different ground to fight on. The country lost several valuable lives through this slight brush with the Indians. The gallant Colonel Gentry, of the Missouri volunteers, was shot through the head; Colonel Thompson, and several other officers, were also among the slain. The enemy had made an excellent choice of ground, and could see our troops while remaining concealed themselves.

I placed myself behind a tree, and Captain Morgan, of the Missouri Spies, was similarly sheltered close by. We were surrounded with Indians, and one was watching, on the opposite side of the tree that protected me, for a chance to get my scalp. A Missourian picked off a fine fat negro who had ensconced himself in a live-oak tree. As he fell to the ground it shook beneath him: the fruit was ripe, but unfit for food.

Seeing the men dropping around, Major Price ordered a retreat. The order was instantly countermanded by Colonel Davenport, who, by so doing, saved many lives.

Colonel Foster had taken a very exposed position on the bough of a tree, where he was visible to all. He ordered his men to lie low and load their muskets; he waited till he saw a favorable opportunity, and then shouted, "Fire, boys, and pour it into the red and black rascals!"

A charge with bayonets was finally ordered, and the Indians, not relishing the look of the sharp steel, retreated; however, not before they had seized a sergeant-major and a private from our line, and scalped them alive.

This was the battle of O-ke-cho-be, which lasted four hours. We lost over a hundred in killed and wounded ; the enemy left nine Indians and a negro dead upon the field. Sam Jones, the half-breed, was only eight miles distant, with a force of a thousand warriors; most providentially he had been dissuaded by the negroes from advancing, who assured him that the whites would not fight on Christmas-day.

It was reported that Colonel Taylor was uncontrollably angry during the battle, and that his aids and other officers had to hold him by main force to prevent him from rushing among the enemy, and meeting certain death. I do not know what truth there was in this, for I saw nothing of it, nor, indeed, did I see the colonel during the whole of the four hours' fighting.

On the conclusion of the action Colonel Taylor wished to send dispatches to Tampa Bay. He requested Captain Lomax to take his company and go with them. The captain refused, for the reason that he and his men would infallibly be massacred. The colonel remarked then, " Since you are all afraid, I will go myself." He sent for me, and demanded if I could raise a sufficient number of brave men among my mountaineers to carry dispatches to the Bay.

I answered, certainly, if I could have his favorite horse, which was the fleetest one in the whole army, and such excellent bottom that he was as fresh after a journey as before. _ I considered that, if I had to run the gauntlet through a host of Seminoles and infuriated negroes, the best horse was none too good, and was, indeed, my only means of salvation.

When ready to start, I applied for the dispatches.

"Where are your men?" asked the colonel.

"My men are in their quarters, colonel," I said. "I am going to carry those dispatches by myself."

"They must go through," he remarked, "and I want them to go well guarded."

"I am not going to fight, colonel," I replied, "I am going to run; and one man will make less noise than twenty. If I am not killed the dispatches shall arrive safe; my life is certainly worth as much to me as the charge I am intrusted with, and for personal safety I prefer going alone."

In our progress out the troops had cut their way through several *hummocks*, and had thrown the bushes up on both sides. I had to pass through some of these lanes. It was night when I started, and as I was riding through one of these excavations at a good pace, I heard a sudden noise in the brush. I saw myself in a trap, and my hair bristled up with affright. I was greatly relieved, however, by the speedy discovery that it was only a deer I had scared, and which was scampering away at its utmost speed. I continued on, resting a short time at each fort, until I arrived in sight of Fort Brooke. As soon as I arrived within hailing distance, I shouted "Victory! victory!" which brought out officers and men, impatient to hear the news. I could not see that O-ke-cho-be was much of a victory;

indeed, I shrewdly suspected that the enemy had the advantage; but it was called a victory by the soldiers, and they were the best qualified to decide.

On my return, I found Colonel Taylor, soon after the battle, had retrograded to Fort Bassinger. We lay at that fort a long while; spies were vigilantly on the look-out, but nôthing very encouraging was reported. I and my company of mountaineers did not encamp with the other troops, but took up our quarters at a considerable distance from the main guard. We were quite tired of inactivity, and wanted to go somewhere or do something. Being quartered by ourselves, we were not subjected to the restrictions and military regulations of the camp; we had our own jollifications, and indulged in some little comforts which the camp did not enjoy. We always would have a large fire when there was need for it, for it destroyed the millions of musquitoes and other vermin that annoyed us; and, as some of our company were always about, the Indians never molested us.

There was a large hummock about four miles distant from the fort which the Indians infested in great numbers, but, as they could not be dislodged without great loss, our colonel was constrained to content himself with closely watching them. One day I proposed to my men to take a stroll, and they fell with great alacrity into the proposition. We passed down to the interdicted hummock, where we shot two deer, and found quite an assortment of stock. We drove them all to the camp before us, to the great admiration of the officers and men present. We had captured quite a drove of hogs, several head of cattle, and a good sprinkling of Seminole ponies. We saw no Indians at the hummock, though certainly we did not search very diligently for them.

During our stay at the fort, the communication between that post and Charlotte's Harbor was closed, and one messenger had been killed. The quartermaster inquired of me if I would undertake the trip. I told him I would; and set one hundred dollars as the price of the undertaking, which he thought quite reasonable. I started with the dispatches, and proceeded at an easy gallop, my eye glancing in every direction, as had been my wont for many years. In casting a look about two gun-shots ahead, I felt sure that I saw some feathers showing themselves just above the palmettos, and exactly in the direction that I was bending my steps. I rode a short distance farther, and my suspicion was confirmed. I immediately stopped my horse and dismounted, as though for the purpose of adjusting my saddle, but in reality to watch my supposed foes. In a minute or two several heads appeared, looking in my direction, and withdrew again in an instant. Immediately the heads declined behind the grass, I sprang upon my horse, and reined him out of the road, taking a wide circuit round them, which I knew would carry me out of danger. I then looked after them, and tantalized them with my gestures in every manner possible, motioning them to come and see me; but they seemed to be aware that their legs were not long enough to reach me, so they digested their disappointment, and troubled me no farther. I arrived safe at the Harbor that same day, delivered my dispatches, and was back at the fort the following night.

We now experienced a heavy rain, which deluged the entire country, and prevented any farther operations against the Indians. The colonel ordered a retreat to Tampa Bay, and, as there was no danger of molestation on the way, many of the officers obtained liberty to gallop on in advance of the army. Colonel Bryant rode a very valuable black charger, acknowledged to be the best horse in camp. After traveling on a while, the colonel said, " I have a notion to ride on and get in to-day, as my presence is required ; you can get in to-morrow at your leisure." A number said, If you can get in to-day, we can, and finally the whole party proposed starting off together.

We at length came to a swampy place in the road, which spread over five miles, and in many places took our horses off their feet. This place forded, there was then a narrow stream, and after that it was all dry land. Having passed the swamp and the stream, and got fairly on to dry land again, I took the saddle off my mule, which example all followed, and, with the assistance of a brother officer, wrung the saddle-blanket as dry as possible, and then spread it out fairly in the sun to dry. In the mean while, the horses helped themselves to a good feed of grass, and we all partook of a hearty lunch likewise.

Thus refreshed, we saddled up and proceeded again. After a few miles travel we discovered the rear of Bryant's party, who were toiling slowly along, and goring their animals' flanks in the vain endeavor to urge them into speed. We passed them with a hearty cheer. We journeyed on until within three miles of the fort, where there was a short bend in the road, and a foot-trail across, which saved about a hundred yards. "Now, gentlemen," said I, "let us raise a gallop, and pass every body on the road." The work was at once accomplished, some of my men deriding those left behind on account of their miserable progress. We then all struck into a gallop, and soon reached the fort, and several of our company found time to get quite intoxicated before the quarter-master arrived. He, however, soon recovered his equanimity of temper, and begged a solution of the mystery how we could come in with our animals fresh, while his and his companions' horses were jaded to death. He was referred by all to the captain of the mountaineers.

I said, " A horse, colonel, is only flesh and blood, and his system requires greater care than that of almost any other animal. We beat your powerful steed with inferior animals by affording them a short rest, with a mouthful or two of grass on the road, and by wringing our blankets after we had passed the water."

Now we had another long interval of inactivity, and I began to grow tired of Florida, with its inaccessible hummocks. It seemed to me to be a country dear even at the price of the powder that would be required to blow the Indians out of it, and certainly a poor field to work in for *renown*. My company and I, its commander, had nothing to do except to carry an occasional dispatch, and I wanted excitement of some kind—I was indifferent of what nature, even if it was no better than borrowing horses of the Black Feet. The Seminoles had no horses worth stealing, or I should certainly have exercised my talents for the benefit of the United States.

The last dispatches that I carried in Florida I bore from Fort Dade to Fort Brooke. In accomplishing this, I traveled with my customary caution, avoiding the trail as much as possible. In a part where I anticipated no danger, I took the trail, and fell asleep on my horse, for I had ridden four days and nights without rest, except what I had snatched upon horseback. Suddenly my horse sprang aside, instantly awaking me. I found I had been sleeping too long, for I had passed the turning-point, and was now near a hummock. To return would cost me several miles travel. My horse's ears informed me there was something in motion near by. I pondered my position, and ultimately resolved to take the chances and go ahead. The road through the hummock was just wide enough to admit the army wagons to pass. I bid my horse go, and he sprung forward with tremendous bounds. He had not reached through this dark and dangerous pass when I saw the flash of several guns, and the balls whizzed harmlessly past me. I discharged my pistols at the lair of my foes, and traveled on in safety to the fort.

I grew tired of this, and informed Colonel Bryant that I wished to resign my task. " Why ?" said he ; " every body who undertakes it gets killed, while you never see any Indians. What are we to do ?"

When in camp, I had frequently seen men come running in half dead with alarm, saying that they had seen Indians, or had been fired upon by Indians. I remarked that they were always ridiculed by the officers ; even the privates disbelieved them. Seeing this, I determined to say nothing about my adventure; for, if they had received my assertion with incredulity, it might have led to an unpleasant scene in the wigwam.

I was determined to return to the "home of the free and the land of the brave," for I felt that the mountains and the prairies of the Great West, although less attended with renown, at least would afford me more of the substantial comforts of life, and suit my peculiar taste better than the service of Uncle Sam in Florida.

The commander of the fort, after reading the dispatch, indorsed on it, " Beckwourth fired on by a party of Indians when near this post." He then returned it to me, and I rode on to Fort Brooke.

Colonel Bryant, having read the dispatch, said, "Ah, Beckwourth, you have been fired on, I see! why did you not tell us so on your arrival?"

I informed him of my reasons, as before stated.

He smiled. "Your word would have been believed by us all," he said; "it is these stupid foreigners that we discredit, who do not know an Indian from a stump; they have deceived us too often for us to put further faith in them."

A Seminole came into the fort a few days subsequent to this, to give himself up, his arm being broken. When questioned about it, he said that a white man had broken it in such a hummock, on such a night. I then knew that my pistols, which I fired at random, had done the mischief.

Alligator, the Seminole Chief, shortly after came in, and informed Colonel Taylor that he and his tribe had concluded to remove to their new home, and requested the colonel to send down wagons to transport their women and children.

"I have fought you a long time," said the Red Man, "but I can not beat you. If I kill ten of your warriors, you send a hundred to replace them; I am now ready to go, and save the rest of my people."

"Yes," the colonel answered, "your talk is good. You can now go to your new home, and be happy. There is a man (pointing to me) who is a great chief of a great nation; you will, for aught I know, be neighbor to his people; he and his people will teach you to hunt the buffalo, and I hope you will be good friends."

While I was with the army a tragedy occurred, which I have never seen in any public print, and I deem it of sufficient interest to make mention of it here. A young private, of very respectable connexions, had been tried for some offense, and sentenced to receive a flogging, which was carried unmercifully into effect. After he had recovered, the surgeon bade him go and report himself fit for duty.

"I will go," said he, "but it will be my last duty."

Accordingly, he fixed his bayonet and repaired to the officers' quarters, where he found the captain and first lieutenant of his company. He advanced upon them, and saying, "You have disgraced me with an inhuman flogging—die!" he shot the captain dead, and plunged his bayonet through the body of the lieutenant, also killing him on the spot.

He straightway gave himself up, was tried by court-martial, and sentenced to be shot. The execution of the sentence was withheld by Colonel Taylor, who had forwarded the particulars of the trial to the department at Washington, and was waiting the result of official investigation. The case was found worthy of executive interference; a pardon was signed by the President and sent on, and the young man was liberated from confinement.

Such inhuman treatment as this poor young soldier received at the hands of his officers has resulted, I have no shadow of doubt, in the death of many an officer on the battle-field.

I remember, at the battle of O-ke-cho-be, a young lieutenant riding up to Colonel Foster, and saying, "Colonel, I have been shot at twice, and not by the enemy either."

"It was by no friend, I will swear," said the colonel; "you can leave the field, and learn to treat your men well in future."

This I witnessed myself; but whether the young "buckskin" profited by the sharp cut of the colonel I am unable to say.

There was a Tennesseean in camp, a great foot-racer, who was incessantly boasting about his wonderful pedestrian powers. He had a valuable horse, which he offered to stake against any person in the camp for a race of sixty yards. As he was considered a "great leg" by all, no one ventured to take up his offer.

I offered myself as a competitor, but all sought to dissuade me. "Don't run against him," said they; "that fellow will outrun Lucifer himself. He has beat every man who has run against him in Florida."

However, I staked a hundred dollars against his horse, and entered the lists. We started together; but, as I did not see my antagonist either ahead of me or by my side, I looked around, and saw him coming up. I went out a good distance ahead of him, and did not exert myself either.

The enemy having submitted to the government, there was nothing more for us to do, and I asked for a furlough to return to St. Louis. I and my company were enlisted for a year; ten months of this time had been served, and I obtained a furlough for the remaining two months. We embarked for New Orleans, Colonel Gates and his regiment taking passage in the same ship. Arriving at my place of destination in safety, I staid but one night in the "Crescent City," and then took the steamer to St. Louis, where we had a good time while steaming up, and I was very well satisfied to jump ashore once again at my old home. My company all returned but two, one of whom died in New Orleans, the other was killed by the Seminoles after I left.

CHAPTER XXX.

Departure for the Mountains.—Severe Sickness on the Way.—Arrival at Bent's Fort.—Arrival at Sublet's Fort.—Interview with the Cheyennes.—Difficulty with a Sioux Warrior.—His Death.—Successful Trade opened with various Tribes.—Incidents.

I STAID but five days in St. Louis, which time I devoted to a hasty visit among my friends. I entered into service with Messrs. Sublet and Vasques to return to the mountains and trade with any tribes I might find on the head-waters of the Platte and Arkansas rivers. This country embraces the hunting-grounds of the Cheyennes, the Arrap-a-hos, the Sioux, and the I-a-tans.

All preliminaries being arranged, which are of no interest to the reader, I bade my friends once more adieu; and, stepping on board a steam-boat bound up the Missouri, we were soon breasting its broad and turbid current. We spent the Fourth on board, amid much noise, revelry, and drunken patriotism. We were landed in safety at Independence, where we received our wagons, cattle, etc., with which to convey the immense stock of goods I had brought through the Indian country. We were very successful in escaping accident in our progress over the plains, until we reached the ridge which passes between the Arkansas and Platte rivers. While ascending this ridge, accompanied with Mr. Vasques, I was sun-struck. We were at that time twenty miles from water; I was burning with thirst, the heat was intolerable, and hostile Indians were before us. After incredible suffering we reached the river bank, and crossed the stream to an island, where I lay me down to die. All our medicines were in the wagons, and two days' journey in our rear. My fatigue and suffering had thrown me into a fever; I became delirious, and grew rapidly worse. I requested my companion to return to the wagons and procure me some medicine; but he refused to leave me, lest I might die in his absence.

I said to him, "If you stay by me I shall certainly die, for you can not relieve me; but if you go, and nature holds out till you return, there is some chance of my gaining relief. Go," I added, "and hasten your return."

He left me at my entreaties, but filled all our vessels with water before he started. I speedily fell asleep, and I know not how long I remained unconscious. When I at length awoke, I drank an inordinate quantity, which caused me to perspire copiously; this relieved me, and my recovery commenced from that moment, although I still suffered from a severe headache. The third day of my friend's absence I could walk about a little, and the fourth day, at noon, I kept a good lookout in the direction I expected succor. Suddenly I saw a head appear, and another, and then another, until four showed themselves. They are Indians, I said to myself; but if there are only four, I stand a passable chance with them, so let them come on. I saw they had discovered me, so I arose and showed myself. With joyous shouts they flew toward me. It was my companion, with three others, who had come either to bury me or to assist me to the wagons. Their joy on beholding me so miraculously restored was unbounded, while my delight at seeing them was almost as great. We remained on the island that night, and the following morning started for the wagons, which we found in two days.

In going for assistance, my friend had a narrow escape. He came suddenly upon a party of Pawnees, and one made a rush for his horse. He discharged his rifle hastily, and missed his mark. He then had to trust to his horse's heels; but, as he was jaded, he did not make very good speed. The Indians were on foot, and gave close chase, but, when they saw his rifle reloaded, they fell back to a wider distance, and plied him with arrows until he was out of reach.

I was placed in a wagon, and attended on as far as our circumstances would admit, until I recovered my accustomed health. We staid one night at Burt's Fort, on the Arkansas, and then moved on to our destination on the South Fork of the Platte. Here we erected suitable buildings within the fort for our proposed trading, and, among others, a barn, which we proceeded to fill with hay for the coming winter.

While staying at the fort, a man inquired of Sublet his reason for bringing up such a rascally fellow as I, to prompt the Indians into rising and massacring all the whites.

"Murray," said Sublet — for that was the man's name—"it is unsafe for you to express such sentiments in relation to Beckwourth; should they reach his ears, he would surely make you rue it. I have heard these foul aspersions upon his character before, and I am in a position to know that they are all unfounded. Had I the least suspicion of his integrity, I should be the last man to take him in my employ."

This conversation was reported to me at some distance from the fort, where Murray was perfectly safe. But these foul reports annoyed me exceedingly. They were like stabs in the dark, for no one ever accused me to my face of such misdeeds.

After having placed things to rights, we were dining together within the fort, when Mr. Sublet rose and said,

"Traders and clerks, you have come here to the mountains to work for me, and I expect every man to do his best. If I am prospered, I will do well by all of you. I desire a regular system established in my business out here, that my interests may be placed upon a secure footing. I am now going to deliver the key of my entire stock of goods to one man among you, in whom I have implicit confidence, and whose long experience and intimate acquaintance with the Indian character pre-eminently entitle him to the trust. This man will have full command of the fort, and full charge of its affairs. I wish you to receive him as a representative of myself, and, whatever orders you receive from him, obey them cheerfully and to the very letter."

All present promised ready acquiescence to the wishes of our chief.

He then delivered the key to me, saying, "Beckwourth, I place this trust in your keeping, believing you to be as morally worthy of the confidence I repose in you, as you are practically qualified to advance my interests. I abandon my affairs to your keeping. Do your best, and I shall be satisfied."

I was so entirely unprepared for this distinguished mark of confidence, that for a moment I was unable to reply. After a momentary irresolution, I said, "Mr. Sublet, you have other men present who are better able to discharge this trust. I thank you for the flattering preference, but I beg to be excused from assuming the responsibility."

" I engaged you," he answered, " to serve me in this capacity, and I wish you to accept the charge."

" In that case," I said, " I will do my best to promote your interest."

Shortly after, he called me apart, and said, " Beckwourth, I am deeply in debt. I have been losing for a long time. If you can replace me in one year, you shall be substantially rewarded, and I shall feel sincerely grateful for your service."

" How much do you owe ?" I inquired.

" Over seventeen thousand dollars."

" Well," said I, " if the men co-operate with me, and carry out my instructions, I feel confident of working you straight."

I forthwith set about establishing sub-posts in various places, with the Siouxs, Arrap-a-hos, I-a-tans, and Cheyennes, and selected the best men at hand to attend them. I placed one at the mouth of Crow Creek, which I called my post, but left a man in charge of it, as I was at present fully occupied in traveling from one post to another."

We had not, as yet, found any customers ; but, as we were in the Cheyenne country, I knew some of that nation could not be very far off. I sent three different messengers in search of them to invite them to trade, but they all returned without having discovered the whereabouts of the Indians. Tired of these failures, I took a man with me, and started in the direction of the Laramie mountain. While ascending the mount, I cast my eyes in the direction of a valley, and discovered buffalo running in small groups, which was sufficient evidence that they had been chased recently by Indians. We went no farther, but encamped there, and at nightfall we saw fires. The next morning a dense smoke hung like a cloud over the village of the Cheyennes; we ate a hasty meal, and started to pay them a visit.

As we approached the village we saw William Bent, an interpreter, entering before us. He visited the chief's lodge; we followed him in, and seated ourselves near him. He looked aghast, and addressed me: "My God! Beckwourth, how dare you come among the Cheyennes? Don't you know that they will kill you if they discover you?"

I replied that I thought not.

He had come on the same errand as ourselves, namely, to induce a portion of the village to remove to the Platte, as buffalo were abundant in that region. After a conversation was held between Bent and a chief, the latter inquired of Bent who we were. He informed him that we were Left Hand's (Sublet's) men.

"What do they want here?" he asked.

"They come for the same purpose that I have," Bent answered, "to have you move on to the Platte."

Bent then inquired of me what account I wished to give of myself, as he would interpret for me; but, preferring to interpret for myself, I asked if there was a Crow among them that I could speak to. At the word "Crow" they all started, and every eye was riveted upon me.

One stepped forward, and said, "I am a Crow."

"You a Crow?"

"Yes."

"How long have you been away from them?"

"Twenty winters."

Bent was in the greatest perplexity. "You are not surely going to tell them who you are, Jim? If you do, you'll cost your friends nothing for your funeral."

This apprehension on the part of Bent proved to me that, although he had lived long among the Indians, he had still much to learn of their real character. I therefore requested him to quiet his fears and bide the result.

Turning to the Crow, I then said, "Tell the Cheyennes that I have fought them many winters; that I have killed so many of their people that I am buried with their scalps; I have taken a host of their women and children prisoners; I have ridden their horses until their backs were sore; I have eaten their fat buffalo until I was full; I have eaten their cherries, and the other fruits of their land, until I could eat no more. I have killed a great Crow chief, and am obliged to run away, or be killed by them. I have come to the Cheyennes, who are the bravest people in the mountains, as I do not wish to be killed by any of the inferior tribes. I have come here to be killed by the Cheyennes, cut up, and thrown out for their dogs to eat, so that they may say that they have killed a great Crow chief."

He interpreted this unreserved declaration faithfully to the chief, and I observed Bent ready to fall from his seat at what he deemed my foolhardy audacity.

"You are certainly bereft of your senses," he remarked; "the Indians will make sausage-meat of you."

Old Bark, the patriarch of the Cheyennes, rose and said: "Warrior, we have seen you before; we know you; we knew you when you came in; now we know you well. We know you are a great brave. You say you have killed many of our warriors; we know you do not lie. We like a great brave, and we will not kill you; you shall live."

I answered, " If you will not kill me, I will live with you; if you become poor, like some of the other tribes; and you need warriors to help you against your enemies, my arm is strong, and perhaps I will assist you to overcome them; but I will not at this time give you my word that I will do so. If you do not kill me, I am going to trade with you for many moons. I will trade with you fairly; I will not cheat you, as some of the traders have cheated you. I have a great many goods over on the Platte, such as you want, more than would fill many of your lodges. They are new, and look well. But, mind you, you must trade fairly with me. I have heard that you sometimes treat your traders badly; that you take away their goods, and whip them, and make them run out of your country to save their lives. Your people must never serve me in that manner; they must pay me for all they get; and if any one strikes me, I shall kill him, and thereby show you that I am brave. If any one should strike me, and I should not kill him, you would call me a woman, and say I was no brave."

They then asked me, through the Crow interpreter, if I was in such and such a battle between their nation and the Crows, all of which questions I answered truthfully.

" Do you remember that in such a battle we lost such a brave?" describing him.

" Yes."

" Who killed him?"

" I did." Or, if I did not kill him, I would tell them the name of the Crow who did.

" Did he fight well?"

" Yes, he fought well."

" He died like a brave man, then!" they would ejaculate.

"Were you in such a battle?" asked another.

"Yes."

"Did you see such a warrior fall?"

"Yes."

"Did he fight strong like a brave?"

"No, he did not fight well."

"Ugh! he was no brave ; he deserved to be killed."

In battle every warrior has his personal device painted on his shield, chosen according to his fancy. My "armorial bearing" was a crescent, with a green bird between the horns, and a star on each side the field. I described my novel device, and there was a great movement among them, for most of them distinctly recollected that shield, and I saw myself rising in their estimation. Their brave hearts rejoiced to have a true warrior before them, for they esteemed me as brave as themselves.

One of their great chiefs, named the Bob-tailed Horse, arose, and asked me if I remembered the battle on Pole Creek. I replied that I did.

"You killed me there," he said, "but I did not die ;" and he pointed out two scars upon his chest, just below the lower rib, where the balls from my gun entered, and which must have killed any body but an Indian.

"Where did I hit you?" he asked.

"Ugh!" said I ; "you missed me."

Old Bark then said, "Warrior, you killed me once too : look here ;" and he withdrew the hair from his right temple, and I saw that his cheek had been badly torn, and his ear was entirely missing. "But," he added, "I did not die. You fought bravely that day."

Had I gone among the Pawnees, the Siouxs, or many other tribes, and held this talk, I should have been

BECKWOURTH AS AN INDIAN WARRIOR, MOUNTED, AND WITH LANCE AND SHIELD.

hewn to pieces in a moment; but the Cheyennes were great braves themselves, and admired the quality in others, the Crows being their only equals.

While I sat talking thus, one of my men entered the village bearing two ten-gallon kegs of whisky. He requested me to take one and sell it out, while he went to the other end of the village, where the Siouxs were encamped, to sell the other. I had hitherto always opposed the sale of liquor to the Indians, and, during my chieftainship of the Crows, not one drop had ever been brought into the village; but now I was restrained by no such moral obligation. I was a mere trader, hazarding my life among the savages to make money for my employers. The sale of liquor is one of the most profitable branches of a trader's business, and, since the appetite for the vile potion had already been created, my personal influence in the matter was very slight. I was no lawgiver; I was no longer in a position to prohibit the introduction of the white man's fire-water; if I had refused to sell it to the Indians, plenty more traders would have furnished it to them; and my conscientious scruples would benefit the Indians none, and would deprive my embarrassed employer of a very considerable source of profit.

Running these things hurriedly over in my own mind, I took the proffered keg, and dealt it all out within two hours. Certainly the rate of profit was high enough; if a man wants a good price for the sale of his soul to his satanic majesty, let him engage in the liquor business among the nations of the Rocky Mountains. Our liquor was a choice article. One pint of alcohol, costing, I suppose, six cents, was manufactured into five times the quantity of whisky, and this was retailed to our insatiate customers at the rate of one pint for each buffalo robe. If the robe was an extra fine one, I might possibly open my heart, and give two pints. But I felt no particular inducement to liberality in my dealings, for I thought the greatest kindness I could show my customers was to withhold the commodity entirely.

Before I had got through with my keg I had a row with an Indian, which cost him his life on the spot. While I was busy in attending the tap, a tall Sioux warrior came into my establishment, already the worse for liquor, which he had obtained elsewhere. He made some formidable strides round and near me, and then inquired for the Crow. I was pointed out to him, and, pot valiant, he swaggered up to me.

" You are a Crow ?" he exclaimed.

" Yes."

" You are a great Crow brave ?"

" Yes."

" You have killed a host of Siouxs ?"

" No; I have killed a host of Cheyennes, but I have only killed fourteen Siouxs with my own hand."

" Look at me," said he, with drunken gasconade; " my arm is strong; I am the greatest brave in the Sioux nation. Now come out, and I will kill you."

" No," I said, " I did not come here to be killed or to kill; I came here to trade. I could kill you as easily as I could kill a squaw, but you know that you have a host of warriors here, while I am alone. They would kill me after I had killed you. But if I should come in sight of your village with twenty of my Crow warriors, you would all run and leave your lodges, women, and children. Go away; I want nothing to do with you. Your tongue is strong, but you are no brave."

I had told the Cheyennes but a few moments previously that I had been among all the nations in the country, and that it had ever been my invariable rule, when struck by a Red Man, to kill him. I was determined to prove the truth of my declaration in this instance. I had my battle-axe hanging from my wrist, and I was ready at a moment's warning. The Sioux continued his abuse of me in his own tongue, which I paid no attention to, for I supposed that, like his white brethren, he might utter a great deal of provocation in his cups, and straightway repent it when he became sober.

Finally, he became so importunate that I saw it was time to take an active part. I said, "You want to kill me, eh?" I would fight with you, only I know I should be killed by the Siouxs afterward, and I should have you for my waiter in the spirit land. I would rather kill a good brave, if I kill any."

This was a very opprobrious speech, for it is their faith that when an Indian is slain who has previously slain a foe, the first-killed warrior becomes waiter in the spirit land to the one who had laid him low. Indeed, it was more than he could endure. He jerked off the cloth that was fastened round his hips, and struck me in the face with it. I grasped my battle-axe, but the blow I aimed was arrested by a lodge pole, which impended over his head, and saved him from immediate death. The lodge pole was nearly severed with the blow. I raised my arm again, but it was restrained by the Cheyennes, who had been sitting round with their heads declined during the Sioux's previous abuse.

The Sioux chief, Bull Bear, was standing near, and was acquainted with the whole particulars of the difficulty. He advanced, and chopped his warrior down, and hacked him to pieces after he fell.

"Ugh!" grunted he, as coolly as possible, "you ought to have been killed long ago, you bad Indian!"

This demonstration on my part had a good effect. The Indians examined the cut inflicted by the edge of my axe on the lodge pole, and declared mine a strong arm. They saw I was in earnest, and would do what I had threatened, and, except in one single instance, I had no farther trouble.

Influenced by my persuasions, two hundred lodges of the Cheyennes started for the Platte, Bent and myself accompanying them. On our way thither we met one of my wagons, loaded with goods, on its way to the North Fork of the Platte. There was a forty-gallon cask of whisky among its contents, and, as the Indians insisted on having it opened, I brought it out of the wagon, and broached it. Bent begged me not to touch it, but to wait till we reached the fort. I was there for the purpose of making money, and when a chance offered, it was my duty to make the most of it. On that, he left me, and went to the fort. I commenced dealing it out, and, before it was half gone, I had realized sixteen horses and over two hundred robes.

While I was busy in my traffic, the Indians brought in four trappers whom they had chanced to pick up. The poor fellows appeared half frightened to death, not knowing what their fate would be. I addressed them in English. "How are you, boys? Where are you bound?"

"These Indians must decide that," they replied. "Are they good Indians?"

"Yes," I replied. "They will not harm you."

They informed me that they were returning from the

mountains with twelve packs of beaver, and, while encamped one night, the Crows had stolen their horses.
They had *cached* their peltry, and now wanted to buy
more horses to carry it to some fort.

I made a bargain with them for their beaver, and,
taking some horses, went with them myself to their late
encampment, for I could not trust them alone for fear
they would take their skins to some other post. We
disinterred the peltry, and with it reached the fort
without accident. The trappers staid with us two or
three weeks, and then, purchasing their outfit and
horses, they again started for the mountains.

We had a prosperous fall and winter trade, and accumulated more peltry than our wagons could transport, and we had to build boats to convey it to St.
Louis. At the settlement of accounts, it was found
that we had cleared sufficient to pay Mr. Sublet's debts,
and enough over to buy a handsome stock of goods
for the next season's trade.

I spent the summer at the fort, while Sublet and
Fitzpatrick went on with the peltry to St. Louis. I
had but little to do, as the Indians had removed to
their summer retreats, and I spent my time very agreeably with the few men remaining behind, in hunting
buffalo for our own use. About the last of August our
goods arrived, and we set ourselves to work again at
business. I put up at the North Fork of the Platte, and
had a busy fall and winter trade, making many very
profitable bargains for the company. The Cheyennes
thought me the best trader that ever visited them, and
would not allow any other company to traffic with their
villages. This sorely vexed my rival traders, and once
or twice I had my life attempted in consequence.
When others came to ask permission to open a trad-

ing-post, the Cheyennes would say, "No; we do all our trading with the Crow. He will not cheat us. His whisky is strong."

When I found I had obtained the confidence of the nation, I told the Cheyennes that if they allowed other traders to come in I should leave them, and they would be cheated by those who sold poor whisky, that would not make them merry half so soon as mine. This may be considered selfish; but I knew that our company was keenly competed with by three or four rival companies, and that the same representations that I used to keep the trade in my hands were freely urged by others to attract it from me. There was also a farther inducement for the Cheyennes to do their business with me, which was founded upon their respect for me as a great brave, who had killed a number of their countrymen. Whether there was diplomatic finesse enough in their minds to reflect that, while I was harmlessly engaged with them, I could not be fighting in the bands of their enemies, and adding to my present number of scalps, I can not pretend to say.

CHAPTER XXXI.

Invitation to visit the Outlaws.—Interview with "the Elk that Calls."
—Profitable Trade with the Outlaws.—Return to the Post.—Great
Alarm among the Traders.—Five Horses killed at the Fort.—Flight
from the Siouxs.—Safe arrival at the Fort.—Trade with the Arrap-
a-hos.—Attacked by a Cheyenne Warrior.—Peace restored.

WHILE in the midst of my occupations, a messenger was dispatched to me by the chief of a Cheyenne village, at that time encamped about twenty miles distant, with an invitation to visit them and trade there. This village was composed of outlaws from all the surrounding tribes, who were expelled from their various communities for sundry infractions of their rude criminal code ; they had acquired a hard name for their cruelties and excesses, and many white traders were known to have been killed among them. The chief's name was Mo-he-nes-to (the Elk that Calls), and he was a terror to all white people in that region. The village numbered three hundred lodges, and could bring from twelve to fifteen hundred warriors into the field —the best fighters of the nation. We called it the City of Refuge.

The messenger arrived at my post, and inquired for the Crow.

" I am the Crow," I answered.

" The great chief, Mo-he-nes-to, wants the Crow to come to his lodge."

" What does he want with me ?"

" He wants to trade much."

" What does he want to trade?"

" He wants much whisky, much beads, much scarlet, much kettles," and he enumerated a list of articles.

" Have your people any robes by them ?"

" Wugh ! they have so much robes that they can not move with them."

" Any horses ?"

" Great many—good Crow horses."

" Well," said I, " I will go straightway, and you must show me the way."

" Who will go to the village of the Elk that Calls ?" I asked ; " I want two men."

Peterson and another volunteered to accompany me ; but by this time the matter in hand had reached Sublet's ears, and he came forward and said,

"You are not going to the village of the Outlaws, Beckwourth?"

"Yes," I replied, "I am."

"Don't you know that they kill whites there?"

"Yes, I know that they have killed them."

"Well, I object to your going."

"Captain Sublet," I said, "I have promised the Indian that I will go, and go I must. There has been no trader there for a long time, and they are a rich prize."

He saw that I was resolved, and, having given me the control of affairs, he withdrew his objection and said no more.

I accordingly prepared for the journey. Ordering the horses, I packed up my goods, together with twenty gallons of whisky, and issued forth on the way to *uncertain* destruction, and bearing with me the means of destruction certain.

The Indian conducted me to the chief's lodge. I dismounted, my two men following my example. The chief came to us, and passed the usual compliments. He desired me to take off my packs, at which request I immediately remounted my horse.

"What is the matter?" inquired the chief.

"When I send for my friends to come and see me," I said, "I never ask them to unpack their horses or to guard them, but I have it done for them."

"You are right, my friend," said he; "it shall be done. Get off your horse, and come into my lodge."

I dismounted again, and was about to follow him. My men, who did not understand our conversation, arrested my path to inquire what was in the wind. I bade them keep quiet, as all was amicable, and then entered the lodge. We held a long conversation together, during which the chief made many inquiries of a similar nature to those addressed me at the first village. In recounting our achievements, I found that I had stolen his horses, and that he had made reprisals upon the Crows, so that we were about even in the horse trade.

At length he wished me to broach the whisky. "No," said I, "my friend, I will not open the whisky until you send for your women to come with their robes, and they have bought what goods they want first. They work hard, and dress all your robes; they deserve to trade first. They wish to buy many fine things to wear, so that your warriors may love them. When they have traded all they wish, then I will open my whisky, and the men can get drunk. But if the men get drunk first, your women will be afraid of them, and they will take all the robes, and the women will get nothing."

"Your words are true, my friend," said the chief; "our women shall trade before the men get drunk; they dress all our robes: it shall be according to your words."

Accordingly, he sent for all the women who had robes and wished to sell, to come and trade with the Crow. They were not long in obeying the summons. Forward they came, some with one robe and some with two. Two was the most that any of them had, as the men had reserved the most to purchase whisky. The trading was expeditiously effected; we did not have to take down and open all our goods, and then sell a skein of thread, and be informed by our customer that she would look elsewhere first, and perhaps call again, which is the practice of many young ladies, especially where there is an attractive shopman. We could hardly hand out things fast enough.

We served all the women to their entire satisfaction, and closed out our stock of dry-goods. We then proceeded to the whisky. Before opening the kegs, I laid down my rules to the chief. I told him that his people might spree as long as they chose, but that they must not obstruct my business, or interfere with me. As the liquor was served out to them, they must carry it out of the lodge, and not stay to be in my way and give me trouble. This was readily assented to, and the sales began.

Whisky will have the same effect every where, and if a man will traffic in the "cursed stuff," he must submit to his share of the mischief he creates. My understanding with the chief was productive of no effect. He came into the lodge, saying, "I have killed an Indian;" I looked, and saw that his battle-axe was dripping with blood. Yells and tumult increased outside; the chief was again making his way toward the lodge, protected by a host of friends, while behind him, and striving to get at him, was an infuriated throng, fighting and yelling like devils. My store in an instant was filled to overflowing with opposing parties, composed of outlaws from a dozen tribes. I sprang to secure my gun; and my companions, mistaking my movement, supposed I had started to run, and they broke out at the back of the lodge, and did not stop until they reached our post on the Platte.

Battle-axes and knives fairly rung through the lodge during the continuance of the fight; but it was over in a few minutes, and they withdrew to the place outside, and renewed it to greater advantage. At the restoration of peace, some ghastly wounds were shown to me, but, singular to say, none of the belligerents were killed.

Mo-he-nes-to, after a short interval, returned, without having received a single scratch, and said all was quiet again, and they wanted more whisky. The women wished to get some also, he informed me. I knew that, if the women were going to join in, I must have another supply, and I told the chief I had not enough left to get the women drunk.

" Send for more, then," said he. " Our women are buried up and smothered with robes, and will buy very much."

I soon found a volunteer to run to the post to carry an order to Sublet to send me twenty gallons more of whisky.

My assistants, after making their hasty exit from the back of the chief's lodge, reported at the post the state of affairs at the village of the Outlaws at the time they left. Guns were being fired, they said, and, beyond all doubt, Beckwourth was killed. No one dared to go and ascertain the result. Sublet was in great trouble. " I did my utmost to prevent his going," he consoled himself by saying, " but he went in opposition to all orders and advice ; so, if he is killed, the responsibility does not rest upon me."

By-and-by my messenger arrived with the order for more whisky. Sublet took the letter and read it. " Ho !" said he, " Jim is not dead yet. He has sent for more fire-water. Who will take it to him ?" Four men volunteered for the errand, and arrived with it next day. The Indians took their horses away from them, and they became alarmed ; but when they shortly after saw me up to my neck in buffalo robes, their fear subsided. These two kegs went off as actively as the preceding, and the robes fairly poured in. The whole village moved on toward the post, singing, dancing, and drinking, and, when I had approached within five miles, I had to send for two kegs more.

In short, the sixty gallons of *fire-water* realized to the company over eleven hundred robes and eighteen horses, worth in St. Louis six thousand dollars.

This trading whisky for Indian property is one of the most infernal practices ever entered into by man. Let the reader sit down and figure up the profits on a forty-gallon cask of alcohol, and he will be thunderstruck, or rather whisky struck. When disposed of, four gallons of water are added to each gallon of alcohol. In two hundred gallons there are sixteen hundred pints, for each one of which the trader gets a buffalo robe worth five dollars! The Indian women toil many long weeks to dress these sixteen hundred robes. The white trader gets them all for worse than nothing, for the poor Indian mother hides herself and her children in the forests until the effect of the poison passes away from the husbands, fathers, and brothers, who love them when they have no whisky, and abuse and kill them when they have. Six thousand dollars' for sixty gallons of alcohol! Is it a wonder that, with such profits in prospect, men get rich who are engaged in the fur trade? or is it a miracle that the poor buffalo are becoming gradually exterminated, being killed with so little remorse that their very hides, among the Indians themselves, are known by the appellation of a pint of whisky?

The chief made me a gratuity of forty robes. On two subsequent visits I paid him on his invitation, he made me further presents, until he had presented me with one hundred and eighty-five robes without receiving any equivalent. The extent of his "royal munificence" seriously alarmed Sublet. It was just this same profuse spirit, he said, that had bred disputes with other traders, often resulting in their losing their lives. It is as well a savage custom as civilized, to expect a commensurate return for any favors bestowed, and an Indian is so punctilious in the observance of this etiquette, that he will part with his last horse and his last blanket rather than receive a favor without requital.

Mo-he-nes-to, without intending it, was rather troublesome on this point. When he became sober after these drunken carousals, he would begin to reflect seriously on things. He would find his robes all gone; his women's labor—for it would take months of toil in dressing and ornamenting these robes—thrown unprofitably away; his people had nothing to show for their late pile of wealth, and their wants would remain unsupplied. They would have no guns or ammunition to fight the Crows, who were always well supplied, and their whole year's earnings were squandered. These reflections would naturally make him discontended and irritable, and he would betake himself to the post for reparation.

"White man," he would say, "I have given you my robes, which my warriors have spent months in hunting, and which my women have slaved a whole year in dressing; and what do you give me in return? I have nothing. You give me fire-water, which makes me and my people mad; and it is gone, and we have nothing to hunt more buffalo with, and to fight our enemies."

The generality of traders will endeavor to make it apparent to him that there was a fair exchange of commodities effected, and that he had the worth of his wares, and they can do no more for him.

This angered him, and in his disappointment and vexation he would raise the war-hoop, his warriors would rush to him, he would harangue them for a moment, an assault would be made upon the trading-post, the goods would be seized, and, in many instances, the trader would be massacred and scalped.

I saw the necessary relation between all these events, and knew that simple justice in exchanges would avoid all such catastrophes. I therefore told Sublet to feel no uneasiness, as I could arrange matters so as to afford general satisfaction.

"Well," said he, "go your own way to destruction."

A day or two after this, Sublet came to inform me that Mo-he-nes-to was on his way to the fort. I looked out, and saw the chief and his wife both approaching on horseback. As he entered, I received him with great ceremony, taking him by the hand, and bidding him welcome to the fort. I had his horses well attended to, a sumptuous supper for himself and wife served up, and, while the meal was preparing, entertained him with liquors fit to make any toper's mouth water. After supper he got gloriously fuddled, and went to bed, ignorant of what was passing in the world around him.

In the morning I inquired of him how he felt.

"Wugh! Much bad! head ache strong!"

I then gave him another whisky punch, well-flavored with spices; he and his lady drank deeply, and then partook of a hearty breakfast. He then felt well again. I next led him into the store, where we had a large assortment of every Indian novelty. I knew he had children, as well as how many; so I selected a five-striped Hudson's Bay blanket for himself, another for his wife, and one for each of his children, besides an extra scarlet blanket for his eldest son, a young warrior. To his wife I also gave a two-gallon brass kettle, and beads enough to last her for a year or two. In fact, I selected more or less of every description of article that I thought would be useful to them, or that I thought an Indian eye could covet. These presents I ceremoniously laid upon the counter, until I had two or three large piles of quite attractive-looking goods.

The chief and his wife had watched me laying all these goods before them. I then asked them if they saw any thing more any where in the store that they thought they would like.

Mo-he-nes-to opened his eyes wide with surprise. "What!" he exclaimed, " are all those things for us?"

" Yes," I said, "they are for you, your wife, and your children—something for you all. When I have a friend, I like to be liberal in my gifts to him. I never rob the Red Men; I never take all their robes and give them nothing but whisky. I give them something good for themselves, their wives, and their children. My heart is big; I know what the Red Men want, and what their families want."

" My friend, your heart is too big; you give me much more than I ever had before; you will be very poor."

" No," I said; " I have many things here, all mine. I am rich, and when I find a good friend, I make him rich like me."

I then bade him look the store carefully through, to see if there was any thing more that he would like. He looked, but saw nothing more that he needed. I then made the same request of his wife, whose satisfaction beamed all over her face, but she too was fully supplied.

I then stepped into another room, and returned with a fine new gun, with a hundred rounds of ammunition, and a new, highly-finished, silver-mounted battle-axe. This was the *comble de bienfaits.* I thought he would not recover from the shock. He took the battle-axe in his hand, and examined it minutely, his face distorted with a broad grin all the while.

"Hugh!" said he; "you give me too much. I gave you no robes, but you have proved that you are my friend."

When they were ready to start, there was an extra horse for him, and a fine mare for his wife, ready waiting at the door.

"There, my friend," said I, "is a good horse for you; he is swift to run the buffalo. Here is a fine mare for you," I said to his wife. "Indian women love to raise handsome colts. I give her to you, and you must not let the Crows steal her from you."

She displayed every tooth in her head in token of her satisfaction, and she mounted to return home. The chief said as he left, "I am going on a war-party, and then to kill buffalo. I will come back again in a few moons. I will then come and see you, and I will kill you—I will crush you to death with robes." And away they went, never better satisfied in their lives.

Now is it to be supposed that the company lost any thing by this liberality? That chief, whose hands were stained with the blood of so many traders, would have defended my life till the last gasp. While I was in his country, no other trader could have bartered a plug of tobacco with him or his people. The company still derived great profits from his trade. Besides the immense returns derived from my transactions with the village, I cleared over five hundred dollars from my exchanges with the chief alone, after the full value of my munificent presents had been deducted.

One day the Cheyenne Dog Soldiers were to have a dance and count their *coos*. I called all the Crows who were in the band, and asked them if the regulations would admit of my joining in the dance.

"Certainly," said they; "nothing will please them more; they will then believe that you have joined them."

Accordingly, I painted myself, and put on a uniform, including a chief's coat, new from the shelves, and painted my white leggins with stripes, denoting a great number of *coos ;* when ready, I walked toward them as great a man as any. On seeing me approach, there was a general inquiry, "Who is that? Where did he come from?" When the ceremonies commenced, I joined in, and danced as hard as any of them. The drum at length sounded, to announce the time to begin to count.

I stepped forward first, and began. "Cheyennes, do you remember that you had a warrior killed at such a place, wearing such and such marks of distinction?"

"Yes, we know it."

"I killed him; he was a great brave."

There was a tap on the drum, and one *coo* was counted. I proceeded until I had counted my five *coos*, which is the limited number between the dances.

Next in turn the Bob-tailed Horse counted his five on the Crows, and to his various allusions I assented with the customary "I remember."

This betrayed who I was, and they were delighted to see one of the Dog Soldiers of the Crows join their band. The Bob-tailed Horse made me a valuable present, and I returned to the fort with six splendid war-horses and thirty fine robes, presented to me at that dance, as my initiation gifts, or bounty-money, I suppose, for joining their army. I was then a Dog Soldier in the picked troop of the Cheyennes, compelled to defend the village against every enemy until I died, like Macbeth, with harness on my back.

The Crows had been informed by sundry persons in the employ of the American Fur Company that I had joined their inveterate enemies. They were satisfied with my proceeding. "The Medicine Calf is a cunning chief," they said; " he best knows how to act. He has joined the Cheyennes to learn all about their numbers, the routes of their villages, and so forth. When he has learned all that he wants, he will return to us, and then we can fight the Cheyennes to greater advantage."

I was now in my second winter with Sublet in the Cheyenne and Sioux country. He had succeeded far beyond his expectation, and he still continued to make money by thousands. We had curtailed the number of sub-posts, and thereby materially reduced his expenses ; indeed, they were now less than half what they were the preceding winter.

Leaving Sublet's, I went down to the South Platte, distant one hundred and fifty miles, and indulged in a short rest, until I heard that the Cheyennes of the Arkansas—those that I first visited—were about to make their spring trade, and I went over to meet them, and bring them to our fort. I found them ; all appeared to be glad to see me, and they returned with me. In crossing the *divide*, or ridge between the two rivers, our spies in advance discovered a party of Pawnees, and a charge was immediately made upon them. We only killed three of the enemy. I counted a *coo* by capturing a rifle. The victim who abandoned it had been already killed.

While we engaged the enemy the village went into camp, and I proposed to my fellow-warriors to return to the village after the manner of the Crows, which was agreed to. There were several in the party, so we could easily raise a good Crow song, and the Cheyenne warriors could join in. We struck up merrily, and advanced toward the village. As soon as the women heard our voices, they ran out to see who were coming. There were several captive Crows among the Cheyennes, who, I supposed, had lived among them ever since I had been sold to the whites. These recognized our stave, and exclaimed, "Those are Crows coming; we know their song." This brought out the whole village, who stood waiting our arrival, in surprise and wonderment. As we drew near, however, they distinguished me in the party, and the mystery was solved. "The Crow is with the Cheyennes."

We performed all kinds of antics; made a circuit round the village, going through evolutions and performances which the Cheyennes had never before seen, but with which they were so highly pleased, that they adopted the dance into the celebrations of their nation. That night the scalp-dance was performed, which I took part in, as great a man as any. I sung the Crow song, to the especial admiration of the fair sex.

The next morning we resumed our journey to the fort, which we reached after three days' travel. The village had brought a great number of robes, together with some beaver, and a great trade was opened with them.

At this time I had a difficulty with a Cheyenne,

the only one I ever had with any of the tribe. I was eating dinner one day, when a great brave came in and demanded whisky. I repaired to the store with him to supply his want, when I found he had no robe to pay for it, and was, besides, intoxicated. I refused to give him the whisky, telling him he must first go and bring a robe. This probably aggravated him, and he made a sudden cut at me with his sword, which I very fortunately dodged, and before he could raise his weapon again I had him between my feet on the ground. I had left my battle-axe on my seat at the table, and I called out for some one to bring it to me, but no one came with it. I at length released him, and he went hooping away, to obtain his gun to shoot the Crow. I seized my own, and waited for him at the door, while all the inmates of the fort begged of me not to shoot him. After some little delay, he appeared, gun in hand; but three Cheyenne warriors interfered to stop him, and he returned into his lodge.

The day following he sent for Sublet and myself to go and dine with him, and we went accordingly. Sublet was apprehensive of mischief from my visit, and endeavored to dissuade me from going; but I foresaw no danger, and knew, farther, that it would be a cause of offense to the Indian to neglect his invitation. When we entered his lodge he was glad to see us, and bade me be seated on a pile of robes. I sat down as desired, and our host, after holding a short conversation with Sublet, turned to me and spoke as follows:

" O-tun-nee" (Crow), " I was a fool yesterday. You spared my life. I do not want you to be angry with me, because I am not angry with you. I was drunk; I had drunk too much of your whisky, and it made my heart black. I did not know what I was doing."

"Very well," said I; "I am not angry with you. When you attempted to kill me I was angry, and if my battle-axe had been in my hand, I should have killed you. You are alive, and I am glad of it."

"Take those robes," he rejoined, "and hereafter you shall be my brother, and I will be your brother. Those robes will make your heart right, and we will quarrel no more."

I took the robes with me, ten in number, and found my heart perfectly mollified.

Messrs. Sublet and Vasques, having realized immense profits during their three years of partnership, disposed of all their interest and effects in the Rocky Mountain fur business, and returned to St. Louis. This threw me entirely out of business, when Messrs. Bent and Saverine wished to engage me in their employ. After some little negotiation with them, I concluded a bargain, and entered into their service in the latter part of the summer of 1840. We immediately proceeded to establish sub-posts in various directions, and I repaired to Laramie Fork.

As soon as it was known among the Indians that the Crow was trading at Bent's post, they came flocking in with their robes. Old Smoke, the head chief of another band of Outlaws, known as Smoke's Band, but claimed by no particular nation or tribe, visited me, with his village, and commenced a great spree. I gave them a grand entertainment, which seemed to tickle their tastes highly. They kept up their carousal until they had parted with two thousand robes, and had no more remaining. They then demanded whisky, and I refused it. "No trust," the motto we see inscribed on every low drinking-saloon in St. Louis, is equally our system in dealing with the Indians.

They became infuriated at my refusal, and clamored and threatened if I persisted. I knew it was no use to give way, so I adhered to my resolution. Thereupon they commenced firing upon the store, and showered the bullets through every assailable point. The windows were shot entirely out, and the assailants swore vengeance against the Crow. According to their talk, I had my choice either to die or give them whisky to drink. I had but one man with me in the store. There had been several Canadians in the fort, but on the first alarm they ran to their houses, which were built around the fort, within the pickets, to obtain their guns; but on the Indians informing them that they would not hurt them, that it was only the Crow that they were after, the *Canadians* staid within doors, and abandoned me to my fate.

I and my companion sat with our rifles ready cocked, well prepared to defend the entrance to the fort. We had plenty of guns at hand ready loaded, and there must a few have fallen before they passed the gate. At dusk I closed the door, but we lay upon our arms all night. The Indians kept up a great tumult and pother, but attempted nothing.

Messrs. Bent and Saverine arrived in the morning, and wanted to be informed of the cause of the disturbance. I acquainted them, and they approved my conduct. They were astonished at my immense pile of robes, and applauded my fortitude.

When the Outlaws became sobered, they expressed contrition for what they had done, and charged their excesses upon John Barleycorn, which plea I admitted. At the same time, it appeared quite inconsistent that I, who was that celebrated gentleman's high-priest, should be set upon and almost murdered by his devotees.

Nothing noteworthy occurred until the following January, when the Indians, being again on the spree, once more attempted my life. I fled to a post in the Arrap-a-ho country, in charge of Mr. Alex. Wharfield, now a colonel in the army; he resigned the post to me, and took my place at Bent's post. I had but little trouble with the Indians here. Cut Nose, an old brave, who, it seems, had been in the habit of obtaining his drams of Wharfield gratis, expected to be supplied by me on the same terms. I resisted this invasion, and seriously ruffled the feathers of the old chief thereby. He left at my refusal, and did not return again that day. During the ensuing night the Pawnees came, and stole both his horses and mine. The old man raised a party, went in pursuit, recaptured all the horses, took two scalps, and returned in high spirits.

He visited the store, and informed me what he had done.

"Well," said I, "that is because I gave you no whisky yesterday. If I had given you whisky, you would have drunk too much, and been sick this morning in consequence. Then you would not have been able to pursue the Pawnees, and you would have lost your horses."

However, I gave him some whisky then in honor of his achievement. This, as I had expected, pleased the old fellow, and he restored me my horses, and charged me nothing for their recapture.

As soon as the spring trade was over, I abandoned that post and returned to the Arkansas. Saverine desired me to go and see if I could open a trade with a village of Arrap-a-hos which he had heard was encamped at forty miles distance. I accordingly started in their direction, accompanied by two men. We journeyed on until we had arrived within a short distance of the village, when we discovered on our road a band of three or four hundred traveling Indians. I saw they were Camanches, and I bade the two men to run for their lives, as I knew the Camanches would kill them. I directed them to the Arrap-a-ho village, and bade them shout their loudest when they came in sight of it. They left me, and ascended a slight eminence a little distance in advance, and then, shouting to the extent of their lungs, they put their horses down at the best speed. I rode up after them, and telegraphed with my blanket to the village to have them come quickly. They obeyed my motions, and fell in with the Camanches on their way to me. The two tribes proved to be friends, and my companions were safe.

On arriving at the village I found abundance of robes, and opened a very successful trade with the people. This finished, I returned to the fort, and assisted the other employés in loading the wagons for their trip to St. Louis.

CHAPTER XXXII.

First Trip to New Mexico.—Return to the Indians with Goods.—Success in Trade.—Enter into Business in St. Fernandez.—Get Married.—Return to the Indians.—The fortunate Speculation.—Proceed to California with Goods.

I HAD now accumulated a considerable sum of money, and thought I might as well put it to some use for my own profit, as risk my life in the service of others, while they derived the lion's share from my industry. It was now about three years since I had left St. Louis on my present excursion, and I began to weary of the monotony of my life. I was within five days' journey of New Mexico, and I determined upon going to take a look at the northern portion of this unbounded territory.

I had but one man with me, named Charles Towne, when I started upon my new exploration. On our road thither we passed near to a Utah village, and two or three of their warriors presented themselves before us to hold a parley, while the chief sat down on a log close by. They said, as we reined in our horses for a moment, "You make our paths bad by coming into our country; you will go back and tell the Cheyennes and Arrap-a-hos where we are; they will then come and kill us, and steal our horses. Come here! our chief wants to see you."

This was spoken in tolerably good Spanish.

"Come on," said I, addressing my companion; "let us not be annoyed by these trifling Indians;" and I urged my horse against the Indian spokesman, knocking him into the dirt. He arose, exclaiming, "Wugh! Shawnee!" We then rode on without further molestation, they evidently mistaking me for a Shawnee. They had robbed several white men, and, after beating them savagely, had liberated them. I had no manner of fear of them, for I knew them to be great cowards; with one hundred and fifty good Crow warriors I would have chased a thousand of them.

We passed on into St. Fernandez, and found quite a number of American traders there, established in business, and supplying both mountaineers and Indians with goods. Here I encountered an old acquaintance, named Lee, with whom I entered into partnership. We purchased one hundred gallons of alcohol, and a stock of fancy articles, to return to the Indian country, and

trade for robes and other peltry. We visited the Cheyennes on the South Fork of the Platte. We passed
Bent's fort on our way thither. He hailed us, and inquired where we were going. I informed him that we
were on our way to the Cheyenne village. He begged
me not to go, as I valued my safety. It was only the
day previous, he said, that he had traded with them,
and bought eighteen horses from their village. They
came the next morning and took them forcibly back,
and threatened him with their guns if he said a word
against their proceedings. I replied to him that I anticipated no danger, and left him to pass on to their
village.

The Indians were delighted at my arrival. I had
heard that the hooping-cough was very prevalent among
the children, and, as we happened to have several
bushels of corn, and beans, and a large quantity of
dried pumpkins, we could not have come at a more opportune moment. I told the Indians, in answer to
their welcome, that I had come back to see them because I had heard their children were all sick. I called attention to my stock of vegetable esculents, as being best adapted for food for their children, and the
best calculated to restore them to health. "Besides,"
I added, "I have brought a little whisky along, to put
good life into your hearts."

They were then in their sobered feelings, which will
return to them after their carousals, and which present so dangerous a time to the trader. Their horses
were all away, their robes were gone, and they had
nothing to show in return for them. Their children
were sick and dying, their wives mourning and half
distracted, and they could obtain nothing at the fort to
alleviate their sufferings. I could understand the whole

corollary of incidents. Like their intemperate white brethren, who will occasionally review matters after a prolonged spree, and who will see the effects of their dissipation in their desolate homes, their heart-broken wives, and their ragged and starving children, what are their feelings at such a contemplation? Unquestionably hostility against the cause of this destitution, whether they recognize it in themselves, the willing instruments, or the liquor that infatuated them, or the dealer that supplied it to them. The Indians seem to have one circle of reasoning, and invariably vent their spleen upon the trader. It was this reactionary feeling that had led the Indians to recover, by force of arms, the horses they had parted with previously. I knew better how to manage them.

I deposited my goods at Old Bark's lodge, who felt highly honored with the trust. The villagers collected round, and a dispute arose among them whether the whisky should be broached or not. Porcupine Bear objected, and Bob-tailed Horse, his brother-in-law, strongly advocated my opening the kegs. This led to a warm altercation between the two warriors, until the disputed question was to be decided by the arbitrament of battle. They both left the lodge to prepare for the combat, and returned in a few minutes fully armed and equipped.

Porcupine Bear argued his cause in the following strain: "Cheyennes, look at me, and listen well to my words. I am now about to fight my brother; I shall fight him, and shall kill him if I can. In doing this, I do not fight my brother, but I fight the greatest enemy of my people.

"Once we were a great and powerful nation: our hearts were proud, and our arms were strong. But a few winters ago all other tribes feared us; now the Pawnees dare to cross our hunting-grounds, and kill our buffalo. Once we could beat the Crows, and, unaided, destroyed their villages; now we call other villages to our assistance, and we can not defend ourselves from the assaults of the enemy. How is this, Cheyennes? The Crows drink no whisky. The earnings of their hunters and toils of their women are bartered to the white man for weapons and ammunition. This keeps them powerful and dreaded by their enemies. We kill buffalo by the thousand; our women's hands are sore with dressing the robes; and what do we part with them to the white trader for? We pay them for the white man's fire-water, which turns our brains upside down, which makes our hearts black, and renders our arms weak. It takes away our warriors' skill, and makes them shoot wrong in battle. Our enemies, who drink no whisky, when they shoot, always kill their foe. We have no ammunition to encounter our foes, and we have become as dogs, which have nothing but their teeth.

"Our prairies were once covered with horses as the trees are covered with leaves. Where are they now? Ask the Crows, who drink no whisky. When we are all drunk, they come and take them from before our eyes: our legs are helpless, and we can not follow them. We are only fearful to our women, who take up their children and conceal themselves among the rocks and in the forest, for we are wolves in our lodges; we growl at them like bears when they are famishing. Our children are now sick, and our women are weak with watching. Let us not scare them away from our lodges, with their sick children in their arms. The Great Spirit will be offended at it. I had rather go to the great and happy hunting-ground now than live and see the downfall of my nation. Our fires begin to burn dim, and will soon go out entirely. My people are becoming like the Pawnees: they buy the whisky of the trader, and, because he is weak and not able to fight them, they go and steal from his lodge.

"I say, let us buy of the Crow what is useful and good, but his whisky we will not touch; let him take that away with him. I have spoken all I have to say, and if my brother wishes to kill me for it, I am ready to die. I will go and sit with my fathers in the spirit land, where I shall soon point down to the last expiring fire of the Cheyennes, and when they inquire the cause of this decline of their people, I will tell them with a straight tongue that it was the fire-water of the trader that put it out."

Old Bark then advanced between the two belligerents and thus spoke: "Cheyennes, I am your great chief; you know me. My word this day shall be obeyed. The Crow has come among us again, and has brought us good things that we need; he has also brought us a little whisky. He is poor, while we are yet strong, and we will buy all he has brought with him. This day we will drink; it will make us merry, and feel good to one another. We will all drink this once, but we will not act like fools; we will not quarrel and fight, and frighten our women and children. Now, warriors, give me your weapons."

This fiat admitted no appeal; it was law and gospel to his people; disobedience to his command subjected the offender to immediate death at the hands of the Dog Soldiers. The warriors delivered up their battle-axes, and the old chief handed them to me. "Crow," said he, "take these weapons that I have taken from

my two children.   Keep them until we have drunk up
your whisky, and let no one have them till I bid you.
Now, Crow, we are ready."

Slim Face and Gray Head, two Dog Soldiers, then
harangued the village, and desired all who wished to
trade to come and bring their robes and horses to Old
Bark's lodge, and to remember that they were trading
with the honest Crow, and not with white men, and
that what they paid him was his.

They answered the summons in flocks, the women
first, according to my established rule.   My corn,
beans, and pumpkins "exhaled like the dew," and I
received in exchange their beautiful fancy robes.   The
women served, the men next came in for whisky.   I
sold on credit to some.   When one wanted thus to
deal, he would tell me what kind of a horse or mule
he had : I would appeal to Old Bark for confirmation
of the statement ; if he verified it, I served the liquor.
They all got drunk, Porcupine Bear, the temperance
orator, with the rest ; but there was not a single fight ;
all passed off harmoniously.

I received over four hundred splendid robes, besides
moccasins and fancy articles.   When I was ready to
leave, thirty-eight horses and mules, a number corresponding to what I had marked, were brought forward.
I packed up my peltry, and sent my partner on in advance with every thing except the horse I rode, telling
him I would overtake him shortly.

I had reserved a five-gallon keg of whisky unknown
to all, and when about to start I produced it and presented it to the crowd.   They were charmed, and insisted on making me a return.   They brought me
over forty of their finest robes, such as the young
squaws finish with immense labor to present to their

lovers. Old Bark gave me a good mule to pack them, and another chief gave me a second. I then took my leave, promising to return by Leaf Fall.

When I passed Bent at his post he was perfectly confounded. He had seen one train pass belonging to me, and now I was conducting another, when, at the same time, he had supposed that there was not a robe in the village.

"Beckwourth," said he, "how you manage Indians as you do beats my understanding."

I told him that it was easily accounted for; that the Indians knew that the whites cheated them, and knew that they could believe what I said. Besides that, they naturally felt superior confidence in me on account of my supposed affinity of race. I had lived so much among them that I could enter into their feelings, and be in every respect one of themselves: this was an inducement which no acknowledged white trader could ever hope to hold out.

I rode on, and overtook my partner in advance. He had had an adventure. A party of Cheyennes, led by a chief named Three Crows, had met him, and rifled him of a three-gallon keg of whisky, which we had reserved for our own use on our way to St. Fernandez. The chief stopped him, and said, "I smell whisky, and we must have some."

My partner told him that he had none.

"Wugh! my nose don't lie, but your tongue does. I smell it strong, and, if you do not hand it out, we shall unpack all your horses and find it."

"Well," said the man, "I have a little, but it belongs to the Crow, and he wants it himself."

"Give it me," said the chief, "and tell him that Three Crows took it."

There was no alternative, and he gave him the keg. They carried it along until they came to a creek, where they sat down and had a jollification. I passed them while they were in the midst of it, but did not see them, although they saw me. When I met the chief some time subsequently, and charged him with the larceny, he gave me ten robes and a good horse to compound the felony.

We shot several buffalo on our way, enough to load all our horses with meat and tallow. We exchanged our effects in Santa Fé for goods, and carried them to St. Fernandez, a distance of sixty miles. Here we established a store as our head-quarters for the Indian trade, where I resided some time, living very fast and happily, according to the manner of the inhabitants. Among other doings, I got married to Senorita Louise Sandeville.

In the fall I returned to the Indian country, taking my wife with me. We reached the Arkansas about the first of October, 1842, where I erected a trading-post, and opened a successful business. In a very short time I was joined by from fifteen to twenty free trappers, with their families. We all united our labors, and constructed an adobe fort sixty yards square. By the following spring we had grown into quite a little settlement, and we gave it the name of Pueblo. Many of the company devoted themselves to agriculture, and raised very good crops the first season, such as wheat, corn, oats, potatoes, and abundance of almost all kinds of vegetables.

When the spring trade was over, I sent all my peltry to Independence, and bought with the proceeds three thousand dollars worth of articles, suitable for the trade in New Mexico. But, on the arrival of the goods, the

JAMES P. BECKWOURTH. 465

whole country was in a ferment on account of Colonel Cook's expedition from Texas, which resulted so disastrously for the parties concerned. This affected the minds of the New Mexicans unfavorably for my interest, inasmuch as their former preference for United States novelties was now turned into strong repugnance for every thing American. I therefore could obtain no sale for my goods, and determined to return to my Indian friends. I bought a load of whisky to trade for horses to pack my goods to California, where I intended removing. I succeeded in my adventure, and obtained forty horses and mules, upon which I packed my merchandise, and quickly found myself on the way to the "golden state."

I started with fifteen men, three of whom were Mexicans. When I reached the Utah country, I found that the Indians were waging exterminating war upon the Mexicans, but I did not learn it in time to save the lives of my three unhappy followers, who, lagging too far in the rear, were set upon by the Indians and slain. In passing through their country I did considerable trading, exchanging my merchandise for elk, deer, and antelope skins, very beautifully dressed.

I arrived in Pueblo de Angeles (California) in January, 1844. There I indulged my new passion for trade, and did a very profitable business for several months. At the breaking out of the revolution in 1845, I took an active part against the mother country, of which I will furnish some details in my next chapter.

CHAPTER XXXIII.

The Californian Revolution.—Rifle Corps.—Position of the two Armies.—Colonel Sutter.—Cannonade.—Flight of Sutter.—His Return.—Trial and subsequent Release.

THE Upper Californians, on account of their great distance from the Mexican government, had long enjoyed the forms of an independent principality, although recognizing themselves as a portion of the Mexican Republic. They had for years past had the election of their own officers, their governor inclusive, and enjoyed comparative immunity from taxes and other political vexations. Under this abandonment, the inhabitants lived prosperous and contented; their hills and prairies were literally swarming with cattle; immense numbers of these were slaughtered annually for their hides and tallow; and, as they had no "Armies of Liberation" to support, and no costly government to maintain in extravagance, they passed their lives in a state of contentment, every man sitting under his own vine and his own fig-tree.

Two years prior to my arrival all this had been changed. President Santa Anna had appointed one of his creatures, Torrejon, governor, with absolute and tyrannical power; he arrived with an army of bandits to subject the defenseless inhabitants to every wrong that a debasing tyranny so readily indulges in. Heavy taxes were imposed for the support of the home government, and troops were quartered to the great annoyance and cost of the honest people. The lives of the inhabitants were continually in danger from the excesses of the worthless vagabonds who had been forced upon them; their property was rifled before their eyes, their daughters were ravished in their presence, or carried forcibly to the filthy barracks. The people's patience became at length exhausted, and they determined to die rather than submit to such inflictions. But they were ignorant how to shake off the yoke: they were unaccustomed to war, and knew nothing about political organizations. However, Providence finally raised up a man for the purpose, General José Castro, who had filled the office of commander under the former system, but who had been forced to retire into privacy at the inauguration of the reign of terror. He stepped boldly forth, and declared to the people his readiness to lead them to the warfare that should deliver their country from the scourge that afflicted them; he called upon them to second his exertions, and never desert his banner until California were purified of her present pollution. His patriotic appeal was responded to by all ranks. Hundreds flocked to his standard; the young and the old left their ranches and their cattle-grounds, and rallied round their well-tried chief.

There was at that time quite a number of Americans in the country, and, according to their interests and predilections, they ranged themselves upon opposing sides. Our present worthy and much-respected citizen, General Sutter, was at that time, if I mistake not, a colonel in the forces of the central government, and at the outbreak of the revolution he drew his sword for Santa Anna, and entered into active service against the rebels in Pueblo de Angeles.

There was an American, long resident in the country, named J. Roland, who sought my co-operation in the popular cause. He said that every American who could use a rifle was a host against the invaders, and besought me to arm in defense, and to influence my* men likewise to espouse the cause. I replied to his solicitations by promising him my active co-operation, and also that I would represent his arguments to the men living with me. Accordingly, I informed my people that I intended to shoulder my rifle in the defense of life and property, and they were unanimous in their resolution to accompany me. Hence there were thirteen riflemen instead of one. We shortly after received an accession of sixty more good frontiersmen, and mustered ourselves for service. The company elected me captain, but I declined the office. Mr. Bell finally assumed the command, with the promise of my unflinching support in extremities. Our company steadily increased in number until we had one hundred and sixty men, including native Californians, who joined us with rifles.

General Castro's first movement was against Pueblo. He entered the place at the head of his forces, and took the fort, arsenal, with all the government arms, ammunition, and stores, with the slight loss of one officer wounded. This enabled the rebels to arm themselves, and he was shortly at the head of a small but well-appointed army. The general highly extolled the rifle battalion, and he looked upon it as a powerful support.

Castro then took a detachment of rebel troops, and proceeded northward to reconnoitre the enemy's position, our main body also moving in the direction of the enemy as far as Monterey, where were the governor's head-quarters. On first hearing the intelligence of the outbreak, the governor had put his forces in motion, and issued orders to shoot the rebels wherever met, and destroy their property of whatever kind. General Castro, having proceeded as far as Santa Barbara, a distance of ninety-six miles, and having obtained full information concerning the movements of the governor, returned and joined the main body. During his expedition he captured five Americans in the Mexican service. He disarmed them, telling them that he had no disposition to injure Americans, and that he would return their arms as soon as he had expelled the enemies of the people.

Our forces were concentrated in a large open prairie, the enemy being stationed at no great distance, likewise on the prairie. I ascended, one morning, the summit of a mountain, which would afford me a fair view of the enemy's camp, just to discover their numbers and strength of position. On my road I encountered two Americans, who were serving in the capacity of spies to the enemy. I accosted them, and expressed surprise to see them in the service of such an old rascal as Torrejon, and recommended them to join the popular cause; but they seemed to have an eye to the promised booty of the rebels, and my arguments could not influence them. I dispatched one of them with a letter to Gant, an American who held the commission of captain in the governor's army, offering him, as we did not wish to fight against our American brethren, to withdraw all the Americans from the rebel ranks, if he would do the same on the side of the governor, and leave the Mexicans and Californians, who were most interested in the issue, to measure their strength. Some Germans who were with us also made the same proposal to Colonel Sutter. Our messenger conveyed the dispatches, and delivered the German's letter to Colonel Sutter, who read both that and our letter to

Captain Gant. He returned for answer that, unless the Americans withdrew from the insurgent army immediately, he would shoot us every one by ten o'clock the next morning. This embittered us the more against the barbarity of the opposing power, and we resolved to make their leaders, not excepting Sutter, feel the effects of our rifles as soon as they placed themselves within range.

On the following morning a weak and ineffective cannonade commenced on both sides. We lay low, awaiting the enemy's charge. As their riflemen had not shown themselves, and we were desirous to obtain a sight of them, myself, with seven or eight others, advanced cautiously in search of them. On our way we discovered a small cannon which the enemy had loaded and was about to discharge upon our ranks. Had there been a gunner among them, it must have done us great injury. We advanced within a few yards of the piece, and had raised ourselves up to shoot the artillerymen, when one of our party arrested our aim by suddenly exclaiming, " Don't shoot! don't shoot!" He then pointed out the enemy's riflemen carefully emerging from a hollow, with the intention of stealing upon our flank and saluting us with a volley of lead. I laid down my rifle, and hailed them to halt. I recognized a number of mountaineers among them, with some of whom I had intimate acquaintance, and I urged them to adopt the cause of the people, for the side they had now espoused was one no American should be seen to defend. They heard me through, and all, or nearly all the Americans were persuaded by my arguments, and returned with me to join our battalion. This assured us of victory. The cannonade was perfectly harmless : some of the balls passed three hundred feet over our heads; others plowed up the prairie as near to their ranks as ours. All the damage we received was one wagon shivered to pieces, and a horse killed under Colonel Price, which animal had been captured by us at Pueblo, and was now serving in the rebel forces with the same rank he had held under government.

The desertion of the riflemen seriously affected the enemy's prospects of victory. Ten o'clock had passed, and Colonel Sutter had not put his threat into execution. The enemy finally retired from the field, and marched in the direction of Pueblo. I took a party, and ascended a mountain to watch the progress of the retiring foe; we staid out some hours, with the view to learn where they encamped. While thus employed, a courier, sent from our commander, brought us orders to return immediately. We instantly obeyed, and found the army gone, with only one man remaining to direct our steps. On coming up with our forces, we found that our colonel had made a movement which cut off all retreat from the enemy, and which must bring him to an engagement, or an unconditional surrender. In the morning, I again took a party with me, and mounted an eminence to reconnoitre the enemy's position. We approached to within five hundred yards of their camp, where we shot a bullock, which we quietly proceeded to dress. While we were thus engaged, I perceived an officer approaching from the enemy's camp to ascertain who we were. I took my rifle, and dodged among the bushes, eager to get a shot at him; but, before I could do so, one of my men prematurely fired, and missed his mark. The officer had dismounted in order to get a nearer view of us, and this admonitory shot warned him back into camp. Myself and another advanced to within fifty rods of it, and boldly seized the officer's horse, and they did not fire a shot at us. We saw their camp was hemmed in on all sides. Our artillery was placed in battery, matches lighted, and men in position—all was ready for action. The enemy, perceiving their desperate condition, sent a flag of truce for a negotiation. Articles of capitulation were eventually drawn up and signed, to the effect that the governor and his forces should immediately lay down their arms, and leave for Acapulco as soon as their embarkation could be accomplished. Accordingly, they laid down their arms, and marched under escort to the Embaradara, distant twenty miles from Pueblo. The governor was not permitted to return to Monterey, but his lady was sent for to the Embaradara, where she rejoined her husband, and they quit the country together.

Colonel Sutter, on the day of embarkation, left his detachment of naked Indians with the army, and proceeded, as we supposed, to his fort on the Sacramento; but he returned the next day, and gave himself up to us. His force of Indians were very well drilled, but would have been far better employed in raising cabbages on his farm than in facing rebel riflemen on the battle-field. A trial was held upon the colonel, which resulted in his full acquittal, with the restoration of all his property fallen into our hands, such as cannon and other military effects, by the surrender of the government forces. The Americans, in jest probably, seemed very desirous to have the prisoner shot, which produced great alarm in his mind, and recalled to his recollection his recent threat to shoot all the Americans in our army.

Our countrymen were almost carried on the shoul-

ders of the Californians, in gratitude for their participation in the revolution ; for, although the victory had
been a bloodless one, they attributed their easily-won
success to the dread inspired by the name of their
American confederates.

After seeing the departure of the government troops,
the rebel army returned to Pueblo, where they elected
Colonel Pico governor ; Colonel, now General Castro,
commander of the forces ; and filled other less important offices. Fandangoes, which were continued for a
week, celebrated our success; and these festivities over,
the insurgents returned to their various homes and occupations.

Some few weeks after, a small proportion of the inhabitants sought to displace our newly-elected chief
magistrate, and appoint some other in his place. I was
sent for during the night to guard the governor's palace
with my corps of rifles, and we succeeded in capturing
the leading conspirators, who were tried and sent to
Acapulco in irons. I had a quarrel with the alcalde
shortly after this service, and he put me in irons for
cursing him. As soon as the governor heard of my
misfortune, he had me immediately discharged from
confinement.

I now resumed my business, and dispatched my partner, Mr. Waters, after a fresh supply of goods; but,
before he had time to return, fresh political commotions
supervened. There still seemed to exist in the minds
of the majority a strong hankering for the domination
of Mexico, notwithstanding they had so recently sided
with the Revolutionists in shaking off the yoke of the
national government. Among other causes of excitement, too, the American adventurers resident there had
raised the " Bear Flag," and proclaimed their intention

of establishing an independent government of their own. This caused us to be closely watched by the authorities, and matters seemed to be growing too warm to be pleasant.

In the midst of this gathering ferment, news reached us from Mazatlan of the declaration of war between the United States and Mexico, and I deemed it was fully time to leave. Colonel Fremont was at that juncture approaching from Oregon with a force, if combined with the Americans resident there, sufficient to conquer the whole country, and I would have liked exceedingly to join his forces, but to have proceeded toward him would have subjected me to mistrust, and consequent capture and imprisonment. If I looked south the same difficulties menaced me, and the west conducted me to the Pacific Ocean.

I had but little time to deliberate. My people was at war with the country I was living in ; I had become security to the authorities for the good behavior of several of my fellow-countrymen, and I was under recognizances for my own conduct. The least misadventure would compromise me, and I was impatient to get away. My only retreat was eastward ; so, considering all things fair in time of war, I, together with five trusty Americans, collected eighteen hundred stray horses we found roaming on the Californian ranchos, and started with our utmost speed from Pueblo de Angeles. This was a fair capture, and our morals justified it, for it was war-time. We knew we should be pursued, and we lost no time in making our way toward home. We kept our herd jogging for five days and nights, only resting once a day to eat, and afford the animals time to crop a mouthful of grass. We killed a fat colt occasionally, which supplied us with meat, and very delicious meat too—rather costly, but the cheapest and handiest we could obtain. After five days' chase our pursuers relaxed their speed, and we ourselves drove more leisurely. We again found the advantage that I have often spoken of before of having a drove of horses before us, for, as the animals we bestrode gave out, we could shift to a fresh one, while our pursuers were confined to one steed.

When we arrived at my fort on the Arkansas, we had over one thousand head of horses, all in good condition. There was a general rejoicing among the little community at my safe arrival, the Indians also coming in to bid me welcome. I found my wife married again, having been deceived by a false communication. Her present husband had brought her a missive, purporting to be of my inditing, wherein I expressed indifference toward her person, disinclination to return home, and tendering her a discharge from all connubial obligation. She accepted the document as authentic, and solaced her abandonment by espousing her husband's messenger. My return acquainted her with the truth of the matter. She manifested extreme regret at having suffered herself to be imposed upon so readily, and, as a remedy for the evil, offered herself back again; but I declined, preferring to enjoy once more the sweets of single blessedness.

I left the fort on a visit to San Fernandez. I found business very dull there on account of the war, and great apprehensions were felt by my friends in règard to the result. Perceiving that was no very desirable place to remove to, I returned to my community.

General Kearney was just then on his march to Santa Fé. I took a drove of my horses, and proceeded down the Arkansas to meet him on his route; for it was probable there might be an opportunity of effecting some advantageous exchanges. The general came up, and found me in waiting with my stock; we had been acquainted for several years, and he gave me a very cordial reception.

"Beckwourth," said the general, "you have a splendid lot of horses, really; they must have cost you a great sum of money."

"No, general," I replied, "but they cost me a great many miles of hard riding."

"How so?" he inquired.

"Why, I was in California at the time the war broke out, and, not having men enough at my command to take part in the fighting, I thought I could assist my country a little by starting off a small drove of the enemy's horses, in order to prevent their being used against us."

"Ah, Beckwourth, you are truly a wonderful man to possess so much forethought," and he laughed heartily. "However," added he, "trade them off as quickly as possible, for I want you to accompany me. You like war, and I have good use for you now."

I informed him that I was ready for service; and, accordingly, I sent all my remaining horses back to my plantation, and went on with the general to Santa Fé, which place submitted without firing a shot. The general sent me immediately back to Fort Leavenworth with dispatches. This was my service during the war. The occupation was a tolerably good one, and I never failed in getting my dispatches through. I enjoyed facilities superior to almost any other man, as I was known to almost all the Indians through whose country I passed.

My partner and I had purchased a hotel in Santa

Fé, and we transacted a very profitable business there. My associate attended to the business of the hotel, while I carried dispatches, and Santa Fé was generally my starting-place. Many messengers lost their lives on the route, as at times there were dispatches to be sent, and I would not be at head-quarters to carry them. The distance from Santa Fé to Fort Leavenworth is nine hundred and thirteen miles. I have frequently made the trip in from twenty to twenty-five days; my shortest trip I accomplished in eighteen. I well knew that my life was at stake every trip that I made, but I liked the employment; there was continual excitement in it, indeed sometimes more than I actually cared about, more particularly when I fell in with the Pawnees. The service furnished an escort of fifteen or twenty-five men, but I always declined the company of troops, as I considered myself safer without them. If I had taken troops with me, it would have led to incessant fights with the Indians; and if they had seen me with white soldiers, they would have been very apt to kill me the first opportunity. Another thing: I did not think the United States regular troops good for any thing against the Indians, for I knew that the Camanches would stand and fight them almost man for man.

I chanced to fall in with Kit Carson one day, as I was about to start from New Mexico to Fort Leavenworth, and he proposed going with me, as he wished to learn my route. I was very much pleased with his proposal, as I thought that with Kit and his men I should go through strong handed. I told him that I should rest at Taos one day to get my horses shod, and that he could easily come up with me there, or on the road thither. I left with two men, and staid at Taos as appointed, but he failed to rejoin us. I rode on as far as my ranch; still he did not appear. I built a large fire before proceeding into the Indian country, thinking to attract him by the smoke, and thus bring him on to our trail, but I saw no more of him, and it was supposed he was lost until he eventually turned up in the City of Washington. We both had a narrow escape from Indians on that trip. I had, contrary to my usual practice, encamped one night in the prairie, and was to start in the morning, when we heard buffalo running close to our camp. On looking out, I saw a great number chased by the Pawnees, although the Indians were not yet in sight. We made all possible haste to the timber, threw our horses on their sides, gagged them and fastened them to the ground, and then secreted ourselves in the willows. The Indians flocked round, busied in their pursuit, and some of the buffaloes they dressed within gunshot of our secret camp. I thought that day the longest I had lived through, and I expect the poor animals thought so too, for they lay in one position the whole time, without food or water, and without being permitted to whisper a complaint. At night we made good our escape, and arrived at the fort without further difficulty.

When I was ready to return to Santa Fé, I could find no one willing to accompany me. The weather was intensely cold, and no inducement that I could offer was sufficient to tempt men to leave their comfortable fires, and encounter the perils of the Indians and Jack Frost in the prairies. Many men had been frozen to death on the route, and a general shudder ran through the company when I proposed the journey to them. I could have been furnished with soldiers in plenty, but I was unwilling to take them, as it imposed so much trouble on the road to stay to bury every man that perished with the hardships of the journey. Important dispatches had arrived from Washington which must go through, and I looked fruitlessly round for a man hardy enough to go with me. At length a boy—a Kentuckian—volunteered. He had followed the army to the fort, and had lived about the barracks until he had become well accustomed to the privations of a camp life. He was an intelligent lad, but, unfortunately, had a malformation of one of his feet, which seriously impeded his walking. However, I liked his " pluck" in proposing, and eventually consented to take him. I went with him to the sutler's store, and procured him the warmest clothing I could, and then bade him repair to my boarding-house, and stay there until I was ready to start.

When I was prepared for departure, I furnished him with a good horse, and, taking an extra one between us, we started on the long journey. I gave him particular directions that if he should become very cold he was to acquaint me, and I would stay and build a fire to warm him by wherever there was any wood; but the proposition he declined.

Three days after we reached the Arkansas, and encamped. Isaac was busied in preparing supper, while I walked to an eminence close by in order to survey the country. I perceived an immense number of Indians approaching directly toward us, and at not more than three or four hundred yards distance. I shouted to Isaac to catch the horses quickly and tether them, and I hastened back to the camp. He inquired what the matter was, and I told him there were a thousand Indians coming after us.

The approaching individuals belonged to the Camanche tribe, and numbered over a thousand warriors. They were in full speed. They dashed through the Arkansas with such precipitation that I thought they would throw all the water out of the channel and hurl it on to the bank. I ran in front of the advance, and challenged them to stop. They halted for a moment, and asked me who I was. I told them the Crow. Thereupon they grabbed me up like a chicken, and carried me into our little camp. They had nine white men's scalps, which, to appearance, were hardly yet cold, and they said they must kill my white boy, and his scalp would just make ten. I told them the boy was my nephew, and that they must not kill him— that great braves never killed boys. They then conversed among themselves a minute or two, and finally said, " He, being your nephew, may live. Tell him to make us some good black soup."

I foresaw that my coffee and sugar must suffer, for by black soup they meant coffee. I directed Isaac to set about making it, but to secrete a little for ourselves, if he could do so unperceived. The Camanches have a great fondness for coffee, and I never fell in with them without having to part with all I had, and I sometimes imagined they preferred my coffee and sugar to my scalp.

The same day, just before dusk, while jogging steadily along, the boy discovered a small party of Pawnees. I hastily dismounted, and tied the heads of our three horses together, to prevent them running, and directed the boy to see that they did not move. I then took his gun and my own, and went away from the horses. As I was leaving, the boy inquired if he should fire too. I told him no, not unless I was killed, and then to defend himself as he best could. I took a secure position and fired. An Indian fell. I fired again, and killed a second. They cracked away at me, but did no harm. I reloaded, and fired again, until I had leveled five of them, they retreating at every discharge. When the fifth warrior fell, the whole party fell back to cry. I knew that, after they had cried for a few minutes, they would make a rush for revenge. Therefore I shouted to the boy to cut the animals loose, and mount in haste. He did so; I sprung on my horse instantly, and we flew away, leaving the mourners to their lamentations. At every foe I shot the boy would ejaculate, "Whoop! you fetched him; he's got his gruel," and other sayings, thereby displaying more bravery than many men would have shown under similar circumstances. Ever afterward he considered that we were a match for any number of Pawnees; and as for the Camanches, I could beat them off with "black soup."

We traveled on for several miles, and then encamped. In the morning I started along a ravine for our horses, which had strayed away. I returned toward the camp, where I found that they had taken themselves up another small ravine, and that I had passed them. While thus pursuing the stray animals, the boy came to acquaint me that he had seen a great number of Indians. I led the horses to the camp, and then mounted a little rise of ground, from whence I descried a large village. I did not know what tribe they belonged to, though I knew they were not Pawnees, for that tribe never visited this country except on war excursions. I took the boy, and walked with him up to the village, but their faces were all strange to me; nor did I like their appearance and movements. On perceiving one at a little distance wrapped in his robe, I thought he might possibly be a chief, and I approached him. He addressed me in Crow, "Ah! my friend, what brought you here?"

I replied that, as I was passing through, I had thought it well to call on him.

" I am glad to see you," said he; "enter my lodge; my warriors are bad to-day."

The Indians were Apaches, and the chief was named Black Shield, an old and intimate acquaintance.

He insisted on my spending the night in the village, which I consented to. He was perfectly rabid toward the whites, and stated his intention to manure the prairie with their bodies the forthcoming season— he would not leave one in the country. I applauded his intention, telling him the whites were unable to fight. Seeing that I was on his side—that is, if my words made me so—he continued, " I have plenty of warriors, and plenty of guns and balls, but I am a little short of powder. When will you return?"

I informed him as nearly as I could calculate, but I added that my return was uncertain.

" Will you bring me some powder?" he inquired.

" I will," I said; " but I shall return by way of the Eagle's Nest Hill."

" That is the very place I am going to from here," he rejoined; " and, if I am not there myself, some of my warriors will be, and they can take it of you."

This afforded me no put-off, and I accordingly promised to furnish him with the powder. If the reader will indulge me in a witticism, I beg to assure him that I carried the powder to the old chief in a *horn !* In the morning he furnished me with meat enough to subsist us for a week, together with new moccasins, and sundry other articles. We then bade him adieu, and proceeded on our journey, arriving at Santa Fé without any farther noteworthy adventure.

On reaching my destination, I informed some of my friends of my promise to the Black Shield, and where they could find him to deliver the powder, to enable him to carry out his commendable resolution. A party started to meet him at the appointed spot; but in delivering the powder they managed to explode it, and he and his warriors only received the bullets, of which they already had plenty.

CHAPTER XXXIV.

Affairs at Santa Fé.—Insurrection at Taos.—Discovery of the Plot.— Battle at the Cañon.—Battles at Lambida, at Pueblo, and at Taos. —A Mexican Woman redeemed from the Indians.—Return to Santa Fé.

ON my arrival at Santa Fé I found affairs in a very disturbed state. Colonel Doniphan had just gained the battle of Brasito, and was carrying all before him in that section of the country. He had forwarded orders to Santa Fé for a field battery, in order to make a demonstration against Chihuahua. Major Clarke was intrusted with the duty of conveying the artillery to the colonel. Scarcely had he departed when we received intelligence of an insurrection in Taos. The information was first communicated by an Indian from a village between Santa Fé and Taos, who reported to General Price that the Mexicans had massacred all the white inhabitants of that place, and that a similar massacre was contemplated in Santa Fé, of which report full information could be obtained by the arrest of a Mexican who was then conveying a letter from the priest in Taos to the priest in Santa Fé. A watch was immediately set upon the priest's house, and a Mexican was seen to enter. The guard approached the door to arrest the man as he issued, but he, being apprised of the action of the authorities, left the house by another door, and escaped.

At night there came a violent rapping at my gate, and on going to open it I perceived my friend, Charles Towne, who, on being admitted, clasped me round the neck, and gave vent to uncontrolled emotion. Perceiving that something alarming had occurred, I invited him into the house, spread refreshments before him, and allowed him time to recover himself. He then informed me that he had escaped almost by a miracle from Taos, where all the American residents had been killed. He was a resident there, having married a girl of New Mexico, and his wife's father had apprised him that he had better effect his escape, if possible, for if he was caught he would be inevitably massacred. His father-in-law provided him with a good horse, and he retreated into the woods, where, after considerable risk and anxiety, he providentially eluded the assassins.

On receiving this alarming information, I lost no time in repairing to the head-quarters of General Price, accompanied by my informant, who related the above particulars. General Price immediately adopted the most effective measures. He assembled his officers, and instructed them to set a close watch upon the house of every Mexican in the city, and to suffer no person to pass in or out; he also ordered that every American should hold himself in readiness for service during the night. Before morning several of the most influential Mexican citizens were placed under arrest.

In searching them, important conspiracies were brought to light. Correspondence, implicating the most considerable residents, was read, and a plot was detected of subjecting Santa Fé to the same St. Bartholomew massacre as had just been visited upon Taos. The city was placed under martial law, and every American that could shoulder a musket was called into immediate service. All the ox-drivers, mule-drivers, merchants, clerks, and commissariat-men were formed into rank and file, and placed in a condition for holding the city. Then, placing himself at the head of his army, four hundred strong, General Price marched toward Taos. On arriving at Canjarra, a small town about twenty miles from Santa Fé, we found the enemy, numbering two thousand Mexicans and Indians, were prepared to give us battle. The enemy's lines were first perceived by our advanced guard, which instantly fell back upon the main body. Our line was formed, and an advance made upon the enemy, the mountaineer company, under Captain Saverine, being placed in charge of the baggage. As soon as battle was begun, however, we left the baggage and ammunition wagons to take care of themselves, and made a descent upon the foe. He fled precipitately before the charge of our lines, and we encamped upon the field of battle. The next day we advanced to Lamboda, where the enemy made another stand, and again fled on our approach. We marched on until we arrived at Taos, and the barbarities we witnessed there exceeded in brutality all my previous experience with the Indians. Bodies of our murdered fellow-countrymen were lying about the streets, mutilated and disfigured in every possible way, and the hogs and dogs were making a repast upon the remains. Among the dead we recognized that of Governor Bent, who had been recently appointed by General Kearney. One poor victim we saw, who had been stripped naked, scalped alive, and his eyes punched out: he was groping his way through the streets, beseeching some one to shoot him out of his misery, while his inhuman Mexican tormentors were deriving the greatest amusement from the exhibition. Such scenes of unexampled barbarity filled our soldiers' breasts with abhorrence: they became tigerlike in their craving for revenge. Our general directed the desecrated remains to be gathered together, and a guard to be placed over them, while he marched on with his army in pursuit of the barbarians.

Late in the afternoon we arrived at Pueblo, where we found the enemy well posted, having an adobe fort in their front. No attack was attempted that evening, and strict orders were issued for no man to venture out of camp.

In the evening I was visited by a man, who informed me that he had a brother at Rio Mondo, twelve miles distant, whom, if he was not already killed, he wished to save from massacre. I determined to rescue him, if possible, and, having induced seven other good and trusty mountaineers to aid me in the attempt, we left the camp unperceived, and proceeded to the place indicated. On our arrival we found two or three hundred Mexicans, all well armed; we rode boldly past them, and they dispersed, many of them going to their homes. We reached the door of the Mexican general Montaja, who styled himself the "Santa Anna of the North," and captured him. We then liberated the prisoner we were in quest of, and returned to Taos with our captive general. At Taos we found our forces, which had retired upon that place from Pueblo, after having made an unsuccessful attempt to dislodge the enemy. We informed our general of our important capture, and he affected great displeasure at our disobedience of orders, although it was easy to see that, in his eyes, the end had justified the means The following morning a gallows was erected, and Montaja was swung in the wind. The correspondence that had been seized in Santa Fé had implicated him in some of the blackest plots, and we thought that this summary disposal of his generalship would relieve us from all further danger from his machinations.

Having procured artillery to bombard the enemy's position, our commander returned to Pueblo. We cannonaded in good earnest, but the pieces were too small to be of much service; but we cut a breach with our axes half way through the six-foot wall, and then finished the work with our cannon. While engaged in this novel way of getting at the enemy, a shell was thrown from a mortar at the fort; but our artillerymen, not being very skillful in their practice, threw the shell outside the fort, and it fell among us. A young lieutenant seized it in his hands, and cast it through the breach; it had not more than struck before it exploded, doing considerable damage in the fort. We then stormed the breach, which was only big enough to admit one man at a time, and carried the place without difficulty.

The company of mountaineers had fallen back midway between the fort and mountain, in order to pick off any Mexican who should dare to show himself. We killed fifty-four of the defenders as they were endeavoring to escape, upon the person of one of whom, an officer, we found one hundred and sixty doubloons. Some of the enemy fired upon us from a position at one corner of the fort, through loop-holes; and while looking about for a covert to get a secure shot at them, we discovered a few of the enemy hidden away in the brush. One of them, an Indian, ran toward us, exclaiming, "Bueno! bueno! me like Americanos." One of our party said, " If you like the Americans, take this sword, and return to the brush, and kill all the men you find there."

He took the proffered sword, and was busy in the brush for a few minutes, and then returned with his sword-blade dripping with gore, saying, " I have killed them."

" Then you ought to die for killing your own people," said the American, and he shot the Indian dead.

The battle lasted through the whole day, and a close watch was set at night to prevent the escape of those yet occupying the fort. The assault was renewed the following morning, and continued during that day also. Toward night several white flags were raised by the enemy, but were immediately shot down by the Americans, who had determined to show no quarter. On the third morning all the women issued from the fort, each bearing a white flag, and kneeled before the general to supplicate for the lives of their surviving friends. The general was prevailed upon, and gave orders to cease firing. The enemy lost severely through their disgraceful cowardice. Our company lost but one man through the whole engagement. Nine of the most prominent conspirators were hanged at Taos, and seven or eight more at Santa Fé. It was about this time that the report reached us of the butchery of Mr. Waldo, with eight or ten other Americans, at the Moro.

After the insurrection was suppressed I started again for Fort Leavenworth. On my way back from the fort I again fell in with Black Shield and his Apaches. I said to him, "You told me false. You said that you would meet me at the Eagle's Nest, but when I went there you were not to be found. I had to throw the powder away that I brought for you, and run for my life; for the whites discovered my errand, and were close at my heels."

"I know it, my friend," said the Black Shield. "We saw your kegs there, but the whites had taken all the powder out. I am sorry they came upon you so suddenly, for we had to run as well as you."

The second day after we left the Apaches we discovered an object in the distance which I at first took for a stump, but still thought it singular that there should be a stump where there were no trees near. As we approached the object moved, and we at length discovered it to be a man of the name of Elliott Lee, who had been wounded by the Apaches three or four days previously, and had not tasted food since. He had belonged to a party of seventeen or eighteen mountaineers, on their way to Santa Fé. They had stopped to rest on the bank of a creek, and were suddenly set upon by the Indians. Several of the party were killed, among whom was my friend Charles Towne, and all the rest were more or less severely wounded. Some few had succeeded in getting away, notwithstanding their wounds; but Mr. Lee had been shot in the thigh, and was unable to crawl along. When we picked him up he was delirious, and his wound was greatly swollen and inflamed. We gave him food, and carried him along with us, until we fortunately came up with his wagons. We then gave him into the keeping of his friends, and proceeded on our way.

On my arrival home I disposed of all my property in Santa Fé, and started to buy horses of the Indians to dispose of to the discharged troops. I had arrived within a short distance of my ranch, when I met a man who advised me to conceal myself. Two rewards had been offered for my apprehension: one of a thousand dollars by Colonel Price, and another of five hundred dollars by Mr. Kissack, Quarter-master. I was accused of confederating with rebels and Indians, and assisting them in stealing horses from the whites, and leading the hostile bands in their warfare upon the American troops.

I listened to his information, and was astonished at the invention. "That is news indeed," I said. "But they shall not have the profit all to themselves; I will immediately go and deliver myself up, and obtain the rewards."

"I advise you, as a friend, not to go," rejoined my interlocutor, "for they will assuredly hang you directly they lay hands upon you."

"Well, hang or not hang," I answered, "I am resolved to go, for I have not been a month absent from Santa Fé, and I can give account of every day and night I have since spent."

At the time I met with my informant, I had an order from Captain Morris, of the United States Army, in my pocket, authorizing me to pick up all the government horses that I might find in my rambles, and bring them in; but up to the time that I was informed of the charges against me, I had found but one horse, the property of Captain Saverine, and it I had restored to the owner. Accordingly, I returned without delay to Taos, where I saw Colonel Willock, who was lieutenant under Colonel Price. Him I acquainted with my determination to proceed to Santa Fé, to deliver myself up for the rewards that were offered for my apprehension, but he urgently requested me not to go. He was about to start with an expedition against the Apaches, and wished to engage me as spy, interpreter, and guide. He promised to forward an exculpatory letter to Santa Fé that should set me all right with the authorities. The letter was sent, but not delivered, as the messenger was shot on the way.

I concluded to accompany the colonel, and aid him to the extent of my ability in the object of his expedition. We started with a small battalion of volunteers for the Apaches. The first day in camp, the common soldier's fare was spread for dinner, which at that time I felt but little appetite for. I informed the colonel that I would go out and kill an antelope.

"Why," said he, "there is not an antelope within ten miles around; the soldiers have scoured the whole country without seeing one."

I told him I felt sure I could find one, and took up my rifle and was about to start.

"Hold on!" cried the colonel; "I will go with you, and will further engage to pack on my back all you kill."

We started, and kept on the road for about half a mile, when I discovered the tracks of three antelopes which had just crossed our path, and gone in the direction of a hill close by. The colonel did not see the tracks, and I did not point them out to him. We passed on a few rods farther, when I suddenly stopped, threw my head back, and began to sniff like a dog scenting his prey.

"What the dickens are you sniffing so for?" asked the colonel.

"I am sure that I smell an antelope," said I.

"You smell antelope!" and the colonel's nostrils began to dilate; "I can smell nothing."

"Well, colonel," I said, "there are antelopes close by, I know, for my smellers never yet deceived me; and now," added I, "if you will start carefully up that hollow, I will go up on the other side, and I am confident that one of us will kill one."

I knew that if the animals were in the hollow they would start at the approach of the colonel, and most probably in my direction, and thus afford me an opportunity of getting a shot at one. I proceeded cautiously along, until, raising my head over a knoll, I saw the three antelopes which had crossed us. Two had already lain down, and the third was preparing to do so, when I sent a leaden messenger which brought him down involuntarily.

The colonel shouted to inquire what I had shot at.

"Antelope," I answered; and he came running at his best speed. There was the very beast, beyond all dispute, to the utter astonishment of the colonel, who regarded for some moments first the game and then the hunter

"And you smelled them!" he pondered; "well, I must confess, your olfactory nerves beat those of any man I ever yet fell in with. Smell antelope! Humph! I will send my boy to carry him in."

"But that was not the bargain, colonel," I said; "you engaged to pack in on your back all I should kill. There is your burden; the distance is but short."

But the colonel declined his engagement. We finally hung the antelope on a tree, and the colonel, on our return to camp, dispatched his servant to fetch it in. He never could get over my smelling antelope, and we have had many a hearty laugh at it since.

The following morning, at daylight, I took five or six men with me, and proceeded on my duty as spy, while the colonel moved on with the troops, we returning to camp every evening at dusk. We frequently saw signs of Indians, but we could make no discovery of the Indians themselves. We continued our chase for nearly a month; our coffee and sugar had given out, and our provisions were getting low; the soldiers could kill no game, and there was a general disposition, especially among the officers, to return.

In leaving the camp, as usual, one morning, I directed the colonel to a camping-ground, and started on my search. Late in the afternoon, I discovered what I supposed to be a large party of Indians moving in our direction. I ran with all possible speed to communicate the information; but, in ascending a small point of land which was in my way, I found a strange encampment of United States troops lying before me. I knew it was not Colonel Willock's command, for these had tents, wagons, and other appointments, which we were unprovided with. When I was first perceived, some of the men pointed me out to their companions; "There's Beckwourth! there's Jim Beckwourth!" I heard whispered around. I found it was a detachment commanded by Colonel Edmondson, who had just returned from Santa Fé with a re-enforcement, having been defeated in an engagement with the Apaches some time previously. When the colonel saw me, he inquired of me my errand.

"I have come after horses," I replied, *en plaisant-ant;* "but I see you have none."

"Beckwourth," said a Captain Donohue, "I have been defending your character for a long time, and I now want you to clear up matters for yourself."

I found I was not in very good savor among the parties present, owing to a mistake in my identity made by one of the soldiers during their late engagement with the Indians. It was supposed I had entered their camp, hurled my lance through a soldier, and challenged another out to fight, telling him he was paid for fighting, and it was his duty to engage me. This suspicion, added to flying reports of evil doings, which derived their origin in the Crow village from my adventure with Fitzpatrick, had associated me in the soldiers' minds with all the horse-raids and white massacres they heard rumors of, and I was regarded by them all as a desperate, lawless character, who deserved hanging to the first tree wherever met.

At this moment two men came running toward the camp at full speed, shouting, " To arms! to arms!" as though the whole Apache nation were behind them.

" Where is your party ?" asked Colonel Edmondson of me.

" Coming yonder, sir," I replied, pointing in the direction of the two approaching heralds; for I supposed it was Colonel Willock's command they had seen, and whom, in their fright, they had mistaken for Indians.

Immediately there was a bustle of preparation to receive the coming foe: muskets were snatched up, and the men fell into line ; but in a few moments the real character of the approaching company was ascertained, and the colonel advanced to greet them. At the junction of the two parties, both engaged on the same errand, matters were discussed by the two colonels, and it was resolved to abandon the expedition, for it was manifest that the Indians were too much on the alert to be taken. I was dispatched to Santa Fé with a letter to Colonel Price from Colonels Edmond-

son and Willock, while they resolved to march back
with their detachments, Colonel Edmondson to Santa
Fé, and Colonel Willock to Taos.

The morning following I again set out for Fort
Leavenworth, having for companion M'Intosh, who,
by the way, was a Cherokee, and known as such to
the Indians whom we fell in with on the road. We
reached the fort without any accident, and delivered
our dispatches safe. On our return we overtook Bullard
and Company's trains of wagons, which were on their
way to Santa Fé with supplies for the army. Bullard
and his partner proposed to leave their charge and go in
with us, if I thought we would be able to keep up with
them. I answered that we would try and keep their
company as far as possible, but that they would be at
liberty to proceed at any time that they considered we
retarded them. They went with us as far as the
Moro, two days' ride from Santa Fé, where we were
compelled to leave them, as they were tired out, and
had already detained us two full days.

My next engagement in the service of Uncle Sam
was a trip to Chihuahua to convey dispatches; but,
previous to starting, Captain Morris wished to engage
me as guide in an expedition against the Utah Indians;
so, preferring the latter service, I transferred my trust
to my brave and faithful friend, M'Intosh, and accompanied Captain Morris. The expedition consisted of
ninety men: the object was a treaty of peace with
the Utahs. We succeeded in finding the Indians;
but, as they supposed our only object was to fight, it
was some time before we could get up to them. We
at length surprised them in a gap in the mountain,
when we succeeded in taking a number of prisoners,
among whom were some chiefs. We explained our

object; they then frankly informed us where their village was; we all repaired to it, and concluded terms of peace. Our approach greatly alarmed the village at first, for they knew that, in conjunction with the Apaches, they had been guilty of many depredations, although it had been their policy to throw all the blame of the mischief upon their allies. Our mission performed, we returned to Taos.

I remained some weeks inactive. Taos was convulsed with continual alarms from reports that Cortez was approaching against us with a great force. The troops were all away at Santa Fé; though, had he visited us, we could have improvised a warm reception. We had a small piece of cannon, with plenty of grape and canister, with which we could have swept the streets. We tried its effect one day, just to satisfy the curiosity of the Mexicans: we put in a heavy charge of grape-shot, and discharged it down the street. The tawny Mexicans were wonder-stricken: they thought an army would stand but a poor chance before such a volcanic belching of iron missiles.

Poultry in the vicinity of Taos became exceeding scarce: it was a rare matter to hear a cock crow. When we did by chance hear the pleasing sound, we would listen for the repetition of it, in order to learn from which direction it proceeded. We would then visit the tell-tale's quarters after dark, as we could obtain our poultry cheaper at night than in the day-time. Orders had been issued to take nothing from the enemy without paying for it, which orders were evidently based upon the assumption that we had money to pay with. Those without money did not feel themselves bound by the injunction. The authorities that issue similar commands in future would do well to insert some clause binding on the *moneyless*, otherwise these orders are all moonshine.

From Taos I proceeded to Santa Fé. I again started, for the last time, to Fort Leavenworth; M'Intosh, having safely returned from Chihuahua, again accompanying me. When we arrived at the Wagon Mound we heard shots fired, and immediately after met a train of mule-teams approaching at their quickest pace. The drivers advised us to return, as they had been attacked by the Apaches, and if we proceeded we could not escape being killed. I thought that my companion and I knew the Indians better than the mule-drivers did, and we bade them good-by and started on. We intended to avoid the Indians by making a circuit away from where we expected they would be, but in so doing we came directly upon the village. We staid all night with them, were well treated, and resumed our journey in the morning. We met a party of Americans who had been attacked by the Camanches, and lost one horse, but we saw no more Indians until we reached the fort.

Many times wonder has been expressed how I could always travel the road in safety while other men were attacked and killed. The only way in which I could account for the marvel was that I knew how to act the "wolf," while the others did not. Of all the dispatches I ever carried, I never lost one; while numbers who have undertaken to bear them lost, not alone the dispatches, but their lives; for, whenever they fell in with the Indians, they were sure to be killed. The Indians knew perfectly well what my business was. They knew that I was conveying orders backward and forward from the great white chief to his war chiefs in New Mexico. They would frequently ask me what the orders were which I had with me. Sometimes I would tell them that the great chief at Washington was going to send on a great host of warriors to rub them all out. They would laugh heartily at the supposition, for they conceived that all the American forces combined would hardly be a circumstance before them. I promised to apprise them when the white warriors were to advance against them, which promise they confidently relied upon. I had to say something to keep on good terms with them, and answer their inquiries to satisfy them, and then proceed with my business. The war between the great white chief and the great Mexican chief interested the Indians but little, though their conviction was that the Mexican chief would be victorious. Their sympathy was with the latter, from motives of self-interest. They were now able to go at any time and drive home all the horses, cattle, and sheep that they wanted, together with Mexican children enough to take care of them. If the white chief conquered, they supposed he would carry all the horses, cattle, and sheep home with him, and thus leave none for them.

The Camanches and Apaches have a great number of Mexicans, of both sexes, among them, who seldom manifest much desire to return home. The women say that the Indians treat them better than they are treated at home. I never met but one exception to this rule, and that was a young Mexican woman captive among the Camanches. She told me that her father was wealthy, and would give me five thousand dollars if I could procure her restoration. I bought her of the chief, and conveyed her to my fort, whence I sent information to her father to acquaint him where he could find his daughter. In a few days her father and her

husband came to her.   She refused to have any thing
to say to her husband, for she said he was a coward.
When the Indians attacked the village, he mounted
his horse and fled, leaving her to their mercy.   Her
father proffered me the promised sum, but I only accepted one thousand dollars, which returned me a very
good profit on the cost of the goods I had given to the
Indians for her ransom.   The woman returned home
with her father, her valorous husband following them.
Shortly after this I returned to Santa Fé.

CHAPTER XXXV.

Departure for California. — Meeting with the Apaches. — Hostile
Threats.—Trouble with the Utahs.—Most terrible Tragedy.—Society in California.—Adventures with Grizzly Bears.

THE last dispatches I bore from Fort Leavenworth
were addressed to California, and I had undertaken to
carry them through.   At Santa Fé I rested a week,
and then, taking an escort of fifteen men, I started on
my errand.   On our arrival at the village of Abbeger,
we found a large party of Apaches, who were in the
midst of a drunken carousal.   We encamped inside the
corral, that being as safe a place as we could select.
Little Joe, an Apache Chief, inquired of me what I was
going to do with these whites.

"I am going to take them to California," I told him.

"No," said he, "you shall never take them nearer
to California than they are now."

"Well, I shall try," said I.

He held some farther conversation with me of a de-
nunciatory character, and then left me to return to the
liquor-shop.

Foreseeing what was likely to result if more liquor was obtained, I visited every place in town where it was kept, and informed every seller that, if another drop was sold to the Indians, I would hang the man that did it without a minute's delay; and I would have been as good as my word, for they were all Mexicans, and I had felt no great liking for them since the awful tragedy at Taos.

"But the priest—" began one or two, in expostulation.

But I cut them short. "I'll hang your priest just as soon as any of you," I said, "if he dares to interfere in the matter."

I suppose they intended to urge that their priest had authorized them to sell liquors to the Indians. My interdict stopped them, for there was no more sold while I was there.

The next day I saw Little Joe in one of the low saloons; the stimulus of the liquor had left him, and he had what topers call the *horrors*. He begged me to let him have one dram more, but I refused.

"Whisky," I said, "puts all kinds of nonsense into your head; you get drunk, and then you are ripe for any mischief."

When he had become perfectly sober, he came to me, and again asked if it were true that I intended taking those whites to California with me.

I told him that it was perfectly true.

"Well," said Joe, "if you attempt it we will kill your whole party, and you with them. You will never listen to us: your ears are stopped. We all love you, but we have told you many times that we hate the whites, and do not want you to lead them through our hunting-grounds, and show them our paths; but you will not listen to us. And now, if you undertake to pass through that *cañon*, we will, without fail, kill you all."

"Well," I replied, "I shall certainly go, so you had better get your warriors ready."

We packed our animals, and I directed my men to travel slowly while I went through the *cañon*. If I wished them to advance, I would climb up and show myself to them as a signal for them to rush through, and reach me as soon as possible. I then went on all alone, as I knew that, if I encountered Indians in the *cañon*, they would not kill me by myself. I passed through without meeting any, and I signaled to the men to come on; they soon joined me, and we issued upon the open prairie. Here we discovered three hundred Apaches, each man leading his war-horse. We numbered eighteen, two of whom were Mexicans. They did not offer to attack us, however, and we continued our route unmolested, although they kept on our trail for twenty miles. A little before dark we rested to take supper, starting again immediately after the meal was finished. We saw no more of the Apaches.

The following afternoon a Utah came to us. I asked him where his village was. He did not know, he said, as he had been away some time. I was going out to shoot game at the time, and I took the Indian with me, lending him a gun belonging to one of my men. I had killed two or three wild turkeys, when my Indian, discovering deer some distance off, went in pursuit. I returned to the camp, but the fellow had not arrived. When we started in the morning he had not shown himself. The second day after the disappearance of the Indian with my gun, I was some distance in advance of the party, when, on ascending a hill, I saw a large party of Utahs ahead. They were looking down, and examining the trail very closely, to see if we had passed. This convinced me that the Indian fugitive had lied to me; that he knew well where his village was, and had, no doubt, been sent out from it as a spy. We held on our way till we came up with them, and, it being then about noon, we halted to take a long rest. The Indians soon came flocking round us, but I gave strict orders to the men to keep a good look-out, and upon no account to let them touch the fire-arms. They swarmed round the camp, entering it one at a time, and I determined to make the first troublesome advance an excuse for getting rid of them.

We packed up, and moved on through the whole mass of Indians, but they did not venture an attack, although it had been their intention to do so if they could have got any advantage over us through our negligence. They were embittered against the whites at that time, on account of a severe whipping that had been recently inflicted upon two of their warriors by Chouteau, who had just passed through them, for a theft from his camp. To receive a whipping, especially at the hands of a white man, is looked upon by them as a lasting infamy, and they would prefer death to the disgrace. The next morning they overtook us again, and the Indian returned me my gun. I mollified them with a few trifling presents, and they finally left us on apparently good terms.

The next hostile country that lay upon our road was that of the Navajo tribe. They followed us through their whole strip of territory, shouting after us, and making insulting gestures; but they took the precaution to keep out of gun-shot range, and I did not think it worth my while to chastise them.

The next tribe on our route was the Pi-u-ches, which is also the last before you reach Pueblo in California. The first Pi-u-ches that we came across were an Indian and his squaw engaged in digging roots. On seeing us approach, the Indian took to his heels, leaving the squaw to take care of herself. I rode up to her and asked where her village was. She pointed in the direction of it, but I could not see it. The next one that I saw stooped and concealed himself in the grass immediately he found himself observed; but I rode up to him, and made him show himself, not wishing to have him think that he could escape our notice so easily. He accompanied me for a short distance, until another of the tribe shouted to him from a hill, and he then left me.

We encamped that night upon the prairie. At dusk we observed the smoke of camp-fires in every direction, and shortly we were visited by hundreds of Indians, who entirely hemmed us in; but, on their finding that we were not Mexicans, they did not offer to molest us. They were hostile on account of the continual abductions of their squaws and children, whom the Mexicans employ as domestic slaves, and treat with the utmost cruelty.

We reached our destination in safety, and I delivered my dispatches. I was now inactive for some time again, and occupied my leisure in rambling about the environs of Monterey. I then engaged in the service of the commissariat at Monterey, to carry dispatches from thence to Captain Denny's ranch, where I was met by another carrier. On my road lay the mission of St. Miguel, owned by a Mr. Reed, an Englishman; and, as his family was a very interesting one, I generally made his home my resting-place. On one of my visits, arriving about dusk, I entered the house as usual, but was surprised to see no one stirring. I walked about a little to attract attention, and no one coming to me, I stepped into the kitchen to look for some of the inmates. On the floor I saw some one lying down, asleep, as I supposed. I attempted to arouse him with my foot, but he did not stir. This seemed strange, and my apprehensions became excited; for the Indians were very numerous about, and I was afraid some mischief had been done. I returned to my horse for my pistols, then, lighting a candle, I commenced a search. In going along a passage, I stumbled over the body of a woman; I entered a room, and found another, a murdered Indian woman, who had been a domestic. I was about to enter another room, but I was arrested by some sudden thought which urged me to search no farther. It was an opportune admonition, for that very room contained the murderers of the family, who had heard my steps, and were sitting at that moment with their pistols pointed to the door, ready to shoot the first person that entered. This they confessed subsequently.

Thinking to obtain farther assistance, I mounted my horse and rode to the nearest ranch, a distance of twenty-four miles, where I procured fifteen Mexicans and Indians, and returned with them the same night to the scene of the tragedy. On again entering the house, we found eleven bodies all thrown together in one pile for the purpose of consuming them; for, on searching further, we found the murderers had set fire to the dwelling, but, according to that Providence which exposes such wicked deeds, the fire had died out.

Fastening up the house, we returned immediately back to the ranch from which I had started with my party, making seventy-two miles I rode that night. As soon as I could obtain some rest, I started, in company with the alcalde, for St. Louis Obispo, where, it was believed, we could get assistance in capturing the murderers. Forty men in detached parties, moving in different directions, went in pursuit. It was my fortune to find the trail, and with my party of six men I managed to head off the suspected murderers so as to come up with them in the road from directly the opposite direction from Reed's house. When I came opposite, one of the men sang out, "Good-day, señors." I replied, but kept on riding in a lope.

The bandits, thrown entirely off their guard, insisted upon entering into conversation; so I had a fair opportunity of marking them all, and discovering among them a horse belonging to the unfortunate Reed. I then rode to Santa Barbara, a distance of forty miles, and, with a party of twenty men, started boldly in pursuit. After much hard travel, we finally came upon the gang, encamped for the night. Without a moment's hesitation, we charged on them, and gave a volley of rifles, which killed one, and wounded all the others, save an American named Dempsey. The villains fought like tigers, but were finally mastered and made prisoners.

Dempsey turned state's evidence. He stated that, on the night of the murder, his party stopped at Reed's; that Reed told them that he had just returned from the mines, whereupon it was determined to kill the whole family and take his gold, which turned out to be the pitiful sum of one thousand dollars. After the confession of Dempsey, we shot the murderers, along with the "state's evidence," and thus ended the lives of two Americans, two Englishmen, and ten Irishmen, they having committed the most diabolical deed that ever disgraced the annals of frontier life.

I continued in this service of carrying dispatches some four months, varying my route with an occasional trip to San Francisco. At this time society in California was in the worst condition to be found, probably, in any part of the world, to call it civilized. The report of the discovery of gold had attracted thither lawless and desperate characters from all parts of the earth, and the government constituted for their control was a weaker element than the offenders it had to deal with. The rankest excesses were familiar occurrences, and men were butchered under the very eyes of the officers of justice, and no action was taken in the matter. What honest men there were became alarmed, and frequently would abandon the richest placers for the mere security of their lives, and leave a whole community of rowdies to prey upon each other. Disorder attained its limit, and some reactionary means would naturally be engendered as a corrective to the existing evils. The establishment of "Vigilance Committees" among the better order of citizens operated as a thunderbolt upon the conniving civil officers and the rank perpetrators of crime. Scores of villains were snatched from the hands of these mock officers, and summarily strung up to the limb of the nearest tree. Horse and cattle thieves had their necks disjointed so frequently that it soon became safe for a man to leave his horse standing in the street for a few moments, while he stepped into a house to call upon his friend, and that widely-practiced business was quickly done away with.

Such sudden justice overtook murderers, robbers, and other criminals, that honest people began to breathe more freely, and acquired a sense of security while engaged in their ordinary pursuits. The *materiel* for crime still existed, and is yet present in California to an alarming extent; but order may be considered as confirmed in the supremacy, though inevitably many social evils still exist, which time alone will remedy.

In the month of April, 1849, the steamship California touched at Monterey, she being the first steam-vessel that had visited there from the States. I, with a party of fifteen others, stepped on board, and proceeded as far as Stockton, where we separated into various parties. I left with one man to go to Sonora, where we erected the first tent, and commenced a business in partnership. I had carried a small lot of clothing along with me, which I disposed of to the miners at what now seems to me fabulous prices. Finding the business thus profitable, I sent my partner back to Stockton for a farther supply, and he brought several mules laden with goods. This lot was disposed of as readily as the first, and at prices equally remunerative. This induced us to continue the business, he performing the journeys backward and forward, and I remaining behind to dispose of the goods and attend to other affairs. Sonora was rapidly growing into a large village, and our tent was replaced with a roomy house. I had a corps of Indians in my employ to take charge of the horses left in my care by miners and other persons, sometimes to the number of two hundred at once. I also employed Indians to work in the mines, I furnishing them with board and implements to work with, and they paying me with one half of their earnings. Their general yield was from five to six ounces a day each man, a moiety of which they faithfully rendered to me. Among my earliest visitors was a party

of eighteen United States dragoons, who came to me
to be fitted out with citizen's clothing, as they had
brought to a sudden period their service to their country. It was an impossible thing at that time to retain troops in California, for the produce of the mines
held out a temptation to desert that none seemed able
to resist, as more gold could be dug sometimes in one
day than would pay a private for a year's service in
the army; even officers of considerable rank not unfrequently threw aside epaulette and sash, and shouldered the pick to repair to the diggings.

While at Sonora I learned that Colonel Fremont
was at Mariposa, and I made a journey over there for
the purpose of seeing him. I was disappointed in my
expectation, and started to return home again. While
proceeding quietly along, having left the main road
and taken up a hollow, I perceived two men approaching me from the opposite direction, running at
the top of their speed, and a crowd of Indians after
them in pursuit. When they came up, they shouted
to me to turn and fly for my life, or the Indians
would certainly massacre me. I bade them stop, and
quiet their fears. Seeing my self-possession, notwithstanding the near approach of the Indians, they at
length halted, and approached close to me for protection against their pursuers. I then commanded the
Indians to stand, telling them that they were my men.
They said they were not aware of that, or they should
not have chased them. The Indians I was acquainted with; they had been frequently to my house to invite me to their village. They wished to purchase
goods of me, and had promised me a mule-load of gold
dust if I would only supply them with what they were
in need of. I accompanied them to their village, but

my two rescued companions were not admitted into their lodges. They then renewed their promise of the mule-load of gold dust if I would bring out the goods they wanted. I never went to them, although it was remiss in me, for they had a great quantity of gold dust. I left after a brief visit, and rejoined the two men. They could not sufficiently express their gratitude to me for their deliverance, as they considered my opportune appearance alone saved their lives.

Becoming tired of my business in Sonora, for inactivity fatigued me to death, I disposed of my interest in it for six thousand dollars, and went on to Sacramento City with the money in my pocket. From this place I traveled on to Murderer's Bar, which lies on the middle fork of the American River; here I found my old friend Chapineau house-keeping, and staid with him until the rainy season set in. Thence I proceeded to Greenwood Valley to establish my winter quarters, but I was seized with an attack of inflammatory rheumatism, and I had a nice time of it that winter. Before I was able to get about, I was called on by the inhabitants to go several miles to shoot a grizzly bear, and as I was unable to walk the distance, several of them volunteered to carry me. The bear was in the habit of walking past a row of cabins every morning on his return to his den, he having issued forth the preceding night to procure his evening meal. They had fired several shots at Bruin as he passed, but he had never deigned to pay any attention to the molestation. I mounted a horse, and rode some distance along his customary path, until I came to a tree which offered a fair shelter to await his approach. I placed my back against it as a support while I awaited his coming, the neighbors drawing off to a safe distance to witness the sport. By-and-by Grizzly came in sight, walking along as independently as an alderman elect. I allowed him to approach till he was within twenty paces, when I called out to him; he stopped suddenly, and looked around to ascertain whence the sound proceeded. As he arrested himself, I fired, and the ball entered his heart. He advanced ten or fifteen paces before he fell; the observers shouted to me to run, they forgetting in their excitement that I had not strength to move. The bear never stirred from where he fell, and he expired without a groan. When dressed, he weighed over fourteen hundred pounds.

The grizzly bear is a formidable animal, and has acted a prominent part among the settlers of California. They are seldom known to attack a man unless wounded; in that case, if a tree is by, the hunter had better commence climbing. They are very plenty from the Sierra Nevada to the coast range of mountains. I have, in the course of my sojourn in the country, killed a great many of them, and met with some singular adventures.

On one occasion, while I was with the Crow Indians, there was a man of the name of Coe who was trapping in one of the neighboring streams, and I became alarmed for his safety, as Black Foot parties were skulking about in all directions, and were sure to kill him if they should find his camp. I found Coe, and told him my fears. He instantly gathered up his traps, and, mounting his horse, started toward me. When within fair gun-shot, an old bear sprang from a thicket, and landed upon the flanks of his horse, applying his teeth to the roots of the poor animal's tail, and holding him as if in a vice. Coe leaned over his horse's neck, and cried out,

ATTACK OF A GRIZZLY BEAR.

" Shoot, Jim! shoot quick!"

I could not help laughing to have saved my life, as he turned from side to side, though his situation was a critical one. I soon got in a favorable position, and put a ball in the animal's head, just behind the ear, when he liberated the horse and his rider, falling on his back apparently stone dead.

There is a story, remembered by the mountaineers, of a person named Keyere. He was a man who never exceeded one hundred pounds in weight, but was clear grit, what little there was of him. He went out one day alone, and his horse came back in the evening without his rider, and we thought that the Indians had made sure of poor Keyere's scalp. The next morning a small party of us started on the horse's trail, and found Keyere lying beside a large dead grizzly bear. Keyere was horribly mutilated and insensible, but still alive, and must have soon died if no one had come to his rescue.

We took him to camp, and nursed him with all possible care. When he recovered sufficiently to tell his tale, his story was received with shouts of laughter, and was rehearsed as a wonderful joke from camp to camp. Keyere stated that, when he saw the grizzly, he got from his horse to shoot him, but unfortunately only wounded the animal. The bear (so Keyere says) caught hold of him, and commenced a regular rough-and-tumble fight; finally Keyere got a good lick at the bear's head, knocked him down with his fist, and then attempted to run away. The bear, however, was too quick, when Keyere, becoming desperate, seized the beast by the tongue, drew his knife, and stabbed the creature to the heart!

Improbable as is the tale, it was a singular fact,

that, when Keyere was found, his knife was up to the
maker's name in the bear's side, and the body showed
the effects of other severe stabs; but whether a man
weighing ninety pounds could knock down the best of
boxers, weighing twelve hundred, the reader can decide; but Keyere ever told the same tale, and became
known far and near as the man that whipped the grizzly
in a stand-up fight.   Probably no man ever recovered who received so many wounds as did Keyere in
this unequal combat.

CHAPTER XXXVI.

Discovery of Beckwourth's Pass.—No pecuniary Reward for public
Services. —Transformation. — A new Character. — Emigrants at
Home and at their Journey's End.—Description of the Happy Val-
ley.—Interesting Reminiscence.

THE next spring I engaged in mining and prospecting in various parts of the gold region.   I advanced as
far as the American Valley, having one man in my
company, and proceeded north into the Pitt River country, where we had a slight difficulty with the Indians.
We had come upon a party who manifested the utmost
friendship toward us; but I, knowing how far friendly
appearances could be trusted to, cautioned my partner
on no account to relinquish his gun, if the Indians
should attempt to take it.   They crowded round us,
pretending to have the greatest interest in the pack that
we carried, until they made a sudden spring, and seized
our guns, and attempted to wrest them from our grasp.
I jerked from them, and retreated a few steps; then,
cocking my gun, I bade them, if they wished to fight,
to come on.   This produced a change in their feelings,

and they were very friendly again, begging caps and ammunition of us, which, of course, we refused. We then walked backward for about one hundred and fifty yards, still keeping our pieces ready should they attempt further hostilities; but they did not deem it prudent to molest us again.

While on this excursion I discovered what is now known as " Beckwourth's Pass" in the Sierra Nevada. From some of the elevations over which we passed I remarked a place far away to the southward that seemed lower than any other. I made no mention of it to my companion, but thought that at some future time I would examine into it farther. I continued on to Shasta with my fellow-traveler, and returned after a fruitless journey of eighteen days.

After a short stay in the American Valley, I again started out with a prospecting party of twelve men. We killed a bullock before starting and dried the meat, in order to have provisions to last us during the trip. We proceeded in an easterly direction, and all busied themselves in searching for gold; but my errand was of a different character: I had come to discover what I suspected to be a pass.

It was the latter end of April when we entered upon an extensive valley at the northwest extremity of the Sierra range. The valley was already robed in freshest verdure, contrasting most delightfully with the huge snow-clad masses of rock we had just left. Flowers of every variety and hue spread their variegated charms before us; magpies were chattering, and gorgeously-plumaged birds were caroling in the delights of unmolested solitude. Swarms of wild geese and ducks were swimming on the surface of the cool crystal stream, which was the central fork of the Rio de las Plumas, or sailed the air in clouds over our heads. Deer and antelope filled the plains, and their boldness was conclusive that the hunter's rifle was to them unknown. Nowhere visible were any traces of the white man's approach, and it is probable that our steps were the first that ever marked the spot. We struck across this beautiful valley to the waters of the Yuba, from thence to the waters of the Truchy, which latter flowed in an easterly direction, telling us we were on the eastern slope of the mountain range. This, I at once saw, would afford the best wagon-road into the American Valley approaching from the eastward, and I imparted my views to three of my companions in whose judgment I placed the most confidence. They thought highly of the discovery, and even proposed to associate with me in opening the road. We also found gold, but not in sufficient quantity to warrant our working it; and, furthermore, the ground was too wet to admit of our prospecting to any advantage.

On my return to the American Valley, I made known my discovery to a Mr. Turner, proprietor of the American Ranch, who entered enthusiastically into my views; it was a thing, he said, he had never dreamed of before. If I could but carry out my plan, and divert travel into that road, he thought I should be a made man for life. Thereupon he drew up a subscription-list, setting forth the merits of the project, and showing how the road could be made practicable to Bidwell's Bar, and thence to Marysville, which latter place would derive peculiar advantages from the discovery. He headed the subscription with two hundred dollars.

When I reached Bidwell's Bar and unfolded my project, the town was seized with a perfect mania for the opening of the route. The subscriptions toward the fund required for its accomplishment amounted to five hundred dollars. I then proceeded to Marysville, a place which would unquestionably derive greater benefit from the newly-discovered route than any other place on the way, since this must be the entrepôt or principal starting-place for emigrants. I communicated with several of the most influential residents on the subject in hand. They also spoke very encouragingly of my undertaking, and referred me, before all others, to the mayor of the city. Accordingly, I waited upon that gentleman (a Mr. Miles), and brought the matter under his notice, representing it as being a legitimate matter for his interference, and offering substantial advantages to the commercial prosperity of the city. The mayor entered warmly into my views, and pronounced it as his opinion that the profits resulting from the speculation could not be less than from six to ten thousand dollars; and as the benefits accruing to the city would be incalculable, he would insure my expenses while engaged upon it.

I mentioned that I should prefer some guarantee before entering upon my labors, to secure me against loss of what money I might lay out.

"Leave that to me," said the mayor; "I will attend to the whole affair. I feel confident that a subject of so great importance to our interests will engage the earliest attention."

I thereupon left the whole proceeding in his hands, and, immediately setting men to work upon the road, went out to the Truchy to turn emigration into my newly-discovered route. While thus busily engaged I was seized with erysipelas, and abandoned all hopes of recovery; I was over one hundred miles away from medical assistance, and my only shelter was a brush tent. I made my will, and resigned myself to death. Life still lingered in me, however, and a train of wagons came up, and encamped near to where I lay. I was reduced to a very low condition, but I saw the drivers, and acquainted them with the object which had brought me out there. They offered to attempt the new road if I thought myself sufficiently strong to guide them through it. The women, God bless them! came to my assistance, and through their kind attentions and excellent nursing I rapidly recovered from my lingering sickness, until I was soon able to mount my horse, and lead the first train, consisting of seventeen wagons, through "Beckwourth's Pass." We reached the American Valley without the least accident, and the emigrants expressed entire satisfaction with the route. I returned with the train through to Marysville, and on the intelligence being communicated of the practicability of my road, there was quite a public rejoicing. A northern route had been discovered, and the city had received an impetus that would advance her beyond all her sisters on the Pacific shore. I felt proud of my achievement, and was foolish enough to promise myself a substantial recognition of my labors.

I was destined to disappointment, for that same night Marysville was laid in ashes. The mayor of the ruined town congratulated me upon bringing a train through. He expressed great delight at my good fortune, but regretted that their recent calamity had placed it entirely beyond his power to obtain for me any substantial reward. With the exception of some two hundred dollars subscribed by some liberal-minded citizens of Marysville, I have received no indemnification for the money and labor I have expended upon my discovery. The city had been greatly benefited by it, as all must acknowledge, for the emigrants that now flock to Marysville would otherwise have gone to Sacramento. Sixteen hundred dollars I expended upon the road is forever gone, but those who derive advantage from this outlay and loss of time devote no thought to the discoverer; nor do I see clearly how I am to help myself, for every one knows I can not roll a mountain into the pass and shut it up. But there is one thing certain: although I recognize no superior in love of country, and feel in all its force the obligation imposed upon me to advance her interests, still, when I go out hunting in the mountains a road for every body to pass through, and expending my time and capital upon an object from which I shall derive no benefit, it will be because I have nothing better to do.

In the spring of 1852 I established myself in Beckwourth Valley, and finally found myself transformed into a hotel-keeper and chief of a trading-post. My house is considered the emigrant's landing-place, as it is the first ranch he arrives at in the golden state, and is the only house between this point and Salt Lake. Here is a valley two hundred and forty miles in circumference, containing some of the choicest land in the world. Its yield of hay is incalculable; the red and white clovers spring up spontaneously, and the grass that covers its smooth surface is of the most nutritious nature. When the weary, toil-worn emigrant reaches this valley, he feels himself secure; he can lay himself down and taste refreshing repose, undisturbed by the fear of Indians. His cattle can graze around him in pasture up to their eyes, without running any danger of being driven off by the Arabs of the forest, and springs flow before them as pure as any that refreshes this verdant earth.

When I stand at my door, and watch the weary, way-worn travelers approach, their wagons holding together by a miracle, their stock in the last stage of emaciation, and themselves a perfect exaggeration of caricature, I frequently amuse myself with imagining the contrast they must offer to the *tout ensemble* and general appearance they presented to their admiring friends when they first set out upon their journey.

We will take a fancy sketch of them as they start from their homes. We will fancy their strong and well-stored wagon, bran-new for the occasion, and so firmly put together that, to look at it, one would suppose it fit to circumrotate the globe as many times as there are spokes in the wheels; then their fat and frightened steers, so high-spirited and fractious that it takes the father and his two or three sons to get each under the yoke; next, the ambitious emigrant and his proud family, with their highly-raised expectations of the future that is before them : the father, so confident and important, who deems the Eastern States unworthy of his abilities, and can alone find a sufficiently ample field in the growing republic on the Pacific side; the mother, who is unwilling to leave her pleasant gossiping friends and early associations, is still half tempted to believe that the crop of gold that waits their gathering may indemnify her for her labors ; so they pull up stakes, and leave town in good style, expecting to return with whole cart-loads of gold dust, and dazzle their neighbors' eyes with their excellent good fortune.

JAMES P. BECKWOURTH IN CITIZEN'S DRESS.

The girls, dear creatures! put on their very best, as all their admiring beaux assemble to see them start, and to give them the last kiss they will receive east of the Nevada Mountains; for their idea is that they will be snatched up and married the moment they step over the threshold into California by some fine young gentleman who is a solid pile of gold, and they joyously start away, in anticipation of the event, their hats decked with ribbons, their persons in long-flowing riding-dresses, their delicate fingers glittering with rings, and their charming little ankles incased in their fashionable and neatly-laced gaiters.

At the close of day, perhaps amid a pelting rain, these same parties heave wearily into sight: they have achieved the passage of the Plains, and their pleasant Eastern homes, with their agreeable, sociable neighbors, are now at a distance it is painful to contemplate. The brave show they made at starting, as the whole town hurraed them off, is sadly faded away. Their wagon appears like a relic of the Revolution after doing hard service for the commissariat: its cover burned into holes, and torn to tatters; its strong axles replaced with rough pieces of trees hewn by the wayside; the tires bound on with ropes; the iron linchpins gone, and chips of hickory substituted, and rags wound round the hubs to hold them together, which they keep continually wetted to prevent falling to pieces. The oxen are held up by the tail to keep them upon their legs, and the ravens and magpies evidently feel themselves ill treated in being driven off from what they deem their lawful rights.

The old folks are peevish and quarrelsome; the young men are so headstrong, and the small children so full of wants, and precisely at a time when every thing has given out, and they have nothing to pacify them with. But the poor girls have suffered the most. Their glossy, luxuriant locks, that won so much admiration, are now frizzled and discolored by the sun; their elegant riding-habit is replaced with an improvised Bloomer, and their neat little feet are exposed in sad disarray; their fingers are white no longer, and in place of rings we see sundry bits of rag wound round, to keep the dirt from entering their sore cuts. The young men of gold, who looked so attractive in the distance, are now too often found to be worthless and of no intrinsic value; their time employed in haunting gaming-tables or dram-shops, and their habits corrupted by unthrift and dissipation.

I do not wish to speak disparagingly of my adopted state, and by no means to intimate the slightest disrespect to the many worthy citizens who have crossed the Plains. I appeal to the many who have witnessed the picture for the accuracy of my portraiture. So much good material constantly infused into society ought to improve the character of the compound, but the demoralizing effects of transplantation greatly neutralize the benefits.

Take a family from their peaceful and happy homes in a community where good morals are observed, and the tone of society exercises a salutary influence over the thoughts of both old and young, and put them in such a place as this, where all is chaotic, and the principles that regulate the social intercourse of men are not yet recognized as law, and their dignity of thought and *prestige* of position is bereft from them. They have to struggle among a greedy, unscrupulous populace for the means of living; their homes have yet acquired no comfort, and they feel isolated and abandoned; and it is even worse upon the children; all corrective influence is removed from them, and the examples that surround them are often of the most vicious and worst possible description. All wholesome objects of ambition being removed, and money alone substituted as the reward of their greed, they grow up unlike their fathers; and it is only those in whom there is a solid substratum of correct feeling that mature into good citizens and proper men.

The girls, too, little darlings, suffer severely. They have left their worthy sweethearts behind, and can not get back to them; and those who now offer themselves here are not fit to bestow a thought upon. Every thing is strange to them. They miss their little social reunions, their quilting-parties, their winter quadrilles, the gossip of the village, their delightful summer haunts, and their dear paternal fireside. They have no pursuits except of the grosser kinds, and all their refinements are roughed over by the prevailing struggle after gold.

Much stock is lost in crossing the Plains, through their drinking the alkali water which flows from the Sierra Nevada, becoming impregnated with the poisonous mineral either in its source or in its passage among the rocks. There are also poisonous herbs springing up in the region of the mineral water, which the poor, famishing animals devour without stint. Those who survive until they reach the Valley are generally too far gone for recovery, and die while resting to recruit their strength. Their infected flesh furnishes food to thousands of wolves, which infest this place in the winter, and its effect upon them is singular. It depilates their warm coats of fur, and renders their pelts as bare as the palm of a man's hand. My faithful dogs have killed numbers of them at different times, divested entirely of hair except on the extremity of the nose, ears, and tail. They present a truly comical and extraordinary appearance.

This general loss of cattle deprives many of the poor emigrants of the means of hauling their lightened wagons, which, by the time they reach my ranch, seldom contain any thing more than their family clothing and bedding. Frequently I have observed wagons pass my house with one starveling yoke of cattle to drag them, and the family straggling on foot behind. Numbers have put up at my ranch without a morsel of food, and without a dollar in the world to procure any. They never were refused what they asked for at my house; and, during the short space that I have spent in the Valley, I have furnished provisions and other necessaries to the numerous sufferers who have applied for them to a very serious amount. Some have since paid me, but the bills of many remain unsettled. Still, although a prudent business man would condemn the proceeding, I can not find it in my heart to refuse relief to such necessities, and, if my pocket suffers a little, I have my recompense in a feeling of internal satisfaction.

My pleasant valley is thirty-five miles at its greatest breadth. It is irrigated by two streams, with their various small tributaries. These form a junction about ten miles from my house up the valley, which, as you remount it, becomes the central fork of the Feather River. All these streams abound with trout, some of them weighing seven or eight pounds. In the main one there are also plenty of otter. Antelopes and deer are to be found the entire year, unless the winter is unusually severe, when they cross the mountains to the eastern slope. Grizzly bears come and disappear again, 'without asking leave of any man. There are wolves of every species, together with foxes, hares, rabbits, and other animals. Of the feathered tribe, we have wild geese, ducks, sage-hens, grouse, and a large variety of smaller birds. Service-berries and cherries are the only kinds of fruit that grow from nature's cultivation.

The growth of timber about the valley is principally pitch-pine, although there is a considerable intermixture of cedar. I have never yet sown any grain, but I have cultivated a small kitchen-garden, and raised cabbages, turnips, and radishes of great size. I have never known the snow to fall to a greater depth than three feet, and when the storms are over it dissolves very rapidly, notwithstanding the elevation is many thousand feet above the level of the Pacific. The snow clings to the mountain peaks that overlook the valley to the eastward the year round, and as it is continually melting and feeding the streams, it keeps the water icy cold all the summer through. About a mile and a half distant from my house there is a large sulphur spring, and on the eastern slope, in the desert, there are copious hot springs, supplying the traveler with boiling water for his coffee without the cost of fuel.

The Truchy rises on the summit of the Sierra Nevada, opposite the head-waters of the Yuba, and runs in an easterly direction until it loses itself in Pyramid Lake, about fifty miles east of this valley. This lake is a great natural curiosity, as it receives not alone the waters of the Truchy, but numerous other streams, and has no visible outlet ; its surcharge of water probably filtering into the earth, like St. Mary's River, and some others I have met with. There is no place in the

whole state that offers so many attractions for a few
weeks' or months' retirement; for its charms of scenery, with sylvan and piscatorial sports, present unusual attractions.   During the winter season my nearest neighbors are sixteen miles away; in the summer
they are within four miles of my house, so that social
broils do not much disturb me.

There is a pleasant historical incident associated
with St. Mary's River, which, as it can be familiar to
but few of my readers, I will relate here.   The St. Mary's River is known to most persons as the River Humboldt, since that is the name that has been since conferred upon it, in honor of the distinguished European
traveler.   I prefer the former name, as being more po-
etical, though less assuming.   An Indian woman, the
wife of a Canadian named Chapineau, who acted as interpreter and guide to Lewis and Clarke during their
explorations of the Rocky Mountains, was suddenly
seized with the pains of labor, and gave birth to a son
on the banks of this mysterious river.   The Red-headed Chief (Clarke) adopted the child thus rudely issued
into the world, and on his return to St. Louis took the
infant with him, and baptized it John Baptist Clarke
Chapineau.   After a careful culture of his mind, the
boy was sent to Europe to complete his education.
But the Indian was ineffaceable in him.   The Indian
lodge and his native mountain fastnesses possessed
greater charms than the luxuries of civilized life.   He
returned to the desert and passed his days with his
tribe.   Mary, the mother of the child, was a Crow,
very pleasing and intelligent, and may have been, for
aught I know, connected with some of my many relatives in that tribe.   It was in honor of this event, and
to perpetuate her memory, that the river received its

original name, St. Mary's, and, as such, is still known to the mountaineers.

CHAPTER XXXVII.

Mistakes regarding the Character of the Indian.—Extent of the Western Tribes.—Their Character.—How a War against them should be conducted.—Reflections.—Closing Address to the Indian Heroine.

As an American citizen, a friend of my race, and a sincere lover of my country, and also as one well acquainted with the Indian character, I feel that I can not properly conclude the record of my eventful life without saying something for the Red Man. It should be remembered, when judging of their acts, that they consider the country they inhabit as the gift of the "Great Spirit," and they resent in their hearts the invasion of the immigrant just as much as any civilized people would, if another nation, without permission, should cross their territory. It must also be understood, that the Indians believe the buffalo to be theirs by inheritance, not as game, but in the light of ownership, given to them by Providence for their support and comfort, and that, when an immigrant shoots a buffalo, the Indian looks upon it exactly as the destruction by a stranger of so much private property.

With these ideas clearly in the mind of the reader, it can be understood why the Indian, in destroying a cow belonging to white people, or stealing a horse, considers himself as merely retaliating for injuries received, repaying himself, in fact, for what he has lost. For this act on the part of the Red Man, the United States troops are often turned indiscriminately upon his race; the innocent generally suffer, and those who have raised the storm can not understand of what crime they can be guilty.

But if the government is determined to make war upon the Western tribes, let it be done intelligently, and so effectually that mercy will temper justice. To attempt to chastise Indians with United States troops is simply ridiculous; the expense of such campaigns is only surpassed by their inefficiency. The Indians live on horseback, and they can steal and drive off the government horses faster than it can bring them together. The Indians having no stationary villages, they can travel faster, even with the incumbrance of their lodges, women, and children, subsisting themselves on buffalo slain on the way, than any force, however richly appointed, the country could send against them. An army must tire out in such a chase before summer is gone, while the Indians will constantly harass it with their sharp-shooters, and, should several powerful tribes unite—not an unusual occurrence—many thousand men would make no impression.

It should also be recollected by our officers sent to fight in the Rocky Mountains, that the Indians have a mode of telegraphing by the aid of robes and mirrors, and thus, by having their spies stationed at convenient distances, they convey intelligence of the movements of their enemies at great distances and in a very few minutes, thus informing villages whether it would be best to retreat or not. Some tribes telegraph by fires at night, and by smoke in the daytime. An officer might hear of a band of warriors encamped at a certain place; he immediately makes a forced march, and when his troops arrive at their destination, those same warriors may be many miles in his rear, encamped on his trail.

A village of three hundred lodges of Crows or Cheyennes could, within thirty minutes after receiving an order to move, have all their lodges struck, the poles attached to the horses, and their men, women, and children going at full speed, and could thus outstrip the best dragoons sent in their pursuit.

I have seen enough of Indian treaties and annuities to satisfy me that their effects for good are worse than fruitless. The idea formed by the Indians is that the annuities are sent to them by the great white chief because he is afraid of them, and wishes to purchase their friendship. There are some of the tribes—a very few—who would keep a treaty sacred; but the majority would not be bound by one, for they can not understand their nature. When caught at a disadvantage, and reduced to enter into a compact, they would agree to any proposals that were offered; but when the controlling power is withdrawn, and they can repeat their depredations with apparent impunity, no moral obligation would restrain them, and the treaty that was negotiated at so much cost to the country proves a mere delusion.

The officer having charge of an expedition against the Indians should rightly understand which *band* of a tribe he is commissioned to punish. The Siouxs, for instance, which, a few years ago, could raise thirty thousand warriors, are divided into many bands, which, at times, are hundreds of miles apart. One band of that tribe may commit a depredation on the emigrant road, and the other bands not even have heard of it: they do not hold themselves amenable for the misdeeds of another body totally distinct from them in social relations, and to inflict chastisement upon them in such a case would be a manifest injustice. But in a case of extreme danger all these bands coalesce.

Other tribes have the same divisions into distinct bands, and many are hence led into the belief that each band is a tribe. The Siouxs range over a territory upward of a thousand miles in extent from north to south, and their country embraces some of the most beautiful spots in the world, as well for natural scenery as for extreme productiveness of soil. The Crows have but one band proper, although they are generally divided into two villages, as being a more convenient arrangement to afford pasture for their immense herds of horses, and also to hunt the buffalo. But these two villages are seldom more than three hundred miles apart, generally much nearer; they come together at least once a year, and have frequent accidental coalitions in the course of their wanderings. They speak the Grovan language, from which nation they are an offshoot.

The Pawnees are probably the most degraded, in point of morals, of all the Western tribes; they are held in such contempt by the other tribes that none will make treaties with them. They are a populous nation, and are inveterate against the whites, killing them wherever met. A treaty concluded with that nation at night would be violated the next morning. Those who engage in warfare with the Western Indians will remember that they take no prisoners except women and children. It has generally been believed that the Siouxs never kill white men, but this is a mistake; they have always killed them. I have seen white men's scalps in their hands, and many still fresh hanging in the smoke of their lodges.

The Western Indians have no hummocks or everglades to fight among, but they have their boundless prairies to weary an army in, and the fastnesses of the

Rocky Mountains to retreat to. Should a majority of those powerful nations coalesce in defense against one common enemy, it would be the worst Indian war—the most costly in blood and treasure that the national government has ever entered into. The coalition tribes could bring two hundred and fifty thousand warriors against any hostile force, and I know I am greatly within the limits of truth in assigning that number to them.

If it is the policy of government to utterly exterminate the Indian race, the most expeditious manner of effecting this ought to be the one adopted. The introduction of whisky among the Red Men, under the connivance of government agents, leads to the demoralization and consequent extermination, by more powerful races, of thousands of Indians annually. Still, this infernal agent is not effectual; the Indians diminish in numbers, but with comparative slowness. The most direct and speedy mode of clearing the land of them would be by the simple means of starvation—by depriving them of their hereditary sustenance, the buffalo. To effect this, send an army of hunters among them, to root out and destroy, in every possible manner, the animal in question. They can shoot them, poison them, dig pit-falls for them, and resort to numberless other contrivances to efface the devoted animal, which serves, it would seem, by the wealth of his carcass, to preserve the Indian, and thus impede the expanding development of civilization.

To fight the Indians *vi et armis*, the government could employ no such effectual means as to take into its service five hundred mountaineers for the space of one year, and any one tribe of Indians that they should fall foul of could never survive the contest.

Such men, employed for that purpose, would have no encumbrance from superfluous baggage to impede them in a pursuit or a retreat over their illimitable plains. The mode of life of a mountaineer just fits him for an Indian fighter, and if he has to submit to privation, and put up with an empty commissariat, he has the means of support always at hand. He is so much an Indian from habit that he can fight them in their own way: if they steal his horses, he can steal theirs in return; if they snatch a hasty repose in the open air, it is all he asks for himself, and his health and spirits are fortified with such regimen. It is only by men possessing the qualities of the white hunter, combined with Indian habits, that the Indians can be effectually and economically conquered.

I have now presented a plain, unvarnished statement of the most noteworthy occurrences of my life, and, in so doing, I have necessarily led the reader through a variety of savage scenes at which his heart must sicken. The narrative, however, is not without its use. The restless youthful mind, that wearies with the monotony of peaceful every-day existence, and aspires after a career of wild adventure and thrilling romance, will find, by my experience, that such a life is by no means one of comfort, and that the excitement which it affords is very dearly purchased by the opportunities lost of gaining far more profitable wisdom. Where one man would be spared, as I have been, to pass through the perils of fasting, the encounters with the savage, and the fury of the wild beasts, and still preserve his life, and attain an age of near threescore, it is not too much to say that five hundred would perish, with not a single loved one near to catch his last whispered accent, would die in the wilderness, either in solitude, or with the fiendish savage shrieking in revolting triumph in his ear.

I now close the chapter of my eventful life. I feel that time is pressing; and the reminiscences of the past, stripped of all that was unpleasant, come crowding upon me. My heart turns naturally to my adopted people. I think of my son, who is the chief; I think of his mother, who went unharmed through the medicine lodge; I think of Bar-chee-am-pe, the brave heroine. I see her, tearful, watching my departure from the banks of the Yellow Stone. Her nation expects my return, that I may be buried with my supposed fathers, but none looks so eagerly for the great warrior as

PINE LEAF, THE INDIAN HEROINE.

I've seen her in her youthful years;
    Her heart was light and free,
Her black eyes never dimm'd with tears,
    So happy then was she.
When warriors from the fight return'd,
    And halted for display,
The trophies that the victors won
    She was first to bring away.

I've seen her kiss her brother's cheek
    When he was called to go
The lurking enemy to seek,
    Or chase the buffalo.
She loved him with a sister's love:
    He was the only son;
And "Pine Leaf" prized him far above
    The warriors' hearts she'd won.

I've seen her in her mourning hours—
    That brother had been slain:
Her head, that oft was decked with flowers,
    Now shed its crimson rain;
Her bleeding head and bleeding hand—
    Her crimson, clotted hair—
Her brother's in the spirit land,
    And hence her keen despair.

I've heard her make a solemn vow—
" A warrior I will be
Until a hundred foes shall bow,
    And yield their scalps to me ;
I will revenge my brother's death—
    I swear it on my life,
Or never, while I draw a breath,
    Will I become a wife."

I've seen her on her foaming steed,
    With battle-axe in hand,
Pursuing at her utmost speed
    The Black Foot and Shi-an.
I've seen her wield her polished lance
    A hundred times and more,
When charging fierce in the advance
    Amid the battle's roar.

I've seen her with her scalping-knife
    Spring on the fallen foe,
And, ere he was yet void of life,
    Make sure to count her coo.
I've seen her, at full speed again,
    Oft draw her trusty bow,
Across her arrow take good aim,
    And lay a warrior low.

I've heard her say, " I'll take my shield,
    My battle-axe, and bow,
And follow you, through glen or field,
    Where'er you dare to go ;
I'll rush amid the blood and strife
    Where any warrior leads :"
Pine Leaf would choose to lose her life
    Amid such daring deeds.

I've heard her say, " The spirit land
    Is where my thoughts incline,
Where I can grasp my brother's hand,
    Extended now for mine.
There's nothing now in this wide world—
    No ties that bid me stay ;
But, a broken-hearted Indian girl,
    I weep both night and day.

"He tells me in my midnight dreams
   I must revenge his fall,
Then come where flowers and cooling streams
   Surround their spirits, all.
He tells me that the hunting-ground,
   So far away on high,
Is filled with warriors all around
   Who nobly here did die.

"He says that all is joy and mirth
   Where the Great Spirit lives,
And joy that's never known on earth
   He constantly receives.
No brother to revenge his wrongs—
   The war-path is my road:
A few more days I'll sing his songs,
   Then hie to his abode."

I've heard her say, "I'll be your bride;
   You've waited long, I know;
A hundred foes by me have died,
   By my own hand laid low.
'Tis for my nation's good I wed;
   For I would still be free
Until I slumber with the dead;
   But I will marry thee."

And when I left the heroine,
   A tear stood in her eye
As last I held her hand in mine,
   And whispered a good-by.
"Oh, will you soon return again?"
   The heroine did say;
"Yes, when the green grass decks the plain,"
   I said, and came away.

THE END.

NOTES

The figures preceding each entry indicate text page and line numbers. In figuring the line number, begin with the first sentence of the text. Chapter headings and summaries preceding the text are not included in the line count. To facilitate locating a note, chapter numbers are given.

CHAPTER I

13: *title* Although the subject was christened James Pierson Beckwith, he will be referred to throughout this work as James Pierson Beckwourth, the name that he preferred to use and made famous.

13:2 No birth certificate verifies the date of April 26, 1798, but it is the date given by W. N. Byers of Denver, a very close friend of Beckwourth, when writing to C. G. Coutant. See C. G. Coutant, *The History of Wyoming*, 3 vols. (Laramie: Chaplin, Spafford & Mathison, 1899), 1:192.

13:3 One wonders if Jennings Beckwith had two families, one in Virginia, the other in St. Louis. Paul Edmund Beckwith, *The Beckwiths* (Albany: J. Munsell & Sons, 1891), pp. 57-58, lists six children but names only four: Richard Marmaduke Barnes Beckwith, a grandnephew of James Madison, who died in 1818 while visiting his father in St. Louis; Edwin Beckwith, killed by pirates on a merchant vessel lost at sea; Malbis Beckwith, who died at his father's home in West Virginia; and a T. W. Beckwith. See also the note for 381:8.

13:7 If it is true that Jennings Beckwith held a major's commission, on which side did he fight? Beckwourth first speaks respectfully of Lt. Col. Banastre Tarleton, commander of the British Legion made up of American Tories, and then asserts that his father fought with General Anthony Wayne. The only available army record states that Jennings Beckwith attained the rank of second lieutenant while serving in the United States Army between April 15, 1814, and June 30, 1816; it makes no mention of his serving in the Revolutionary War. Francis B. Heitman, *Historical Register and Dictionary of the United States Army 1789-1903*, 2 vols. (Urbana: University of Illinois Press, 1965), 1:205. Sir Jennings Beckwith, as Jim's father was called, was a native of Richmond County, Virginia, and worked as an overseer on a plantation. The title "Sir" came from Jennings Beckwith's great-grandfather, who was created a baronet by Charles II of England in 1681. Although officially all inherited titles were given up in America after the War of Independence, often they continued to be used. Beckwith, *The Beckwiths*, pp. 57-58.

13:21   The reference is to the replacement by the Tories at Charleston of Lt. Col. Banastre Tarleton's cavalry horses which died on the voyage from England.

14:11   General Anthony ("Mad Anthony") Wayne (1745-96). For an account of the battle of Stony Point, see I. W. Sklarsky, *The Revolution's Boldest Venture* (Port Washington, N. Y.: Kennikat Press, 1965).

14:18   Jennings Beckwith purchased from Louis Labeaume 1,130 arpens of land located twelve miles east of St. Charles, Missouri, at what was called "The Point." Deed Record B, Recorder of Deeds Office, St. Charles County, Missouri, pp. 104-108.

14:19   Although the text suggests that the date of the move was 1805-1806, the deed mentioned above is dated April 21, 1810.

16:31   Portage des Sioux.

17:25   I can find no mention of Blondo; Blondeaux might be a closer approximation of the spelling.

18:17   Judging by the date of the deed to his father's land, Beckwourth was at least twelve or thirteen years old, not ten, when he started to school. His school days could not have lasted long, however, for he was unable to write his name until very late in his life.

18:20   Casner and Sutton are mentioned as owners of one of the three major blacksmith shops in St. Louis. J. Thomas Scharf, *History of St. Louis City and County,* 2 vols. (Philadelphia: Louis H. Everts & Co., 1883), 1:198. See also Lewis H. Garrard, *Wah-To-Yah and the Taos Trail,* ed. Ralph P. Bieber (Glendale: Arthur H. Clark Co., 1938), p. 310, and Frederic L. Billon, *Annals of St. Louis in its Territorial Days From 1804 to 1821* (St. Louis: Printed for the author, 1888), p. 156. James Haley White, a friend of the Beckwith family in St. Louis, states that Beckwourth was first apprenticed to a man named Bueron who was killed by his son-in-law. Beckwourth then finished his apprenticeship in the shop of John Sutton. See James Haley White, "St. Louis and Its Men Fifty Years Ago" (Unfinished manuscript, St. Louis History Papers, Missouri Historical Society), p. 3.

18:29   A letter from C. A. Peterson dated March 15, 1907, St. Louis, Missouri Historical Society Library, seems to bear out the story of Jim's love affair. Peterson writes that "Jim Beckwith, (or Beckwourth,) of Crow Indian fame, early in the 19th century, paired with a slave woman named 'Amy,' belonging to the Draper family, living on 'The Point' in St. Charles Co., Mo. and of this temporary union a boy was born—a slave, named 'Alvin'—said to have been a man of superior intellect, in later life." The letter is printed in Nolie Mumey, *James Pierson Beckwourth, 1856-1866* (Denver: Old West Publishing Co., 1957), pp. 41-42.

20:15   Beckwourth never mentions his mother, but she was of Negro heritage and might have been a slave. White, "St. Louis and Its Men," p. 3, states she was a mulatto: Beckwith, *The Beckwiths,* p. 57, refers to her only as a Miss Kill; Col. Henry Inman, *The Old Santa Fe Trail* (Topeka: Crane & Co., 1916), p. 337, says: "The woman who bore [Beckwourth] played in her childhood beneath the palm trees of Africa." Although the amount of Negro blood in Beckwourth is not known, the epithet "famous Mulatto of the Plains," coined by M. J. Carrington in her *Ab-Sa-Ra-Ka, Home of the Crows* (Philadelphia: J. B.

Lippincott & Co., 1868), p. 131, seems to have stuck to him. See also T. D Bonner, *The Life and Adventures of James P. Beckwourth*, ed. Charles G. Leland (London: T. Fisher Unwin, 1892), p. 9, and Hubert Howe Bancroft, *The Works of Hubert Howe Bancroft*, 39 vols. (San Francisco: History Co., 1882-91), 25:352.

20:22   According to one source, a Colonel Johnson from Kentucky started mining near Fever River in 1823. Charles R. Tuttle, *An Illustrated History of the State of Iowa* (Chicago: Richard S. Peale & Co., 1876), p. 74. A second source mentions that in 1822 a Kentuckian named James Johnson opened a lead mine on Fever River near present Galena, Illinois, and that after his success others soon began mining. Cyrenus Cole, *I Am a Man—The Indian Black Hawk* (Iowa City: State Historical Society of Iowa, 1938), p. 78. The *Harper's Magazine* reviewer of Beckwourth's dictated autobiography in 1856 claims that Col. R. M. Johnson was the Richard Mentor Johnson who served as vice-president of the United States under Martin Van Buren from 1837 to 1841. "The Life and Adventures of James P. Beckwourth," *Harper's Magazine* 13 (September 1856) : 456.

CHAPTER II

21:17   A Col. Willoughby Morgan of the United States Army is mentioned as being in the Fever River area in 1822. William T. Hagan, *The Sac and Fox Indians* (Norman: University of Oklahoma Press, 1958) p. 90.

21:24   The treaty was signed in 1816 by the same Keokuk who figured in the Black Hawk War. His son Moses Keokuk did not take his father's place until his father died in 1848. Ibid., p. 233.

23:19   Beckwourth must have joined the Rocky Mountain Fur Company in the late winter of 1823 or early in the spring of 1824. There is no mention of his participating in William H. Ashley's second expedition, which left in the spring of 1823.

23:21   It has been estimated that the company consisted of twenty-four or twenty-five men, not twenty-nine. Charles

L. Camp, ed., *James Clyman, Frontiersman* (Portland: Champoeg Press, 1960), pp. 35, 97.

23:22 Beckwourth's date of October 11 is wrong. The expedition left St. Louis two days after William H. Ashley received his license to trade with the Indians, and the license was issued by William Clark, superintendent of Indian affairs, on September 24, 1824. Ibid., p. 35.

23:31 Moses Harris, sometimes referred to as Black Harris, was used as a courier for the fur company. For additional information, see Jerome Peltier, "Moses 'Black' Harris," in *The Mountain Men and the Fur Trade of the Far West,* ed. LeRoy R. Hafen, 8 vols. (Glendale: Arthur H. Clark Co., 1965-71), 4:103-17

24:6 Beckwourth's chronology is confused here. The journey he describes took place in the winter of 1825 during his second trip to the Rockies. For an account arranged in the proper chronology, see Delmont R. Oswald, "James Pierson Beckwourth, 1798-1866" (Master's thesis, Brigham Young University, 1967).

24:10 Jedediah Smith headed the 1825 expedition, but Beckwourth never mentions him by name. See Dale L. Morgan, *Jedediah Smith and the Opening of the West* (New York: Bobbs-Merrill Co., 1953), p. 175. There seemed to be some antagonism between the two men and Beckwourth's refusal to mention Smith probably was his way of getting even. Consigning an enemy to anonymity, to a man like Beckwourth, was the worst thing that could be done to him.

26:1 The Pawnee villages were located in present Nebraska on the south side of the Republican River where it runs closest to the Kansas border.

26:26 The Grand and Republican bands were break-offs from the Black Pawnee group. The Pawnee Pics, or Piques, sometimes were called the Wichita Indians. The Loup Pawnees were called the Skidis but lived along the forks of the Loup River in present Nebraska. For an excellent study of the tribe, see George E. Hyde, *Pawnee Indians* (Denver: University of Denver Press, 1951), pp. 49-87.

26:34 The total population of the Pawnee tribe for the years

from 1820 to 1825 is estimated to have been between
6,500 and 10,250. The number of warriors would have
been between 2,000 and 2,050. Ibid., p. 292.

27:16 "Some thirty-two years ago" refers to the date that
Beckwourth began dictating his memoirs, not to the 1824
trip to the mountains.

27:17 I can find no reference to a Pawnee chieftain named Two
Axe and no verification for the story of his visit to President Monroe.

CHAPTER III

28:13 The Big Nemaha is a branch of the Missouri River in
present southeastern Nebraska.

29:17 "Ely's" refers to the trading post operated by Cyrus
Curtis and Michael Eley at the mouth of the Kansas
River. See Louise Barry, "Kansas Before 1854," *Kansas
Historical Quarterly* 27 (1961): 516-17.

32:10 The Kansa Indians were distinct from the Osage Indians
but related to them. They were of southern Siouian
stock and were generally at peace with the whites.

32:24 G. Chouteau probably is Francis Gesseau Chouteau. The
"Kansas Post" of the Chouteaus was on an island in the
Missouri about three miles below the mouth of the
Kansas River.

32:34 There is no evidence that Ashley had planned a spring
expedition in 1826. Someone, probably Moses Harris, had
carried him word that his help was needed. Because of
the poor conditions existing in Smith's party when Beckwourth and Harris left, it is unlikely that they would
wait until spring to carry the message to Ashley. According to the *Missouri Advocate and St. Louis Enquirer*,
March 11, 1826, as cited in Dale L. Morgan, ed., *The
West of William H. Ashley* (Denver: Old West Publishing
Co., 1964), p. 142, Ashley left St. Louis on March 8; thus
he could not have waited for Beckwourth to arrive with
the spring thaw. One wonders if perhaps it was Beckwourth, not Harris, who gave out first.

33:5 There were only 25 men, not 120. Ibid.

33:24 Thomas Fitzpatrick was often called "Broken Hand,"

"Bad Hand," and "White Head" by the Indians. For a brief account of his life, see LeRoy R. and Ann W. Hafen, "Thomas Fitzpatrick," in *The Mountain Men and the Fur Trade*, 7:87-105.

33:32   William H. Ashley married Eliza Christy on October 26, 1825. See *Missouri Intelligencer*, Franklin, Missouri, November 11, 1825, as quoted in Donald McKay Frost, *Notes on General Ashley, the Overland Trail, and South Pass* (Barre, Mass.: Barre Gazette, 1960), p. 134.

34:19   The Padouca Indians often were referred to as the Ietans.

34:31   This adventure did not occupy "nearly the whole summer"; Beckwourth and his group reached Smith's party early in April, according to the "Narrative of Robert Campbell" in Morgan, ed., *The West of Ashley*, p. 143.

35:7   Campbell was making his first trip to the mountains to recover from tuberculosis. In 1832 he joined with William Sublette to form the Campbell and Sublette Fur Company, and later became a prominent banker in St. Louis.

35:8   The Loup Fork is a branch of the Platte River.

35:23   The statement that Harris rejoined the company may possibly refer to Beckwourth's own reunion with the party as it passed Chouteau's fort.

36:33   I find no evidence which would either support or disprove the theft of the horses by the two Spaniards.

CHAPTER IV

37:3   If only twenty-six men remained with Smith, there must have been a good many deserters, for no deaths are recorded. According to Robert Campbell, "A good many of the men—about 25 or 30—had deserted. They were sick of the trip, having suffered like the rest, almost to the verge of starvation." See Morgan, ed., *The West of Ashley*, p. 145.

37:23   James Clyman, in his account of the 1824-25 expedition, verifies the scantness of the rations. See Camp, ed., *James Clyman, Frontiersman*, p. 36.

42:24   William H. Ashley died of pneumonia on March 26, 1838.

43:14   I can find no mention of Two Axe or Antoine Behele.

45:17 "The Ashley Narrative" in Morgan, ed., *The West of Ashley*, pp. 101-02, follows Beckwourth's account rather closely.

CHAPTER V

46:27 Ashley makes no reference to any difficulty between himself and Beckwourth. The only suggestion of any adverse feelings toward Ashley on the part of his men occurs in Robert Campbell's note that when there were not enough horses "everybody walked except Ashley." See Morgan, ed., *The West of Ashley*, p. 145.

50:1 There is mention of an experienced mountain man named Basil Lajeunesse, who was hired along with Louis Vasquez in 1833 by Robert Campbell to help keep his caravan organized, and also of a Francois Lajeunesse, who was in the fur trade. See Mae Reed Porter and Odessa Davenport, *Scotsman in Buckskin* (New York: Hastings House, 1963), pp. 35, 37. Whether either of these men might be Baptiste La Jeunesse is still a question.

50:20 Perhaps Le Pointe is a misspelling of La Bonte, but which La Bonte? See Morgan, ed., *The West of Ashley*, p. 291.

51:19 The "hermitage" was located near present Portola, California.

52:31 The party followed the southern branch of the Platte. The complete route of the expedition can best be seen in the map at the end of Morgan, ed., *The West of Ashley*, and can be followed in the "Ashley Diary" and "Narrative."

53:4 Beckwourth's account of the Crows stealing their horses is confirmed by the "Ashley Diary"; however, it happened at Steamboat or Table Mountain, not Pilot Butte. See Morgan, ed., *The West of Ashley*, p. 105. There is no mention in other accounts of Ashley's having been seriously ill.

53:31 The Green River was often referred to at this time by its Crow Indian name "Seeds-ke-dee-agie," or Prairie Hen River. This point was reached on April 19, 1825.

57:21   The division into parties occurred about fifteen miles
        above the mouth of the Sandy River on April 22, 1825.
        Morgan, ed., *The West of Ashley*, pp. 106-7.

57:33   Flaming Gorge near Henry's Fork.

58:32   A Paul Dorio or Dorion is listed on Ashley's payroll in
        1827 and an M. Derochae is mentioned in his accounts
        with Smith, Jackson and Sublette. See Morgan, ed., *The
        West of Ashley*, pp. 172, 196.

59:32   Beckwourth's error in placing the point of departure of
        the separate companies at the "Suck" may be because he
        needed it for the setting of his claimed rescue of Ashley.
        He has clearly amplified an incident that Ashley must
        have related at the rendezvous of 1825 and made himself
        the hero. Ashley makes no reference anywhere to being
        saved by Beckwourth. Ibid., p. 111.

61:12   Beckwourth would have been about twenty-seven years
        of age.

CHAPTER VI

62:4   Beckwourth is wrong. The rendezvous was not held at
        the "Suck." See note for 73:23.

62:7   "Clements" is James Clyman. See Camp, ed., *James Cly-
        man, Frontiersman*, p. 38.

63:6   The creek upon which they camped has since that time
        been known as La Barge Creek. It is located near present
        Viola, Wyoming.

64:21   The identity of Le Brache is not known. Dale Morgan
        says he may have been Charles La Barge. See Morgan,
        ed., *The West of Ashley*, p. 271.

66:19   These Indians probably were from either the Arapaho or
        Gros Ventre tribe. The fact that they did not continue
        to attack the trappers when they outnumbered them seems
        to substantiate Beckwourth's account. See also Camp, ed.,
        James Clyman, Frontiersman, p. 38.

67:28   The "supposed enemy" probably was the party of John
        H. Weber, which had been out since 1822. It is doubtful
        that Beckwourth would have known any member of their
        company.

69:17   The year was 1825, not 1822. Beckwourth's party awaited

Ashley and the others at the mouth of Henry's Fork, below the "Suck."

CHAPTER VII

73:9   Beckwourth probably derived his story of saving Ashley at the "Suck" from one of these incidents. There has also been much controversy over Beckwourth's account of Ashley's emergence from the canyons of the Green River and his meeting with Etienne Provost. With the discovery of "Ashley's Diary," however, has come some vindication for Beckwourth, for the two accounts closely parallel each other. Beckwourth colors the story but the essential truth is there. See Morgan, ed., *The West of Ashley*, pp. 116-17, 284-85.

73:15   For verification, see Ted J. Warner, "Peter Skene Ogden and the Fur Trade of the Great Northwest" (Master's thesis, Brigham Young University, 1958), pp. 51-53.

73:23   Recognizing that the mouth of Henry's Fork was not the best site for the rendezvous, Ashley decided to hold it on the right bank of Henry's Fork, a few miles above its junction with the Green River. LeRoy R. Hafen, "A Brief History of the Fur Trade and the Far West," in *The Mountain Men and the Fur Trade*, 1:82.

74:29   "Sublet" is William L. Sublette. For a description of his activities, see John E. Sunder, *Bill Sublette, Mountain Man* (Norman: University of Oklahoma Press, 1959).

74:34   There are no other accounts of this skirmish taking place at this time. Sublette's biographer claims he may have been wounded in such a way after the rendezvous, on Ashley's return trip to St. Louis. John E. Sunder, "William Lewis Sublette," in *The Mountain Men and the Fur Trade*, 5:350.

75:6   Generals Winfield Scott and Zachary Taylor.

75:13   Peter Skene Ogden's party.

75:22   Ashley states that there were about 120 men present, but this figure does not include Indians. There were probably fewer than at later rendezvous, however, since it was such a new institution. "The Ashley Narrative," in Morgan, ed., *The West of Ashley*, p. 118.

75:34   The number of pelts was close to nine thousand, so Beck-wourth's figures are exaggerated. See Morgan, ed., *The West of Ashley*, p. 129. The Rocky Mountain Fur Company paid in trade by the pound or about five dollars per pelt. Beaver pelts did not bring a great deal more in St. Louis, the profits being made in the markup of trade goods freighted to the mountains. Still, profits could be made on the pelts if prices happened to go up in St. Louis. See Morgan, *Jedediah Smith*, pp. 230-31.

76:12   According to Ashley, this rendezvous lasted only one day and his return trip began the next, July 2, 1825. Morgan, ed., *The West of Ashley*, p. 129.

76:19   Ashley agrees with Beckwourth on the number of men leaving the rendezvous with him. In "The Ashley Narrative" he states that "I set out on my way homewards with 50 men, 25 of whom were to accompany me to a navigable point of the Big Horn River thence to return with the horses employed in the transportation of the furs." Ibid.

77:11   Beckwourth's chronology of events is wrong. On the return journey Ashley split his party at a point near where Wind River enters the Big Horn Mountains. Beckwourth and the larger party continued on over Bad Pass, while Ashley and twenty men detoured to raise a cache of forty packs of fur buried by either Jedediah Smith or John H. Weber the year before. Ashley's party was attacked by Blackfoot Indians and the ensuing skirmish closely resembled the one described by Beckwourth earlier, in which Sublette was wounded (see note for 74:34). Having lost most of his horses, Ashley sent for help from the main party. Beckwourth probably returned with the relief unit and was with Ashley when they encountered the Crow Indians. After this episode they rejoined the main party a short distance below present Thermopolis, Wyoming. See Oswald, "James Pierson Beckwourth, 1798-1866," pp. 37-40, and Morgan, ed., *The West of Ashley*, p. 130. Concerning the cached furs, Dale Morgan believes that they were Jedediah Smith's, gathered in the winter of 1823-24. LeRoy Hafen states that Smith's furs were sent down river with Fitzpatrick in 1824 and that these pelts

must have belonged to John H. Weber. See Morgan, ed.,
The West of Ashley, p. 118 and Hafen, ed., *The Mountain
Men and the Fur Trade*, 1:78-79.

77:22   Caleb Greenwood, an experienced mountaineer, had been
trapping and exploring in the West since 1808. For an
account of his life, see Charles Kelly and Dale L. Morgan,
Old Greenwood (Georgetown, California: Talisman Press,
1965).

77:28   This figure, like many in Beckwourth's account, is greatly
exaggerated. The figures he gives will not always be an-
notated because it is impossible to know exactly how many
Indians he actually saw, but the reader should keep in
mind that generally Beckwourth overestimates.

80:6   In 1833 Captain Bonneville also called it Bad Pass, and
Nathaniel Wyeth describes the pass in his diary without
giving it a name. For an explanation of the earliest maps
mentioning the pass, see Morgan, ed., *The West of Ashley*,
p. 296.

80:19   Stephen W. Kearny confirms this bear story in his diary;
he writes that on August 19 one of Ashley's men had
been attacked and severely injured by a white bear.
Stephen W. Kearny MS Diary, Kearny Papers, Missouri
Historical Society, as cited in Morgan, ed., *The West of
Ashley*, p. 296.

81:17   The slain trappers have not been identified, but both the
Henry Atkinson Journal, entry of August 14, 1825, and
Stephen W. Kearny's Diary for the same date offer proof
that trappers were in the area at this time. Both manu-
scripts are in the Missouri Historical Society. See also
Morgan, ed., *The West of Ashley*, p. 297.

81:33   Gen. Henry Atkinson.

82:6   Gen. William Selby Harney gives an account of the meeting with Ashley's men which is similar to Beckwourth's
but does not mention an overturned boat. L. U. Reavis,
*The Life and Military Services of General William Selby
Harney* (St. Louis: Bryan, Brand & Co., 1878), pp. 67-68.

83:2   Gen. Henry Atkinson records the incident of the amok
buffalo in his journal entry for Thursday, September 1,
1825. However, he states that the bull was shot and taken

in the river. "Henry Atkinson Journal," in Morgan, ed., *The West of Ashley*, p. 133.

83:12 Atkinson verifies this statement. Ibid., p. 135.

83:15 Fort Clark was just north of present Bismarck, North Dakota, on the west side of the river.

83:30 Benjamin O'Fallon was the United States Indian agent of the upper Missouri agency.

83:32 Edward Rose was a famous mulatto of the fur trade whose exploits have sometimes been mixed with Beckwourth's. Often referred to as Cut Nose, he, like Beckwourth, lived with the Crow Indians. His reputation was not the most savory during his life, but recent studies have helped to prove that he was more reliable than many of his contemporaries. See note for 195:31.

84:13 Long Hair was also called Red Feather at the Temple. Since his hair was considered part of his medicine, he never cut it but wore it in a bundle at his back. It is said to have measured eleven feet in length. See Edward S. Curtis, *The North American Indian*, 20 vols. (Cambridge: University Press, 1909-30), 4:28-30, 47-48. Other accounts say his hair measured from 9 feet 11 inches to 10 feet 7 inches and that it was carried in a ten-inch container which he carried under his arm or in his clothing. Robert H. Lowie, *The Crow Indians* (New York: Farrar & Rinehart, 1935), pp. 83-84.

85:17 Fort Look-out was located just above the mouth of the White River in present South Dakota; it is also called Fort Kiowa.

85:19 "Pitcher" is Joshua Pilcher, a prominent St. Louis fur trader, who succeeded Manuel Lisa as head of the Missouri Fur Company. For a brief account of his life, see Ray H. Mattison, "Joshua Pilcher," in *The Mountain Men and the Fur Trade*, 4:251-60.

86:5 Beckwourth arrived at Council Bluffs on September 19, 1825. See Dwight L. Clarke, *Stephen Watts Kearny, Soldier of the West* (Norman: University of Oklahoma Press, 1961), p. 32.

86:27 Charles Wahrendorff and Edward Tracy were two of the

major creditors of General Ashley in St. Louis. See Morgan, ed., *The West of Ashley*, pp. 300, 312.

87:10   Jennings Beckwith sold the last of his property at St. Charles to Daniel Griffith on May 15, 1823. See Deed Record G-546, St. Charles County, St. Charles, Missouri.

87:16   There seems to be no record of these men being in Ashley's pay. Possibly Beckwourth's spelling, La Roche, might disguise Polette Labross, a mulatto killed in Jedediah Smith's party in the Mojave Massacre; but Pellow remains a mystery.

89:3   Major Thomas Biddle died August 30, 1830 as a result of a duel with one Spencer Pettis. There seems to be no verification for the story about the bear. Billon, *Annals of St. Louis in its Territorial Days From 1804-1821*, p. 361.

CHAPTER VIII

90:7   There is no record of a thousand-dollar offer being made to Beckwourth. Robert Campbell states that it was Jedediah Smith and Moses Harris who were sent ahead to search out the parties in the mountains and arrange for a rendezvous. See the "Narrative of Robert Campbell," in Morgan, ed., *The West of Ashley*, p. 145. Still, one cannot rule out entirely Beckwourth's claim that he was sent ahead with two others. His account of events in Cache Valley during the winter of 1825-26 is amazingly accurate. The names La Roche and Pellow might have been substituted for Smith and Harris for obvious reasons. Beckwourth could not name Harris because it would throw doubt on his story of outwalking Harris to St. Louis. As for Jedediah Smith, Beckwourth never uses his name and often attributes Smith's actions to Ashley.

92:24   Beckwourth's story is garbled. The expedition of 1825-26 left St. Louis with approximately sixty men on October 30, 1825. Morgan, ed., *The West of Ashley*, p. 138. Ashley stayed in St. Louis and married Eliza Christy (see note for 33:32). After much deprivation, which Beckwourth described as occurring on the 1824-25 expedition, he and Harris were sent back to St. Louis for help. It was when Ashley returned with them to the Platte River with relief for Smith's stranded group that Smith and Harris (and possibly Beckwourth) were sent ahead to Cache Valley. See Oswald, "James Pierson Beckwourth, 1787-1866," pp. 45-53. "Robert Campbell's Narrative," dictated in 1870, claims that Beckwourth was not sent ahead to Cache Valley. Morgan, ed., *The West of Ashley*, p. 145.

93:6   1825, not 1823.

93:18   Cache Valley was sometimes referred to as Willow Valley.

93:22   Weber River.

93:30   "Punnacks" was the Shoshoni name for the Bannock Indians.

94:6   For an account of the life of Bridger, one of the most famous of the mountain men, see J. Cecil Alter, *Jim Bridger* (Norman: University of Oklahoma Press, 1962).

94:23   I could find no other account of this raid.

94:25   The Snakes were also known as the Shoshonis.

95:30   Beaverhead River.

95:33   Sheep Mountain is located near Bear River just west of present Alexander, Idaho.

95:34   Correctly spelled Portneuf River. It runs through southeastern Idaho.

96:15   Bear Lake.

96:18   The journey was made during the winter of 1826-27, not 1825-26. Harris "gave out" with a sprained ankle at the Kansas Indian villages. Sublette, trading a pistol for a horse for Harris, left him to come at his own speed while he raced on to St. Louis. Perhaps this is the source of Beckwourth's story of Harris's failing to make the journey. John E. Sunder, *Bill Sublette, Mountain Man* (Norman: University of Oklahoma Press, 1959), p. 72.

96:21   The second rendezvous was held at Cache Valley in late May and early June of 1896. Trading lasted two weeks. Morgan, ed., *The West of Ashley*, p. 145.

96:25   Warren Angus Ferris gives an account of the cave-in but dates it in the spring of 1827. He claims that only one Canadian was killed and that rather than dig him up and let the Indians bury him, the party left him where he was and proceeded to dig another cache elsewhere. Warren Angus Ferris, *Life in the Rocky Mountains* (Salt

Lake City: Rocky Mountain Book Shop, 1940), p. 43. Because of this incident and because there were so many caches dug in the area, the trappers soon changed the name of the valley to Cache Valley. Beckwourth seems to be the first to use it in reference to the area instead of the older name Willow Valley. See Alter, *Jim Bridger*, p. 83.

96:27   Tree burial was not a custom of the Shoshoni Indians. Beckwourth seems to have attributed to them a Crow custom.

CHAPTER IX

98:7   At the rendezvous of 1826 the Rocky Mountain Fur Company changed hands. The new owners divided the trappers into three groups for the fall hunt. One party, under Jedediah Smith, set out toward the southwest. The others, under David E. Jackson and William L. Sublette, turned north. Beckwourth seems to have been with the Sublette group. It is strange, however, that he makes no mention of the sights of present Yellowstone Park which were seen by this group.

100:6   Daniel Potts, a member of the group in 1827, records that the party was daily harassed by the Blackfeet. Letter from Daniel Potts to Robert T. Potts at Sweetwater Lake [Bear Lake] on July 8, 1827, in Frost, *Notes on General Ashley*, pp. 63-64.

100:16   The Ephraim Logan party seems to have consisted of Logan himself, Jacob O'Hara, William Bell, and James Scott. Ashley mentions only these four in his letter to Thomas H. Benton, St. Louis, January 20, 1829, cited in Morgan, ed., *The West of Ashley*, pp. 186-87. These men left together to trap after the 1827 rendezvous, so Beckwourth's chronology must again be corrected. Whether they were killed by the Blackfeet or the Snakes is still not known. Ibid., p. 289.

100:28   Portuleuse is unidentified.

100:34   Beckwourth's chronology is badly garbled. He has squeezed the events of three years into one, at the same time scrambling them. This statement would refer to

Sublette's returning from St. Louis in the spring of 1827.
101:11 Beckwourth probably means Etienne Provost, or Provot, and perhaps Jean B. Gervais. It is questionable, however, if Provot was in the area after 1826. See Morgan, ed., *The West of Ashley*, p. 279.

103:23 I find no other references to Eroquey.

104:29 This battle takes place along the shore of Bear Lake just prior to the rendezvous of 1828. Robert Campbell's account corresponds closely to Beckwourth's except that Campbell claims that he and a Spaniard rode through to the rendezvous area, not Beckwourth. But since Campbell was the leader of the party, it seems likely that he would have stayed and sent someone else for help. See Morgan, ed., *The West of Ashley*, pp. 314-15, and Daniel T. Potts's letter to Robert Potts, St. Louis, October 13, 1828, in Gerald C. Bagley, "Daniel T. Potts, Chronicler of the Fur Trade, 1822-1828" (Master's thesis, Brigham Young University, 1964), pp. 138-39. See also Ashley's letter to Thomas H. Benton, January 20, 1829 in U.S., Congress, Senate Documents, 20th Cong., 2d sess., 67, serial 181, p. 14.

105:32 Jedediah Smith refers to Bollìere as François Bouldeau. William H. Ashley calls him Lewis "Boldue" and "Bolduke." See Morgan, ed., *The West of Ashley*, pp. 186-87, 314.

106:1 The only loss mentioned by Ashley is "Boldue."

107:7 Again an exaggerated number.

107:17 About one hundred mules, not three hundred. See Morgan, ed., *The West of Ashley*, p. 165.

107:27 The rendezvous of 1827 was the biggest and most elaborate trade fair yet held, lasting from about June 22 until July 13. It was held unwittingly on Mexican soil near present Lakewood, Utah. Ibid., p. 169.

107:34 Having sold the Rocky Mountain Fur Company to Smith, Jackson and Sublette at the rendezvous of 1826, Ashley did not come to the 1827 rendezvous, but he did maintain the right to supply it with trade goods and sent his caravan under the direction of James B. Bruffee and Hiram Scott. Ibid., pp. 150-52, 158, 164-66.

CHAPTER X

108:11 This is the only use of the name "Cut Face" for Sublette; later Beckwourth refers to him as "Left Hand." Chittenden says that the Indians called him "Fate." Hiram M. Chittenden, *The American Fur Trade of the Far West*, 2 vols. (New York: Barnes & Noble, 1935), 1:255.

109:7 A slam at Ashley.

109:15 Cecil Alter believes that the battle scene was at the mouth of Weber Canyon. He could be correct, but the canyon mouth is not on the border of the lake. Alter, *Jim Bridger*, p. 81.

110:33 This battle closely resembles the one described by Daniel T. Potts in his letter dated Sweet Lake, July 8, 1827, in Bagley, "Daniel T. Potts," pp. 134-35. Beckwourth's figures are again exaggerated.

111:32 If Ashley made such a speech, it would have been at the 1826 rendezvous.

112:10 This burst of praise for Ashley is certainly puzzling. Perhaps Ashley did compliment Beckwourth as he left.

113:21 The invitation was quite a concession for the Blackfeet, who had been enemies of the Americans since the Lewis and Clark expedition. Ashley partially verifies the chief's invitation in his letter to Thomas H. Benton, St. Louis, January 20, 1829, cited in Morgan, ed., *The West of Ashley*, pp. 186-88. The Indians were probably Piegans, a branch of the Blackfeet less bloodthirsty than the Bloods. Dale Morgan believes that perhaps it was Robert Campbell's party who traded with the Blackfeet. Ibid., p. 315.

113:32 The Beaverhead River, which runs through present Dillon, Montana.

114:8 I can find no reference to a Blackfoot chief named Asasto.

114:18 If this story has any basis in fact, the scalps might have been taken from the Logan party. See note for 100:16.

121:30 Cloth for dresses.

CHAPTER XI

122:2 The Black Foot Buttes, sometimes called the Twin Buttes, are located between present Arco and Idaho Falls, Idaho.

123:17   Alexander is unidentified. If Beckwourth invented the episode, he may have taken the name from an acquaintance of his, one Alexander Harvey, but there is no connection with the Swiss.

124:25   It seems likely that if such a marvelous feat had been performed someone in Sublette's party would have recorded it, or at least told of it at one of the rendezvous, but no record except Beckwourth's own exists. Many writers have speculated that he simply appropriated the John Colter "Run-for-life" episode. See Burton Harris, *John Colter: His Years in the Rockies* (New York: Charles Scribner's Sons, 1952), pp. 124-31. J. M. Letts in 1849 related that Beckwourth's legs looked as if they were bound with cords under the skin because of a general rupture of the blood vessels. He says Beckwourth claimed the rupture was due to a ninety-mile run from the Indians. J. M. Letts, *California Illustrated: Including a Description of the Panama and Nicaragua Routes* (New York: R. T. Young, 1853), pp. 92-94.

126:11   The Snake River.

126:27   Generally, it was the custom for Indians to place their clothes on anthills to rid them of vermin.

128:21   This battle is not described elsewhere. Again Beckwourth's count of the Indians involved must be reduced.

128:28   The identity of Le Blueux is not known. The name closest in sound is that of Morris Ladue, listed on Ashley's 1827 payroll. Morgan, ed., *The West of Ashley*, p. 172.

133:6   Godin's River, or Lost River, seems more accurate.

133:24   "Cotton" is Joseph Coté or Coty. The place of Coty's death is believed to be on Birch Creek in southeast Idaho. Morgan, ed., *The West of Ashley*, pp. 186, 314.

134:18   Ashley merely says Coty was shot "while at his post on guard." Ibid., p. 314.

137:16   If this episode occurred, it would probably have been on the Snake River.

137:29   Beckwourth's story is shaky, for only a year later Peter Skene Ogden records meeting the "Lower Snakes," or Bannocks, on Camas prairie and estimates their number at three hundred lodges. T. C. Elliott, ed., "The Peter

Skene Ogden Journals, Snake Expedition, 1827-1828," *Oregon Historical Society Quarterly* 11 (December 1910): 362-72. Such a massacre did take place on the Green River in 1837, with Jim Bridger involved. See Osborne Russell, *Journal of a Trapper; or, Nine Years in the Rocky Mountains, 1834-1843* (Boise: Syms-York Co., 1921), pp. 45, 62-63, and Stanley Vestal, *Jim Bridger: Mountain Man* (New York: William Morrow & Co., 1946), pp. 122-24.

138:12 The Blackfoot River near present Blackfoot, Idaho.

139:2 Again, exaggerated numbers.

139:31 Caleb Greenwood was not present at this encampment. Kelly and Morgan, *Old Greenwood*, pp. 85-87.

CHAPTER XII

144:28 There is no corroboration for this story.

147:20 What actually happened was doubtless much more mundane. Beckwourth probably just signed a note acknowledging his indebtedness to the Rocky Mountain Fur Company and then moved in with the tribe. This would be January 6 or February 6, 1829. The original IOU is in the Sublette Papers in the Missouri Historical Society. Another story told among the trappers of how Beckwourth came to be admitted into the Crow tribe is as follows: "A very large grizzley bear had been driven into a cave and Beckwourth asked a great many Crows, who were present, whether any one of them would go in and kill the creature. All declined, for it seemed to be certain death. Beckwourth stripped himself naked, and wrapping a Mexican blanket around his left arm and holding a strong, sharp knife, he entered the cave and after a desperate fight, killed the bear. Beckwourth came out of the cave all torn and bleeding. He looked like an evil demon, if ever a man did. The Crows were so much pleased at this that he was declared a subject on the spot." George C. Mansfield, "James P. Beckwourth, Indian Scout and Discoverer of the Beckwourth Pass," *The Feather River in '49 and the Fifties* (Oroville, California: By the author, 1924), pp. 19-20. Charles G. Leland claimed this story came from an eyewitness to the act. Bonner, *The Life and Adventures of James P. Beckwourth,* ed. Leland, pp. 8-9. This is probably one of the stories that Francis Parkman found so hard to believe.

149:19 This custom is verified by Robert H. Lowie, a leading authority on the Crow Indians, who believes that Beckwourth's account contains some good general information concerning Crow life. He states: "Whether the mulatto Beckwourth was or was not a chief, he lived among the Crow for many years and while a Münchhausen in the recital of his own deeds, he reproduces with admirable correctness the martial atmosphere of the Crow life in the 'twenties and 'thirties of the last century . . . . Every once in a while the genuineness of the record is forcibly demonstrated, as when a maiden promises to marry Beckwourth 'when the pine leaves turn yellow,' an expression still in vogue. The book [Beckwourth's] is disappointing on Crow religion. While Beckwourth repeatedly notes the planting of sacred Tobacco and essays a description of the Sun Dance, he evidently does not know clearly what it is all about. Nevertheless, for the latter ceremony the recital of coups, the sham battle, and the part played by a virtuous woman are registered." Lowie, *The Crow Indians,* pp. 30-31, 335-36. Another excellent, earlier study of the Crow Indians which verifies much of Beckwourth's information is volume four of Curtis, *The North American Indian.*

151:30 I have found no verification of this episode.

152:18 Arthur Wellesley, 1st duke of Wellington (1769-1852).

CHAPTER XIII

153:18 Hiram Chittenden mentions that the Indians recognized the white man's intelligence in military matters and thus when they found one who could enter easily into their way of life they would accept and honor him. Chittenden, *American Fur Trade of the Far West,* 2:675.

153:26 "With black face" was a common expression meaning a victorious return. Lowie, *The Crow Indians,* p. 225.

155:8   Lowie mentions thirteen such clans which were divided by exogamous maternal lines. Ibid., p. 9.

156:8   When two Crows form such a friendship, each becomes the others *Irapaíse*. Loyalty to each other takes precedence over all other loyalties. Ibid., p. 42.

158:4   According to Lowie, when the time came for battle each warrior also "tied sacred objects to his body and painted his face according to the rules associated with them." Ibid., p. 220.

158:22   The correct spelling is Assiniboine. The Milk River runs through northern Montana and southern Alberta, Canada.

159:12   A brave's social standing and the possibility of chieftain-ship were dependent entirely on military prowess. The property he distributed was booty from successful raids and no accomplishment was a substitute for a man's record as a great fighter and warrior. Lowie, *The Crow Indians*, p. 215.

159:34   See note for 34:19.

160:5   South Park, Colorado. The headwaters of the South Platte were extremely rich in beaver.

161:2   With no fear of anyone disputing his stories, Beckwourth goes to great lengths to stress his bravery. How much is true and how much is fable can only be guessed at.

162:11   Gros Ventre.

162:21   James Kipp built Fort Clark near the Mandan villages in the spring of 1831. The fort referred to here was prob-ably Fort Floyd, later known as Fort Union. For a brief biography of Kipp, see Ray H. Mattison, "James Kipp," in *The Mountain Men and the Fur Trade*, 2:201-05.

162:24   Arikara Indians. Beckwourth's figures are again doubtful.

163:16   Lowie verifies this custom. Lowie, *The Crow Indians*, pp. 68, 240.

163:23   Often, if there were no trees, a scaffold would be built to hold the remains. When a great chief died, his lodge was painted with horizontal red stripes and the corpse placed on a platform with its feet to the east inside the lodge. Everything was then left to be destroyed by the elements. Ibid., pp. 66-69.

163:29   1830 or 1831, not 1826.

165:2   Even young boys were often spared and adopted into the
          tribe, although their foreign origin was remembered. But
          the Crows were not above torture if they were angered
          by their own losses. Lowie, *The Crow Indians*, pp. 229-30

165:10   Incessant warfare was known to have depleted the Crows'
          numbers considerably. If all the Crow warriors had
          joined together, it is doubtful that they would have com-
          prised a fifth of Beckwourth's figure of sixteen thousand.

169:12   Although a long life to the Indians was contemptible and
          a valiant death in battle every warrior's ideal, avoiding
          waste of human life was still an accepted value. Lowie,
          The Crow Indians, p. 227.

169:21   Beckwourth was named after his adopted father.

170:16   Crow girls were often married before puberty. Menstru-
          ation was considered a contamination and often a girl's
          playmates would tease and ridicule her if she were still
          single at the time of her first menses. Lowie, *The Crow
          Indians*, p. 45.

171:13   Women played important parts in the Sun Dance and also
          could become directors of the Tobacco Ceremony or act
          as hostesses in the Cooked Meat Festival. While their
          roles were often more conspicuous than the men's, they
          had to be highly respected and sexually moral individuals,
          and such women were the exception rather than the rule.
          Ibid., p. 61.

172:20   See note for 197:34.

175:33   Each spring a military society was appointed by the chief
          to act as policemen for the tribe. The chief might pick
          different societies or the same one several times in a row.
          Their most important duty was to serve as game wardens,
          prior to the communal buffalo hunt. Anyone guilty of
          a premature attack was punished by a whipping, de-
          struction of his weapons, and confiscation of the game
          he had illegally killed. The appointed society also regu-
          lated war parties, settled disputes, and generally tried to
          maintain order. Lowie, *The Crow Indians*, p. 5.

176:33   There is no mention of powder stains in later descriptions
          of Beckwourth.

178:20   There is no record of Sublette's reporting Beckwourth's
          death.

179:26 John Jacob Astor and Stephen Girard.

182:23 I can find no record of a party of trappers like this one mentioning Beckwourth.

183:20 These fraternal organizations had their ups and downs in popularity and membership. For an excellent description of their organization and purpose, see Lowie, *The Crow Indians*, pp. 172-214.

187:14 After the Sand Creek Massacre in 1864 the chieftainship of the Cheyennes was temporarily taken from Black Kettle and given to Leg-in-the-Water and Little Robe. When Beckwourth tried to make peace with the Cheyennes, Leg-in-the-Water rejected his overtures. Whether he is the same Leg-in-the-Water as the one mentioned here is not known. Since Beckwourth's manuscript was published before the Sand Creek Massacre, perhaps there is some basis for this story if it is the same man and if Beckwourth really did see Leg-in-the-Water in this battle and knew him well enough later to counsel with him. U.S., Congress, Senate, *Report of the Secretary of War*, 39th Cong., 2d sess., Senate Executive Doc. no. 26, pp. 73-74.

CHAPTER XIV

189:4 Tongue River Mountain possibly is Bear's Paw Mountain in present central Montana.

189:11 Beckwourth's figure of ten thousand for the community is exaggerated. A closer estimate was made by Zenas Leonard who claimed that in the winter of 1832-33 the Crow nation numbered from seven to eight thousand people, divided equally into two separate bands. Zenas Leonard, *Adventures of Zenas Leonard, Fur Trader and Trapper, 1831-1836*, ed. W. F. Wagner (Cleveland: Burrows Brothers Co., 1904), p. 255.

190:25 Robert Meldrum and Beckwourth both worked for the American Fur Company and both attempted to gain the Crows' trade for the company. Alter believes that Beckwourth probably was Meldrum's subordinate. Alter, *Jim Bridger*, p. 106.

193:19 See note for 84:13.

195:27 Meldrum claimed that in all his fights among the Indians he was never wounded. Lewis Henry Morgan, *The Indian Journals, 1859-62,* ed. Leslie A. White (Ann Arbor: University of Michigan Press, 1959), p. 192.

195:31 Another account of this battle is given in Zenas Leonard, *Adventures of Zenas Leonard,* pp. 261-70. Wagner states that the Negro mentioned in Leonard's account was Edward Rose, but the facts seem to point to Beckwourth. First of all, as Camp notes, Rose died in 1833 and this battle took place in 1834. Camp also notes that "Beckwourth had been associated with 'Mackinney,' Kenneth Mackenzie, Rose had not; Beckwourth gives an account of the stealing of Bonneville's horses which Leonard and others mention as occurring in the latter part of the year 1832; Beckwourth was eleven years older than Dr. Wagner makes him out to be and could have been called an 'Old Man' as were some trappers even younger than he; finally, the storming of the Blackfoot fort, which Leonard claimed to have witnessed, is an incident not only described similarly and in detail by Beckwourth but which Parkman, who got the story from the son of old Pierre Dorion in 1846, did not believe until he had 'heard it confirmed from so many independent sources that [his] skepticism was almost overcome.'" Camp, *James Clyman, Frontiersman,* pp. 33-34. If this account of Beckwourth is true, it would certainly lend more credibility to his other claimed exploits with the Indians.

197:34 Robert H. Lowie records the "Honors" a man had to receive in order to become a chief in the Crow tribe as follows: "There were the four standard deeds of valor grouped under the head of the probably synonymous terms ackýape or araxtsí, a man with claims to any one of them being an araxtsíwice, honor-owner. The touching of an enemy—whether he was hurt or not—counted as the 'coup' proper, dáḱce. Four men might count coup on the same enemy, but the honor diminished with each successive blow. Also, in any one engagement only one man ranked as the striker of the first-coup; in other words, the first striking of other foemen was not so rated. Snatching away a bow or gun in a hand-to-hand encounter was a second honor; and the theft of a horse picketed in a hostile camp so that it had to be cut loose was still another. Being the pipe-owner or raid-planner was the fourth deed that counted toward the chieftainship; and a 'chief' was simply a man who had achieved at least one of each of these four feats." Lowie, *The Crow Indians,* p. 216. See also Curtis, *The North American Indian,* 4:12-13.

CHAPTER XV

202:29 There are legends telling of a woman of the tribe who went to war, and other women were known for striking coups. Lowie, *The Crow Indians,* p. 215.

205:11 A common Crow saying. Ibid., p. 205

206:5 Little Big Horn River.

207:34 Kenneth MacKenzie was largely responsible for the success of the American Fur Company on the upper Missouri. His organization and leadership helped to eliminate any competition.

208:3 Samuel P. Winter, like Robert Meldrum and Beckwourth, was an employee of the American Fur Company. Robert Campbell mentions him in his journal under the date of September 26, 1833. George R. Brooks, "The Private Journal of Robert Campbell," *Bulletin of the Missouri Historical Society* 20 (October 1963): 7-8.

212:11 For a study of the exogamic nature of the Crows see Lowie, *The Crow Indians,* pp. 18-32.

212:24 The reference is to Fort Cass, built in 1832 by Samuel Tullock, sometimes referred to as A. J. Tullock. Beckwourth probably was consulted on the location of the fort and perhaps helped on its construction, but he was not in charge. See Charles Larpenteur, *Forty Years a Fur Trader on the Upper Missouri,* ed. Elliot Coues (Minneapolis: Ross & Haines, 1962), 1:46-47. See also Annie Heloise Abel, *Chardon's Journal at Fort Clark, 1834-1839* (Pierre: Department of History, State of South Dakota, 1932), p. 236. Fort Cass was abandoned in 1838 for Fort Van Buren farther down the Yellowstone.

212:30 Other sources say that forty men, not fifty, were sent. Ibid.

213:19 If the fort took twelve months to construct, Beckwourth must have left on a trip before it was completed. The records of Fort Tecumseh state that on Thursday, November 1, 1832, "A. [Alexander] Harvey and Beckwourth arrived here from Fort Lookout on their way to the mandans (both Freemen.)" "Records of Fort Tecumseh," *South Dakota Historical Collections,* vol. 9 (Pierre: Hipple Printing Co., 1918), p. 93.

213:33 As previously mentioned, A. J. Tullock was in charge.

214:6 Rosebud River.

214:14 Probably exaggerated figures again.

216:21 The Indians' boldness is one reason the fort was deserted for Fort Van Buren in 1835.

218:8 A statement by Charles Larpenteur may refer to such a scare at Fort Cass. He says: "We learned that this was a very dangerous post; they had had some men killed by the Blackfeet, and were even afraid to go out to chop wood." Larpenteur, *Forty Years a Fur Trader,* 1:47.

218:33 Beckwourth probably means Fort Union. Fort Clark was near the Mandan villages.

CHAPTER XVI

220:3 Lewis Cass (1782-1866), governor of Michigan Territory (1813-31), who was made secretary of war by President Andrew Jackson in 1831.

220:13 The degree of Beckwourth's influence is still a matter of controversy. Robert Meldrum was said to have stated that Beckwourth had very little influence and was not as respected by the Crows as he tried to make people believe. Morgan, *The Indian Journals, 1859-62,* p. 191. J. Lee Humfreville, a captain in the United States Cavalry who claimed to have known Beckwourth while he lived with the Crows, said that he was very highly respected by them and did wield considerable influence. J. Lee Humfreville, *Twenty Years Among Our Hostile Indians* (New York: Hunter & Co., 1903), p. 227. Others say that Beckwourth had influence but did not always use it for good ends. Porter and Davenport, *Scotsman in Buckskin,* p. 73.

221:12 Little Big Horn River.

222:24 It was common practice for men to take a new name after some creditable deed. Lowie, *The Crow Indians*, p. 43.

225:1 A misprint in the original. "Red-handed" should be "red-headed."

226:5 For descriptions of the horse dance and the scalp dance, see Lowie, *The Crow Indians*, pp. 225, 245-57.

226:10 The Kootenay, or Kootenai, Indians were not part of the Blackfoot nation; they belonged to a separate language group.

227:9 I cannot identify "the head-hunter of the fort."

227:18 "Pompey's Tower" today is called Pompey's Pillar; it is located about thirty miles northeast of Billings, Montana.

228:2 No other source confirms that Beckwourth held the office of counselor. No such hierarchical structure of government as that described by Beckwourth is mentioned by Lowie; but it is mentioned by Zenas Leonard, Beckwourth's contemporary. Leonard, *Adventures of Zenas Leonard*, pp. 258-59.

228:21 The penalty for disobeying orders is verified by Leonard, ibid., pp. 257-58, and by Lowie, *The Crow Indians*, pp. 219 ff.

CHAPTER XVII

231:16 Fort Laramie is located at the mouth of the Laramie River where it joins the North Fork of the Platte River in southeastern Wyoming.

233:2 Zenas Leonard mentions finding a "Negro Man" among the Crows in the winter of 1832-33, and says that he proved to be a great help to his group who had lost some horses. If the man were Beckwourth it would help to substantiate his claim of saving life and property, but some writers believe the reference is to Edward Rose. Leonard, *Adventures of Zenas Leonard*, p. 255.

233:25 Ute Indians.

237:23 Although I cannot identify the persons involved, it is unlikely that Beckwourth would have related the incident and explained the mistake unless he was reporting an actual occurrence.

238:8 Beckwourth's explanation of the Crow government compares favorably with that in Lowie, *The Crow Indians*, p. 5.

241:22 See note for 80:6.

243:18 The ideal of a Crow warrior was to die in battle. Often the older warriors would take chances that the younger men would not, expecting to die for their cause. Lowie, *The Crow Indians*, pp. 330-31.

244:31 This poem probably was supplied by Bonner. It has not been identified.

245:25 Both the Mussel Shell and Judith rivers run into the Missouri River in Montana. When Beckwourth says "a little below the mouth of the Judith," he means about eighty miles.

247:19 Edwin Sabin mentions two sons of Beckwourth by Crow women, one called "Panther" and the other "Kit," after Kit Carson. Beckwourth makes no mention of a friendship with Carson this early, however. The children of such matches were generally left with the mothers. Edwin L. Sabin, *Kit Carson Days, 1809-1868*, 2 vols. (New York: Press of the Pioneers, 1935), 1:150-51. See also Mumey, *Beckwourth*, p. 104.

247:34 David Adams was one of Bonneville's lieutenants in the 1832 expedition to the Rockies. For a full account of his story, which is similar to that told by Beckwourth although it does not mention him, see Washington Irving, *The Adventures of Captain Bonneville U.S.A.*, ed. Edgeley W. Todd (Norman: University of Oklahoma Press, 1961), pp. 150-53.

248:9 Whether the mulatto referred to is Edward Rose or another of the mulatto trappers is not known. One wonders if perhaps Beckwourth is trying to cover up his own participation in this event by attributing his actions to another. He was working for the American Fur Company and Adams's party was looked upon as a rival or interloping group.

252:23 This story of Beckwourth's taking another man's wife could be true. Sometimes the men's societies would compete with one another in wife-stealing. Nothing was more disgraceful than to take back a stolen woman, however. Lowie, *The Crow Indians*, pp. 186-92.

253:4   Cutting off noses was a Blackfoot custom which Beckwourth falsely attributes to the Crows.

253:14   Johnson Gardner was noted for despoiling Peter Skene Ogden's fur operation in the Salt Lake Valley and for naming Gardner's Hole. He died a horrible death, tortured by his mortal enemies, the Arickaras. Aubrey L. Haines, "Johnson Gardner," in *The Mountain Men and the Fur Trade*, 2:157-59.

254:1   The three men were Hugh Glass, Edward Rose, and one Menard. Letter, John F. A. Sanford to William Clark, July 26, 1833 (National Archives, Office of Indian Affairs, Letters Received, 1823-40).

254:27   Antoine Garro possibly is Pierre Garreau who spoke the Arickara language fluently because his mother was an Arickara woman. No other account mentions his being with this Arickara band, however. Larpenteur, *Forty Years a Fur Trader*, 1:125-26.

256:6   Prince Maximilian of Wied, who became acquainted with Gardner on a boat trip down the Missouri, relates this story but adds that the two Indians were killed with a knife when they attempted to escape. Maximilian, Prince of Wied, *Travels in the Interior of North America, 1832-34*, in *Early Western Travels, 1748-1846*, ed. Reuben G. Thwaites, 31 vols. (Cleveland: Arthur H. Clark Co., 1906), 24:102-3. The account circulated in the West is closer to Beckwourth's, the difference being that the Indians were supposed to have been scalped first. Prince Maximilian claims that Gardner gave him the scalp of one of the Indians. When Gardner was caught by the Arickaras he was scalped and killed. Haines, "Johnson Gardner," in *The Mountain Men and the Fur Trade*, 2:159.

257:19   The men were probably from the Johnson Gardner party. Ibid.

258:17   For an excellent brief account of Hugh Glass, see Aubrey L. Haines, "Hugh Glass," in *The Mountain Men and the Fur Trade*, 6:161-71.

259:8   Edward Rose.

CHAPTER XVIII

259:16 Tobacco is essential to the Crows. It has traditionally played an important part in their folklore from their creation epic to their modern-day revelations, and it is still a major element in their medicine. The holy tobacco used in their ceremonies is *Nicotina multivalvis,* or "short tobacco." For the best detailed account of the organization of the Tobacco Society and its purposes, see Lowie, *The Crow Indians,* pp. 274-96.

261:23 Arapooish, or Rotten Belly, is still honored by the Crow nation as one of its greatest chiefs. He was killed by the Blackfeet late in the summer of 1834. Abel, *Chardon's Journal at Fort Clark, 1834-1839,* p. 275. See also the Fort Union Letters of September 17, 1834, Pierre Chouteau Collection, Missouri Historical Society.

262:12 Among the Crows a man no longer interested in living was called a "Crazy-dog-wishing-to-die." He pledged himself to foolhardiness in battle or in his everyday actions, but was highly respected by the tribe. Lowie, *The Crow Indians,* pp. 330-34.

262:23 The circular shield served the Crows as their only defensive weapon and was also a very important religious symbol. A shield was held to be part of its owner's medicine and the designs painted on it were usually revealed to the owner during a vision. The shield was always scrupulously cared for and was never supposed to touch the ground. One of Arapooish's shields used in prophecying was said to have the black figure of a man with disproportionately large ears painted on it. Another represented the Seven Stars. Ibid., pp. 86, 234-35.

264:9 Because the shield was a sacred symbol of the owner, to receive another's shield, particularly that of a great chief, was a high honor. The medal referred to was supposed to have been one given out by William Clark on the Lewis and Clark Expedition.

264:22 Another account of Arapooish's death supposedly was translated from the Crow account by Beckwourth while he was still living among them and related to J. Lee Humfreville. The account varies somewhat from the one printed here: it states that Arapooish was killed by a lance and that the killing occurred during a full-scale battle with the Blackfeet from which the Crows withdrew upon the death of their chief. Humfreville, *Twenty Years Among Our Hostile Indians*, pp. 227-29.

267:9 The Rosebud River is a tributary of the Yellowstone River.

267:17 It is doubtful that Beckwourth was more than a subchief in the tribe. The Crows recognized two head chiefs only during the time of Arapooish and Long Hair. At the death of Arapooish, Long Hair, or Red-Feather-at-the-Temple, became the recognized head chief. He was succeeded by Hair-on-Top and Twists-His-Tail. Twists-His-Tail was head chief in 1866 when Beckwourth died. Curtis, *The North American Indian*, 4:28-30, 47-48. Zenas Leonard mentions two chiefs leading the Crow tribes, Long Hair and Grizzly Bear. Leonard, *Adventures of Zenas Leonard*, p. 255.

268:15 The law limiting the nation to two villages was in effect before Arapooish's death. Arapooish and Long Hair were the two head chiefs. Edwin Thompson Denig states the limitation on the number of villages was put into effect to protect the Crows after the ravages of smallpox weakened their numbers in 1833. Edwin Thompson Denig, *Five Indian Tribes of the Upper Missouri*, ed. John C. Ewers (Norman: University of Oklahoma Press, 1961), pp. 169-70.

269:22 Ten thousand is too high a figure. Counting children and women, eight thousand would still be giving Beckwourth the benefit of a doubt. See Leonard, *Adventures of Zenas Leonard*, p. 255.

270:5 For verification of mourning practices, see Lowie, *The Crow Indians*, pp. 67-68, 179.

270:23 Assiniboine is the accepted spelling.

272:6 A. J. Tullock is sometimes referred to as Samuel Tullock. See note for 212:24.

272:12 The company payroll lists Beckwourth's wages at $800 per annum, a good salary for the time. Bernard De Voto, *Across the Wide Missouri* (Boston: Houghton Mifflin Co., 1946), p. 128.

CHAPTER XIX

274:12 Sir William Drummond Stewart was traveling as a guest with Thomas Fitzpatrick at this time. He had fought at Waterloo under Wellington and was well respected as a soldier. He seemed to have been well liked by most of the mountain men, Beckwourth being an exception.

274:15 Dr. Benjamin Harrison, son of President William Henry Harrison, seems to have taken this journey in order to cure his alcoholism. Porter and Davenport, *Scotsman in Buckskin*, p. 28.

274:16 I have found no information on Mr. Brotherton. The only other person with the group mentioned by name was Edmund Christy of St. Louis. Ibid., p. 35.

278:8 Charles A. Warfield, trapper and military man better known for his participation in the Mexican War. LeRoy R. and Ann W. Hafen, eds., *Rufus B. Sage: His Letters and Papers, 1836-1847*, 2 vols. (Glendale: Arthur H. Clarke Co., 1956), 1:18, 2:206-7 and passim. See also David Lavender, *Bent's Fort* (Garden City: Doubleday and Co., 1954), pp. 217-23.

282:13 Beckwourth seems to have appropriated another story concerning Stewart to make his account more exciting. Sometime in the spring of 1834 Stewart's Indian servant stole his horse and best rifle. Greatly angered, Stewart offered a reward of five hundred dollars for his scalp. A man named Markhead took Stewart seriously, found the Indian, killed and scalped him, and returned the horse and rifle for the reward. Porter and Davenport, *Scotsman in Buckskin*, p. 74.

282:34 Fitzpatrick wrote a letter of complaint about this incident to General Ashley, then in Congress, blaming the theft on the American Fur Company and on one of the company's agents living with the Crows, who perpetrated it, but he does not mention Beckwourth's name. The fact that the Indians did return some guns, horses, and traps may indicate that someone with influence intervened, but this is only a supposition. The accuracy of Beckwourth's account, however, indicates that he was either with the Crows or at least close to the vicinity of the theft, even if he preferred to remain hidden. For accounts of the robbery, see Chittenden, *The American Fur Trade of the Far West*, 1:302-3; De Voto, *Across the Wide Missouri*, pp. 127-31; Irving, *Adventures of Captain Bonneville*, pp. 207-8; Porter and Davenport, *Scotsman in Buckskin*, pp. 71-73; Francis Fuller Victor, *The River of the West* (San Francisco: R. J. Trumbull & Co., 1870), pp. 160-61, and LeRoy R. Hafen and W. J Ghent, *Broken Hand* (Denver: Old West Publishing Co, 1931), pp. 110-11.

284:12 Perhaps this massacre of Crow warriors did occur, but no record exists of Fitzpatrick's men taking part in it.

285:32 Long Grass Creek is in present Wyoming.

287:1 The reference is probably to Fort Piegan at the mouth of the Marias River.

288:24 "Poo-der-ee" perhaps comes from the French word *poudrerie* for gunpowder factory or *poudrìere* for powder-magazine.

290:23 "Mildrum" is Robert Meldrum, but Cross's identity is not known.

CHAPTER XX

291:25 Moses Harris.

293:13 Beckwourth's description is of the Crow Sun Dance, which was essentially a ritual representing a prayer for vengeance. For the best detailed account of a ritual which includes elements described here by Beckwourth, see Lowie, *The Crow Indians*, pp. 297-326.

294:14 Lowie does not mention such extreme punishment for an unvirtuous woman who seeks to be the Tree-Notcher in the Sun Dance, but he verifies the rest of Beckwourth's account. Ibid., pp. 312-13.

297:13 The Gros Ventre Indians have traditionally been grouped with the Blackfoot nation, while the Crows are said to have been separated from the Hidatsa. Sometimes the name Gros Ventre has been applied to the Hidatsa, but it is no longer so used scientifically. Ibid., pp. 154, 343. The Gros Ventre of the Missouri of whom Beckwourth speaks would be more closely associated with the Arapahos.

298:2 The term "Absaroke" means Sparrowhawk or Bird People, and through some corruption in translation the appellation of "Crow" was given to the tribe. The land they inhabited was called "Absaroka," meaning "Home of the Bird People" or "Home of the Crows." Frederick Webb Hodge, *Handbook of American Indians North of Mexico*, 2 vols. (Washington: Government Printing Office, 1912), 1:367-68.

298:4 "Fort" is probably a misprint in the original edition. It should read Clark's Fork, referring to a branch of the Yellowstone River.

299:8 Located near the Mandan villages in present North Dakota.

299:13 James Kipp. See note for 162:21.

CHAPTER XXI

303:8 A misprint in the original edition. "Red-handed" should read "red-headed."

303:15 Larpenteur mentions that some men were killed by the Blackfeet, but does not say how many. Larpenteur, *Forty Years a Fur Trader*, p. 47. Fort Cass was abandoned in 1835. Chittenden, *The American Fur Trade of the Far West*, 2:938.

303:25 The reference is to Fort Van Buren, built by Tullock in the fall of 1835 near the mouth of the Tongue River, and used until 1843. It was named after Martin Van Buren, at that time vice-president and subsequently president of the United States. Ibid., pp. 938-39. The fort across from the mouth of the Rosebud was Fort Alexander; it was not constructed until 1839.

305:3 Zenas Leonard mentions an acquaintance named Kean who was killed at the battle of Pierre's Hole in 1832— too early to be the man referred to here unless Beckwourth's chronology is again in error. Leonard, *Adventures of Zenas Leonard*, p. 114.

312:2 The moccasin-bearer was generally a long-limbed dog which had been gelded. These dogs accompanied war parties to carry special moccasins which were part of the warrior's medicine. Lowie, *The Crow Indians*, pp. 91,

220. In this passage, however, Beckwourth speaks as if he were referring to a young boy.

312:6   I have not identified Hunter.

314:22   Since Beckwourth could not read, this quotation probably was added by T. D. Bonner. The entire poem, entitled "Alknoomook," by a Mrs. Hunter, wife of a famous English physician, was quoted by C. G. Leland in the 1892 edition of Bonner, *Beckwourth*, p. 206. It is given there as follows:

The sun sets at night and the stars shun the day,
But glory remains though the light fades away;
Begin ye tormentors, your threats are in vain,
For the son of Alknoomook shall never complain.

Remember the wood where in ambush we lay,
And the scalps which we bore from your nation away;
Why so slow, do you wait till I shrink from my pain?
No, the son of Alknoomook shall never complain.

Remember the arrows he shot from his bow,
Remember the chiefs by his hatchet laid low,
Remember his war-whoop again and again;
The son of Alknoomook shall never complain.

I go to the land where my father has gone,
And his ghost shall rejoice in the fame of his son;
Now the flame rises bright, I am freed from my pain,
And the son of Alknoomook hath ceased to complain.

CHAPTER XXII

317:25   The "meteoric shower" was called the "Great Shower of the Leonids." Robert Campbell mentions it in his journal under the date of November 13, 1833, describing it as follows: "About one o'clock I was waked to witness a most extraordinary spectacle in the heavens. A number of meteors or *falling stars* were seen shooting in all directions and 10, 15 and 20 visible at a time. They continued without intermission until morning and became larger, some remaining suspended as it were two minutes, beautiful and bright." Brooks, "The Private Journal of Robert Campbell," pp. 19-20. Other accounts of this phenomenon are given in Zenas Leonard, *Adventures of Zenas Leonard,*

p. 187, and Hiram M. Chittenden, *History of Early Steamboat Navigation on the Missouri River* (Minneapolis: Ross & Haines, 1962), pp. 40-41.

319:8 The Sulphur River is possibly the Stinking River, or Shoshone as it is called today, a branch of the Bighorn River.

321:23 Indian forts were generally just rough breastworks of timber and brush or natural rock formations used by Indian parties for protection and as corrals for horses when they were not traveling with their villages.

324:17 Fort Van Buren.

CHAPTER XXIII

325:3 Tobacco was considered a sacred plant and was said to have come from the stars. Consequently, at its planting there were many ceremonies, such as fasting, praying, the seeking of visions, and self-purification. The Crows believed that planting tobacco was synonymous with the continued welfare of their people. Lowie, *The Crow Indians*, p. 295.

327:3 Kootenay, or Kootenai, are the accepted spellings of this tribal name.

327:9 The Assiniboine River empties into Lake Winnipeg, which drains into Hudson Bay.

328:22 The fact that Beckwourth's horse-stealing trip lasted for more than a year casts doubt on his story of being head chief of his village. If he were responsible for the welfare of an entire village, he could not have stayed away such a length of time. Beckwourth's account of this extended trip seems to be a cover-up for a horse-stealing venture into California in 1835 with Thomas ("Peg-Leg") Smith and the Ute Chief Walkara. Taking furs and Indian slaves for barter, they enjoyed the pleasures of the Spanish settlements. When attempts to buy the Californians' horses proved unsatisfactory, Walkara and his Indian band drove off over six hundred head, and because Beckwourth and Smith fled with them they were branded as thieves by the Spanish. The two trappers wintered in the Salt Lake area and then drove their share of the horses to

Bent and St. Vrain's Fort on the South Platte, where they disposed of them for a good price. Beckwourth returned to the Crows for a brief time in the spring of 1836. Oswald, "James Pierson Beckwourth, 1798-1866," pp. 83-84.

329:8　I find no fort called Fort Row in this area. Possibly Beckwourth means the site of Fort Rouge, founded by Verendrye in 1734 at the confluence of the Assiniboine and Red rivers. It was a famous historical point even in Beckwourth's day. Elliott Coues, ed., *New Light on the Early History of the Greater Northwest: The Manuscript Journals of Alexander Henry and David Thompson* (New York: Francis P. Harper, 1897), p. 43.

329:12　The Piegan Indians are a branch of the Blackfeet.

329:33　The spotted horses probably were the famous Appaloosa horses of the Nez Perce Indians, of which the Kootenay had their share. They were called the "Tilamselp Shikam" by the Nez Perce. Thwaites, ed., *Early Western Travels,* 30:276.

331:5　It is difficult to identify this mountain spur from Beckwourth's brief account. If the party was returning from the Assiniboine River area, it is doubtful that they would cross a spur of the Rockies unless an extensive detour was made.

331:13　If Beckwourth made such a journey it probably would have been during the winter of 1834-35, but if the story is to cover up his trip to California it would have been the winter of 1835-36. See note for 328:22.

332:24　Lewis Henry Morgan describes medicine shields thus: "They are made of a circle of raw hide about two feet in diameter, made by means of an outside cover of big horn (sheep) or elk skin, tanned white to assure a convex form next to the body and a flat surface outside, so as to make them about four inches thick in the center. Whether there is anything between the skins I know not, but I think from the weight there must be several thicknesses of rawhide. . . . They have connected medicine performances with these shields and thus they attach to them a fictitious value." Morgan, *The Indian Journals,* p. 191.

334:19 Painting one's face for a specific occasion was common among the Crows. While the result may have looked like Satan's face to a white man, face-painting was only a means of decoration to the Indian. Lowie, *The Crow Indians*, pp. 170, 182.

CHAPTER XXIV

339:7 The falling off in trade and profits is perhaps another explanation for the abandonment of Fort Cass for Fort Van Buren. Beckwourth's chronology is again garbled for he has already mentioned the construction of Fort Van Buren. See Chapter XXI.

339:34 A common saying of that day, but probably written by Bonner rather than Beckwourth.

341:28 The Crows were not exempt from most of the vices common to other tribes. Perhaps they drank less alcohol, but to claim that they never drank at all is too absolute a statement to be believed. Chittenden, *The American Fur Trade of the Far West*, 2:842-44. However, for a statement that agrees with Beckwourth's, see note for 460:7.

342:27 Another exaggerated estimate.

345:10 Andrew W. Sublette.

CHAPTER XXV

348:9 Another contemporary account of coal in the area is given by Col. Henry B. Carrington. He says: "Coal is exhaustless. It can be found all along the route from Powder River to the Upper Yellowstone, and the red buttes which dot the country for miles northward are grand repositories of the same article. Lignite and the lower grades of wood coal are the prevailing type; but a vein was opened close to Fort Philip Kearney, soon after its establishment, in 1866, which was advantageously used in welding of iron, and will prove no less valuable for winter fires." Col. Henry B. Carrington, *Ab-Sa-Ra-Ka, Land of Massacre* (Philadelphia: J. B. Lippincott & Co., 1879), p. 35

349:18 The correct spelling is Commanche.

351:8 Bernard De Voto questions this story. He believes that the Commanches would have followed the tracks of the horses, if they were that close behind, and would not have run into the Cheyennes. De Voto edition of Bonner, *Beckwourth*, p. 404.

351:13   The Powder River is a branch of the Yellowstone, but its headwaters are near the headwaters of the Platte in Wyoming. Beckwourth probably is referring to the river Ashley called the Cache La Poudre River, which runs close to Long's Peak in northern Colorado.

351:26   North Park, a title given to the famous trapping area of the Colorado Rockies extending from Long's Peak into southern Wyoming.

CHAPTER XXVI

360:12   Jacob Halsey, a clerk and partner of the Upper Missouri Outfit, was stationed mainly at Fort Pierre and Fort Union. In 1837 he was the first at Fort Union to get smallpox; the epidemic soon spread to the Indians. Chittenden, *The Fur Trade of the Far West*, 2:615-17, and Larpenteur, *Forty Years a Fur Trader on the Upper Missouri*, 1:131-35.

362:25   I cannot identify Fuller.

366:31   I can find nothing to verify the statement that two hundred lodges of the Snakes joined the Crows.

371:34   For an account of where Beckwourth ended his days and was buried, see the Epilogue.

375:32   The five-thousand-dollar figure probably is exaggerated.

CHAPTER XXVII

377:11   Charles Larpenteur states that a Dutchman and a Mexican stole two of Alexander MacKenzie's best horses sometime in July of 1836. After failing in their plans to leave the mountains, they gave themselves up and were flogged. When Beckwourth arrived and expressed his intention of going back to the States, it was decided that these two should accompany him so that they would cause no more trouble. Larpenteur, *Forty Years a Fur Trader on the Upper Missouri*, 1:104-5.

377:18   Chardon's journal states: "Thursday 28—Beckwourth and Co. started for St. Louis—sent P. Garreau with them as far as the Little Miss. (Bad River) with letters to Mr.

Papin—the river rising." Abel, *Chardon's Journal at Fort Clark*, p. 74. Nothing is said about the subsequent adventure with the Arickaras.

377:21 "Bellemaire" is Michel Bellehumeur. Ibid., p. 310.

377:26 Antoine Garreau.

377:33 Pierre Garreau. Larpenteur, *Forty Years a Fur Trader on the Upper Missouri*, 1:125-26.

378:10 Joseph Garreau.

378:20 Beckwourth seems to be recounting a story he had heard, perhaps from Larpenteur, who gives it with much more detail. Ibid., 1:124-30.

378:28 Fort Canaille is unidentified. "Mr. Pappen" is probably Pierre Didier Papin. If Papin's son accompanied Beckwourth, he must have joined the party somewhere near Fort Tecumseh or White River.

379:16 Fourteen years is incorrect. It was not over eleven years since Beckwourth had been in St. Louis.

381:8   James Haley White, a personal acquaintance of the Beckwith family in St. Louis, states that Beckwourth was the third of four children, having an older brother and sister and a younger sister. According to White, Jim's "brother Lemuel learned the Barbar trade with a white man by the name of Hoffa; his youngest sister Ranaye was raised as a servant in a family by the name of Dunlevy, and his oldest sister, Winney, was a woman of the town." White, "St. Louis and Its Men Fifty Years Ago." There is also mention of a brother named Pedro. J. M. Manzanares, "Colorado Recollections of a Centenarian," *Colorado Magazine* 10 (May 1933): 114. See also note for 13:3.

381:22 Probably Pierre Chouteau, Jr.

381:31 Jennings Beckwith sold the last of his land to Daniel Griffith on May 15, 1823, and probably left for Virginia soon after—perhaps even before James left to go with Ashley to the mountains. See note for 87:10.

CHAPTER XXVIII

387:2   I can find neither proof nor disproof of this story.

387:11 Forsyth and Kinney are unidentified.

388:5   William L. Sublette.

394:1   A. J. Tullock was referred to as "The Crane" by the Crow tribe because of his tall slender build. Larpenteur, *Forty Years a Fur Trader*, 1:46.

394:15 Beckwourth's Indian son could have been at most only five or six years of age, and it is doubtful that he would be given authority to "harangue the people."

394:16 Joseph Papin.

404:6   Beckwourth's account of a return trip to the Crows has been seriously questioned by Bernard De Voto, but J. Lee Humfreville, who is very critical of Beckwourth's reputation, believes that he did return under such circumstances and further states that he made the journey of more than twenty-seven hundred miles in fifty-three days, a feat in itself. Humfreville, *Twenty Years Among Our Hostile Indians*, p. 227.

CHAPTER XXIX

404:15 Gen. Edmund P. Gaines had surrendered command of the army in Florida on March 7, 1836, and proceeded to the St. Louis area to recruit volunteers. John T. Sprague, *The Origin, Progress and Conclusion of the Florida War* (New York: D. Appleton & Co., 1884), p.113.

405:22 There seems to be no record of Beckwourth's being made captain, and, for that matter, no record except his own account that he even participated in the Florida War. His accurate knowledge of the men involved, the geography, and the fighting conditions, however, is sufficient to substantiate his participation. Moreover, there is no evidence of Beckwourth's presence and activity elsewhere during this time period.

407:6   Major Bryant is unidentified. Zachary Taylor mentions a Major Brant in the quartermaster's department at Tampa Bay, who was very efficient. Sprague, *The Florida War*, p. 211.

407:14 Gen. Thomas Sidney Jesup.

407:17 Col. Zachary Taylor.

408:9   The reference is to Fort Brooke, located at present Tampa, Florida, at the head of Tampa Bay.

411:2   Colonel Taylor reports 1,032 men. "Colonel Zachary Taylor's Report, Fort Gardiner, January 4th, 1838," in Sprague, *The Florida War*, p. 203. Beckwourth's account of this battle very closely parallels Colonel Taylor's report. Both give the right date and mention Morgan's Spies, the death of Colonel Gentry, the bayonet charge, etc.

411:4   Forts Fraser, Gardiner, and Basinger were established on this march. Holman Hamilton, *Zachary Taylor, Soldier of the Republic* (Hamden, Connecticut: Archon Books, 1966), pp. 127-30.

411:18   Col. Richard Gentry.

411:20   Lt. Col. Alexander R. Thompson.

411:24   Major Alexander G. Morgan.

411:32   Lt. Col. Sterling Price.

411:34   Lt. Col. William Davenport.

412:1   Lt. Col. William Sewell Foster.

412:13   Taylor's figures are 26 killed, 112 wounded. Sprague, *The Florida War*, p. 208.

412:14   Taylor agrees that ten of the enemy dead were left upon the field. Ibid.

412:14   Arpeika, Arpeik, or Sam Jones, as he was more commonly known, was about seventy years of age and declared himself to be a prophet and medicine man. He would plan the war parties and accompany the young warriors to the scene of the battle, giving encouragement by his incantations which made use of roots, bark, skins of animals, snakes, and songs. Taylor also states Jones took part in this battle. Ibid., pp. 97-100.

412:28   Captain Lomax has not been identified.

413:21   Large clumps of swamp grass and trees which made excellent hiding places for the Indians.

414:5   Fort Basinger was located on the Kissimmee River in De Soto County, Florida.

414:16   The Missouri Volunteers were paid the same as the regular army, but they received a few extra benefits because of their voluntary status. Sprague, *The Florida War*, pp. 102-3.

415:2   Charlotte's Harbor was located directly south of Tampa Bay.

417:28   Fort Dade was located about thirty-five miles north of Tampa Bay.

419:18   The head chief of all the Seminoles was known as Mica-nopy, but the four more prominent war chiefs were Osceola, Arpeika (Sam Jones), Coacooche (Wild Cat), and Halpatter Tustenuggee (Alligator). Alligator was considered to be the shrewdest and craftiest and the best military strategist among the Seminoles. Sprague, *The Florida War*, pp. 97-100.

420:23   I find only one account of a private shooting a superior officer: Private S. Wright shot 1st Sergeant John Williams at Fort Marion on April 5, 1836. However, this was before Zachary Taylor was given a command in Florida. Sprague, *The Florida War*, p. 530.

421:22   Fighting continued on through the year 1842.

421:25   The length of service for volunteers was generally from three to six months, but some volunteered for twelve months. Sprague, *The Florida War*, p. 102.

421:26   Colonel Bates is unidentified.

CHAPTER XXX

422:3   Andrew W. Sublette and Louis Vasquez.

424:14   Probably Bent's Fort.

424:16   Fort Vasquez, the first fort built on the South Platte River, was located about one and one-half miles south of present Platteville, Colorado.

424:24   Probably Lucas Murray, better known as "Goddamn" Murray because of his constant use of the word. David Lavender, *Bent's Fort* (Garden City, New York: Doubleday & Co., 1954), pp. 170, 181.

427:4   William Bent was a respected man among the Cheyennes and had married the daughter of one of their chiefs. Bent, his brother Charles, and Ceran St. Vrain composed the chief trading opposition to Sublette and Vasquez. Samuel P. Arnold, "William W. Bent," in *The Mountain Men and the Fur Trade*, 6:61-84.

428:28   "Old Bark," or "Ugly Face" as he was sometimes called, is mentioned as one of the leading chiefs of the Cheyennes. See Charles Preuss, *Exploring with Frémont: The Private*

Diaries of Charles Preuss, trans. and ed. Erwin G. and Elizabeth K. Gudde (Norman: University of Oklahoma Press, 1938), p. 138, and Donald J. Berthrong, *The Southern Cheyennes* (Norman: University of Oklahoma Press, 1963), pp. 91, 94, and passim.

430:19 George Bird Grinnell refers to an old Cheyenne warrior named Bob-tailed Horse who had taught Little White Man how to make a Crazy Dog Society rattle. While this may not be the Bob-tailed Horse mentioned by Beckwourth, it proves, at least, that the name was in use within the tribe. Often a name was _passed down from grandfather to grandson or from uncle to nephew. George Bird Grinnell, *The Cheyenne Indians,* 2 vols. (New Haven: Yale University Press, 1924), 1:107-8; 2:124.

434:1 Often grain alcohol was used as a base for whiskey. Traders steeped plugs of tobacco in it to give it color and flavor, diluted it with spring water, and sold it to the Indians. Other trade items were sold to the Indians for profits that ranged from 200 to 2,000 percent.

434:11 John C. Frémont mentions that the Sioux and the Cheyennes traveled together. John Charles Frémont, *Narrative of the Exploring Expedition to the Rocky Mountains in the Year 1842, and to Oregon and North California in the Years 1843-44* (London: Wiley & Putnam, 1843), p. 317.

437:19 Beckwourth exaggerates how well he did for Sublette and Vasquez. Their complete accumulation for the winter of 1839-40 was recorded at seven hundred robes and four hundred buffalo tongues. Bent and St. Vrain sent more than twenty times as many robes and tongues to St. Louis the same year. Lavender, *Bent's Fort,* p. 184.

438:21 Col. Henry Inman agrees with Beckwourth's estimate of himself as a trader, although Lavender questions it somewhat. (See note for 437:19.) Inman says: "His [Beckwourth's] success as a trader among the various tribes of Indians has never been surpassed; for his close intimacy with them made him know what would best please their taste, and they bought of him when other traders stood idly at their stockades; waiting almost hopelessly for customers." Inman, *The Old Santa Fe Trail,* p. 339.

CHAPTER XXXI

439:11 I can find no mention of a village of outlaws or of a chief named Mo-he-nes-to, but there was an outlaw group of Cheyennes led by Porcupine Bear. See note for 459:19.

439:32 I cannot identify Peterson.

444:5 See note for 437:19.

444:14 See note for 434:1.

446:34 The more stripes, the more prestigious the blanket.

448:6 *comble de bienfaits:* showering of kindness.

449:5 For a full account of the history and characteristics of the Dog Soldiers, see Grinnell, *The Cheyenne Indians,* 2:63-72.

450:8 It is possible that Beckwourth did join the Dog Soldiers of the Cheyennes; any brave warrior living with them was eligible. Grinnell mentions that the group often was referred to as the Cheyenne-Sioux because so many were half-breed Sioux. Ibid., p. 68.

450:22 See note for 437:19.

450:28 Beckwourth did not spend as much time trading for Sublette and Vasquez as he claims. In the summer of 1839 he once again joined his notorious cronies, Peg-leg Smith and the Ute Chief Walkara, and he spent the following winter making plans and participating in another horse-stealing expedition into California. Oswald, "James Pierson Beckwourth," pp. 98-102.

451:26 I can find no verification of the statement that the dance was adopted by the Cheyennes.

453:14 A combination of factors brought about the decision of Vasquez and Sublette to sell their holdings: they were unable to meet the competition of the Bent brothers and Ceran St. Vrain; their overhead was growing; and the demand for beaver fur declined with the advent of the silk hat. The new owners, Lock and Randolph, took over in the summer of 1840, but failed to make all their payments. Lauren C. Bray, "Louis Vasquez, Mountain Man," *Denver Westerners' Monthly Roundup* 15 (July-August 1959) :12.

453:16   "Messrs. Bent" were Charles, William, George, and Robert Bent. "Savarine" is a phonetic rendering of Ceran St. Vrain.

453:25   I can find no other mention of Old Smoke or Smoke's Band.

455:4   Charles A. Warfield. See note 278:8.

455:7   I can find no other mention of Cut Nose.

CHAPTER XXXII

457:5   Charles Town was a well-known trader among the Ute Indians. Janet Lecompte, "Charles Town," in *The Mountain Men and the Fur Trade*, 1:391.

457:27   Beckwourth was also an accomplice to their chief Walkara on two horse-stealing ventures into California. See notes for 328:22 and 450:28.

457:28   St. Fernandez de Taos.

457:32   Probably Stephen Louis Lee. Lee's partnership with Alexander Branch had ended with Branch's death in 1840 and he was trading independently when he entered into partnership with Beckwourth. David J. Weber, "Stephen Louis Lee," in *The Mountain Men and the Fur Trade*, 3:183-4.

458:3   The reference probably is to William Bent.

458:15   I can find no other mention of a serious outbreak of whooping cough among the Cheyennes in 1841.

459:19   Porcupine Bear was considered an outlaw Cheyenne. In 1837, while chief of the Dog Soldiers, he had participated in the killing of a tribesman and was forced to give up his chieftainship and leave the main tribe to live as an outlaw. Perhaps Beckwourth has confused his name with those of the outlaws he calls Mohenesto and Old Smoke. Grinnell, *The Cheyenne Indians*, 1:256-58; 2:52, and Lavender, *Bent's Fort*, pp. 186-87. See notes for 439:11 and 453:25.

460:7   Rufus B. Sage verifies this comment on the Crows' abstemiousness. In 1842 he stated that the Crow Indian not only didn't drink but would take any whiskey brought into his territory, by force if necessary, and pour it on the ground. The Crows' attitude was said to be a result of their seeing how foolishly they acted when under the influence of alcohol. Hafen and Hafen, eds., *Rufus B. Sage, His Letters and Papers, 1836-1847,* 1:335-36.

462:4   The reference must be the same Slim Face who accompanied William Bent to St. Louis in 1844 to see what could be done to stop the whiskey traffic of the traders. Lavender, *Bent's Fort,* pp. 230-32, and Berthrong, *The Southern Cheyennes,* pp. 101-2. Grinnell mentions a Gray Head who created a scandal in the tribe in 1865 by having a thunder-bow made for him, even though he was married. Grinnell, *The Cheyenne Indians,* 2:84.

463:22   I find no other mention of Three Crows.

464:17   The name Louise Sandeville is sometimes spelled Luisa Sandoval. Frémont mentions seeing her on his first expedition west at Charbonneau's camp on the Platte River. In his report for July 9, 1842, he says: "The people in his [Jean Baptiste Charbonneau, son of Sacajawea] employ were generally Spaniards, and among them I saw a young Spanish woman from Taos, whom I found to be Beckwourth's wife." Frémont, *Narrative of the Exploring Expedition to the Rocky Mountains,* p. 31.

464:21   Beckwourth claims sole credit for the building of the first post at what became the city of Pueblo, Colorado; however, George Simpson, J. B. Doyle, and Alexander Barclay appear to be entitled to as much credit for it as Beckwourth. Lavender, *Bent's Fort,* pp. 212-13. Chittenden, in tracing the history of Pueblo, agrees with Beckwourth that 1842 was the year the fort was built, but suggests that others were involved. Chittenden, *The American Fur Trade in the Far West,* 2:942-43.

464:26   Pueblo's reputation was not the best. It was a haven for the disreputables of the area and a center of distribution for smuggled liquor called "Taos Lightning." Hafen and Ghent, *Broken Hand,* pp. 205-6. See also Letter from Charles Bent to D. D. Mitchell, January 1, 1843, Clark Letter Books, 8:92-93, Kansas State Historical Society. Beckwourth's reputation at Pueblo was not the best either, according to David Lavender. In a story never mentioned by Beckwourth, Lavender relates that Jim got some Indians drunk and began cheating them by trading one quart of Taos Lightning for three buffalo robes and two beaver pelts. Old Bill Williams, whose reputation was none too honorable, allegedly sneered, "No one but a low-down half-breed nigger Frenchman would stick an Indian that way." This brought Jim up fighting, but Williams beat him unconscious. Lavender, *Bent's Fort*, p. 213.

465:2 Lt. Col. Philip St. George Cooke. For an account of this expedition, see Philip St. George Cooke, *The Conquest of New Mexico and California* (New York: G. P. Putnam's Sons, 1878), pp. 6-35.

465:9 Since Colonel Cooke did not march to Santa Fe until 1846 and Beckwourth left for California in 1844, probably his reason for leaving was simply that he could not compete with the Bent brothers. Francis T. Cheetham, "The Early Settlements of Southern Colorado," *Colorado Magazine* 5 (February 1928): 4.

465:16 Jim Waters was with Beckwourth on this trip. Arthur Woodward, "Trapper Jim Waters," *Los Angeles Corral Westerners Publication No. 23* (January-February 1954): 9. They had a caravan of forty horses and mules.

CHAPTER XXXIII

466:19 "Torrejon" is Gov. Manuel Micheltorena.

467:11 Although Beckwourth mentions only Gen. José Castro, this civil war in California was also directed by Juan Bautista Alvarado.

467:27 John Sutter's name has become famous because of the discovery of gold near his fort on the American River, January 24, 1848.

467:33 J. Roland is the John Rowland who gave his word as security to José Castro for John Sutter's release into his custody. Erwin G. Gudde, *Sutter's Own Story* (New York: G. P. Putnam's Sons, 1936), pp. 131-32.

468:13 The leader of the American forces was William O'Fallon. Perhaps Beckwourth substituted the name Bell because he was jealous of O'Fallon. He openly admits he is seeking renown (see p. 405), yet he says he turned down this opportunity to gain it and gave the leadership of the

American forces to an unknown man.

468:18 Estimates place the number of mountain men under O'Fallon at about 30 or 40, not 160. Gudde, *Sutter's Own Story*, p. 129.

468:19 Probably a reference to the pueblo of Buena Ventura.

469:24 Captain John Gantt was a mountaineer who had been dismissed from the United States Army. Gudde, *Sutter's Own Story*, p. 113.

469:32 Sutter states that the messenger was the mistress of Alvarado; she was accompanied by a little boy who carried the letter to Captain Gantt in a bag of tortillas. He makes no mention of a letter to himself, only the one to Gantt. Ibid., p. 126.

470:10 The battle of Cahuenga Pass in the San Fernando Valley began on February 20, 1845.

470:33 Credit for this action belongs not to Beckwourth, but to John Marsh, a rebel infiltrator among Micheltorena's forces. George D. Lyman, *John Marsh, Pioneer* (New York: Charles Scribner's Sons, 1930), p. 260.

471:7 One wonders if Beckwourth is implying that stolen United States government horses had been brought to California and sold.

471:12 Pueblo de Angeles.

472:33 Sutter mentions that many Americans wanted to kill him. Gudde, *Sutter's Own Story*, pp. 134-35.

473:8 Governor Pio Pico.

473:24 I can find no verification for Beckwourth's story of protecting Governor Pio Pico.

473:26 Jim Waters.

474:8 Col. John Charles Frémont.

474:27 LeRoy Hafen questions whether it was Beckwourth ("who was never unduly modest in reporting his achievements") or Joseph Walker who led this group of horse thieves. It is possible that Beckwourth and Waters joined Walker's band of horse thieves, which was active at that time. LeRoy R. and Ann W. Hafen, *The Old Spanish Trail, Santa Fe to Los Angeles* (Glendale: Arthur H. Clark Co., 1954), pp. 190, 245-47.

475:2 Jim Waters stated that many horses also were killed by the Piutes, who managed to get six or seven head a night. Letter from Norris Colburn to the *Missourian Republican*, July 17, 1846, as cited in Dale L. Morgan, *Overland in 1846*, 2 vols. (Georgetown, California: Talisman Press, 1963), 2:645.

475:10 If Beckwourth was with Walker's band, then there were only about five hundred head, not over one thousand. Edwin Bryant, *What I Saw in California . . . in the Years 1846, 1847* (New York: D. Appleton & Co., 1848), p. 143.

475:26 Beckwourth had a daughter named Matilda from this marriage. Matilda's daughter, Anna Waite LaNiece, was interviewed by LeRoy R. Hafen on February 6, 1951. Mrs. La Niece said her grandmother (Louise Sandeville) had married John Brown, a fur trapper who became a well-known spiritualist. In 1849 Louise Sandeville sold her horses and property at Pueblo and financed the moving of Brown and their family to Santa Barbara, California. Counting Matilda, the Browns had eleven children. Interview between LeRoy R. Hafen and Anna Waite LaNiece, February 6, 1951. Private Papers of LeRoy R. Hafen, Provo, Utah. For a history and writings of John Brown, see John Brown, *Mediumistic Experiences of John Brown, the Medium of the Rockies*, ed. J. S. Loveland, 3d ed. (San Francisco: Office of the Philosophical Journal, 1897).

475:32 General Stephen Watts Kearny (1794-1848).

476:33 There seems to be no proof that Beckwourth joined Kearny except his own word. He did leave Hardscrabble Settlement on August 4, 1846. "The Journal of Alexander Barclay," as cited in Morgan, *Overland in 1846*, 2:769. Kearny left Bent's Fort for Santa Fe on August 2. Perhaps Beckwourth took his horses to his ranch and then caught up with Kearny as he entered Santa Fe. This would account for his not being mentioned in the journals of the expedition, if he did volunteer to help. Kearny's biographer, Dwight L. Clarke, doubts Beckwourth's story. See Clarke, *Stephen Watts Kearny*, p. 164.

476:34 Beckwourth's partner was probably Jim Waters. Lewis H. Garrard states that "Beckwourth kept the best-furnished saloon in the place—the grand resort for liquor-imbibing, monte-playing, and fandango-disposed American officers and men." Garrard, *Wah-To-Yah and the Taos Trail*, pp. 309-11.

478:7   An item in the *Jefferson Inquirer*, July 22, 1848, partially verifies Beckwourth's story of traveling with Kit Carson. It states: "Jim Beckwith and three others crossed the plains with an express, represent the Indians as collecting in large bodies. Kit Carson with eight men were to have left Taos the day after Beckwith." M. Morgan Estergreen states, in *Kit Carson, A Portrait in Courage* (Norman: University of Oklahoma Press, 1962), p. 196, that Beckwourth traveled with Carson in late June of 1848; and Carson's autobiography verifies that Carson made the trip and followed a new route, perhaps proposed by Beckwourth. Milo Milton Quaife, ed., *Kit Carson's Autobiography* (Lincoln: University of Nebraska Press, Bison Books, 1966), pp. 124-25. But the question arises: who was with Carson? I do not believe that Beckwourth was in the party. See Oswald, "James Pierson Beckwourth, 1798-1866," p. 118 n.

William N. Byers, an old friend of Beckwourth, related the following incident in which supposedly both Carson and Beckwourth figure: "In later years, when the Kansas slavery question was at the border on the west line of Missouri, Beckwourth joined a party of Kit Carson's men to escort a wagon train to the Missouri River. Arriving at their destination, Beckwourth was left to guard the horses and camp, while his comrades made a reconaissance for game. Suddenly two men, coming from the Missouri side, rushed upon Beckwourth, and, after a struggle, put hand-cuffs upon him, meanwhile telling him that he was a d - - - d nigger; that he had run away and they had come to catch him. At the moment he was about to be led away, Kit Carson's men appeared upon the scene, among them O. P. Wiggins of Denver, and ordered them to desist. With their guns and a show of authority as fugitive slave catchers, the Missourians defied the mountaineers and declared they would take the 'nigger' and that opposition was useless. Wiggins was the first to speak. He cocked his rifle, and instantly four guns were pointed at the breasts of the desperadoes. They unlocked the hand-cuffs, and the moment he was free Beckwourth picked up a gun and killed the two bloodhounds which the men had brought. This so infuriated the Missourians that one of them recklessly fired upon Beckwourth and missed him. Then they ran. Beckwourth fired and killed his man. Another shot from one of Beckwourth's party killed the other. The United States Marshal and his posse followed them westward for a week, but were finally obliged to give up the chase." William N. Byers, *Encyclopedia of Biography of Colorado*, 2 vols. (Chicago: Century Publishing & Engraving Co., 1901), 1:20. Stories of this sort about Beckwourth and Carson apparently were related by Oliver P. Wiggins, who has been shown to be an unreliable source. Lorene and Kenny Englert, "Oliver Perry Wiggins," *Denver Westerners Monthly Roundup* 20 (February 1964) : 3-14.

479:6   I have not identified the Kentuckian. An account of this journey in the winter of 1847-48 was printed in the *Santa Fe Republican*, February 12, 1848. The newspaper account mentions only the incident with the Pawnees; it says nothing of the meetings with the Commanches and Apaches that Beckwourth describes here.

481:5   Beckwourth is quoted as believing that he killed two and wounded three. Ibid.

482:9   I can find no mention of an Apache chief named Black Shield, although there was a Chief Black Knife. According to the *Santa Fe Republican*, at the Mermeho River Beckwourth and his companion met with a party of Bent's and St. Vrain's men, and they were pursued by Apaches to the town of Moro. Ibid.

CHAPTER XXXIV

483:12 Col. A. W. Doniphan fought the battle of Brazito on December 21, 1846.

483:16 Major M. L. Clark.

483:22 Col. Sterling Price.

484:9   Lewis H. Garrard verifies that Charles Town brought the news of the Taos insurrection on January 20, 1847. Garrard, *Wah-To-Yah and the Taos Trail*, pp. 309-11.

485:12 Beckwourth's figure of 400 is not exaggerated. Other accounts place the number of men at between 350 and 450.

485:13 Canjarra is La Cañada, or present Santa Cruz.

485:24 When a detachment of Mexicans tried to capture the ammunition wagons, St. Vrain with Beckwourth and the other mountain men scattered them and gave chase. Seeing that their charge had taken them to an unguarded flank of the rebel forces, St. Vrain ordered his men to attack on the enemy's rear. The Mexican army retreated leaving thirty-six dead, including their leader, General Tafoya. Lavender, *Bent's Fort*, p. 290.

485:26 A stand was made at El Embudo ("Lamboda"), the narrowest part of the trail leading to Taos.

486:1   Charles Bent.

486:8   The victim was the circuit attorney, James White Leal.

486:14 The reference is to the pueblo, or town, of the Pueblo Indians sometimes called Pueblo de Taos, not to the town of Pueblo where Beckwourth's ranch was located.

486:30 Gen. Pablo Montoya. James Madison Cutts claims that the leaders of the rebellion were turned over to Col. Sterling Price after the battle at Pueblo de Taos. James Madison Cutts, *The Conquest of California and New Mexico* (Philadelphia: Carey & Hart, 1847), p. 234.

487:7   The date of the hanging was February 7, 1847.

488:25 For two accounts of this battle which closely parallel Beckwourth's, see Edward D. Mansfield, *The Mexican War: A History of Its Origin and a Detailed Account of the Victories which Terminated in the Surrender of the Capital, with the Official Dispatches of the Generals*, 10th ed. (New York: A. S. Barnes & Co., 1850), pp. 99-102, and the report of Col. Sterling Price in Cutts, *The Conquest of California and New Mexico*, pp. 223-31.

488:31 L. L. Waldo, younger brother of William and David Waldo, was one of the Americans killed on January 19, 1847. Another was Benjamin Prewitt. Cutts, *The Conquest of California and New Mexico*, p. 233.

489:32 This Apache attack occurred in May or June of 1848. For verification and an excellent discussion of the sources, see Janet Lecompte, "Charles Town," in *The Mountain Men and the Fur Trade*, 1:395-97.

490:6 I cannot identify Kissack.

490:10 The accusations were reported by John Brown (possibly the same John Brown who married Louise Sandeville), the regular correspondent from Santa Fe, in a letter to the *St. Louis Reveille*, June 7, 1847. Brown's story was refuted in the *Santa Fe Republican*, September 17, 1847.

490:24 A Capt. Lewis N. Morris was killed in the battle of Monterey in 1846, but possibly Beckwourth was referring to the Captain Morin who attacked the town of Moro. Cutts, *The Conquest of California and New Mexico*, p. 233. The most likely guess, however, is that Beckwourth means Brevet Capt. R. M. Morris who took over the command of the Gunnison Expedition after Capt. John Williams Gunnison was killed by the Utes.

490:30 Lewis Garrard gives fuller information on the return of St. Vrain's horse. In early May of 1848 he met Beckwourth near Raton Pass. He reports that Beckwourth "was a large, good-humoured fellow; and while listening to the characteristic colloquy, I almost forgot that he was of a race who, in the mind of the much boasted land of liberty, are an inferior, degraded people. With their caballada, we found a horse of Mr. St. Vrain, which we drove to our own band, without a previous by or leave or a single complement to Jim's honesty. Hatcher [John Hatcher] thought that the party was upon a horse-stealing expedition, to which propensity, however, in the mountains, small blame should be imputed." Garrard, *Wah-To-Yah and the Taos Trail*, pp. 309-11.

490:31 Lt. Col. David Willock, or Willoch, of Missouri.

491:4 The expedition is mentioned in the *Santa Fe Republican*, September 17, 1847.

493:23 Major Benjamin B. Edmonson. An account of his defeat at Red River Cañon, May 29, 1847, is given in Cutts, *The Conquest of California and New Mexico*, p. 237.

493:30 I cannot identify Captain Donohue.

495:5   The *St. Louis Union,* July 20, 1848, lists Charles McIntosh, a half-breed Cherokee, and Henry Hamilton as men who accompanied Beckwourth on a trip from Chihuahua to Fort Leavenworth.

495:10   I can find no mention of Bullard and Company.

496:10   The threat posed by Gen. Manuel Cortes is explained in the report of 2d Lt. J. J. Bourman, dated Santa Fe, August 4, 1847, in Cutts, *The Conquest of California and New Mexico,* pp. 238-40. Cortes had participated in the battle of Pueblo de Taos but had escaped.

497:6   Located near the present town of Wagon Mound, New Mexico.

499:9   I can find no evidence for this ransom story except Beckwourth's own account.

CHAPTER XXXV

499:14   Beckwourth signed up as a member of a protective escort for Orville C. Pratt, a young military lawyer traveling to Los Angeles. Hafen and Hafen, *The Old Spanish Trail,* pp. 344-58.

499:15   Probably Abiquiú, an outpost on the old Spanish Trail.

499:19   I can find no mention of an Apache chief named Little Joe.

501:2   The location described apparently is the point where the Old Spanish Trail crosses the Continental Divide in northern New Mexico.

501:22   Pratt mentions Apache threats in his diary. Hafen and Hafen, *The Old Spanish Trail,* pp. 344-45.

502:21   Probably B. Chouteau, who gave a log of the Old Spanish Trail route to Orville Pratt. Ibid., pp. 365-69.

502:26   According to the entry in Pratt's diary for Sunday, September 2, 1848, a Ute Indian who had stayed with the party for a time stole a rifle, giving as an excuse that he intended to hunt for game. Pratt states that the rifle belonged to a man named Wilson. Ibid., p. 345.

503:1   Paiutes.

503:2   Pueblo de Angeles.

503:24   For accounts of Mexican abductions of squaws and children, see Hafen and Hafen, *The Old Spanish Trail*, pp. 259-83.

503:30 I cannot identify Captain Denny. The ranch belonging to Albert H. Denny was not established in the Shasta Valley until 1852.

503:32 William Reed and Don Petronelo Rios purchased the Mission of San Miguel and its lands in 1845. The Reed family lived in the mission itself. Bancroft, *The Works of Hubert Howe Bancroft*, 22:639.

504:28 The victims were Reed; his wife, Maria Antonia Vallejo; her unborn child; their son, aged two or three; Mrs. Reed's brother José Ramon; Josefa Olivera, a midwife who had come to attend Mrs. Reed; the midwife's fifteen-year-old daughter and four-year-old nephew; an Indian servant and his nephew; and a Negro cook. Ibid., p. 640.

506:2 Bancroft states that there were only five murderers, not fourteen. One unnamed individual was fatally wounded in the chase; Samuel Brenard jumped into the sea and drowned; and Joseph Lynch, Peter Remer or Raymond, and Peter Quin were executed at Santa Barbara on December 28, 1848. Ibid. In an account given by the granddaughter of Don Petronelo Rios, it is stated that one of the murderers, an Irishman, confessed and then was shot. Charles Francis Saunders and J. Smeaton Chase, *The California Padres and Their Missions* (Boston: Houghton Mifflin, 1915), p. 259. Another contemporary account is William A. Streeter, "Recollections of Historical Events in California: 1843-1878," *California Historical Society Quarterly* 18 (1939): 265-66. Beckwourth is not mentioned in any of these accounts. The leader of the group credited with the capture of the murderers was Don Cesareo Lataillade.

507:8 The *California* reached San Francisco on February 28, 1849. If Beckwourth traveled on her, as he claims, he must have paid dearly for his ticket, for the gold fever was spreading and hundreds were awaiting passage from Panama north. Bancroft, *The Works of Hubert Howe Bancroft*, 23:129-30, 133-38.

508:12 John C. Frémont had a very lucrative gold mine near Mariposa.

509:13 When Beckwourth arrived in Sacramento, he spent his entire earnings in a week, buying whiskey for himself and anyone who wanted a drink. He signed on to carry mail from Sacramento to Santa Fe but was too drunk to undertake the assignment, and was jailed for failing to meet his deadline. Letts, *California Illustrated,* p. 100. Letts, who kept a store at Mormon Bar, has left the following account of a meeting with Beckwourth:

> About nine in the morning I saw, approaching the store, a strange looking being, mounted on a grey horse, a *poncho* thrown over his shoulder, over which was slung a huge rifle, skins wrapped around his legs, a pair of Mexican spurs on and a slouched hat which partially obscured his copper complexion. As he rode up, Tracy recognized him as an old mountaineer, whom he had seen in Santa Fe. After the recognition, Tracy says, "Jim, whose horse is that?"
>
> Jim—"How do I know whose horse it is?"
>
> Tracy—"Where did you get him?"
>
> Jim—"I stole him from an Indian, of course."
>
> I have no doubt his declarations were true, for he claimed the credit (and I was informed he deserved it) of being the most accomplished horse-thief in all New Mexico. He informed Tracy that he was "dead broke" and hungry, and wished him to ask me for something to eat. I requested Prince to get him some breakfast, after which he was rich as Croesus, and commenced giving me his life. . . .
>
> Jim's legs had the appearance of being bound with cords under the skin, in consequence of the general rupture of the blood vessels. He says he was taken prisoner by the Indians, and making his escape was chased ninety miles, without stopping for food and rest. The condition of his limbs then compelled him to stop and secrete himself, where, in consequence of his lameness, he was obliged to remain for three weeks subsisting on roots. Jim, with his other ac-

complishments, was considered one of the best "*monte*" dealers in Mexico.

Some three weeks after Jim's departure, as I was sitting in the store, in the after part of the day, I heard a peculiar whoop, and looking up the side of the mountain I saw a cloud of dust, and something flying in the air that had the appearance of a sail that had broken loose from its lower yard during a gale; then there were four legs and two other legs, all of them seemed to be running races whether on the ground or in the air it was difficult to tell. I soon came to the conclusion that it was a trial of speed between Old Grey and Jim; they both arrived about the same time; Jim a little ahead; as between his poncho and Old Grey's latter extremity it was about an even race, and they both settled down quietly, as if glad the race had ended. As Jim drew up to the door he dismounted and throwing on the counter a large handkerchief filled with gold and silver said: "Well, I vow, captain, I've made a raise," he then untied his handkerchief; there were twenty or thirty dollars in silver, the balance in gold coin; the former he insisted upon my accepting, assuring me that it was not of the least value to him. He had been up the river twenty miles, had fallen in with a Mormon who had some money, and who proposed that Jim should deal "monte" and share the profits; in a few nights they had won $13,000; the half of this was more money than he cared to have by him at any one time, and he was on his way to Sacramento City to spend it. He felt in high spirits, and as there were two gamblers along in the evening, who wished to open a "monte bank," he wished me to allow them to do so, which I did; they had the capital of a few hundred dollars, and Jim was to try his luck at betting, which by the way, he understood as well as the other branch of the game. He watched the run of the cards for some time, then wished to cut them; soon he made a small bet—it won; he made a larger bet, and won it also; after making a few successful bets, he "tapped the bank" and won it; at about midnight he mounted Old Grey for Sacramento City, with as much money as he could conveniently carry. Ibid., pp. 92-94, 98-99.

509:16 Jean Baptiste Charbonneau, James Haley White recorded staying at a hotel kept by Beckwourth and Charbonneau in 1849. White, "St. Louis and Its Men Fifty Years Ago," p. 3.

509:18 Greenwood Valley, named after Caleb Greenwood, prior to 1848 was called variously Long Valley, Green Valley, and Lewisville. Bancroft, *The Works of Hubert Howe Bancroft*, 23:353-54, 482.

510:23 I can find no reference to Coe or to the incident described.

513:9 I can find no reference either to Keyere or to the bear story related by Beckwourth. A Sebastian Keyser settled on the Bear River, a branch of the Feather River, but I find nothing about him and a bear fight. Ibid., 23:16.

CHAPTER XXXVI

514:14 The Pitt River is a northern branch of the Sacramento River.

515:8 See map for location of "Beckwourth's Pass."

515:14 The reference is to Mount Shasta.

515:19 Beckwourth's chronology places this event in 1850, but it is said that there were no bullocks in the American Valley until 1851. *Illustrated History of Plumas, Lassen and Sierra Counties, with California from 1515 to 1850* (San Francisco: Fariss & Smith, 1882), p. 257.

515:34 Feather River.

516:8 Truckee River.

516:21 The Turner brothers did not settle their American Ranch until late summer of 1850; thus it is more likely that Beckwourth discovered the pass in 1851. Perhaps he gives the date as 1850 to substantiate his claim that he was the first to discover the pass. A. P. Chapman, George F. Kent, and William E. Jones were said to have seen it in June of 1850 before Beckwourth. *Illustrated History of Plumas*, pp. 257-59.

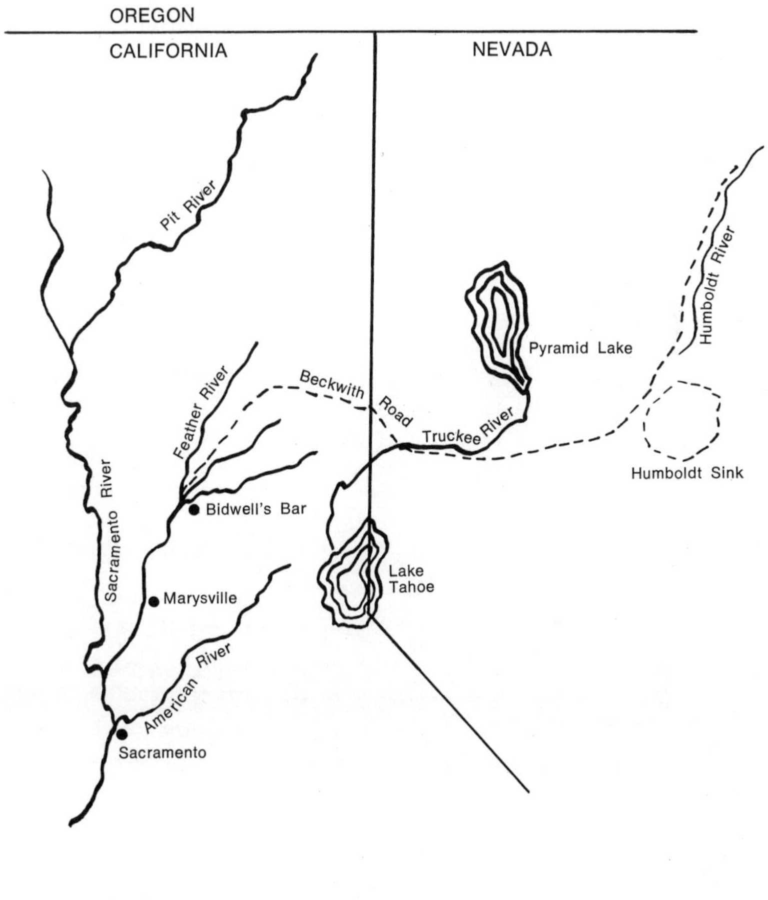
OREGON
CALIFORNIA
NEVADA
Pit River
Feather River
Beckwith Road
Truckee River
Pyramid Lake
Humboldt River
Humboldt Sink
Sacramento River
Bidwell's Bar
Marysville
American River
Sacramento
Lake Tahoe

517:12   S. M. Miles, the first mayor of Marysville, was not elected until March of 1851. This is further evidence that Beckwourth discovered the pass in 1851, not 1850.

518:14   Ina Coolbrith, poet laureate of California, recalls that the wagon train in which she, then a ten-year-old girl, and her parents were traveling was led by Beckwourth across the pass he had discovered, and that he carried her part way on his horse. See personal interviews with Miss Coolbrith in George Wharton James, *Heroes of California* (Boston: Little, Brown & Co., 1910), pp. 111-12 and George R. Stewart, *The California Trail* (New York: McGraw-Hill Book Co., 1962), pp. 302-3.

518:27   Marysville burned on August 31, 1851. *Illustrated History of Plumas*, p. 258.

519:18   A. W. Keddie, a prominent civil engineer, known as "Father of the Western Pacific," furnishes one of the best descriptions of the actual route of the Beckwourth Road: "Beginning at Beckwourth Pass, on the main summit of the Sierra Nevada Range, which is the divide between the waters of the Pacific and the Great Basin, the Beckwourth Trail went about due west through the northern edge of Beckwourth Valley—now called Sierra Valley—to its outlet at the Beckwourth Ranch. Thence the trail turned to the left, and went down the hill to Spring Garden Valley; then followed Spring Garden Creek to American Valley; thence to the American Valley Ranch, now Quincy. From Quincy the trail turned to the right, and went in a northwesterly direction across the American Valley to Elizabethtown; thence westerly, up Emigrant Hill and on to Snake Lake Valley; thence southwesterly to Spanish Ranch and Meadow Valley. From Meadow Valley the trail followed about the line of the present wagon road to a point about a mile and a half beyond Meadow Valley, where it turned to the left, and reached the summit east of Buck's Ranch, by way of what is now known as the Edman Mine. From the Summit east of Buck's Ranch the trail—as near as I can determine—followed about the line of the present traveled wagon road through Buck's Ranch, Buckeye, Mountain Horse, and on to Oroville."

George C. Mansfield, *History of Butte County, California, With Biographical Sketches* (Los Angeles: Historic Record Co., 1918), pp. 50-51. The Western Pacific tracks were laid over Beckwourth Pass. Francis P. Farquhar, "Exploration of the Sierra Nevada," *California Historical Society Quarterly* 4 (March 1925): 10.

519:21 Beckwourth's hotel and store was the first commercial building in the valley. Soon other buildings began to grow around it. First named Jones Station, in 1869 the town changed its name to commemorate its founder and became known as Beckwourth. It is located near present Portola, California. *Illustrated History of Plumas*, p. 260.

526:24 Granville Stuart, a miner traveling through the valley in 1852, confirms that Beckwourth was open handed. Granville Stuart, *Forty Years on the Frontier*, ed. Paul C. Phillips, 2 vols. (Cleveland: Arthur H. Clark Co., 1925), 1:52-53.

528:24 Beckwourth has garbled the story of Jean Baptiste Charbonneau. Charbonneau's mother was Sacajawea, a Shoshoni Indian who gave birth to Jean Baptiste on February 11, 1805, at Fort Mandan in present North Dakota. R. G. Thwaites, ed., *Original Journals of the Lewis and Clark Expedition, 1804-1806*, 8 vols. (New York: Dodd, Mead, and Co., 1904-1905), 1:257-58. See also Ann W. Hafen, "Jean Baptiste Charbonneau," in *The Mountain Men and the Fur Trade*, 1:205-24.

529:2 Now called the Humboldt, the river was first named Ogden's River after its discoverer, Peter Skene Ogden. It then became known to trappers as Mary's River, after Ogden's Indian wife; why this was changed to St. Mary's River is not known. Frémont later named it the Humboldt after Baron Alexander von Humboldt, although Humboldt had never seen it. Dale L. Morgan, *The Humboldt* (New York: Farrar & Rinehart, 1943), pp. 5-6.

CHAPTER XXXVII

532:17 Both the Gros Ventres and the Crow Indians were related to the Hidatsa group. Hodge, *Handbook of American Indians North of Mexico*, 1:367, 508.

532:24 Beckwourth's assessment of the Pawnees is a personal opinion and does not square with other judgements of the tribe.

535:3 Beckwourth began dictating his story to an acquaintance named Philip Stoner during the winter of 1849-50, but for some unknown reason they parted ways. Boutwell Dunlap, "Some Facts Concerning Leland Stanford and His Contemporaries in Placer County," *California Historical Society Quarterly* 2 (October 1923) : 204-05. While at Indian Bar on the Feather River, Beckwourth met an itinerant justice of the peace, sometimes referred to as the "Squire," whose real name was Thomas Daniel Bonner. Finding that Bonner had been a newspaperman before the gold rush and was always open to a money-making proposition, Beckwourth asked him to write his memoirs at his dictation. Bonner accepted the proposal, and Beckwourth's dream of gaining "renown" was on its way to realization. Carl I. Wheat, ed., *California in 1851: The Letters of Dame Shirley*, 2 vols. (San Francisco: Grabhorn Press, 1933), 1:87-88, 88-93. See also the contract drawn for the publication of the first edition of this book printed in Mumey, *Beckwourth*, pp. 26-28.

EPILOGUE

IN THE SPRING OF 1853, James Beckwourth moved to his ranch at the lower end of Beckwourth Valley. Here, near the outlet of Grizzly Creek, he built a log cabin and settled down to raising cattle[1] and guiding parties over Beckwourth Road. The only available figures concerning the traffic on the road were published in 1854. In that year, according to the *Butte Record*, "12,000 head of cattle, 700 sheep, 500 horses and mules, and 1,200 emigrants, including 200 families" used this route. With the opening of the Isthmian Railroad in 1855 the number of emigrants going overland was considerably reduced, and those who did travel overland preferred the Hangtown Route into California because of rumors of cattle killed by poisonous plants along the Beckwourth Road.[2]

Little is known of Beckwourth's activities in California from 1853 to 1858. In 1854 the contract for the publication of his autobiography was drawn up and signed by Beckwourth, T. D. Bonner, and Joseph L. Davis. The contract defined the responsibility of each of the respective parties: Beckwourth was to dictate his life story as accurately as he could remember it, Bonner was to write

1. Beckwourth had dealings in cattle as early as 1851, but they were not always of the most respectable kind. See Letter from Jacob Hall to Manuel Alvarez, February 1, 1852, quoted in a review of the 1931 edition of Beckwourth. Lansing P. Bloom, "The Life and Adventures of James P. Beckwourth," *New Mexico Historical Review* 6 (October 1931) : 419-20.

2. George C. Mansfield, *History of Butte County, California, with Biographical Sketches* (Los Angeles: Historic Record Co., 1918), p. 51.

it, and Davis was to pay the publication costs. The three men were to share equally in the profits.[3] Beckwourth and Bonner spent the winter of 1854 and almost all of 1855 at Beckwourth's ranch preparing the manuscript for publication. Their attitude toward their work is suggested in a story that circulated in the Feather River area to the effect that Jim's bravado and the number of Indians he killed grew in proportion to the amount of rum that he and Bonner consumed. Beckwourth, it was said, slapped his collaborator on the knee and commanded, "Paint her up, Bonner! Paint her up!"[4]

In 1856, when the book was published, many of his acquaintances considered it something of a joke. One story, often told but possibly apocryphal, gives this account of its reception:

> There was a camp of miners in California to whom Beckwourth was well-known, and when his life appeared they commissioned one of their number, who was going to San Francisco to obtain stores, to purchase the book. Not being very careful, he got by mistake a copy of the Bible. In the evening, after his return, the messenger was requested to read aloud to the rest from the long-expected work. Opening the volume at random, he hit upon and read aloud the story of Samson and the foxes. Whereupon one of the listeners cried: "That'll do! I'd know that story for one of Jim Beckwourth's lies anywhere!"[5]

3. The contract is in the Henry E. Huntington Library, San Marino, California. It is reprinted in Nolie Mumey, *James Pierson Beckwourth, 1856-1866* (Denver: Old West Publishing Co., 1957), pp. 27-28.

4. Carl I. Wheat, ed., *California in 1856: The Letters of Dame Shirley*, 2 vols. (San Francisco: Grabhorn Press, 1933), 1:146-47.

5. T. D. Bonner, *The Life and Adventures of James P. Beckwourth*, ed. Charles G. Leland (London: T. Fisher Unwin, 1892), p. 8. See also the *Richmond* (Missouri) *Mirror*, September 25, 1858.

Although there seems to be no record of Beckwourth's activities during his last two years in California, he may have been engaged in some questionable enterprise, for it is said that he came under the surveillance of the vigilantes.[6] The last mention of his presence in California is found in the diary of a Marysville lawyer, Charles E. DeLong, who says he visited with Beckwourth on November 10, 1858.[7] After that nothing is known of his movements until the fall of 1859, when he was recognized in Kansas City.[8]

In Kansas City, Beckwourth apparently made plans to visit his Crow Indian family and then continue on to California. However, when trying to lasso some mules while riding bareback, he was thrown from his horse and suffered severe bruises about the hips and shoulders.[9] During his convalescence he changed his plans and agreed to work for his old friend Louis Vasquez. On October 2 he set out with Vasquez's caravan for Denver.[10] The following letter, written by an observer who saw the caravan enter the city, and who talked with Vasquez's men, describes the trip and how Beckwourth conducted himself upon his arrival:

> Mr. Vasquez's train of wagons with goods from the States arrived yesterday, in charge of Dr. Lee, a former resident of Santa Fe, and a good physician. Mr. Tom Duncan, brother-in-law of your Capt. Scott

6. Hubert Howe Bancroft, *The Works of Hubert Howe Bancroft*, 39 vols. (San Francisco: History Co., 1882-1891), 25:352.

7. Carl I. Wheat, ed., "California's Bantam Cock: The Journals of Charles E. DeLong, 1854-1863," *Quarterly of the California Historical Society* 9 (December 1930) : 368.

8. *Kansas City Journal of Commerce*, September 28, 1859. In the Private Papers of LeRoy R. Hafen, Provo, Utah.

9. Ibid., September 29, 1859.

10. *Rocky Mountain News*, November 24, 1859.

of the steamboat Twilight came along with him. They are sorry to relate that a Mr. A. S. Jenny, who accompanied them from Kansas City, accidently shot himself on the route, through the discharge of a loaded rifle while taking it out of a wagon. Also Jim Beckwith, the well-known mountaineer and formerly chief of the Crow Indians, arrived. He got a little jolley on his arrival the first night, perhaps, because, as he said, he had just come to one of his old camping grounds, and he might be d——d if he knew an individual in it!—that he was an "honest Indian," and herefore kept "ahead of the hounds," but now, by George, we have stole a March on him and passed his time![11]

Soon after the arrival of the wagon train, Beckwourth helped unload the goods at the Vasquez store on Ferry Street[12] and at the office of the *Rocky Mountain News,* where he made an important friend in the editor, William N. Byers.[13] That winter Beckwourth worked as a storekeeper selling groceries and provisions for A. Pike Vasquez and Company. In December he purchased a lot in the present north Denver area from Charles P. Marion for one hundred dollars cash. There he built himself a home, and for the next two years he continued to buy land from Louis Vasquez.[14] While working in the Vasquez

11. A letter from Auraria and Denver, Territory of Jefferson, in the *Missouri Democrat,* December 10, 1859, as quoted in LeRoy R. and Ann W. Hafen, *Reports from Colorado: The Wildman Letters, 1859-1865, with Other Related Letters and Newspaper Reports, 1859* (Glendale: Arthur H. Clark Co., 1961), pp. 214-15.

12. Ferry Street is now Eleventh Street, West Denver. LeRoy R. Hafen, "The Last Years of James P. Beckwourth," *Colorado Maga zine* 5 (August 1928) : 134-35.

13. *Rocky Mountain News,* December 1, 1859.

14. The original bill of sale is in the Beckwourth Papers, Folio #3, Brigham Young University. See also Interview with Frank S. Byers, son of William N. Byers, by E. C. McMechen, February 20, 1934, in Private Papers of LeRoy R. Haven, Provo, Utah. Accord-

store, Beckwourth made friends quickly and easily with the Indians who came to trade. Because of his capacity to understand their problems he gained their respect and soon found himself acting as mediator between the redmen and the people of Denver. In this connection his friendship with Byers proved extremely helpful, for Byers printed articles and letters explaining the Indians' situation to the whites. A typical example is the following item which appeared in the *Rocky Mountain News*, April 4, 1860:

> Capt. James Beckwourth called upon us on Saturday evening last, and with an expression of warmest sympathy for his old, and now neglected friends, the Cheyenne Indians, . . . related the following affecting interview with nine of them whom he met in our streets on Friday evening: "My chief, we are glad to see you—although we do not like to see you among the pale faces. In passing through our hunting grounds, many a pale face has been lost, but never has one come to a Cheyenne lodge without getting plenty to eat, and being set on the right road to his people. Last night I arrived here; have not eaten a mouthful, and the pale-face has not asked me to eat. Chief, I am hungry." Whereupon the Captain took them to his boarding house, where they partook of a hearty meal.

Because of the great number of Indians who had settled around Denver, conflict between them and the whites was inevitable. On April 14 a group of drunken white men entered an Arapaho camp near the town and, finding the men of the village gone, raped several of the women and stole three mules. When the men returned and discovered

---

ing to this interview, "Beckwourth's homestead adjoined that of William N. Byers, lying south of it. Both were west of Broadway. He gave the location of Beckwourth's cabin as on the South side of Virginia Ave. 150′ east of the Platte River Drive."

the outrage, they threatened reprisals. As soon as Beck-wourth learned of the situation he went to the Arapaho chief in an attempt to calm the tribe down. He then dictated a letter to the *Rocky Mountain News* with the object of informing responsible Denver citizens of the injustice which had been perpetrated. He denounced all "drunken devils and bummers," and warned that "the Indians are as keenly sensible to acts of injustice as they are tenacious of revenge."[15] As a result of his letter, a public meeting was called, and a committee, which included Beckwourth and four others, was appointed to investigate the outrage against the Indians and bring the guilty parties to justice.[16] Because of a lack of substantial proof no one was brought to trial, but presents were given to the Indians and for a time they were mollified. After this seeming success, it was suggested at another public meeting that a memorial to Congress be drafted asking for Beckwourth's appointment as Indian agent for Colorado Territory.[17] However, A. G. Boone, a grandson of Daniel Boone, already had been appointed agent, so the memorial was dropped.

Although he was sixty-two years old, Beckwourth was still very alert and active and had not lost his eye for women. He made the acquaintance of Elizabeth Lettbetter, daughter of the first laundress in Denver, and asked her to marry him.[18] On June 21, 1860, they were joined as man and wife by A. O. McGrew, the famous "Wheelbar-

15. *Rocky Mountain News,* April 18, 1860. The language of the letter suggests that Beckwourth had help in its composition.

16. Ibid., April 25, 1860.

17. Ibid., May 2, 1860. The Cheyenne Indians also seemed to be in favor of the appointment.

18. Hafen, "Last Years of Beckwourth," p. 137.

row Man" of the 1859 Pike's Peak gold rush.[19] We have
the following description of Beckwourth at this time:
"Here is a well-formed elderly man, with a devil-may-care
expression, but a face full of character and of wonderful
perceptive faculties; long black hair, complexion like a
Mexican, and eyes like an Indian. . . . His body is scarred
from wounds received 'In worst extremes and on the
perilous edge of battle, when it raged.' But he is the very
pink of courtesy and specially devoted to a comely young
wife whom he invariably dignifies with the title of
'Lady Beckwourth.' " [20]

Beckwourth and his bride continued to manage the A.
Pike Vasquez store and took on as well the responsibility
of a company farm two and a half miles south of Denver.
Here they set up housekeeping and entertained some of
the most influential men in the territory. William Byers
was a frequent visitor, and Gen. William Larimer, one
of the founders of Denver, also traveled to their home to
"eat possum" with them. Beckwourth evidently could not
resist telling him a tall story, for Larimer records that

> Jim had passed through many adventurous exper-
> iences, of which perhaps none was more thrilling or
> more dangerous than that of his sixteenth year. It
> was the "Massacre of the Alamo"—that tragic event
> in the history of the southwest. . . . The Negro, a
> 16-year-old valet to Colonel Travis, who went out
> behind Mrs. Dickinson on the horse, became after-
> wards the chief of the Crow tribe of Indians in the

19. *Rocky Mountain News*, June 27, 1860. See also *Freedom's
Champion*, Atchison City, Kansas, July 14, 1860, quoted in Mumey,
Beckwourth, p. 104. A. O. McGrew attempted to cross the plains
from Missouri to Pike's Peak pushing a wheelbarrow.

20. Albert D. Richardson, *Beyond the Mississippi* (Hartford:
American Publishing Co., 1867), p. 299.

Crow nation, and was known throughout all the Western country by the name of Beckwith.[21]

Mining was then the main industry in Colorado, but Beckwourth decided to stay with the Vasquez Company and in consequence became one of the city's pioneer farmers. Although farming was a relatively tranquil life for a man of his background, it was not entirely dull. One night some stock belonging to a group of people who were encamped near his ranch broke into the garden and did extensive damage to his produce. Beckwourth and his wife drove the stray animals into a corral and barred the gate. When the owners arrived the next morning and demanded their animals, Beckwourth refused to release them until he had received compensation for the damage. After a price had been agreed upon, some of the owners refused to pay and drew their guns, attempting to intimidate him. But, according to witnesses, "the old war horse stood his ground, rifle in hand, and they were finally glad to compromise and pay the damages agreed upon." [22]

Louis Vasquez believed that his Denver business was not doing as well as it should, and late in the fall he decided to dissolve his partnership with his nephew, A. Pike Vasquez. Writing to Beckwourth from Westport, Missouri, he gave him power of attorney and asked him to settle all debts and affairs of the company.[23] Beckwourth immediately began to dissolve the firm, and at the same time he was called upon by his old friend Jim Bridger

21. Herman S. Davis, comp., *Reminiscences of General William Larimer and of His Son William H. H. Larimer* (Lancaster, Pa.: New Era Printing Co., 1918), p. 208.

22. *Rocky Mountain News*, September 11, 1880.

23. This document and other letters from Vasquez to Beckwourth are in the Beckwourth Papers, Folios #4 and #8.

to act for him in collecting seven hundred dollars which Vasquez owed to Bridger. Although Beckwourth was representing both the debtor and the creditor in this transaction, both Vasquez and Bridger trusted Beckwourth's judgment and honesty. Indeed, Bridger was so satisfied that the next spring he asked Jim to dispose of some Denver property for him.[24] He even notified Beckwourth of the discovery of a new gold field in Montana which he was willing to share.[25]

One of Beckwourth's tall stories about Bridger concerned an occasion when he and Bridger were

> piloting a small outfit across the plains. They had one day reached the grounds over which both the Sioux and the Pawnees roamed and hunted, and in the morning [Beckwourth] and Bridger had beat off a force of some fifty Pawnees, and afterward continued their journey along the Republican River for some hours, without molestation.
>
> Late that afternoon, however, they had run into a band of about fifty Sioux. Although they succeeded in defeating this band also; yet he now saw that they were in for trouble. "I seen," said he, "that the Pawnees would get together a big lot of their warriors and follow after us, and the d——d Sioux, I knowed, would do the same thing, so I soon saw that we'd have about a thousand Injuns after us, and we wouldn't be a taste for 'em. I seen this wouldn't do, so I says to Jim Bridger, says I, "Jim, what we goin ter do?" "Damfino," said Jim, says he, "fight till the reds down us, I reckon, and then go under like men." All this time, bless your soul, them pilgrims what we was guidin', they was in the wagons cryin', d—— me, if they wasn't!

24. Ibid., Folio #15.

25. *Rocky Mountain News*, December 12, 1860.

"Well, sir, I jest made up my mind that I did'nt intend to give my har to no d——d Injun jest then, so I calculates about whar the two parties of red devils would meet, and when we got thar we drove over a raise in the plain, and jest waited. It wasn't more'n two hours till I seen the dust raisin' to the East. Them's Pawnees, by G——, says I, and then I looked to the West, and thar the dust was a raisin', too. Them's Sioux, says I, and be d——d to 'em! Well, after waitin' some time, the Injuns they seen each other, and of all the d——d yelling you ever heard, it was thar. I jest laid back and laughted, and Bridger, he done some tall chucklin', too, when them two bands come together. It was lively times, you bet.

"The Injuns did'nt have many guns them days, but you kin just rest sure they used their arrows for what was out. Thar they went circlin' around each other, bendin' under their horses' necks and lettin' the arrows fly. At one time the air was filled so full of arrows, that they shut out the sunlight and made a cloud. Their dogs was full of 'em, their ponies was full of 'em, and every Injun in the gang had a lot of 'em stickin' inter him. I seen one of 'em, a big, fat feller, a riding off on his stomach with two long arrows stickin' inter the seat of his buckskins, and it put me so much in mind of a big Dutch pincushion, that I like ter die a laughin'." In describing this unique combat, the old liar waxed lurid in his profanity, and wound up with the information, that he "believed them Injuns was a runnin' from each other yit."

I once heard old Jim Beckwith tell a pilgrim how his right leg came to be afflicted with varicose veins. "I was out on foot one day, about thirty miles from camp, (the Crow village), and on the other side of the mountain, when a hundred Blackfeet jumped me. Well, sir, they was armed only with bows and arrows, (arrers, Jim called them), and I had my rifle with me. I shot down their chief, and then I seen I had to make a race for camp. Every d——d one of them Injuns was mounted, and so I took up the mountains, but when I got half way up I found they was a gainin' on me.

"Look here, Jim," says I to myself, "this here won't never do, so I jest thought that I'd try runnin' around the hill, as I had an idea that it would strain their horses some. It was a success. As soon as I began streakin' it around the mountain I began to gain on 'em, and I just kept up my lick until I got inter camp. Yer see, the mountain jest circled around to our village, and when I got thar, I jest mounted a lot of my warriors, and that night one hundred Blackfeet scalps was a dryin' in the village. Yer see, their horses was wore out a chasin' me around the mountain, and when they got down inter the plain to escape, I'll be blamed if them horses hadn't stretched all of their legs on the right side so that they couldn't run at all on level ground, and we jest picked 'em all up. But I tell yer what it is, stretchin' this here leg of mine in that thirty-mile race strained it so I've had them big veins ever since." [26]

During the summer of 1860 Beckwourth continued to counsel the Indians living near Denver. When about five hundred members of the various tribes in the area decided to unite in a general assault on the Ute tribe located in South Park, both Beckwourth and Kit Carson advised them against it. But their words went unheeded. The Indians marched into South Park and attacked a camp of Utes, killing many and driving the rest into the hills. After the battle the allied Indian forces withdrew a safe distance and camped at a spring. Meanwhile the Utes had reorganized with reinforcements and they counterattacked when the allies were off guard, sweeping down

26. Colonel Frank Triplett, *Conquering the Wilderness* (Chicago: National Book & Picture Co., 1883), pp. 463-66.

and slaughtering them at will. After suffering heavy
casualties, the remnants of the allies retreated to Denver.[27]

In 1862 Beckwourth claimed legal ownership of a
160-acre farm located about a mile south of the farm
that he had managed for A. Pike Vasquez.[28] Since he
needed to fence his new property, he "borrowed" some
lumber from a nearby fence belonging to the Hydraulic
Ditch Company. The company sent him a bill for twenty-
five dollars and Beckwourth paid it, to avoid the wrath
of the local sheriff.[29] It was one of the few occasions when
he backed down.

After the outbreak of the Civil War, Beckwourth at-
tempted to secure a commission in the Second Colorado
Regiment but did not succeed.[30] In 1862 he served briefly
as an army guide for E. L. Berthoud and for the Colorado
Second Infantry, along with Tim Goodale and Uriel M.
Curtis.[31] Gov. William Gilpin, anticipating a possible
Confederate invasion, established Camp Weld just outside
Denver, near Beckwourth's ranch, to serve as a mobili-
zation point for the newly recruited Territorial Volun-

27. *Rocky Mountain News*, June 20, 1860.

28. The claim and the deed to the property are in the Beckwourth Papers, Folio #2. According to Nolie Mumey, the boun-
daries of the ranch today are "West Virginia Avenue as the northern boundary, South Broadway on the east, West Kentucky Avenue
on the south, and Huron Street on the west. The southern boundary was about one mile north of Overland Park." Mumey, *Beckwourth*, pp. 94-95.

29. The receipt from the Hydraulic Ditch Company is in the
Beckwourth Papers, Folio #3.

30. *Rocky Mountain News*, March 4, 1862.

31. Statement from E. L. Berthoud to Professor F. W. Cragin in
1903, in Cragin Collection, Pioneers Museum, Colorado Springs,
Colorado, as quoted in Mumey, *Beckwourth*, p. 121.

teers. There were many indictments against civilians for thefts of livestock and equipment, and Beckwourth was charged with "larceny and receiving stolen goods," including a saddle, bridle, and blankets. Soon after his arrest he and two friends, Mitchell Goldbaum and Nicholas Noire, posted a five-hundred-dollar bond. Arraigned in open court on February 28, 1863, Beckwourth pleaded not guilty and produced two witnesses, Moro J. Adams and Jessie Kelsey, on his behalf. The prosecution brought in eight witnesses of its own. The jury could not reach a decision and the court decided to grant a new trial, but before it could take place the government dropped all charges against Beckwourth.[32]

On April 29, 1864, Beckwourth's infant daughter died,[33] leaving him and "Lady Beckwourth" with only one child, a son named George.[34] By spring of that year Beckwourth had remodeled his home outside Denver, converting part of it into a saloon. Here another incident occurred which involved him with the law. On Saturday night, May 14, William Payne, commonly known as "Nigger Bill," a blacksmith for the Holladay stage lines, stopped in to see his wife, who was staying with Mrs. Beckwourth. In an argument between Payne and his wife, he tried to force a ring off her finger. Her screams

32. United States Criminal Records, City Hall of the City and County of Denver, pp. 38-41, as quoted in Mumey, *Beckwourth*, pp. 105-11.

33. *Rocky Mountain News*, April 29, 1864. The cause of death was not recorded.

34. J. W. Taylor Manuscript, State Historical Society of Colorado, as quoted in Mumey, *Beckwourth*, pp. 104-5. According to this source, in 1875 George Beckwourth carried the first mail to the Uncompahgre Agency. That winter he was kicked to death by a horse and was buried there.

alarmed the house and brought Beckwourth, who asked Payne to leave. After some hard words and a brief scuffle, both men grabbed for a double-barrel gun standing in a corner of the room. N. A. Fairchilds and John McGuire were in the barroom at the time, and came to Beckwourth's aid. They took the gun away and pushed Payne out of the house. But he was wild with anger and not to be put off so easily. Breaking open the door, he attempted again to go for Beckwourth, and Jim picked up the gun and shot him, killing him almost instantly. With the arrival of the sheriff, Beckwourth was again arrested, and this time he had to remain in jail until his trial.[35]

Public opinion in Denver was with Beckwourth. According to the *Rocky Mountain News*, August 16, 1864,

> The unanimous voice of the people is that he did a good job, and will be at once cleared. Indeed this sentiment was so universal that you would hear nothing but "bully for Beckwourth, if he ever runs for Indian chief again, we sign his papers of recommendation." Also the expressions, "a Payne-ful funeral," there was a "black-berrying" party today at the graveyard, etc., were in many men's mouths, who are noted for principles of charity, justice, right and order.[36]

At the trial, Beckwourth argued that he had acted in self-defense, and after only a few minutes' deliberation the jury rendered a verdict of not guilty.[37]

Next Beckwourth was confronted with marital difficul-

35. *Rocky Mountain News*, May 16, 1864.

36. For additional documents concerning this case, see Mumey, *Beckwourth*, pp. 113-17.

37. Verdict of the Jury, filed August 13, 1864. Case no. 153, District Court of Records, City and County of Denver, quoted in Mumey, *Beckwourth*, p. 117.

ties which he was unable to resolve. Shortly after being acquitted of the manslaughter charge, he left "Lady Beckwourth" and took an Indian woman named Sue as his common-law wife. They lived together Indian-fashion while he ran the ranch, did some placer mining, and even hunted a few beaver. His friend William Byers has described Beckwourth at this time as having "a rather gruff voice. He always wore a cap and ball six-shooter and a butcher knife and when he wore a coat it was of buckskin, decorated with fringes and beadwork, as he was fond of fancy trappings. Indians often visited the Beckwourths and fifteen or twenty teepees were frequently set up about their cabin." Beckwourth and Sue often took Byers' son Frank trapping on the Platte and its tributaries, setting their traps under the water near the beaver slides. When a beaver was caught, "Jim would haul it out, knock it in the head, release it from the trap and Sue would take out her butcher knife and skin it then and there." [38]

In November Beckwourth was hired by Col. George L. Shoup to be a guide to the Third Regiment of Colorado Volunteer Cavalry under Col. J. M. Chivington on their march against the Cheyennes at Sand Creek.[39] He accepted the post although it was an early winter in 1864 and the weather was extremely cold for an elderly man with rheumatism. As they marched toward Sand Creek the troops fought cold winds and encountered snow-drifted gulches where horse and rider would nearly sink from sight. In the face of these harsh conditions Beckwourth

38. Hafen, "Last Days of Beckwourth," p. 138.

39. U.S., Congress, Senate, *Report of the Secretary of War*, 39th Cong., 2d sess., Senate Executive Doc. no. 26, p. 68.

was in bad shape by the time the party reached Fort Lyon and collapsed "so stiff he had to be lifted from his horse." [40] To help him with his duties Chivington impressed into service an unwilling half-breed guide, Robert Bent, whose mother was a Cheyenne.

Since Chivington's plan was to march all night and catch the unwary Indians at dawn, the soldiers left Fort Lyon at dark on November 28. Nineteen years later, in an address to the Pike's Peak Pioneers of 1858, Colonel Chivington stated that "about midnight, the guide (Robert Bent) reported himself lost, and said that Jim Beckwourth, on whom he had depended for the last part of the route, was so blind from age and cold, that he was not willing to proceed further till daylight." [41]

Early the next morning Beckwourth guided the troops to the Indian village at Sand Creek. They immediately surrounded the village and began to fire, shooting at anything that moved. As Robert Bent told the story,

> I saw five squaws under a bank. When troops came up to them they ran out and showed their persons to let the soldiers know they were squaws and begged for mercy but the soldiers shot them all. I saw one squaw lying on a bank whose leg had been broken by a shell. A soldier came up to her with drawn sabre. She raised her arm to protect herself when he struck, breaking her arm; she rolled over and raised the other arm which he struck breaking it; then he left without killing her. . . . Some thirty or

40. David Lavender, *Bent's Fort* (Garden City: Doubleday & Co., 1954), p. 358.

41. William M. Thayer, *Marvels of the New West* (Norwich, Conn.: Henry Bill Publishing Co., 1887), p. 242. The original manuscript of the address is in the Library of the State Historical Society of Colorado.

forty squaws, collected in a hole for protection . . .
sent out a little girl about six years old with a white
flag on a stick. She was shot and killed. . . . I saw one
squaw cut open with an unborn child lying on her
side. I saw a little girl who had been hid in the sand.
Two soldiers drew their pistols and shot her, and then
pulled her out of the sand by her arm. I saw quite a
number of infants in arms killed with their mothers.[42]

Beckwourth himself admits that he participated in the
massacre, although he professed disgust at the atrocities
committed. Even those few Indians taken prisioner were
not safe from the blood-crazed soldiers. Beckwourth tells
of the death of a captive half-breed, Jack Smith, after
the battle was over:

He (Jack Smith) was sitting in the lodge with
me; not more than five or six feet from me, just
across the lodge. There were from ten to fifteen
soldiers came into the lodge at the time, and there
was some person came on the outside and called
to his father, John Smith. He, the old man, went
out, and there was a pistol fired when the old man
got out of the lodge. There was a piece of the lodge
cut out where the old man went out. There was a
pistol fired through this opening and the bullet
entered below his right breast. He sprung forward
and fell dead, and the lodge scattered, soldiers,
squaws, and everything else. I went out myself; as
I went out I met a man with a pistol in his hand.
He made this remark to me: he said, "I am afraid
the damn son of a bitch is not dead, and I will finish
him." Says I, "let him go to rest; he is dead." That
is all that occurred at that time. We took him out

42. Lavender, *Bent's Fort*, pp. 359-60. Although Robert Bent may
have exaggerated somewhat because of his connection with the
tribe, many details of his account have been verified by others.

and laid him out of doors. I do not know what they did with him afterwards.[43]

The day after the battle Beckwourth returned with the troops to Denver where he spent nearly a month resting and regaining his strength. He then prepared to make a reconnaissance trip on his own to the Cheyenne camp. With no official authorization, he set out to find the Cheyennes, in January, 1865, guided by reports of Indian depredations and retaliatory attacks against ranchers, and soon located the Cheyennes at White Man's Fork. Once in camp he was allowed to meet with Chief Leg-in-the-Water,[44] who was acting head of the tribe until Black Kettle returned from a journey to the Sioux. With the expectation of perhaps gaining more "renown" by obtaining a peace settlement, Beckwourth tried to persuade the Indians to negotiate. But the Indians, whose attitude now was kill or be killed, would not listen, and his attempt at truce-making ended in failure.

In March Congress decided to investigate the Sand Creek Massacre, and Beckwourth, as one of the major

43. Testimony of James P. Beckwourth given before a military commission investigating the Sand Creek affair, in *Report of the Secretary of War*, 39th Cong., 2d sess., Senate Executive Doc. no. 26, p. 71. John Smith, who worked as a trader for William Bent, married a Cheyenne woman and became a subchief known as "Blackfeet" or "Grey Blanket." He helped Kit Carson and the Bent traders build the first Fort Adobe on the South Canadian River. In 1847 he commanded Fort Mann but quit and was hired by Thomas Fitzpatrick in Santa Fe. Smith was the first white man met by the gold-rush emigrants at Cherry Creek in 1858 and helped to build the first log cabin in Denver. He left Denver to live with the Cheyennes and served as their interpreter at the Treaty of Fort Wise in 1860. Stan Hoig, *The Sand Creek Massacre* (Norman: University of Oklahoma Press, 1961), pp. 14-16.

44. See note for 187:14.

witnesses, was called to testify. His testimony was heard, along with that of nearly thirty others, and recorded by the commission.[45] Thus once again Beckwourth figured in an episode that would leave his name recorded in the pages of history, but this time it was not an involvement of which he was proud.

For a time after the Sand Creek investigation Beckwourth remained in Denver, but the life of a farmer-rancher was too quiet for him. He felt that the pressures and restrictions of civilization limited his freedom. His instinctive love for his old ways of outdoor living grew so strong that he decided to return once more to the wilds, and he moved out of his home, settling with Sue in a tent on Monument Creek about two miles south of present Monument, Colorado.[46]

In the spring of 1866 he completely abandoned his farm and returned with four other trappers to his trapping grounds on the headwaters of the Green River. While they were there, three of the group—Burns, Williams, and Dave Clayton—were killed by Indians. Beckwourth surmised that the murderers were his old enemies, the Blackfeet. On the trip back to Denver with the other survivor, John Simmons, tragedy struck again. As they were crossing the Green River most of their traps and furs were washed away in the current, and Simmons was drowned attempting to save them. Beckwourth barely managed to save himself and the 280 pelts which were not washed away. After caching the pelts, he rode to the Pass

45. *Report of the Secretary of War*, 39th Cong., 2d sess., Senate Executive Doc. no. 26.

46 Statement of Amos Welty of Colorado Springs to Professor F. W. Cragin in 1902, as quoted in Mumey, *Beckwourth*, p. 158.

Creek Station where he was able to get enough horses to carry the furs to Denver.[47]

Whether he was impelled by a desire to see his Indian family and friends, to help settle the disputes between the Crows and the United States government, or to join in the Montana gold rush is not known, but in late July of 1866 Beckwourth set out for Montana Territory. Upon his arrival he was employed as a scout and messenger at Fort Laramie for a salary of $75.00 a month. His money must have gone for debts or gambling, for when he arrived he gave the sutler at the post, Seth Ward, a note for $93.70 worth of goods.[48] Because of the recent unrest among the Crows, Beckwourth soon left Fort Laramie and was employed as guide and interpreter by Col. Henry B. Carrington, the district commander in charge of pacifying the tribe.[49]

Before Beckwourth was sent out to counsel with the Indians, it is likely that he helped to build Fort C. F. Smith. According to government records, he was employed at five dollars a day from August 13 to August 31, the period during which Carrington had the fort constructed.[50] In early September Beckwourth's presence at the fort was recorded by Ambrose Bierce, a journalist and author who was traveling with Gen. W. B. Hazen on an inspection tour of the northwestern army posts. Probably Beckwourth was assigned by Colonel Carrington to act as their guide while they inspected the forts in the area,

47. *Rocky Mountain News*, June 20, 1866; *Placer Herald*, Auburn, California, July 21, 1866.

48. The note is in the files of the Wyoming State Archives and Historical Department, Cheyenne, Wyoming.

49. Mumey, *Beckwourth*, p. 164.

50. Files of the Quartermaster General, National Archives, Washington, D.C.

for Bierce wrote the following account of an incident involving Jim:

At irregular intervals we hear the distant howling of a wolf—now on this side and again on that. We check our talk to listen; we cast quick glances toward our weapons, our saddles, our picketed horses; the wolves may be of the variety known as Sioux, and there are but four of us.

"What would you do, Jim," said Hazen, "if we were surrounded by Indians?"

Jim Beckwourth was our guide—a lifelong frontiersman, an old man "beated and chapped with tanned antiquity." He had at one time been a chief of the Crows.

"I'd spit on that fire," said Jim Beckwourth.[51]

At this time the majority of the Indian tribes in the region were causing a great deal of trouble for the whites, and it was feared that the construction of Fort C. F. Smith on the Crows' land might cause them to join the rest of their red brothers. In an attempt to avoid such a development, Colonel Carrington determined to open lines of communication with the tribe. The Crow chiefs agreed to talks, and when they learned that Beckwourth was in the area they asked specifically that he be the intermediary.[52] Carrington acceded to their request, ar-

51. Ambrose G. Bierce, *Collected Works of Ambrose Bierce*, 12 vols. (New York: Neale Publishing Co., 1909), 1:383. According to the diary of Lt. George M. Templeton, who was stationed at Fort C. F. Smith at this time, Beckwourth was with the Hazen party from late August to September 9, 1866. Beckwourth is mentioned in the diary under the entries for September 1, 5, and 9. See The Templeton Diaries, as quoted in Mumey, *Beckwourth*, pp. 168-69.

52. U. S., Congress, Senate, *Report of Henry B. Carrington, Colonel Eighteenth U. S. Infantry, to Major H. G. Litchfield*, dated Fort Philip Kearny, Dakota, November 5, 1866, 50th Cong., 1st sess., Senate Executive Doc. no. 33, p. 21.

ranging for Beckwourth to go to counsel with the Crows and through them to find out the disposition of Red Cloud and his Sioux bands.[53] Although Jim was offered a detachment of soldiers to escort him to the Crow village at Pryor's Creek, he declined the offer and asked for only one man. James W. Thompson, Company D, 27th Infantry, was assigned to accompany him.[54] It was a mission from which Jim was not to return.

Because of several conflicting points in the various accounts of Beckwourth's death, it is fairly difficult to determine what actually happened. Perhaps the most popular story, although it seems to have no foundation, was written by Beckwourth's friend William N. Byers. According to this story,

> the Crows, who had removed as far north as the headwaters of the Missouri, had not forgotten nor lost their affection for their whilom chief. They had even kept track of him through all these years, and when they were fully appraised of his situation in Denver, they sent envoys to persuade him to make them a visit. He yielded to the influence and went to the encampment of the Crows. They entertained him with all the honors an Indian can bestow. He remained many days with them. During the time they used every means and argument to persuade him to again become their chief. Upon his final refusal and his preparation to return to his home, the Indians honored him with a great farewell dog feast. The meat that was served to him was poisoned and he died on the spot. The Crows freely acknowledged the crime saying; "He has been our good medicine. We have been more successful under him

---

53. Ibid., p. 20.

54. James D. Lockwood, *Life and Adventures of a Drummer-Boy* (Albany: Published by John D. Skinner, 1893), pp. 156-59.

than under any chief." Their excuse was that if
they could not have him living it would be good medicine to them to have him dead.[55]
Byers' account, with its heroic and mythical overtones,
would have pleased even Beckwourth.

Another story, which seems to have been mostly
hearsay, was related to Granville Stuart By Tom H.
Irving, one-time sheriff of Custer County, Montana. In
1876 (actually 1866), Irving stated, Beckwourth was

> back on the Big Horn River in Montana with
> Captain John W. Smith, post-trader at Fort C. F.
> Smith. Beckwith had regained some of his former
> influence among the Crows. As soon as the troops
> came to the fort, Smith sent him to the river to
> bring up a large party of Crows that was camped
> there for the purpose of trading with them. Beckwith,
> who was getting old, was mounted on a spirited
> cavalry horse and seeing a small herd of buffalo he
> determined to kill one. His companions tried to
> persuade him not to attempt to run buffalo on such
> a horse, but he would not listen to them and started
> in pursuit. He soon was in the midst of the buffalo
> herd. His frightened horse became unmanageable,
> plunging and rearing among the running buffalo,
> and the old man was thrown and seriously injured.
> Some Indian women picked him up and placing him
> on a travois, started with him for camp, but he died
> before reaching it. He was buried on the Big Horn
> in the hunting grounds of his adopted people.[56]

55. William N. Byers, *Encylopedia of Biography of Colorado*, 2
vols. (Chicago: Century Publishing & Engraving Co., 1901), 1:20-
21. See also Hafen, "Last Years of Beckwourth," p. 139, and John
G. Neihardt, *The Splendid Wayfaring* (New York: Macmillan Co.,
1927), pp. 171-72.

56. Granville Stuart, *Forty Years on the Frontier*, ed. Paul C.
Phillips, 2 vols. (Cleveland: Arthur H. Clark Co., 1925), 1:52-53.

Another account has it that Beckwourth perished on a travois while returning to Fort C. F. Smith escorted by his Indian friends,[57] and still another holds that he sickened and died before ever reaching the Crow village. According to the latter,

> Beckwourth became ill and was unable to travel. He asked [James W.] Thompson to provide him with wood and water for his use, then sent Thompson on alone to complete the mission. After a day's ride, the soldier reached the Indian village. He used signs and gave them Beckwourth's Indian name, Etsedscarsha, which means antelope. Some of the Indians were induced to accompany him to the place where he had left the old trapper. When they arrived they found Beckwourth dead. The Indians grieved and mourned over the body, then they gave the old scout a fine funeral in the form and dignity of a chief, wrapping the body in a buffalo robe, and hoisting it upon a platform in the branches of a tree, where the remains of the old scout found their last resting place.[58]

Perhaps the most accurate information comes from the diaries of Lt. George M. Templeton, an acquaintance of Beckwourth stationed at Fort C. F. Smith. According to Templeton, Beckwourth and Thompson left for the Crow village the night of September 29. The Crows came to the fort on October 30, and Thompson, who was the only white man present when Beckwourth died, gave an account of the death which Templeton wrote down. He recorded Thompson's statement as follows:

57. M. A. Leeson, comp., *History of Montana, 1739-1885* (Chicago: Warner, Deers & Co., 1885), p. 199, as quoted in Mumey, *Beckwourth*, p. 168.

58. Lockwood, *Life and Adventures of a Drummer-Boy,* quoted in Mumey, *Beckwourth,* pp. 165-66.

He [Beckwourth] complained of being sick on the same evening that he left here, and soon after commenced bleeding at the nose. On his arrival at the village he and Thompson were taken into the lodge of "The Iron Bull" and were his guests while they remained. There Beckwourth died and was buried by his host.[59]

So it would seem that James P. Beckwourth ended his long and eventful life buried as a Crow Indian on a platform in a treetop. His last expedition was not without its measure of achievement, for before he died Beckwourth secured the Crows' promise to send one to two hundred warriors to help the white man fight the Sioux.[60] The Crow village itself moved to the vicinity of Fort C. F. Smith and the inhabitants remained friendly to the whites.[61]

By the terms of Beckwourth's will, drawn up in Denver on May 18, 1864, all of his property and possessions, after payment of his debts, were left to his wife, Elizabeth.[62] There is no record of what happened to Sue, his last Indian mate. No doubt like other Indian women in her circumstances she quietly returned to live with her own people.

59. The Templeton Diaries, in Mumey, *Beckwourth*, pp. 171-73. The only date given for Beckwourth's death, October 14, 1866, is written on the back of the IOU of Beckwourth to Seth E. Ward. See note 48, above.

60. Templeton says that about one hundred young warriors were pledged to help the whites against the Sioux; Carrington says about two hundred and fifty. Mumey, *Beckwourth*, p. 174; and see *Report of Henry B. Carrington*, 50th Cong., 1st sess., Senate Executive Document no. 33, p. 30.

61. U. S., Congress, Senate, Letter from Colonel Henry B. Carrington to Major H. G. Litchfield, dated Fort Philip Kearny, Dakota, November 14, 1866, 50th Cong., 1st sess., Senate Executive Doc. no. 33, p. 35.

62. Beckwourth Papers, Folio #1.
Phillips, 2 vols. (Cleveland: Arthur H. Clark Co., 1925), 1:52-53.

Regardless of the diverse opinions about Beckwourth and the incidents of his life, historians must recognize that he was indeed remarkable, perhaps more of a truth-stretcher than many of his contemporaries, but not unworthy of their companionship. Perhaps his best eulogy was written by the noted historian Hubert Howe Bancroft:

> Beckwourth was by no means a bad man, though he had his faults, the greatest of which was being born too late. He should have swam the Scamander after Grecian horses, captured Ajax when calling for light, or scalped Achilles in his tent. Then had not been denied him the honor of dying like a Roman on his shield, in a lightening of lances, or a storm of Blackfoot braves.[63]

63. Bancroft, *Works*, 28:449.

ACKNOWLEDGMENTS

In preparing this edition for publication I have incurred a debt to many people and institutions. First of all, I would like to thank Dr. LeRoy R. Hafen who so freely gave of his time and his private papers to encourage me not only in this work but in the scholarly world of Western Americana in general. I am grateful to Dale L. Morgan and Nolie Mumey whose works saved me many hours by pointing the way to sources. And special thanks must go to my wife, Jean, without whose faithful support and proofreading the task would have been impossible, and to my parents, Mr. and Mrs. Philip F. Oswald, for their constant encouragement and unstinting help.

I must thank also the secretaries of the Department of History at Brigham Young University and commend them for their excellent work, especially Mrs. Mariel Budd, who gave much time and effort to the typing of the manuscript. I acknowledge the assistance of the library staffs at the following institutions: J. Reuben Clark Library, Brigham Young University; California State Library, Sacramento; Missouri Historical Society, St. Louis; State Historical Society of Colorado, Denver; Wyoming State Historical Department, Laramie; Bancroft Library, University of California at Berkeley; Recorder of Deeds Office, St. Charles County, Missouri; National Archives, Washington, D. C.; and Chicago Historical Society.

D. R. O.

INDEX